BUDDHA

OSAMU TEZUKA

VERTICAL.

3: Devadatta

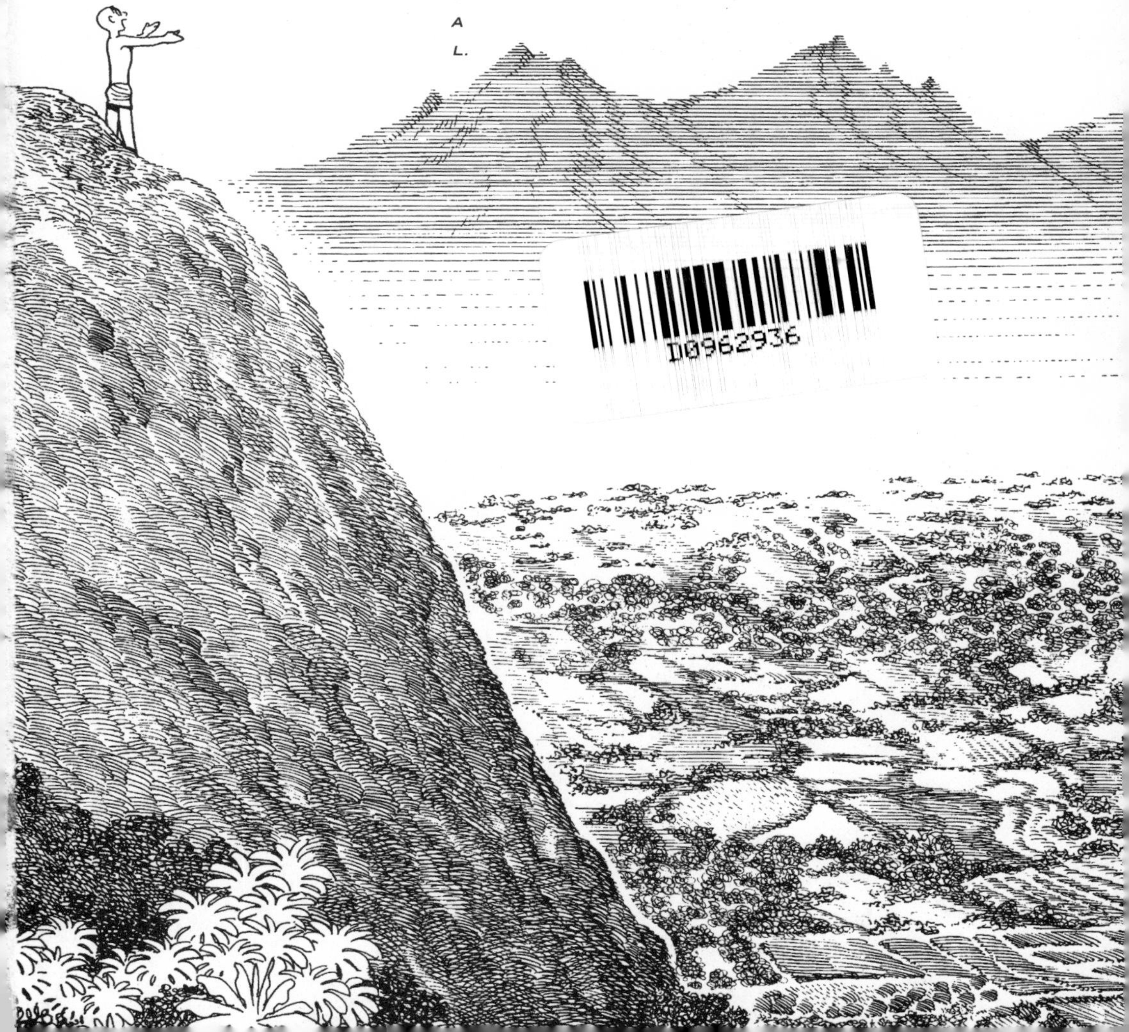

THE JOURNEY

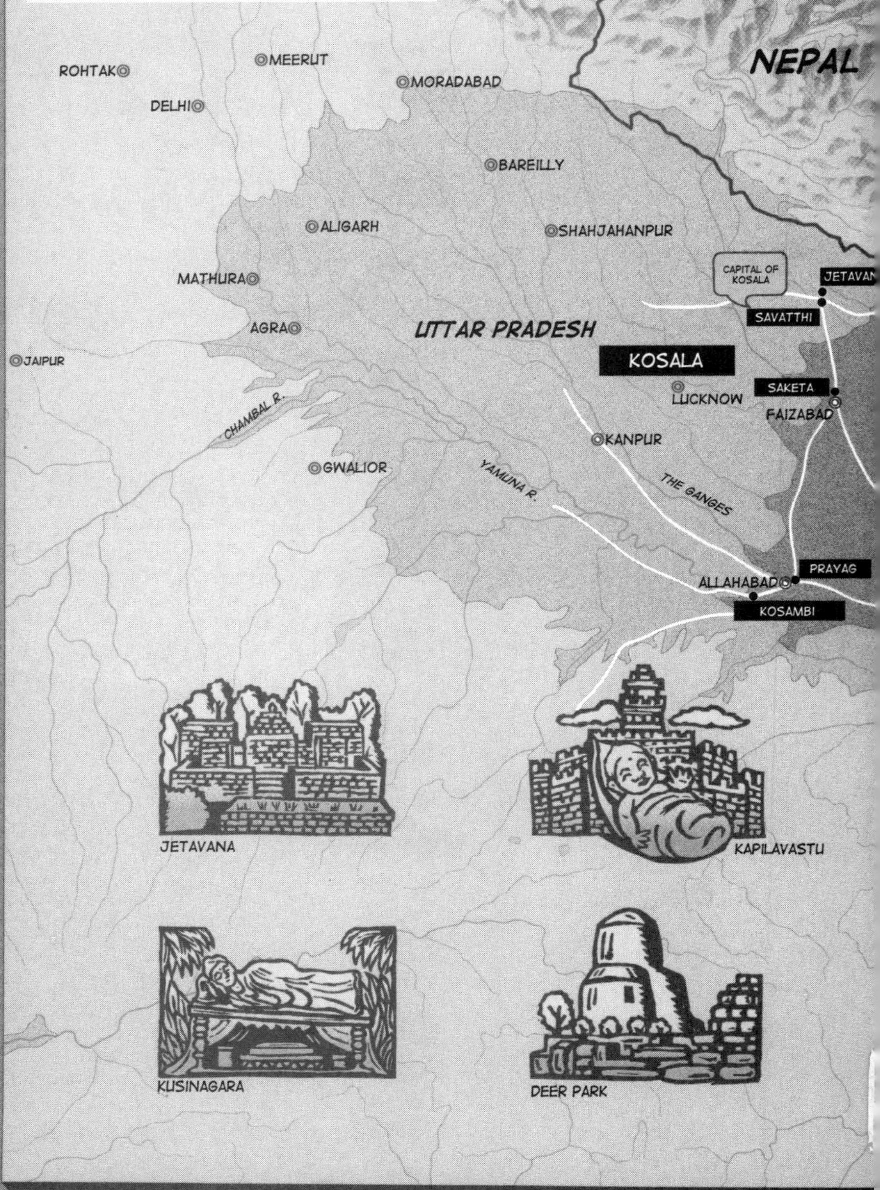
NEPAL
ROHTAK
MEERUT
MORADABAD
DELHI
BAREILLY
ALIGARH
SHAHJAHANPUR
CAPITAL OF KOSALA
JETAVAN
MATHURA
SAVATTHI
AGRA
UTTAR PRADESH
JAIPUR
KOSALA
SAKETA
LUCKNOW
FAIZABAD
CHAMBAL R.
KANPUR
GWALIOR
YAMUNA R.
THE GANGES
PRAYAG
ALLAHABAD
KOSAMBI
JETAVANA
KAPILAVASTU
KUSINAGARA
DEER PARK

LUMBINI ANCIENT PLACE NAMES — MAJOR ROUTES • PLACES VISITED BY THE BUDDHA

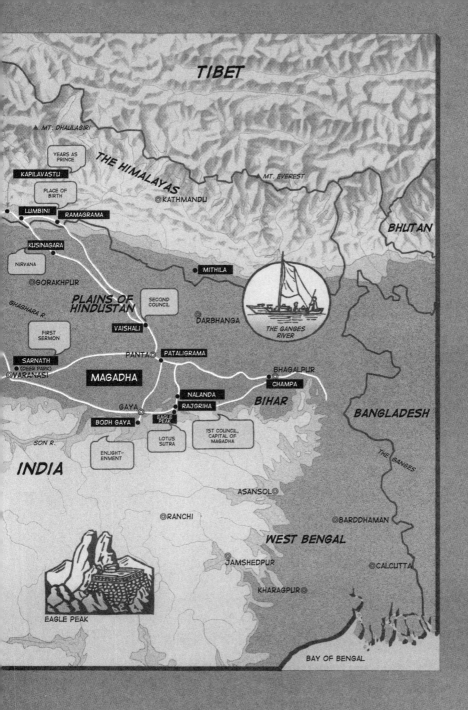

TIBET

MT. DHAULAGIRI

THE HIMALAYAS

MT. EVEREST

YEARS AS PRINCE

KAPILAVASTU

PLACE OF BIRTH

KATHMANDU

LUMBINI   RAMAGRAMA

BHUTAN

KUSINAGARA

NIRVANA

GORAKHPUR

MITHILA

GHAGHARA R.

PLAINS OF HINDUSTAN

SECOND COUNCIL

DARBHANGA

THE GANGES RIVER

FIRST SERMON

VAISHALI

PANTA   PATALIGRAMA

SARNATH (DEER PARK)

VARANASI

MAGADHA

BHAGALPUR

CHAMPA

NALANDA

RAJGRIHA

BIHAR

GAYA

BODH GAYA

EAGLE PEAK

LOTUS SUTRA

1ST COUNCIL, CAPITAL OF MAGADHA

BANGLADESH

THE GANGES

SON R.

ENLIGHT-ENMENT

INDIA

ASANSOL

RANCHI

BARDDHAMAN

WEST BENGAL

JAMSHEDPUR

CALCUTTA

KHARAGPUR

EAGLE PEAK

BAY OF BENGAL

PUBLISHED BY VERTICAL, INC., NEW YORK.

ORIGINALLY PUBLISHED IN JAPANESE AS *BUDDA DAI SANKAN DAIBADATTA* BY USHIO SHUPPANSHA, TOKYO, 1987.

ISBN 978-1-932234-58-9

MANUFACTURED IN THE UNITED STATES OF AMERICA

FIRST PAPERBACK EDITION. THE ARTWORK OF THE ORIGINAL HAS BEEN PRODUCED AS A MIRROR-IMAGE IN ORDER TO CONFORM WITH THE ENGLISH LANGUAGE. THIS WORK OF FICTION CONTAINS CHARACTERS AND EPISODES THAT ARE NOT PART OF THE HISTORICAL RECORD.

SEVENTH PRINTING

VERTICAL, INC.
451 PARK AVENUE SOUTH 7TH FLOOR
NEW YORK, NY 10016
WWW.VERTICAL-INC.COM

CONTENTS

PART THREE

PART THREE

CHAPTER ONE

THE ORDEALS

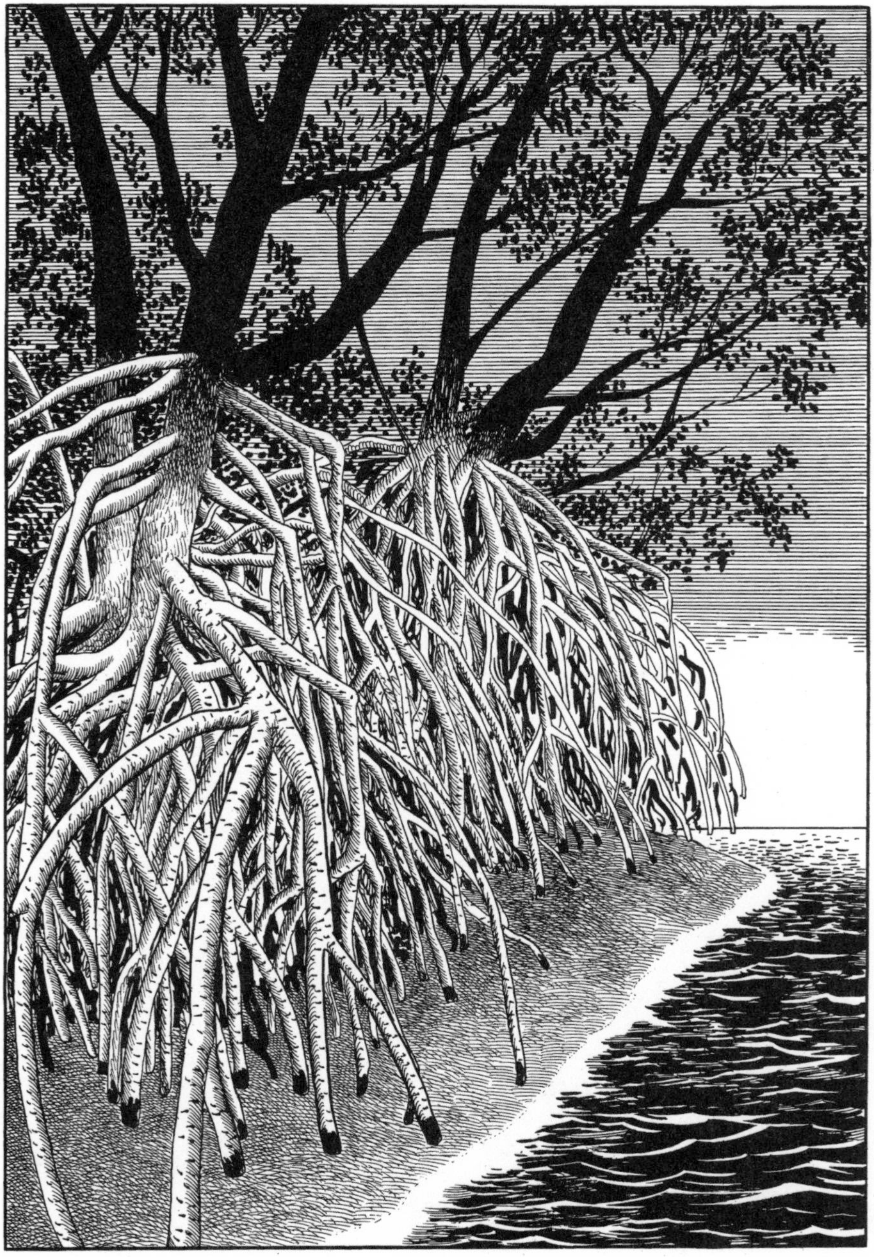

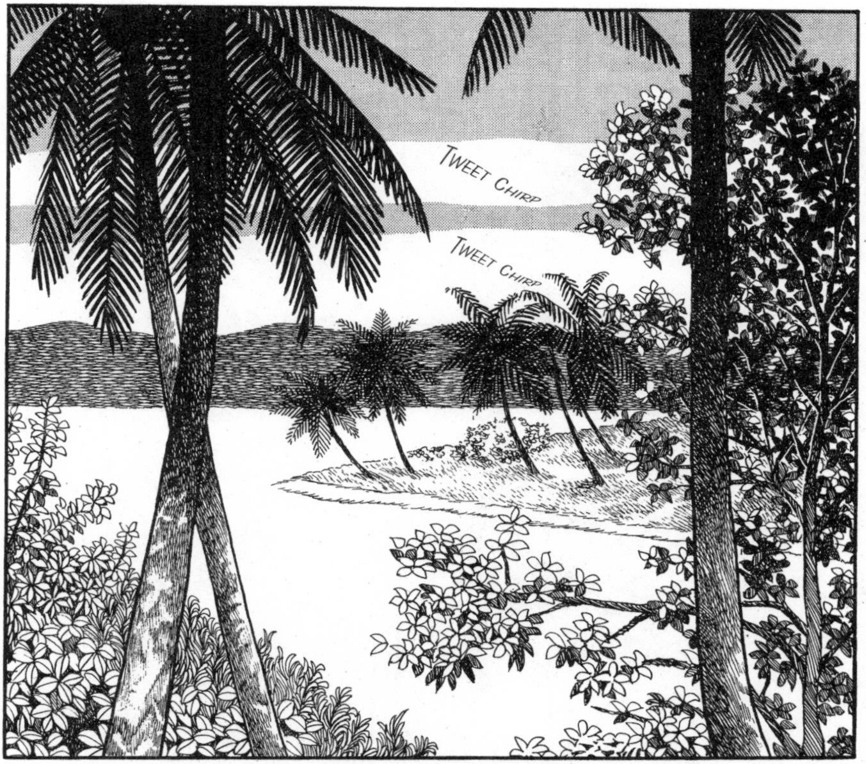
TWEET CHIRP
TWEET CHIRP
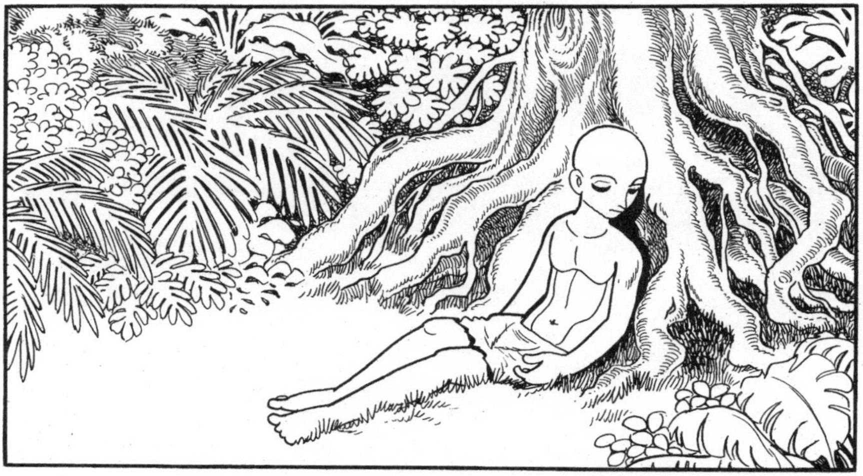

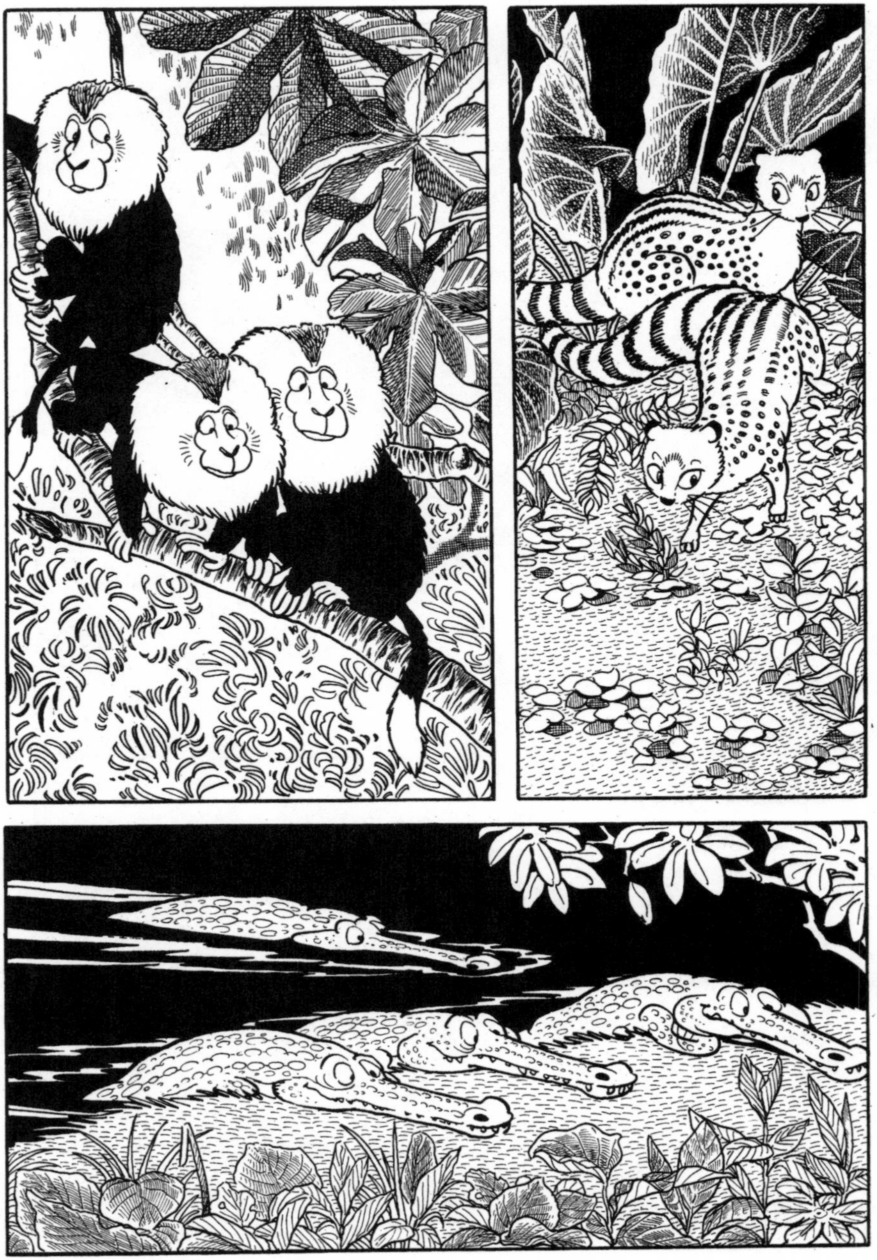

WHAT A GLORIOUS DAY...

THE MOST SPLENDID ONE I'VE WOKEN TO IN MY LIFE.

11

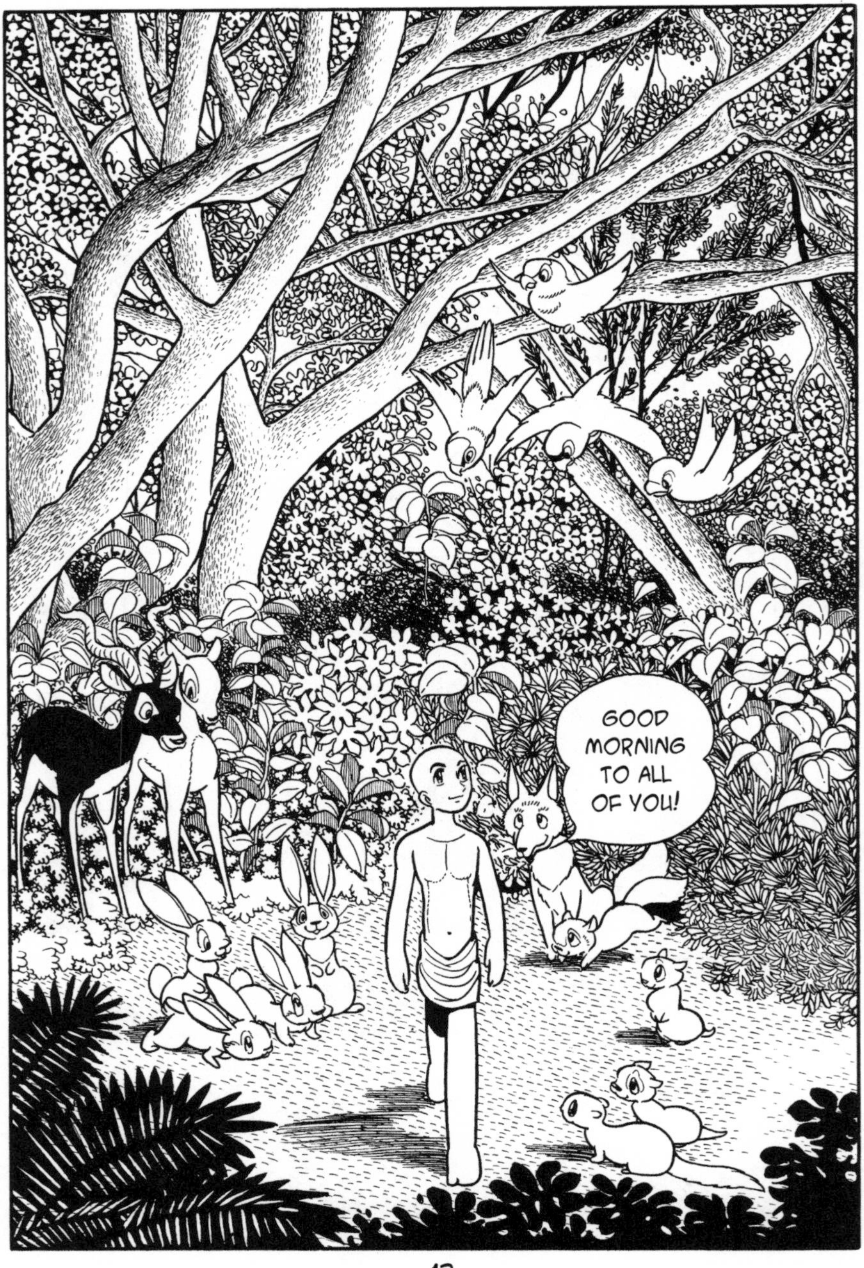
GOOD MORNING TO ALL OF YOU!

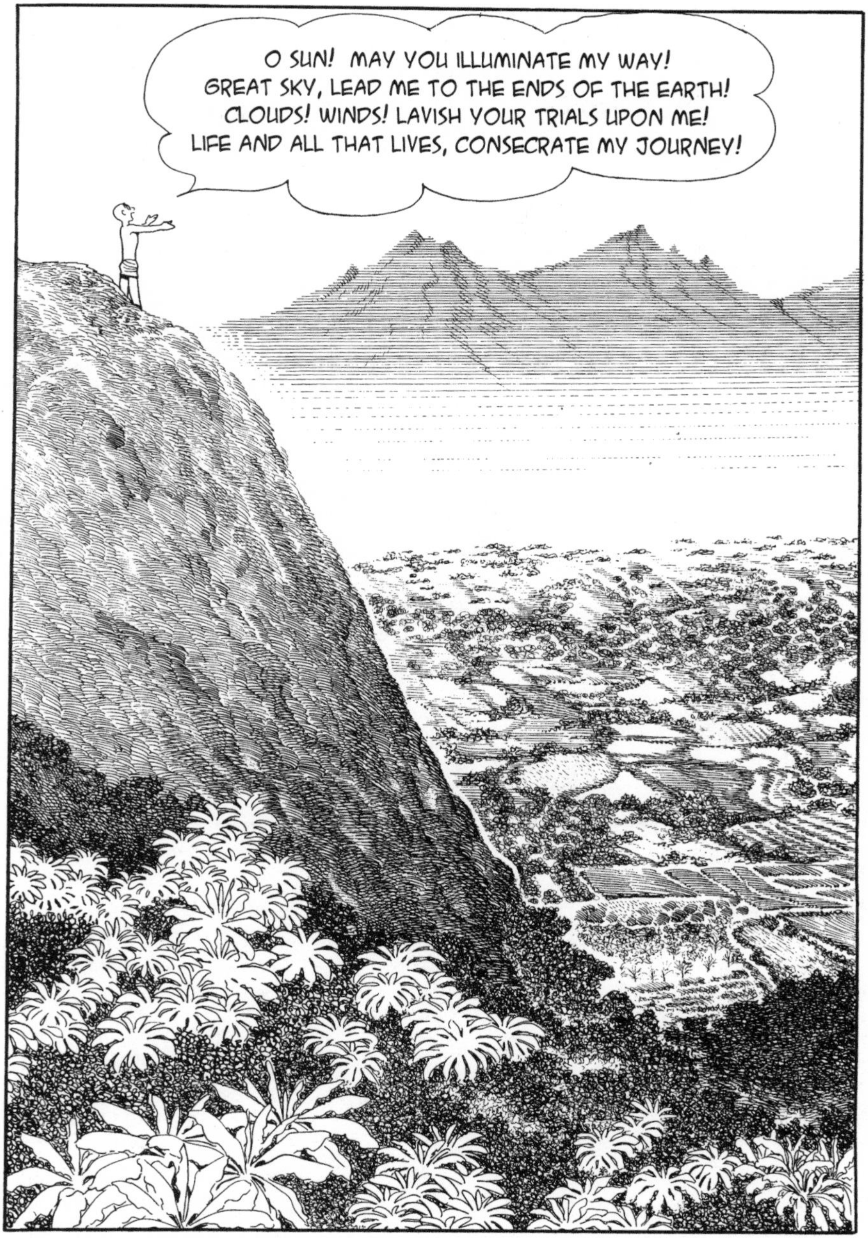
O SUN! MAY YOU ILLUMINATE MY WAY! GREAT SKY, LEAD ME TO THE ENDS OF THE EARTH! CLOUDS! WINDS! LAVISH YOUR TRIALS UPON ME! LIFE AND ALL THAT LIVES, CONSECRATE MY JOURNEY!

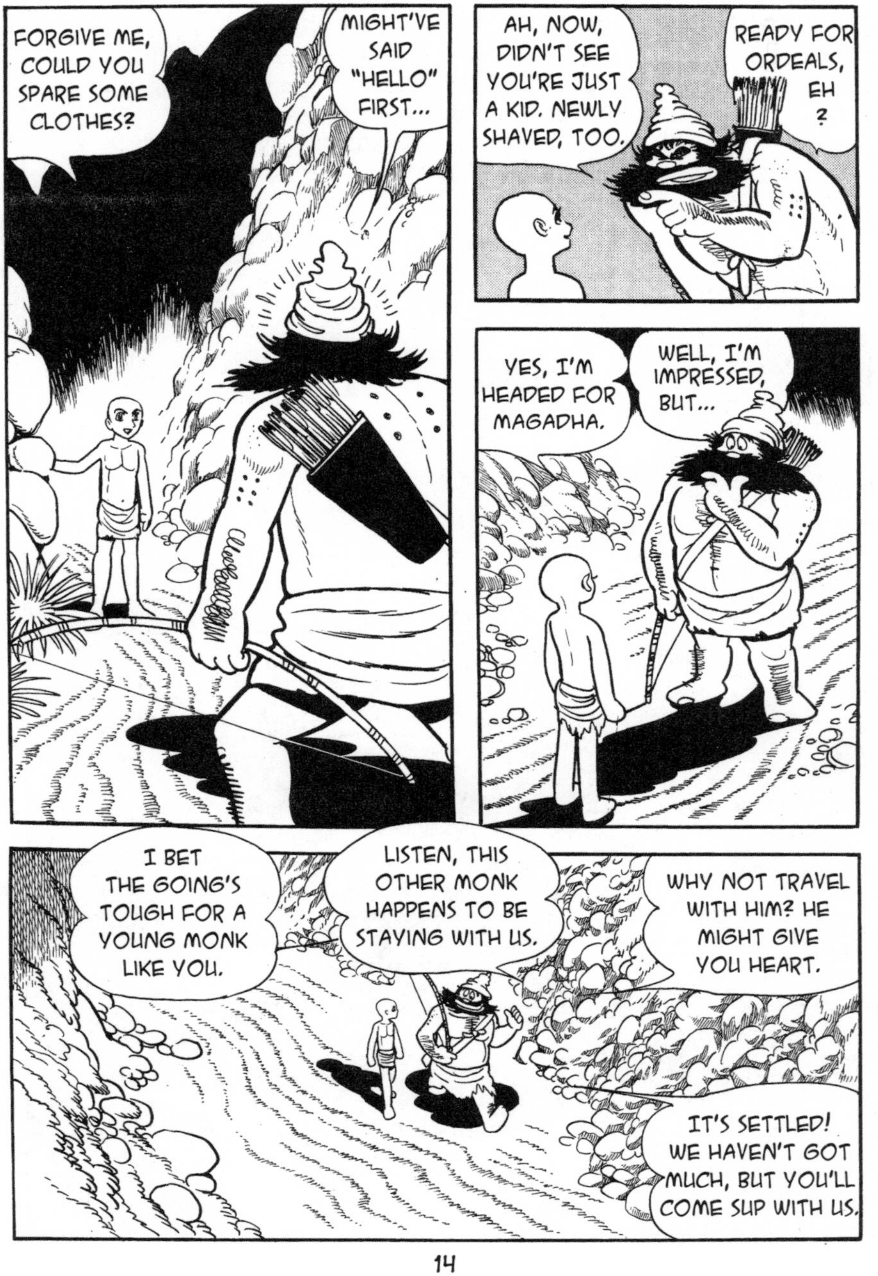
FORGIVE ME, COULD YOU SPARE SOME CLOTHES?
MIGHT'VE SAID "HELLO" FIRST...
AH, NOW, DIDN'T SEE YOU'RE JUST A KID. NEWLY SHAVED, TOO.
READY FOR ORDEALS, EH ?
YES, I'M HEADED FOR MAGADHA.
WELL, I'M IMPRESSED, BUT...
I BET THE GOING'S TOUGH FOR A YOUNG MONK LIKE YOU.
LISTEN, THIS OTHER MONK HAPPENS TO BE STAYING WITH US.
WHY NOT TRAVEL WITH HIM? HE MIGHT GIVE YOU HEART.
IT'S SETTLED! WE HAVEN'T GOT MUCH, BUT YOU'LL COME SUP WITH US.

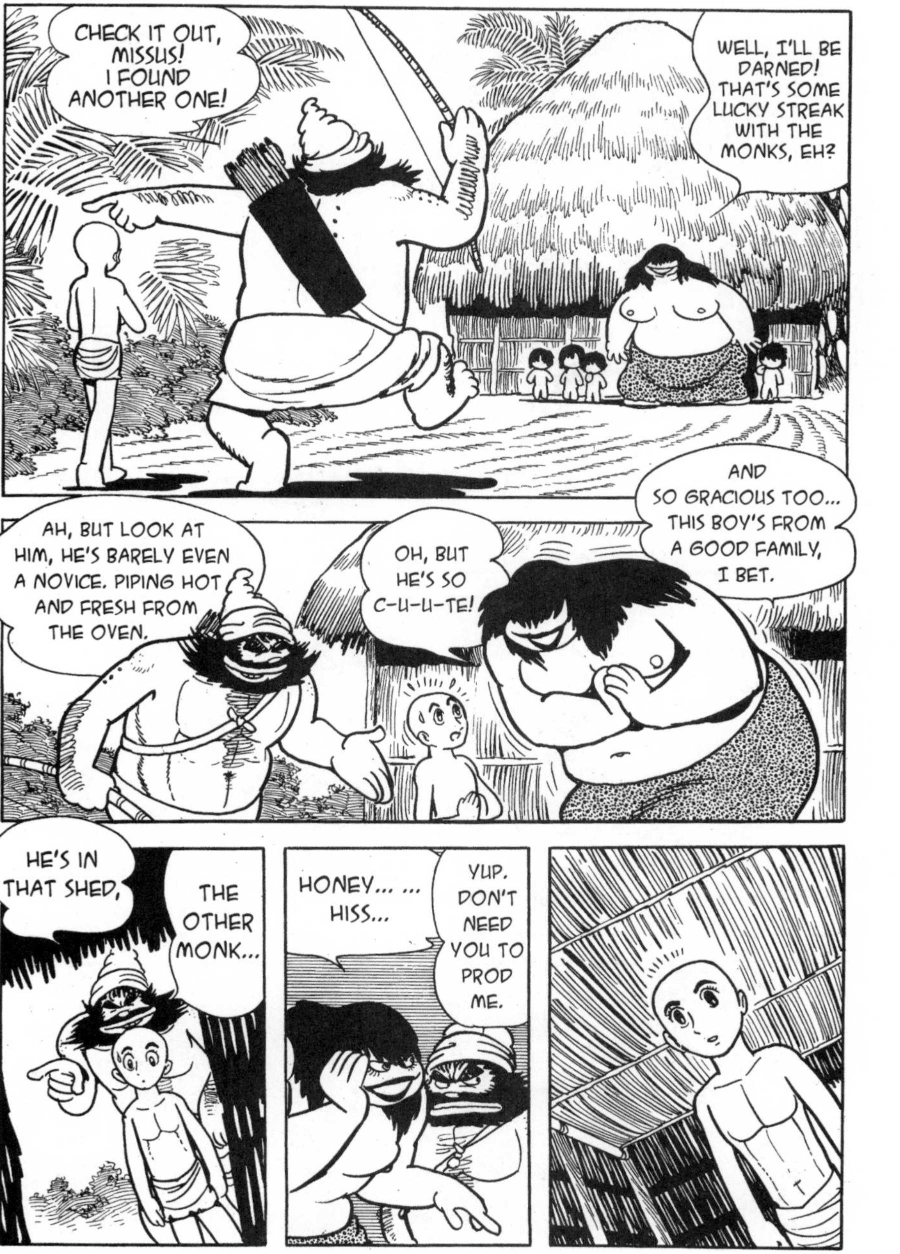
CHECK IT OUT, MISSUS! I FOUND ANOTHER ONE!
WELL, I'LL BE DARNED! THAT'S SOME LUCKY STREAK WITH THE MONKS, EH?
AH, BUT LOOK AT HIM, HE'S BARELY EVEN A NOVICE. PIPING HOT AND FRESH FROM THE OVEN.
OH, BUT HE'S SO C-U-U-TE!
AND SO GRACIOUS TOO... THIS BOY'S FROM A GOOD FAMILY, I BET.
HE'S IN THAT SHED,
THE OTHER MONK...
HONEY... ... HISS...
YUP. DON'T NEED YOU TO PROD ME.

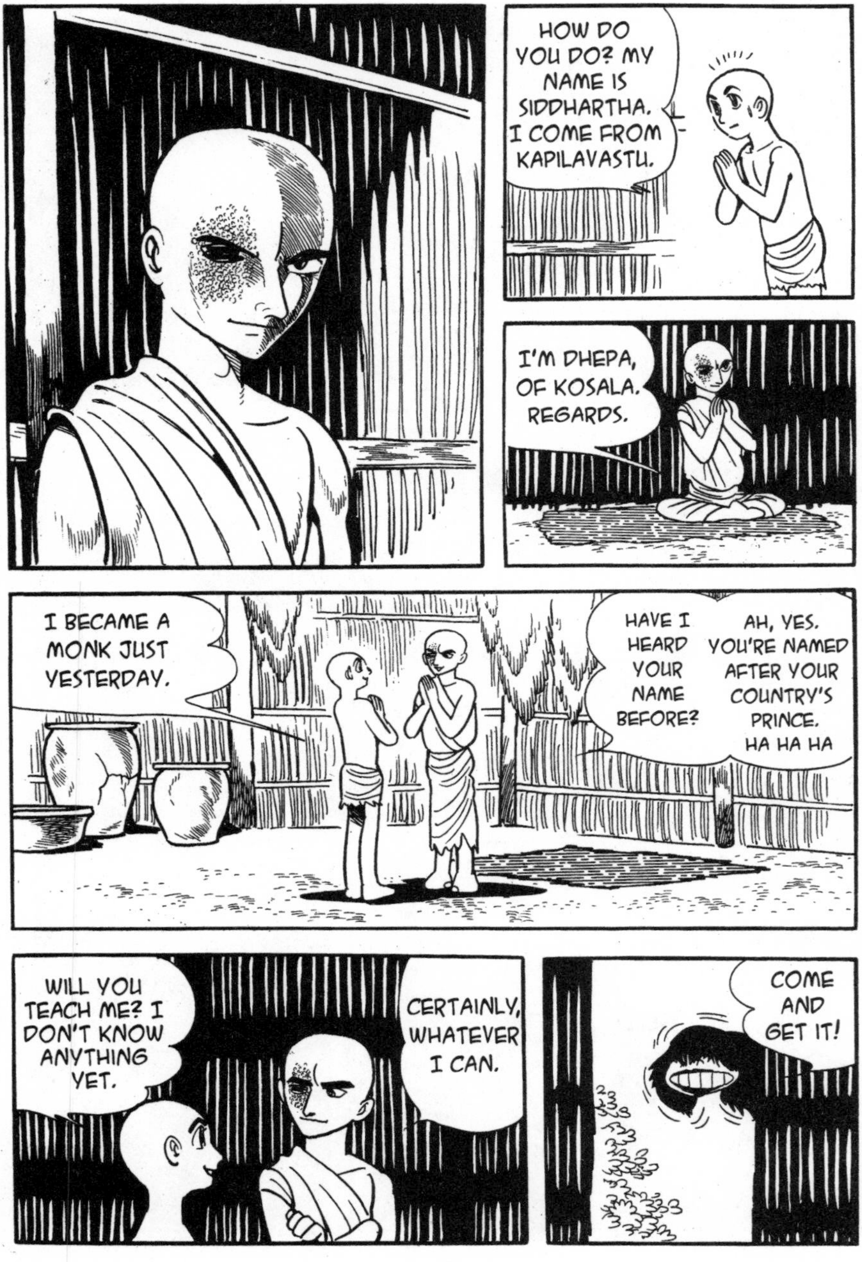

HOW DO YOU DO? MY NAME IS SIDDHARTHA. I COME FROM KAPILAVASTU.
I'M DHEPA, OF KOSALA. REGARDS.
I BECAME A MONK JUST YESTERDAY.
HAVE I HEARD YOUR NAME BEFORE?
AH, YES. YOU'RE NAMED AFTER YOUR COUNTRY'S PRINCE. HA HA HA
WILL YOU TEACH ME? I DON'T KNOW ANYTHING YET.
CERTAINLY, WHATEVER I CAN.
COME AND GET IT!

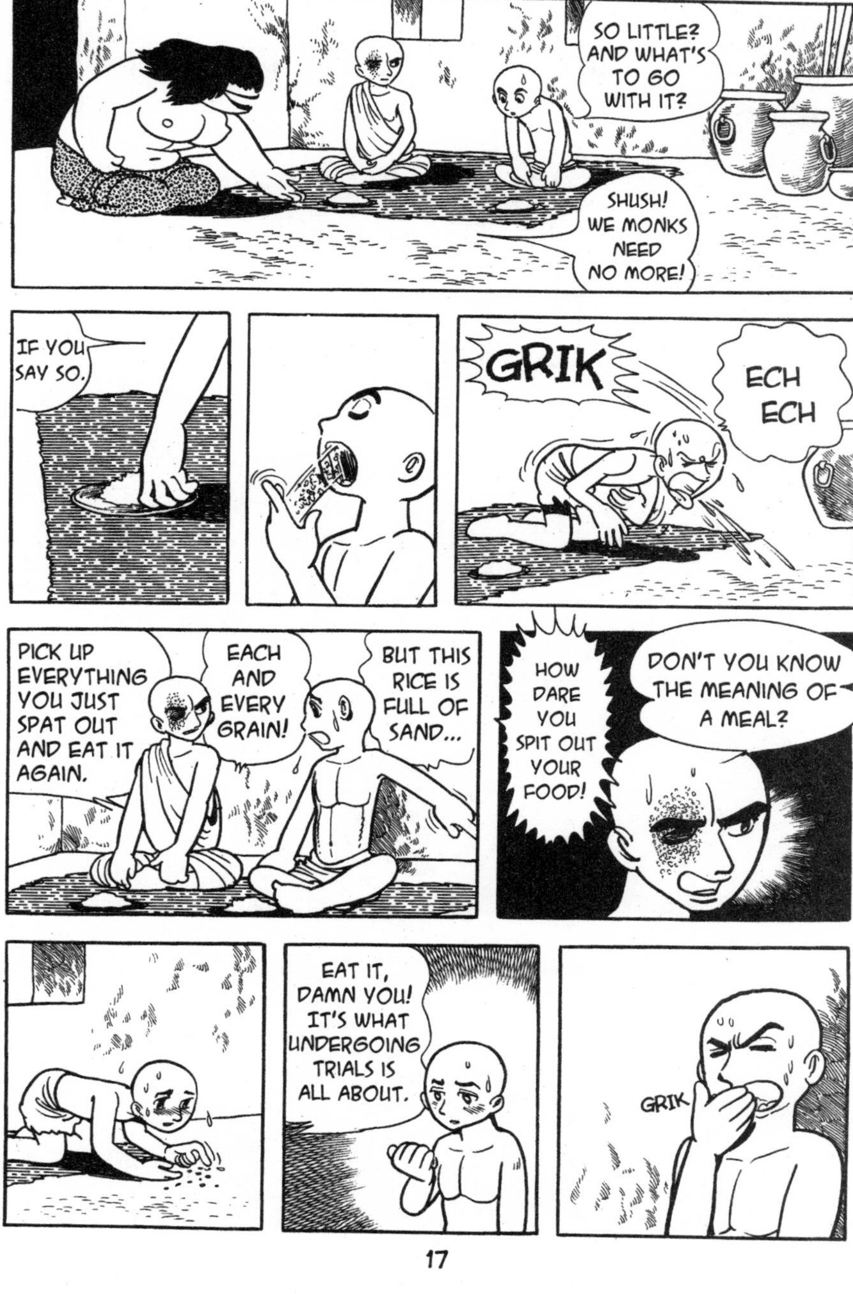
SO LITTLE? AND WHAT'S TO GO WITH IT?
SHUSH! WE MONKS NEED NO MORE!
IF YOU SAY SO.
GRIK
ECH ECH
PICK UP EVERYTHING YOU JUST SPAT OUT AND EAT IT AGAIN.
EACH AND EVERY GRAIN!
BUT THIS RICE IS FULL OF SAND...
HOW DARE YOU SPIT OUT YOUR FOOD!
DON'T YOU KNOW THE MEANING OF A MEAL?
EAT IT, DAMN YOU! IT'S WHAT UNDERGOING TRIALS IS ALL ABOUT.
GRIK

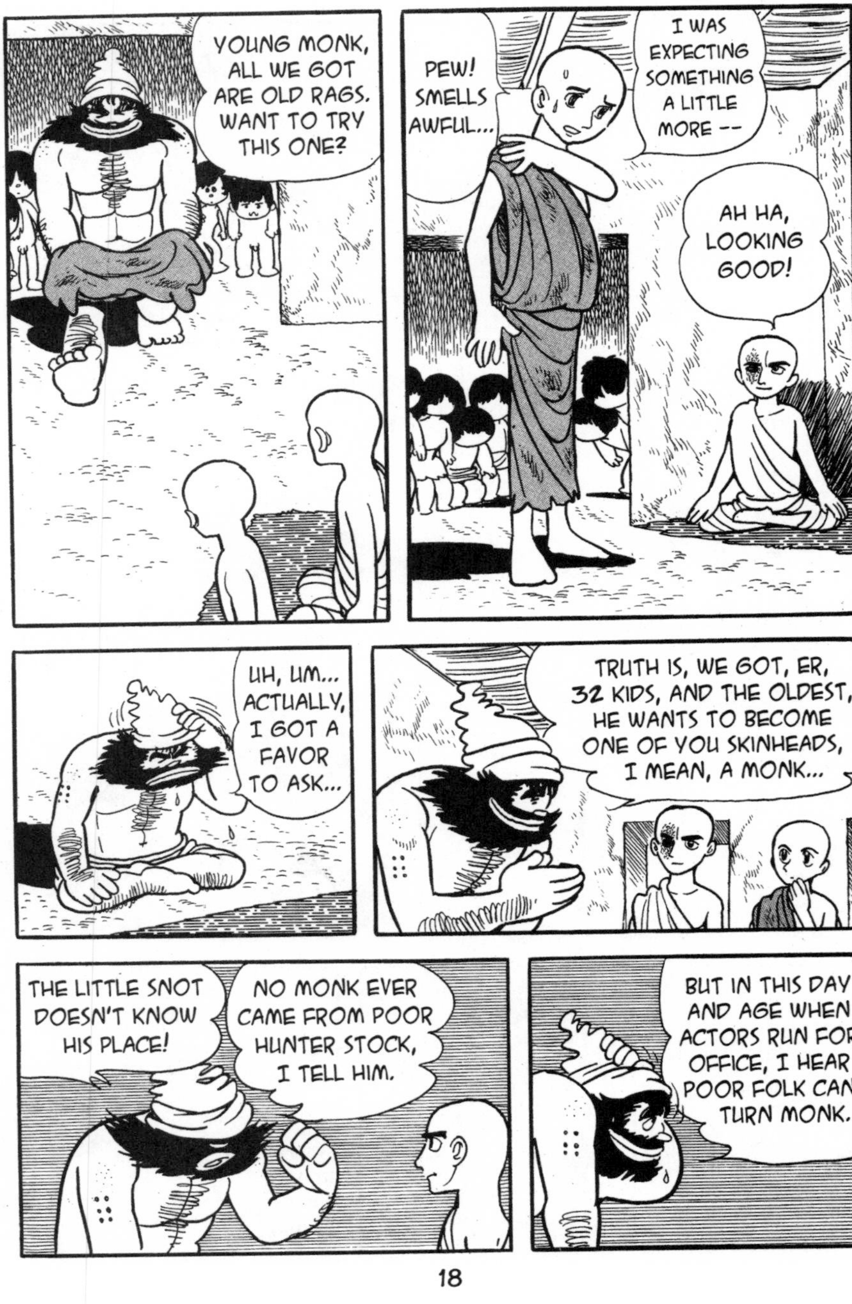
YOUNG MONK, ALL WE GOT ARE OLD RAGS. WANT TO TRY THIS ONE?
PEW! SMELLS AWFUL...
I WAS EXPECTING SOMETHING A LITTLE MORE --
AH HA, LOOKING GOOD!
UH, UM... ACTUALLY, I GOT A FAVOR TO ASK...
TRUTH IS, WE GOT, ER, 32 KIDS, AND THE OLDEST, HE WANTS TO BECOME ONE OF YOU SKINHEADS, I MEAN, A MONK...
THE LITTLE SNOT DOESN'T KNOW HIS PLACE!
NO MONK EVER CAME FROM POOR HUNTER STOCK, I TELL HIM.
BUT IN THIS DAY AND AGE WHEN ACTORS RUN FOR OFFICE, I HEAR POOR FOLK CAN TURN MONK.

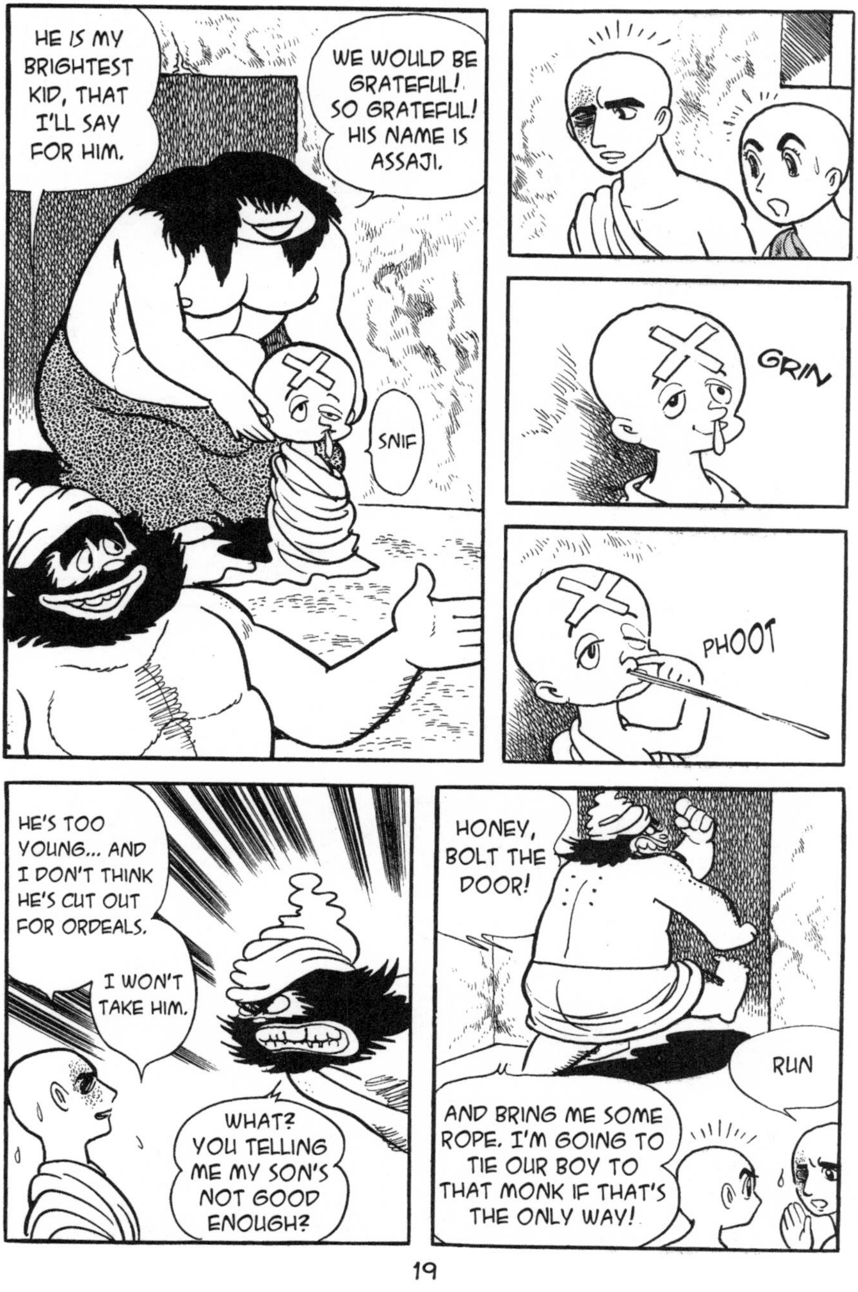
HE IS MY BRIGHTEST KID, THAT I'LL SAY FOR HIM.
WE WOULD BE GRATEFUL! SO GRATEFUL! HIS NAME IS ASSAJI.
SNIF
GRIN
PHOOT
HE'S TOO YOUNG... AND I DON'T THINK HE'S CUT OUT FOR ORDEALS.
I WON'T TAKE HIM.
WHAT? YOU TELLING ME MY SON'S NOT GOOD ENOUGH?
HONEY, BOLT THE DOOR!
AND BRING ME SOME ROPE. I'M GOING TO TIE OUR BOY TO THAT MONK IF THAT'S THE ONLY WAY!
RUN

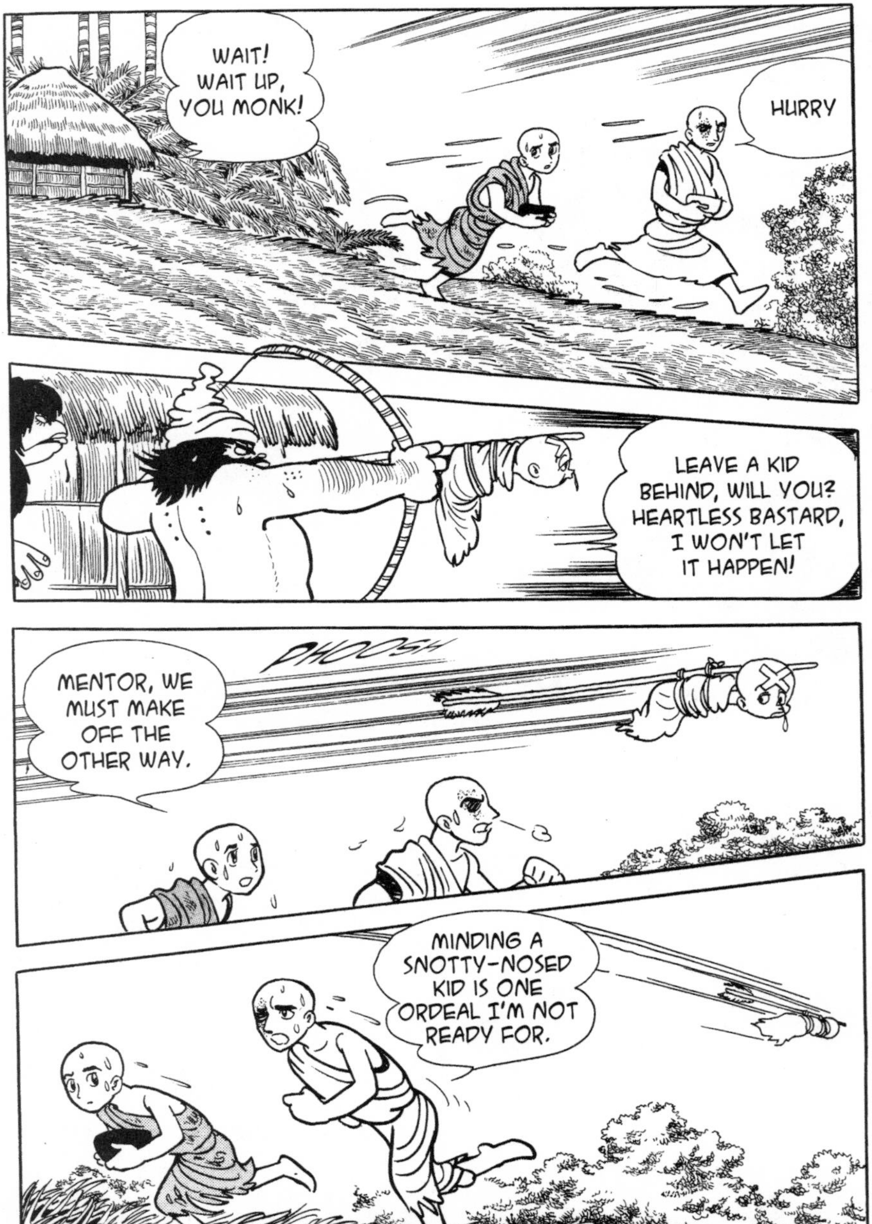
WAIT! WAIT UP, YOU MONK!
HURRY
LEAVE A KID BEHIND, WILL YOU? HEARTLESS BASTARD, I WON'T LET IT HAPPEN!
PHOOSH
MENTOR, WE MUST MAKE OFF THE OTHER WAY.
MINDING A SNOTTY-NOSED KID IS ONE ORDEAL I'M NOT READY FOR.

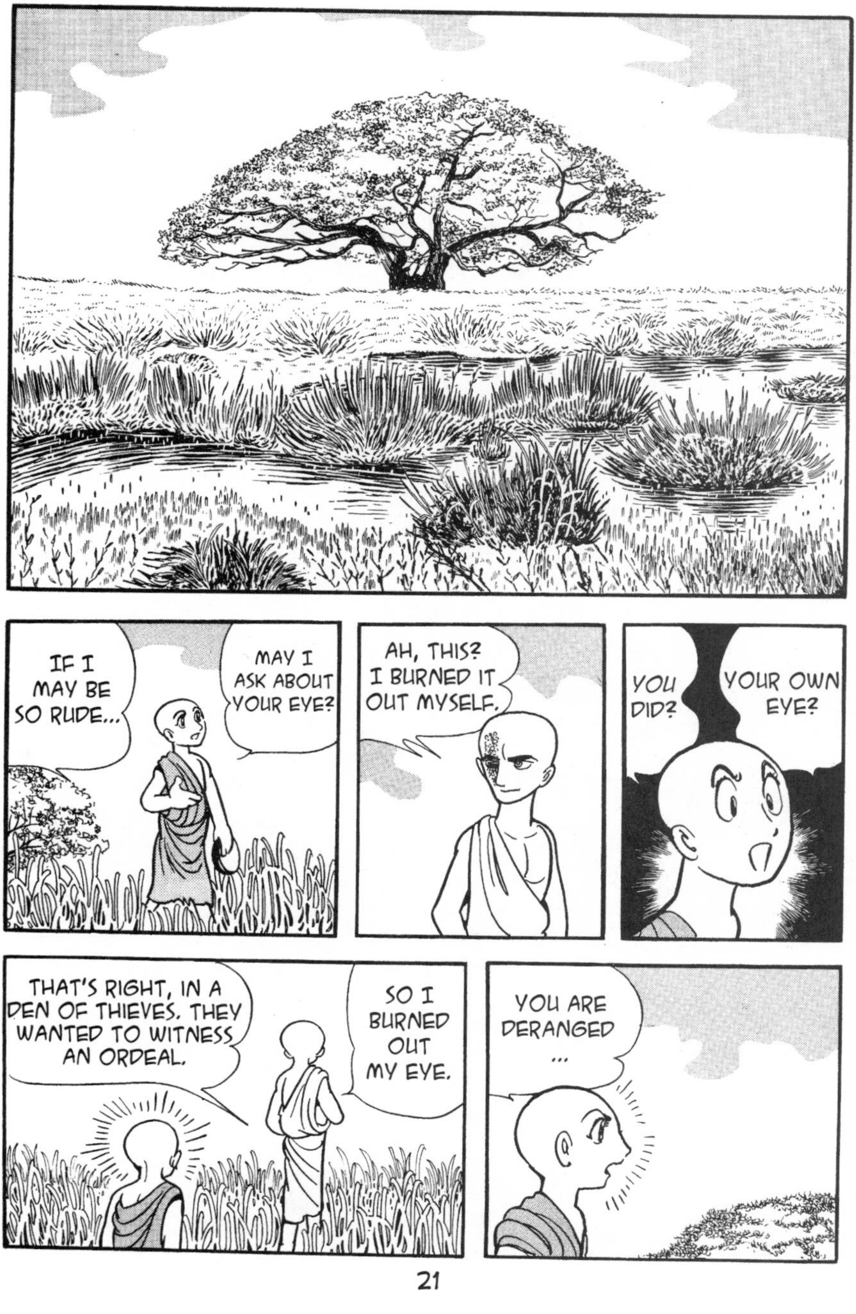
IF I MAY BE SO RUDE...
MAY I ASK ABOUT YOUR EYE?
AH, THIS? I BURNED IT OUT MYSELF.
YOU DID?
YOUR OWN EYE?
THAT'S RIGHT, IN A DEN OF THIEVES. THEY WANTED TO WITNESS AN ORDEAL.
SO I BURNED OUT MY EYE.
YOU ARE DERANGED ...

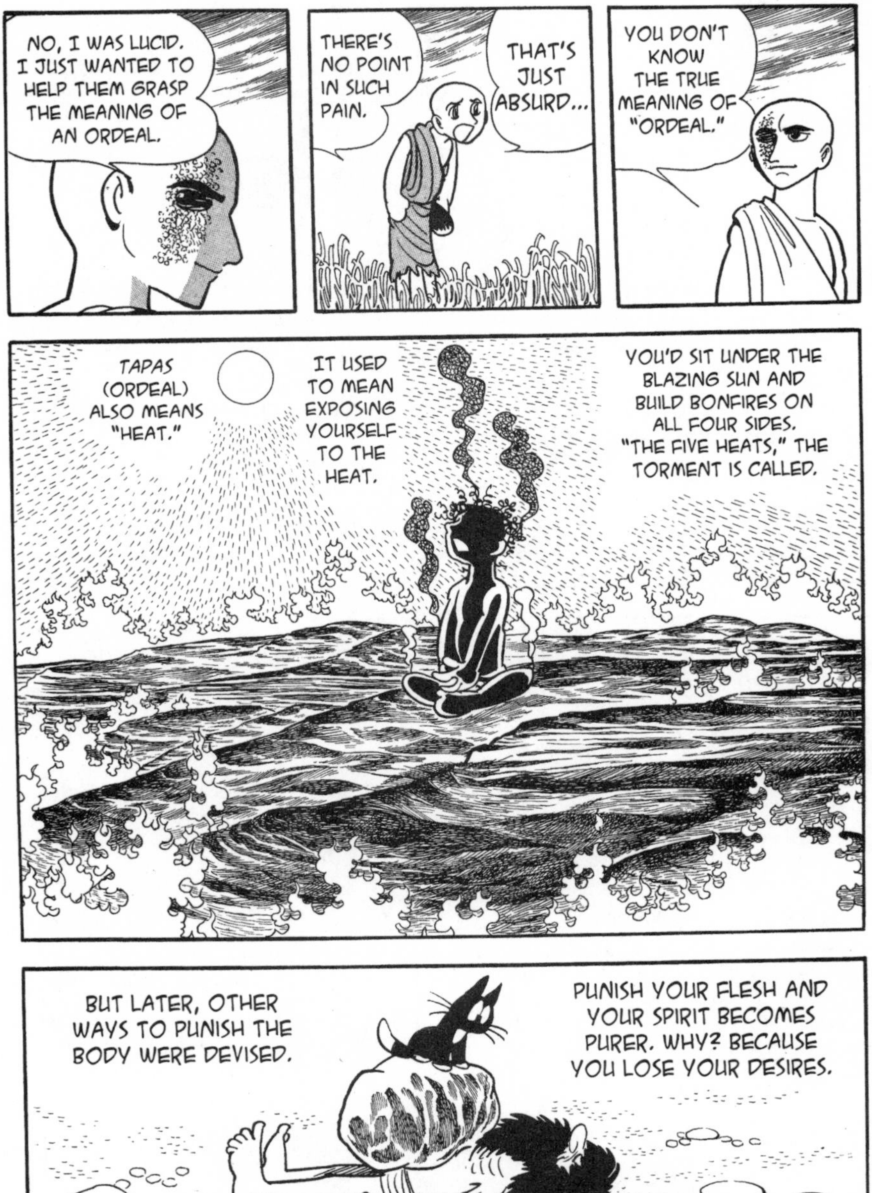
NO, I WAS LUCID. I JUST WANTED TO HELP THEM GRASP THE MEANING OF AN ORDEAL.
THERE'S NO POINT IN SUCH PAIN.
THAT'S JUST ABSURD...
YOU DON'T KNOW THE TRUE MEANING OF "ORDEAL."
TAPAS (ORDEAL) ALSO MEANS "HEAT."
IT USED TO MEAN EXPOSING YOURSELF TO THE HEAT.
YOU'D SIT UNDER THE BLAZING SUN AND BUILD BONFIRES ON ALL FOUR SIDES. "THE FIVE HEATS," THE TORMENT IS CALLED.
BUT LATER, OTHER WAYS TO PUNISH THE BODY WERE DEVISED.
PUNISH YOUR FLESH AND YOUR SPIRIT BECOMES PURER. WHY? BECAUSE YOU LOSE YOUR DESIRES.

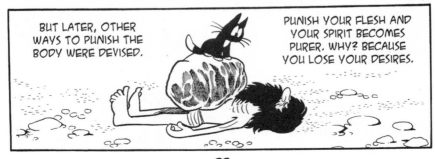

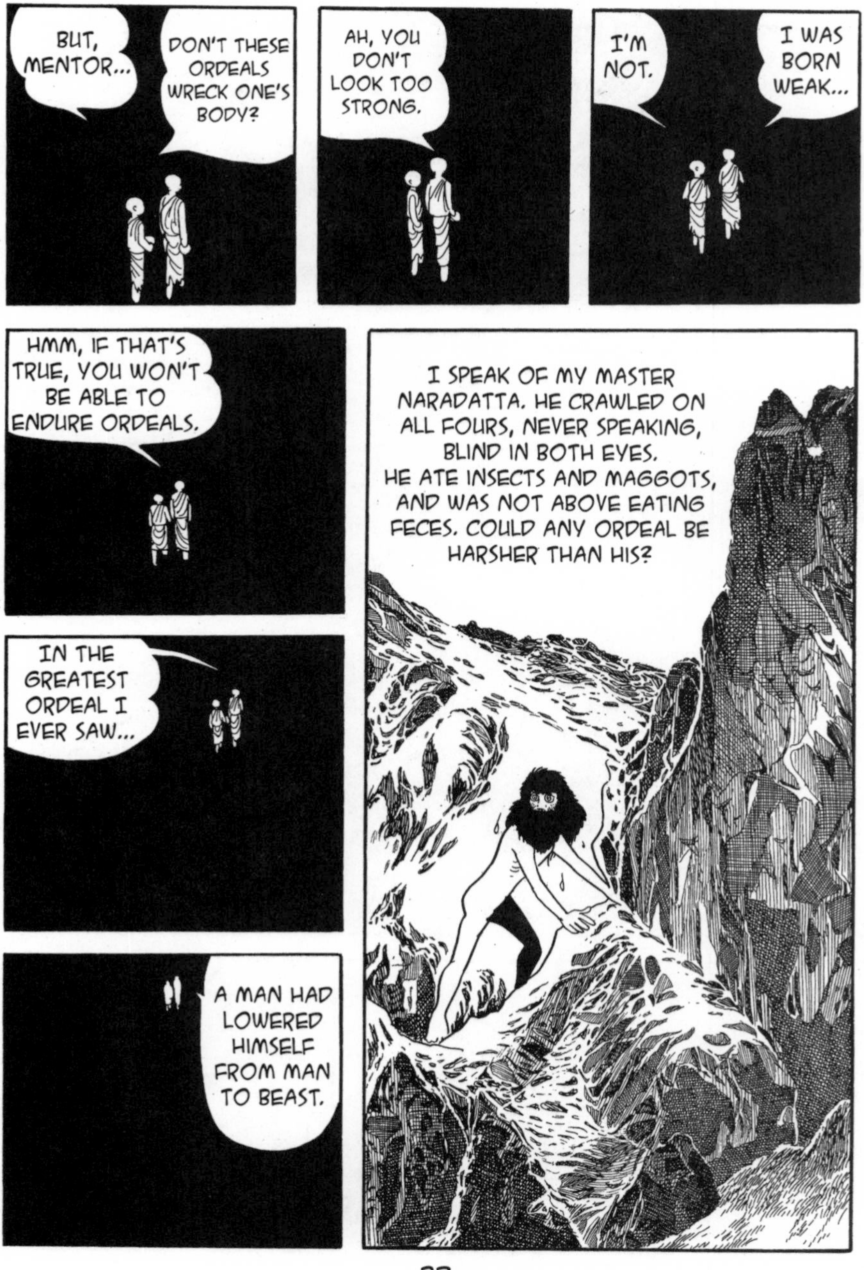
BUT, MENTOR...
DON'T THESE ORDEALS WRECK ONE'S BODY?
AH, YOU DON'T LOOK TOO STRONG.
I'M NOT.
I WAS BORN WEAK...
HMM, IF THAT'S TRUE, YOU WON'T BE ABLE TO ENDURE ORDEALS.
IN THE GREATEST ORDEAL I EVER SAW...
A MAN HAD LOWERED HIMSELF FROM MAN TO BEAST.
I SPEAK OF MY MASTER NARADATTA. HE CRAWLED ON ALL FOURS, NEVER SPEAKING, BLIND IN BOTH EYES. HE ATE INSECTS AND MAGGOTS, AND WAS NOT ABOVE EATING FECES. COULD ANY ORDEAL BE HARSHER THAN HIS?

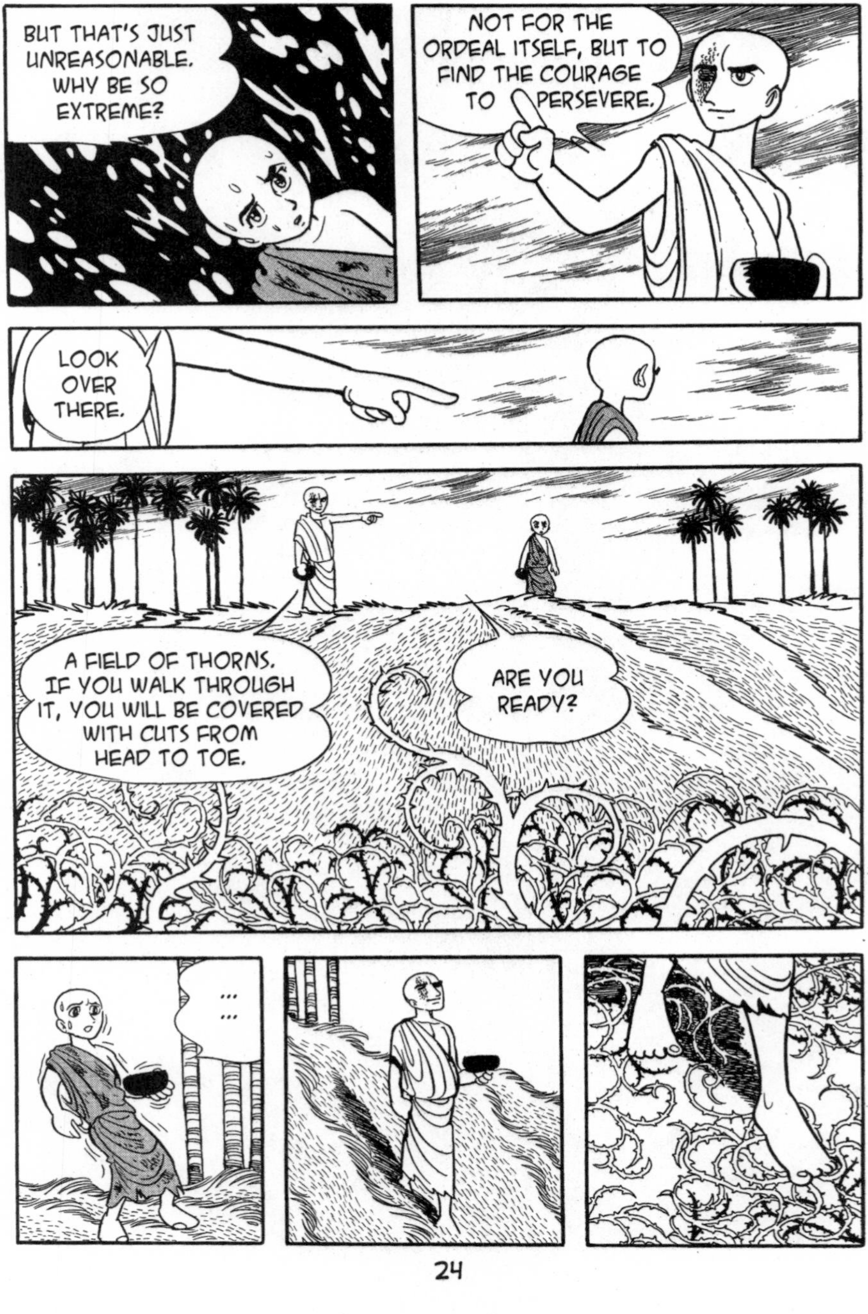
BUT THAT'S JUST UNREASONABLE. WHY BE SO EXTREME?
NOT FOR THE ORDEAL ITSELF, BUT TO FIND THE COURAGE TO PERSEVERE.
LOOK OVER THERE.
A FIELD OF THORNS. IF YOU WALK THROUGH IT, YOU WILL BE COVERED WITH CUTS FROM HEAD TO TOE.
ARE YOU READY?
...
...

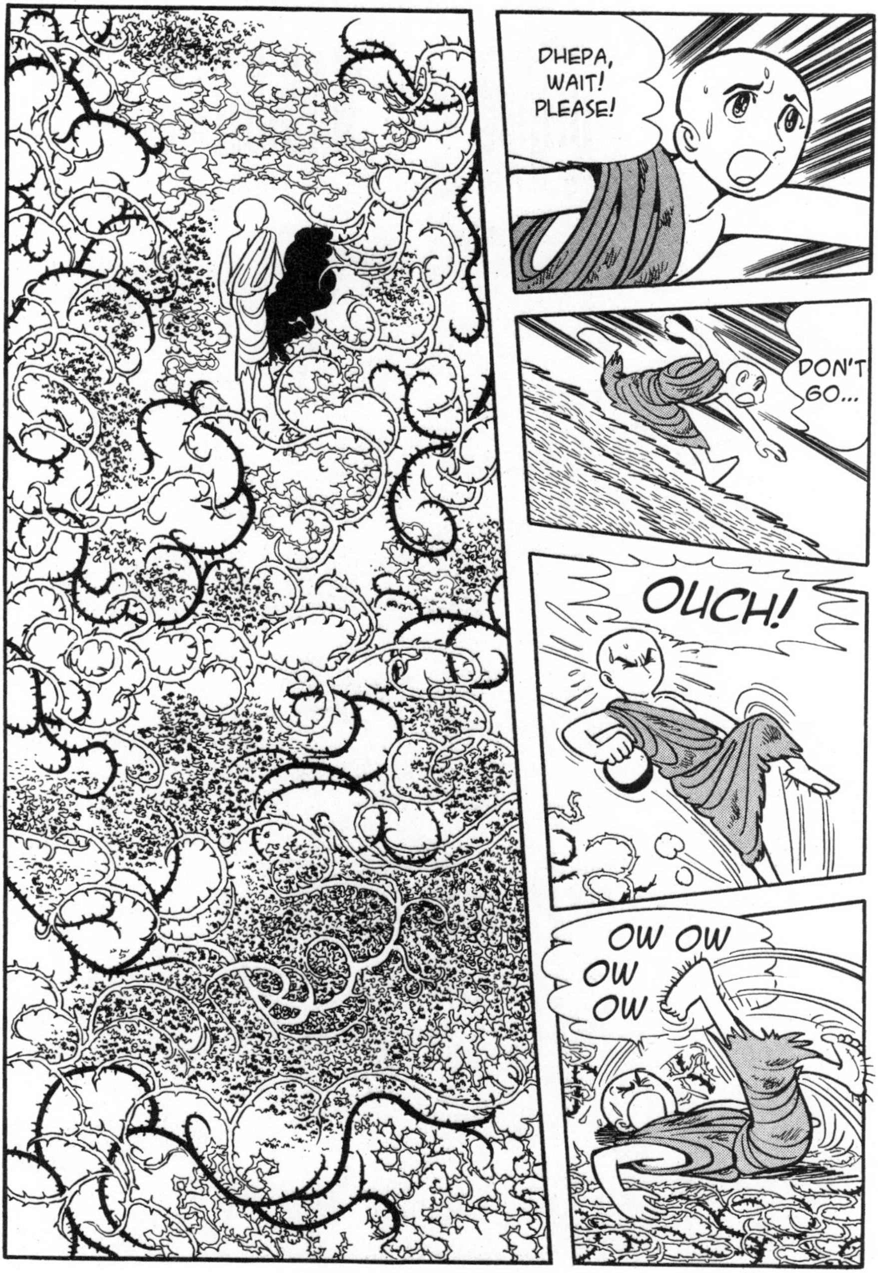
DHEPA, WAIT! PLEASE!
DON'T GO...
OUCH!
OW OW OW OW

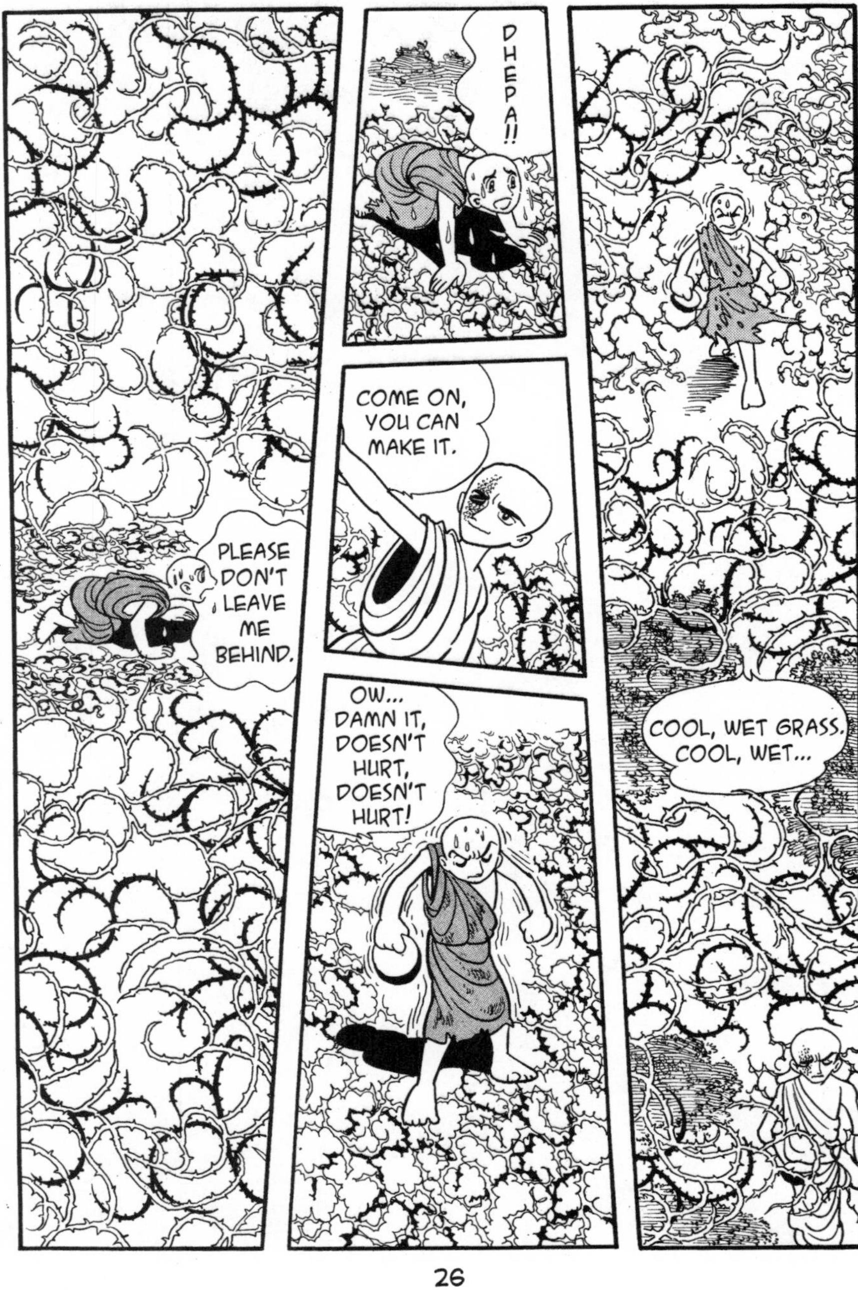
PLEASE DON'T LEAVE ME BEHIND.
DHEPA!!
COME ON, YOU CAN MAKE IT.
OW... DAMN IT, DOESN'T HURT, DOESN'T HURT!
COOL, WET GRASS. COOL, WET...

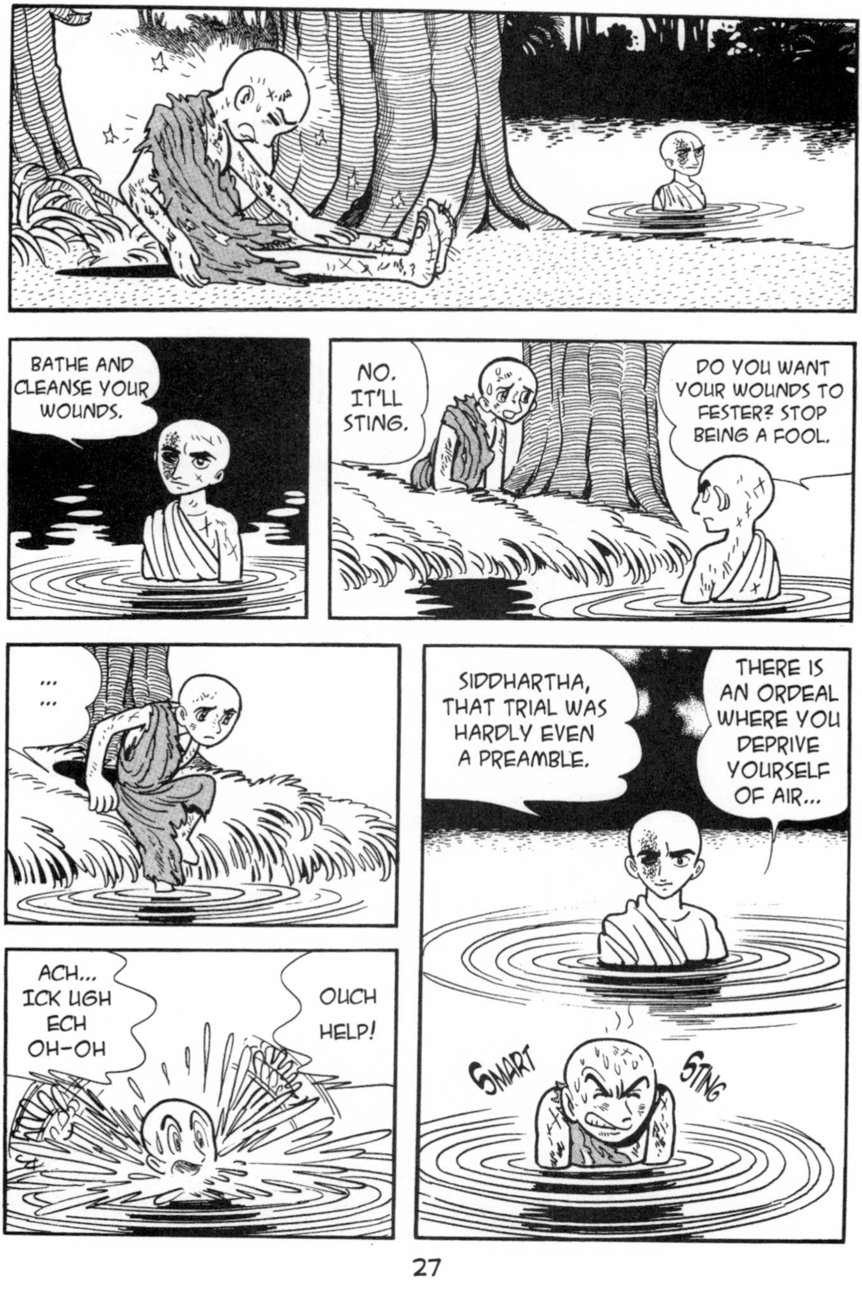
BATHE AND CLEANSE YOUR WOUNDS.
NO. IT'LL STING.
DO YOU WANT YOUR WOUNDS TO FESTER? STOP BEING A FOOL.
... ...
SIDDHARTHA, THAT TRIAL WAS HARDLY EVEN A PREAMBLE.
THERE IS AN ORDEAL WHERE YOU DEPRIVE YOURSELF OF AIR...
ACH... ICK UGH ECH OH-OH
OUCH HELP!
SMART
STING

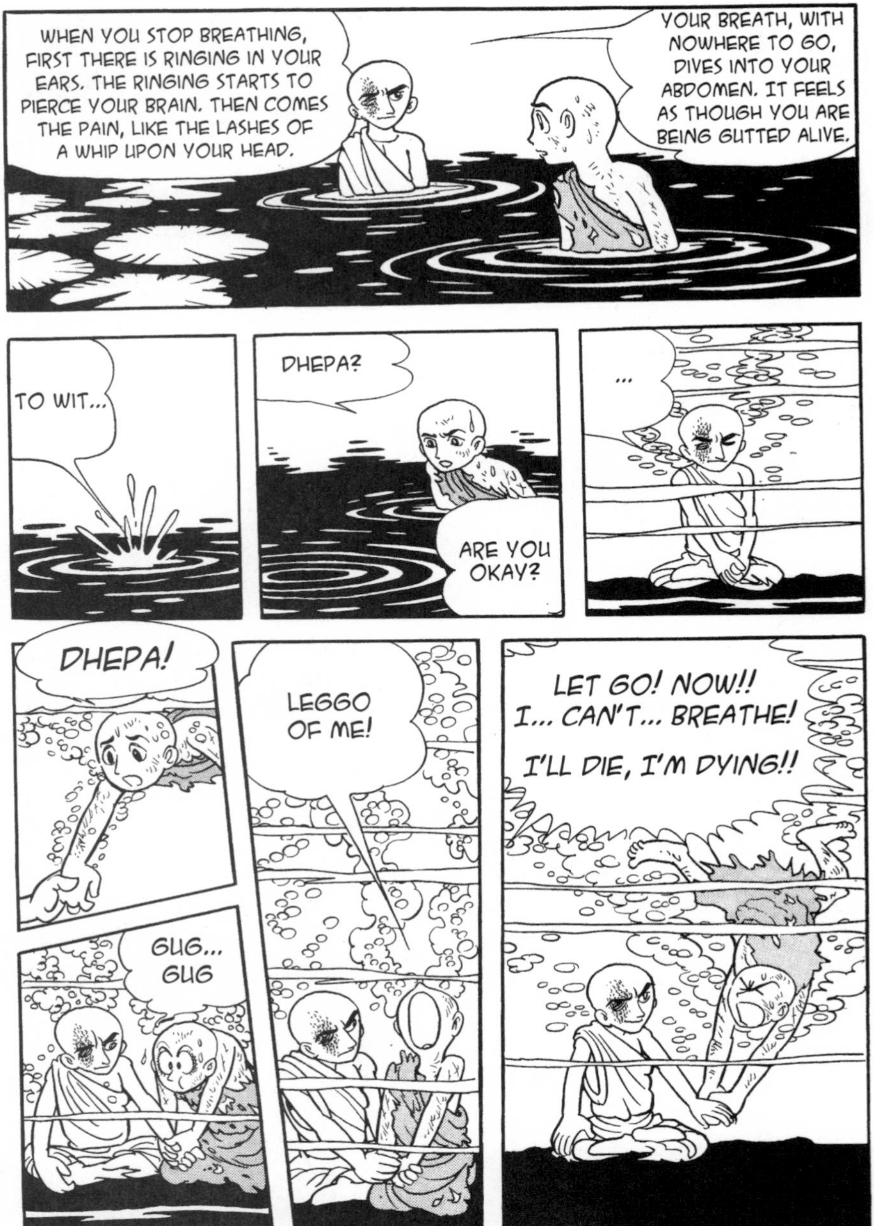
WHEN YOU STOP BREATHING, FIRST THERE IS RINGING IN YOUR EARS. THE RINGING STARTS TO PIERCE YOUR BRAIN. THEN COMES THE PAIN, LIKE THE LASHES OF A WHIP UPON YOUR HEAD.
YOUR BREATH, WITH NOWHERE TO GO, DIVES INTO YOUR ABDOMEN. IT FEELS AS THOUGH YOU ARE BEING GUTTED ALIVE.
TO WIT...
DHEPA?
ARE YOU OKAY?
...
DHEPA!
GUG... GUG
LEGGO OF ME!
LET GO! NOW!! I... CAN'T... BREATHE!
I'LL DIE, I'M DYING!!

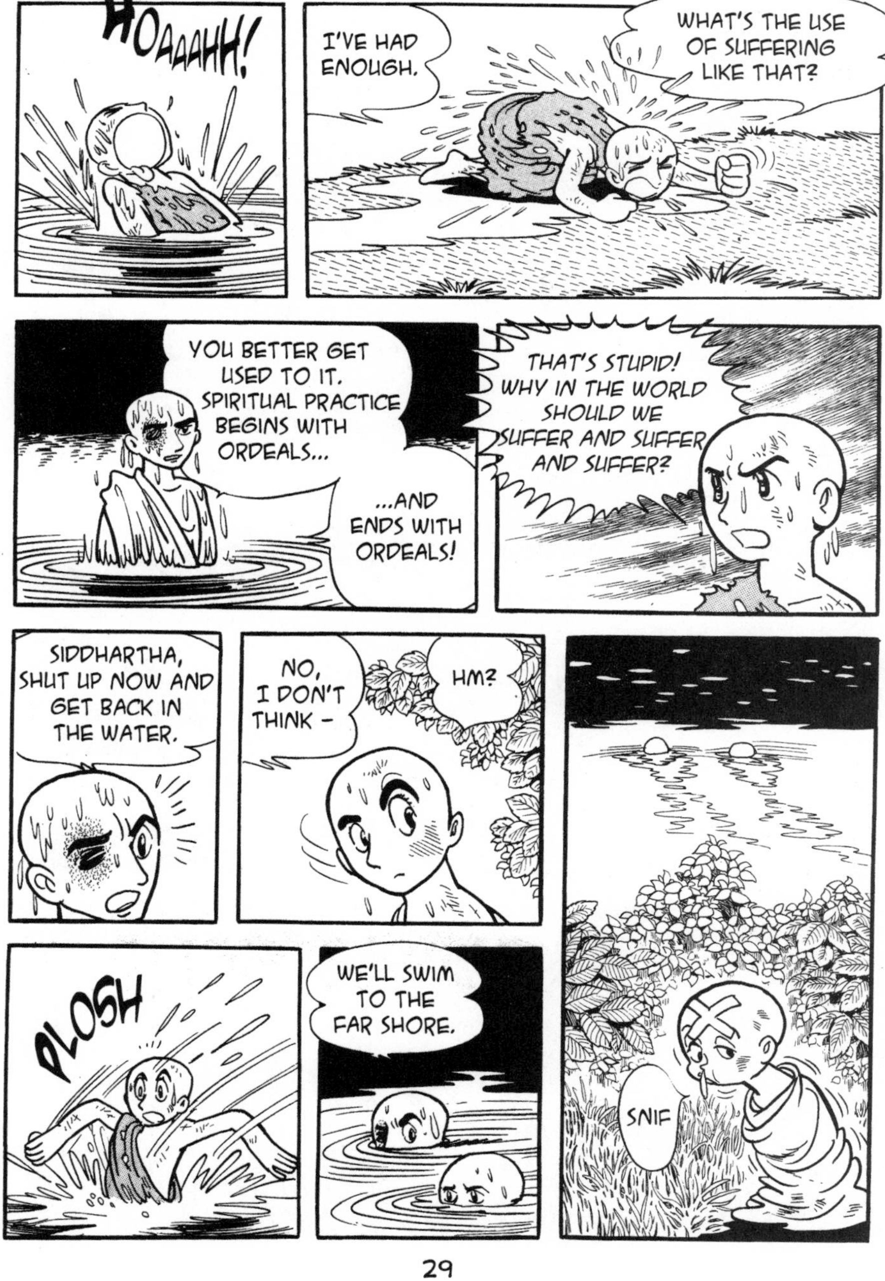
HOAAAHH!
I'VE HAD ENOUGH.
WHAT'S THE USE OF SUFFERING LIKE THAT?
YOU BETTER GET USED TO IT. SPIRITUAL PRACTICE BEGINS WITH ORDEALS...
...AND ENDS WITH ORDEALS!
THAT'S STUPID! WHY IN THE WORLD SHOULD WE SUFFER AND SUFFER AND SUFFER?
SIDDHARTHA, SHUT UP NOW AND GET BACK IN THE WATER.
NO, I DON'T THINK –
HM?
PLOSH
WE'LL SWIM TO THE FAR SHORE.
SNIF

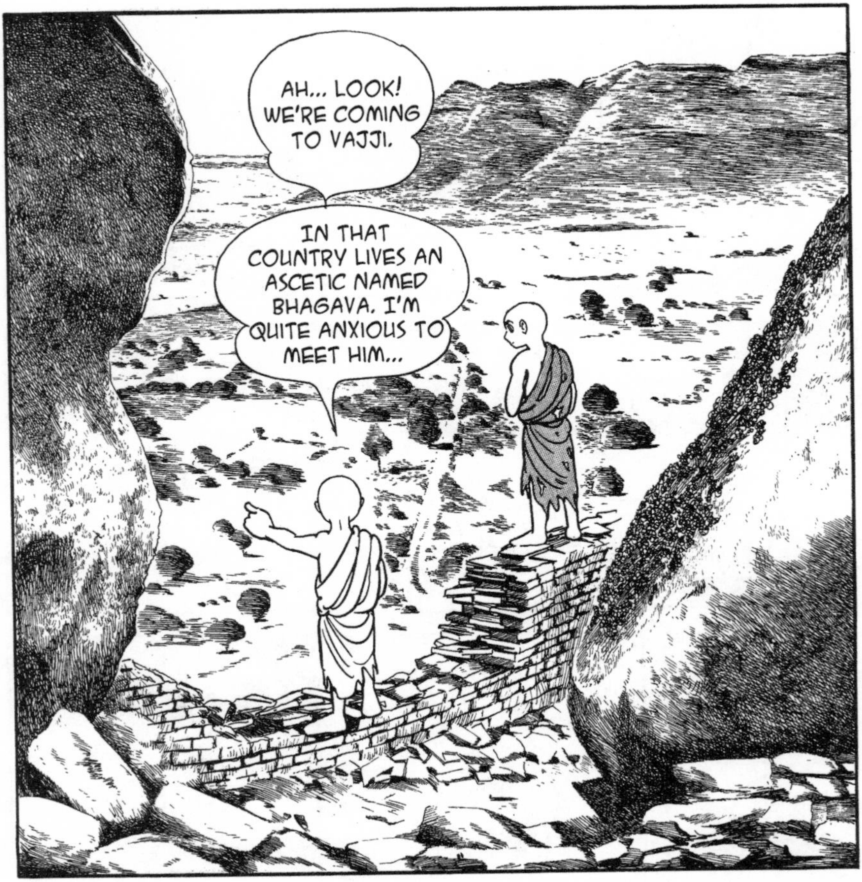
AH... LOOK! WE'RE COMING TO VAJJI.
IN THAT COUNTRY LIVES AN ASCETIC NAMED BHAGAVA. I'M QUITE ANXIOUS TO MEET HIM...

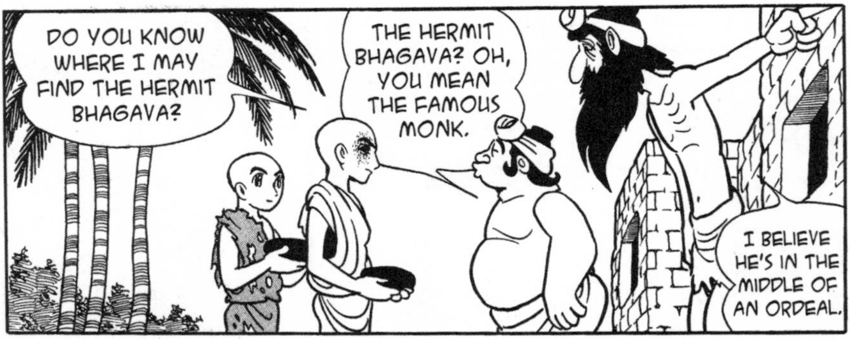
DO YOU KNOW WHERE I MAY FIND THE HERMIT BHAGAVA?
THE HERMIT BHAGAVA? OH, YOU MEAN THE FAMOUS MONK.
I BELIEVE HE'S IN THE MIDDLE OF AN ORDEAL.

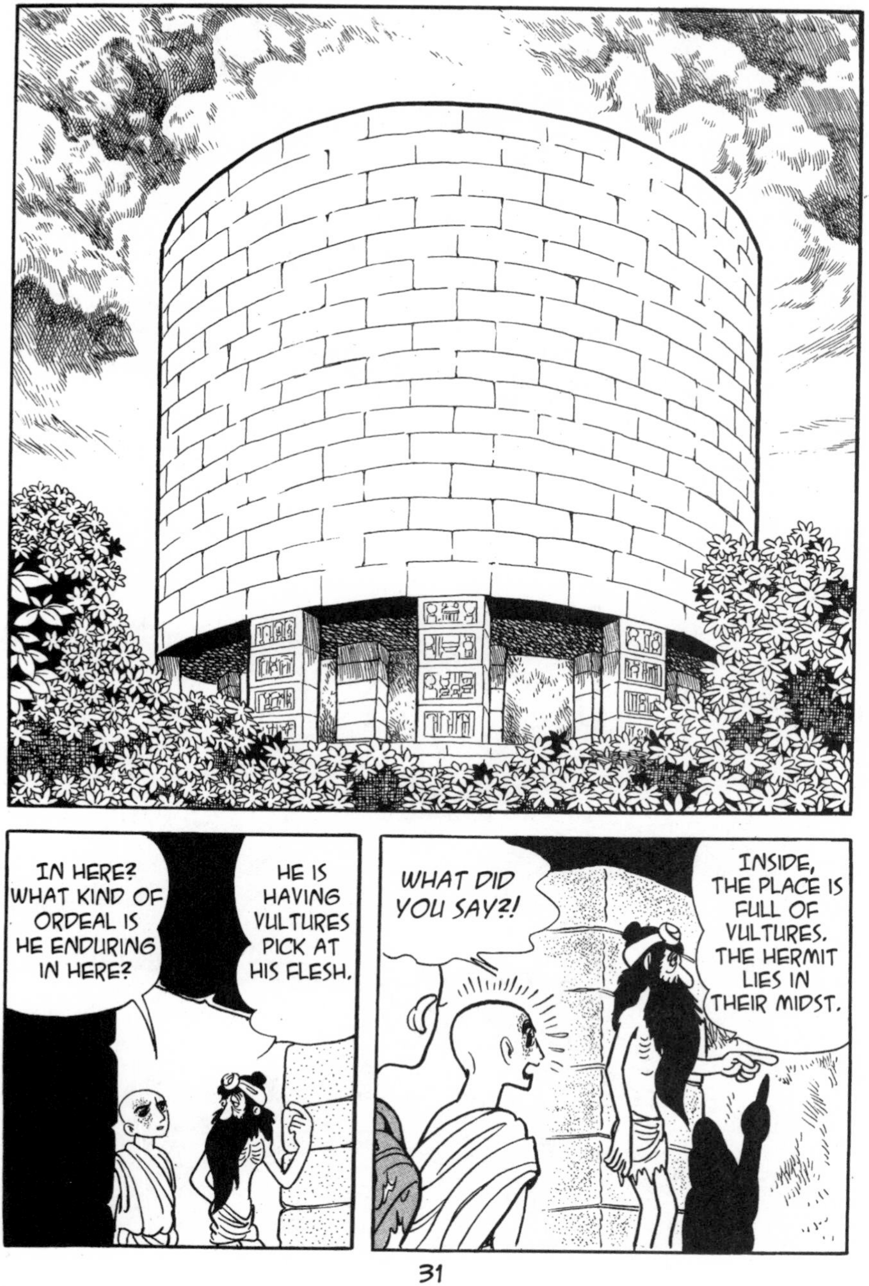
IN HERE? WHAT KIND OF ORDEAL IS HE ENDURING IN HERE?
HE IS HAVING VULTURES PICK AT HIS FLESH.
WHAT DID YOU SAY?!
INSIDE, THE PLACE IS FULL OF VULTURES. THE HERMIT LIES IN THEIR MIDST.

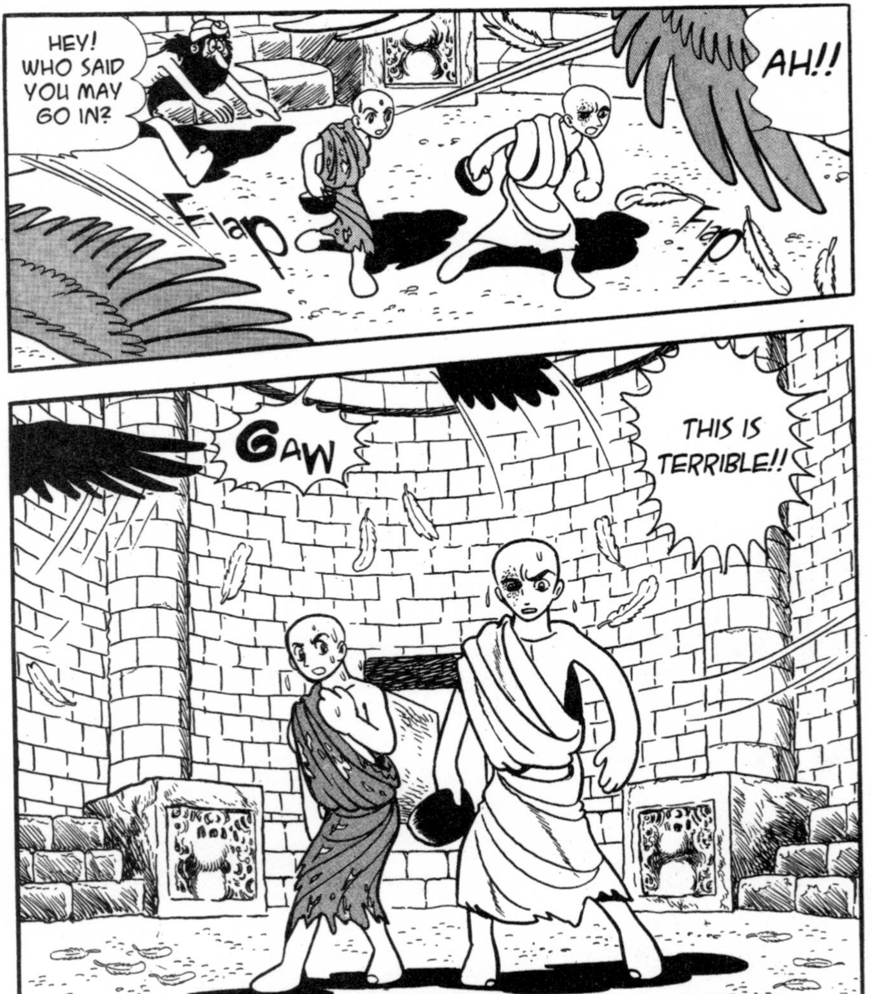
HEY! WHO SAID YOU MAY GO IN?
AH!!
Flap
Flap
GAW
THIS IS TERRIBLE!!

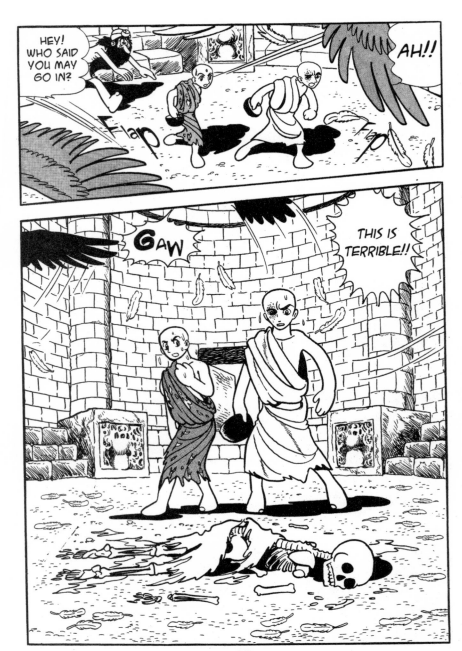

THESE BONES ARE HIM?

WHAT GOOD DID IT DO HIM IF IT ENDED UP KILLING HIM?

THIS IS WHAT YOU GET FOR ALL YOUR SUFFERING?

TELL ME, DHEPA.

NOW YOU SEE WHY I'M SKEPTICAL OF ORDEALS.

YOU HAVEN'T GOT A CLUE, HAVE YOU?

TO DIE IN AN ORDEAL IS PURE GREATNESS! IT IS THE SUPREME IDEAL!

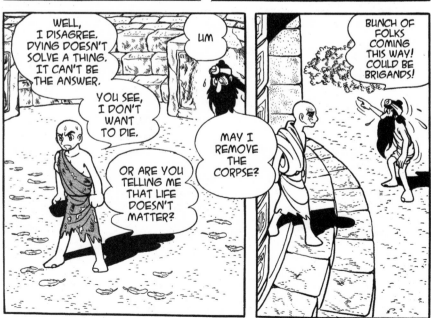

WELL, I DISAGREE. DYING DOESN'T SOLVE A THING. IT CAN'T BE THE ANSWER.

YOU SEE, I DON'T WANT TO DIE.

OR ARE YOU TELLING ME THAT LIFE DOESN'T MATTER?

UM

MAY I REMOVE THE CORPSE?

BUNCH OF FOLKS COMING THIS WAY! COULD BE BRIGANDS!

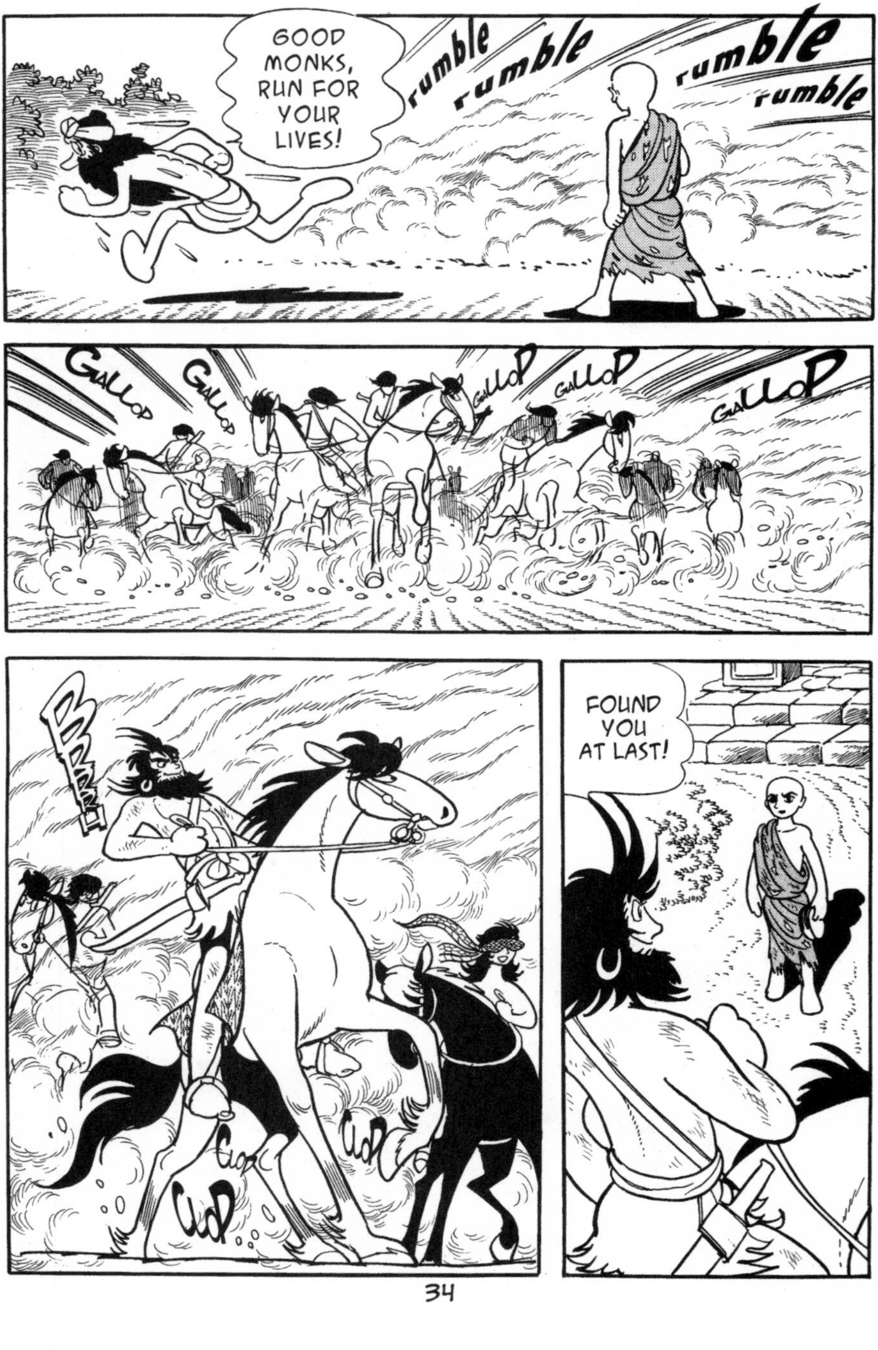
GOOD MONKS, RUN FOR YOUR LIVES!
rumble
rumble
rumble
rumble
GALLOP
GALLOP
GALLOP
GALLOP
GALLOP
CLOP
CLOP
CLOP
CLOP
FOUND YOU AT LAST!

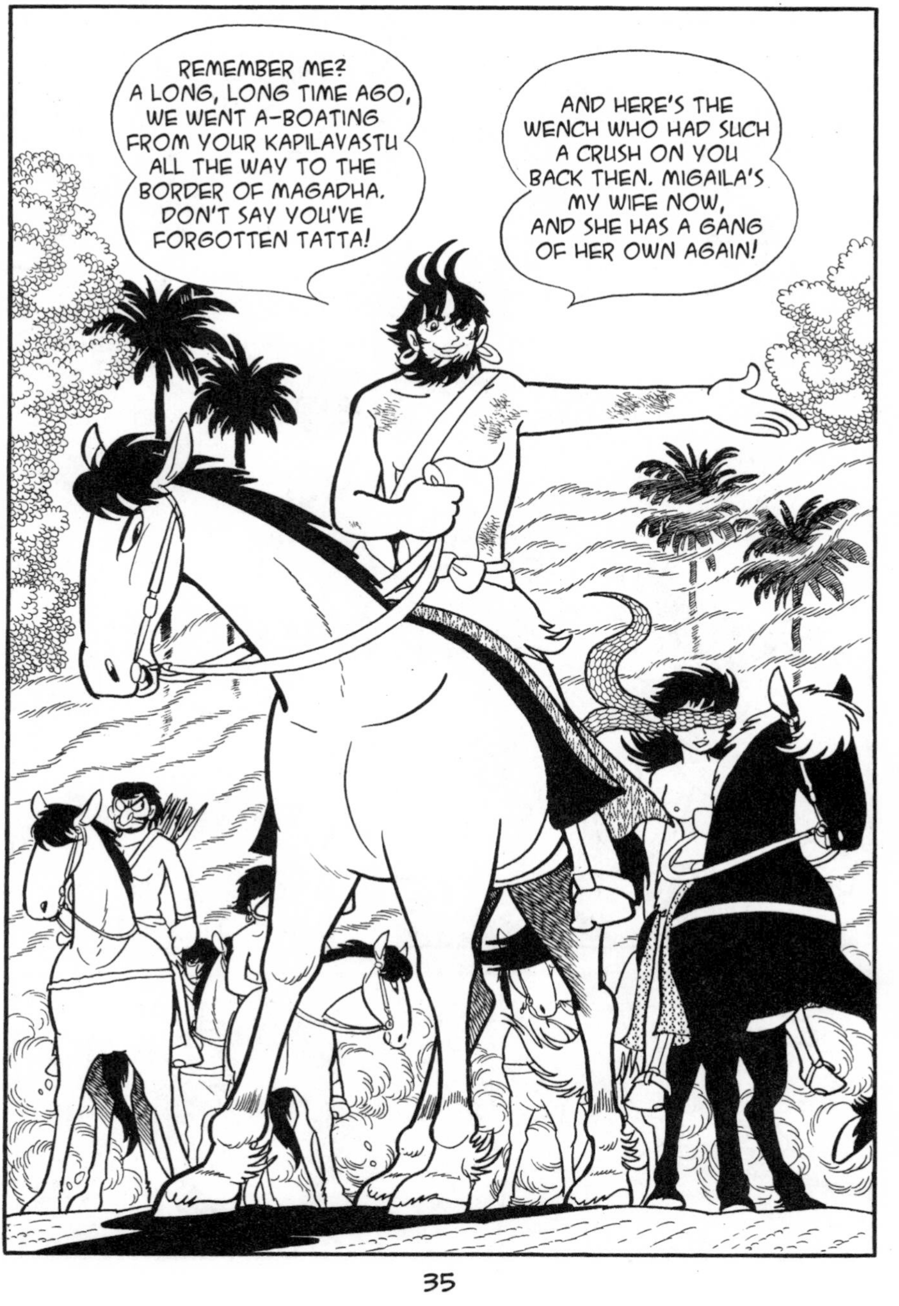
REMEMBER ME? A LONG, LONG TIME AGO, WE WENT A-BOATING FROM YOUR KAPILAVASTU ALL THE WAY TO THE BORDER OF MAGADHA. DON'T SAY YOU'VE FORGOTTEN TATTA!
AND HERE'S THE WENCH WHO HAD SUCH A CRUSH ON YOU BACK THEN. MIGAILA'S MY WIFE NOW, AND SHE HAS A GANG OF HER OWN AGAIN!

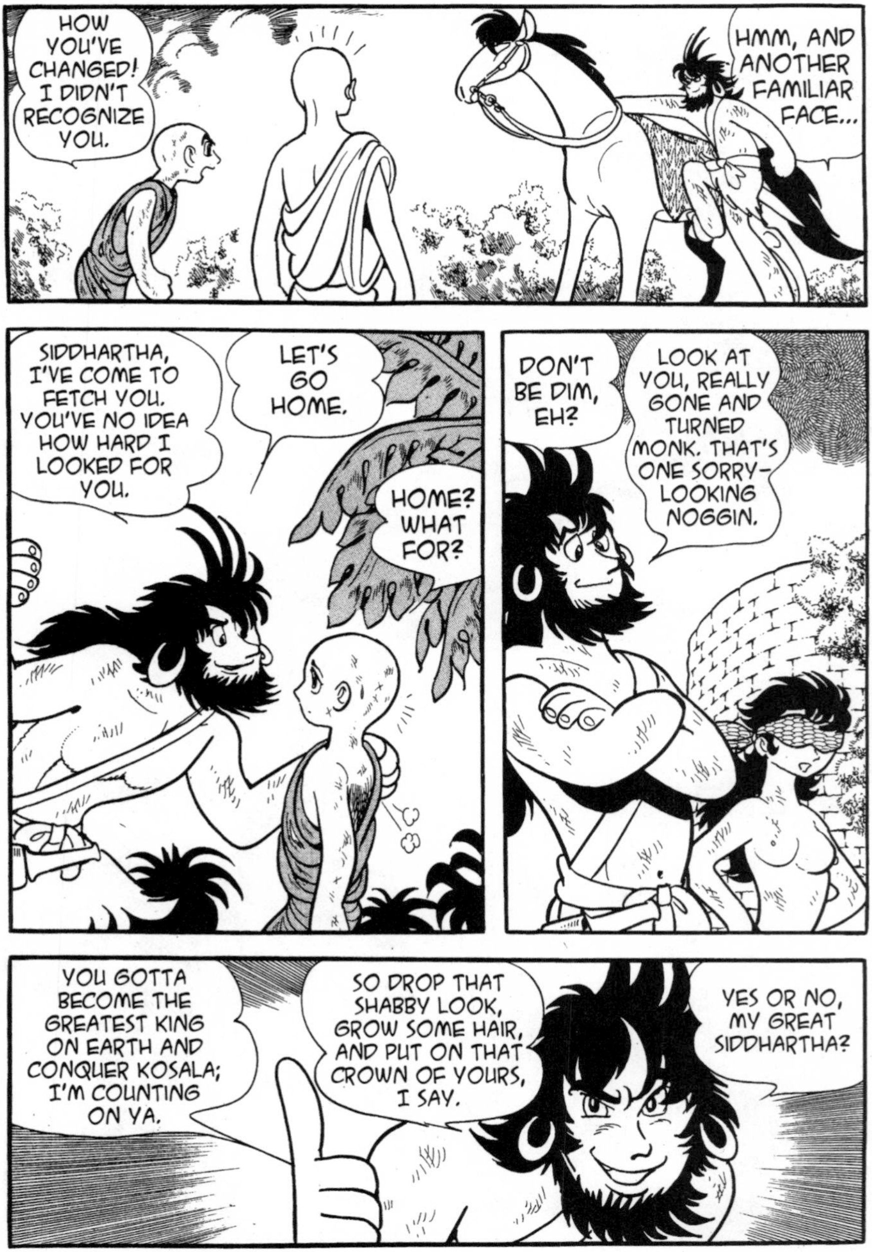
HOW YOU'VE CHANGED! I DIDN'T RECOGNIZE YOU.
HMM, AND ANOTHER FAMILIAR FACE...
SIDDHARTHA, I'VE COME TO FETCH YOU. YOU'VE NO IDEA HOW HARD I LOOKED FOR YOU.
LET'S GO HOME.
HOME? WHAT FOR?
DON'T BE DIM, EH?
LOOK AT YOU, REALLY GONE AND TURNED MONK. THAT'S ONE SORRY-LOOKING NOGGIN.
YOU GOTTA BECOME THE GREATEST KING ON EARTH AND CONQUER KOSALA; I'M COUNTING ON YA.
SO DROP THAT SHABBY LOOK, GROW SOME HAIR, AND PUT ON THAT CROWN OF YOURS, I SAY.
YES OR NO, MY GREAT SIDDHARTHA?

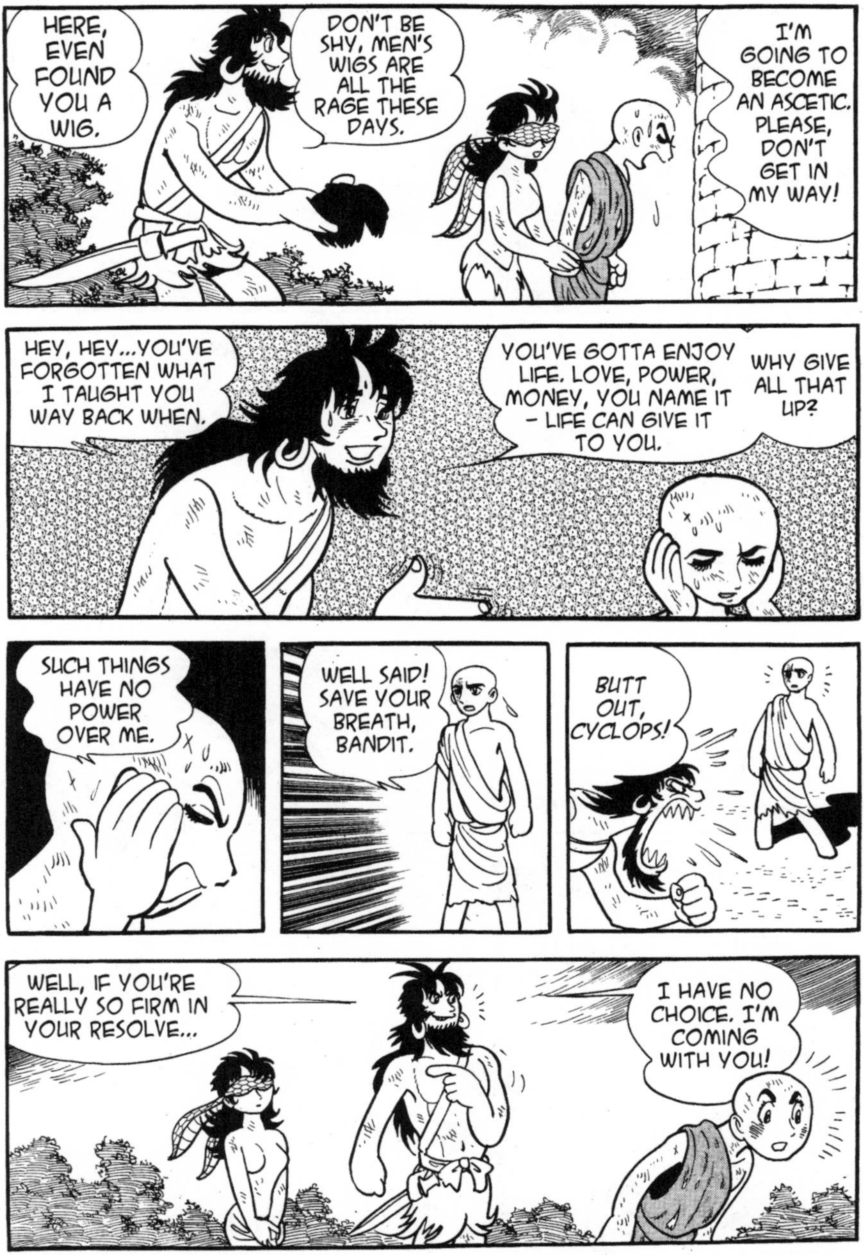
HERE, EVEN FOUND YOU A WIG.
DON'T BE SHY, MEN'S WIGS ARE ALL THE RAGE THESE DAYS.
I'M GOING TO BECOME AN ASCETIC. PLEASE, DON'T GET IN MY WAY!
HEY, HEY...YOU'VE FORGOTTEN WHAT I TAUGHT YOU WAY BACK WHEN.
YOU'VE GOTTA ENJOY LIFE. LOVE, POWER, MONEY, YOU NAME IT - LIFE CAN GIVE IT TO YOU.
WHY GIVE ALL THAT UP?
SUCH THINGS HAVE NO POWER OVER ME.
WELL SAID! SAVE YOUR BREATH, BANDIT.
BUTT OUT, CYCLOPS!
WELL, IF YOU'RE REALLY SO FIRM IN YOUR RESOLVE...
I HAVE NO CHOICE. I'M COMING WITH YOU!

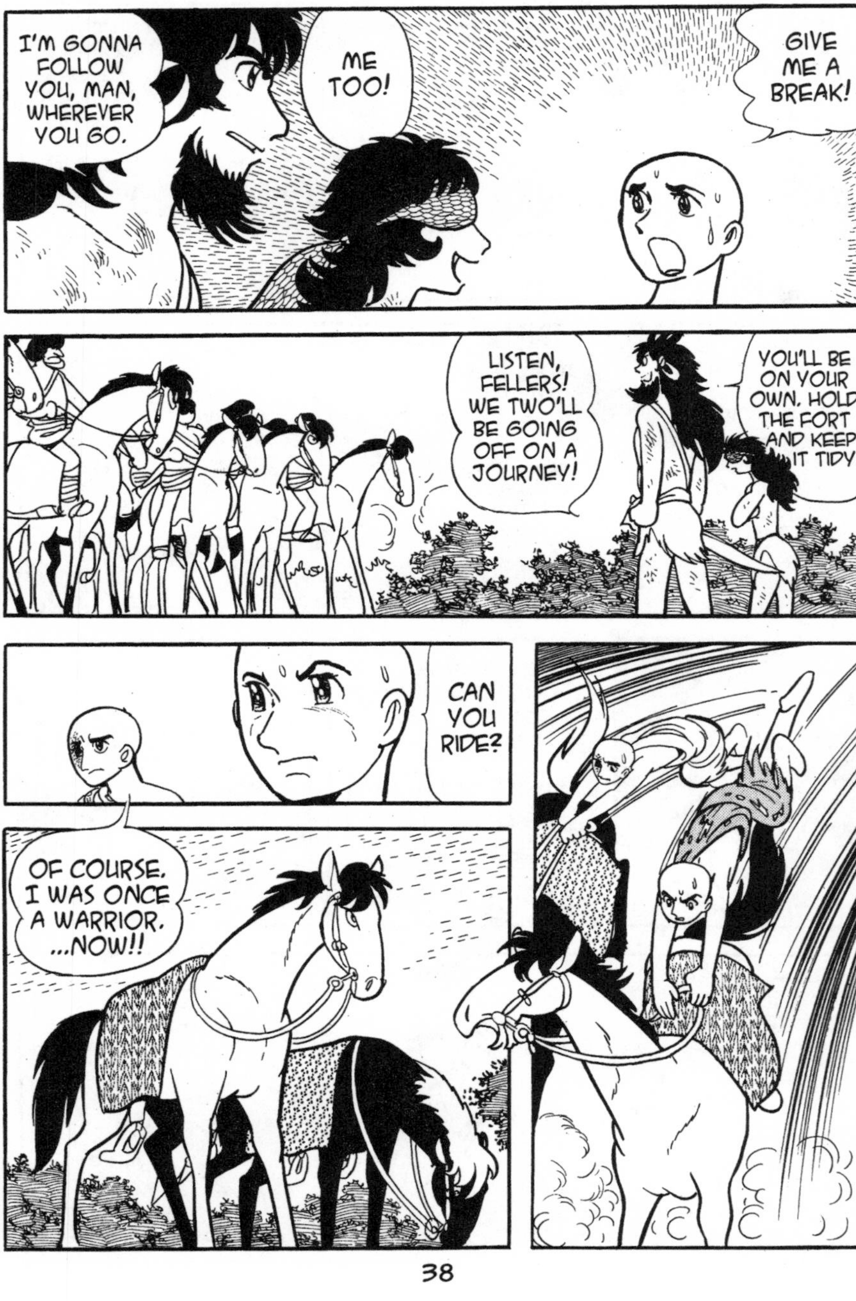
I'M GONNA FOLLOW YOU, MAN, WHEREVER YOU GO.
ME TOO!
GIVE ME A BREAK!
LISTEN, FELLERS! WE TWO'LL BE GOING OFF ON A JOURNEY!
YOU'LL BE ON YOUR OWN. HOLD THE FORT AND KEEP IT TIDY.
CAN YOU RIDE?
OF COURSE. I WAS ONCE A WARRIOR. ...NOW!!

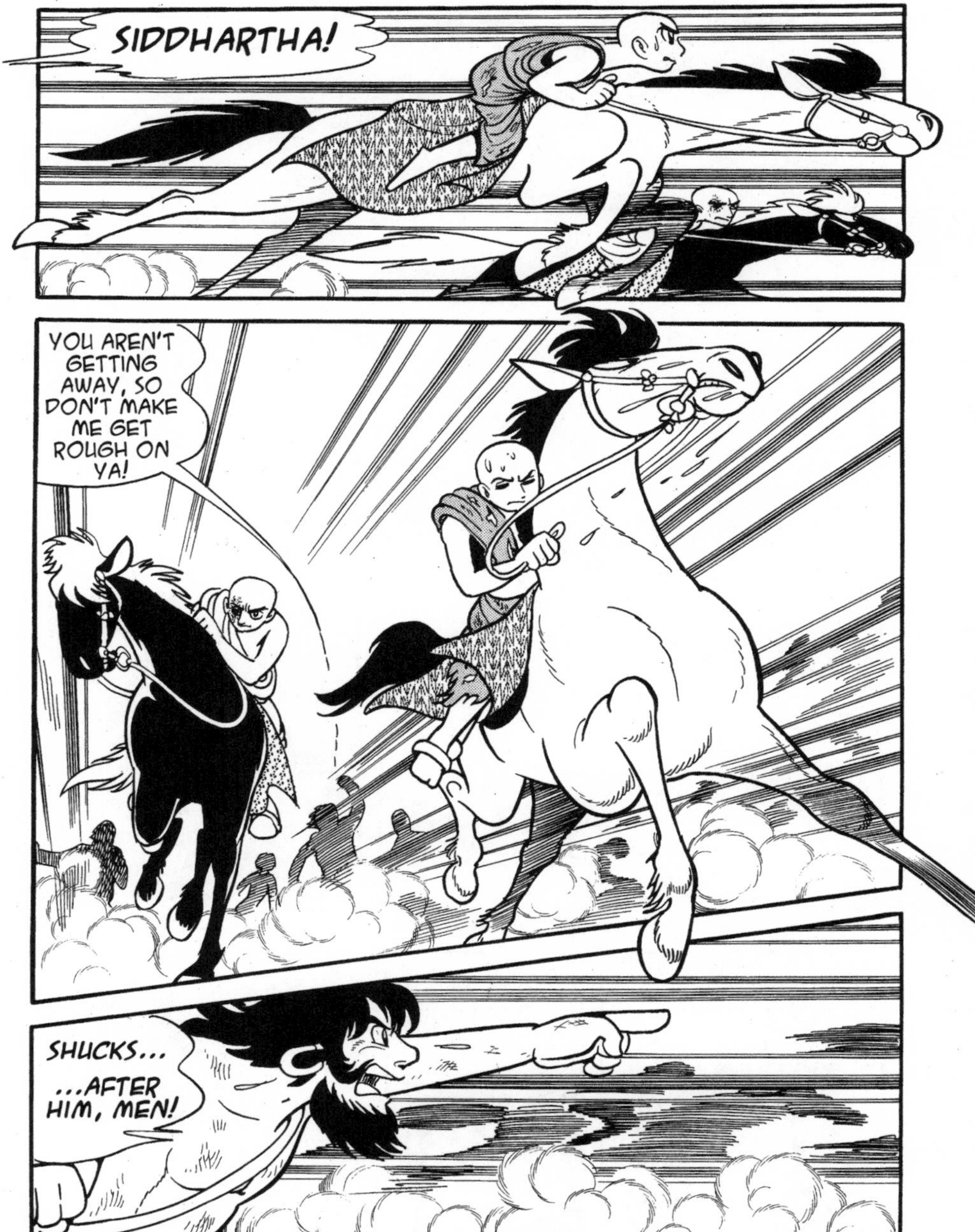
SIDDHARTHA!
YOU AREN'T GETTING AWAY, SO DON'T MAKE ME GET ROUGH ON YA!
SHUCKS...
...AFTER HIM, MEN!

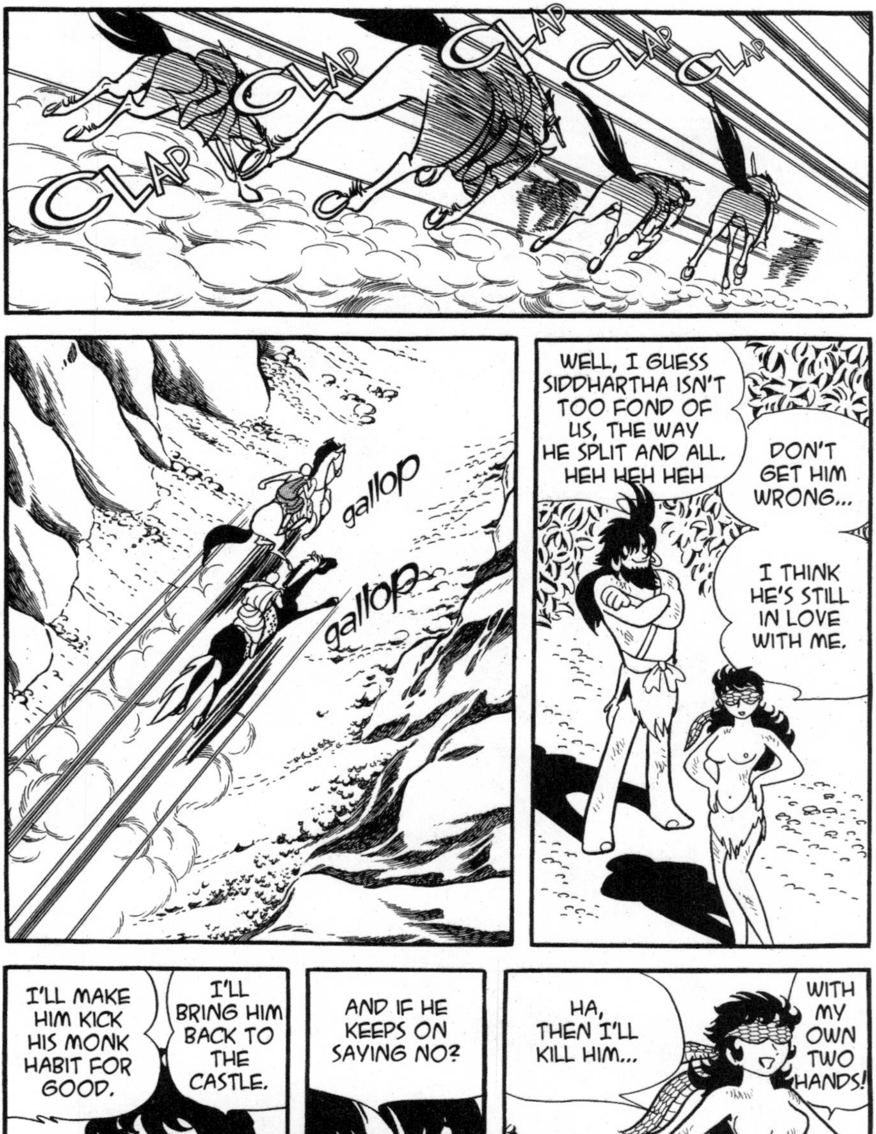
CLAP CLAP CLAP CLAP CLAP
gallop gallop
WELL, I GUESS SIDDHARTHA ISN'T TOO FOND OF US, THE WAY HE SPLIT AND ALL. HEH HEH HEH
DON'T GET HIM WRONG...
I THINK HE'S STILL IN LOVE WITH ME.
I'LL MAKE HIM KICK HIS MONK HABIT FOR GOOD.
I'LL BRING HIM BACK TO THE CASTLE.
AND IF HE KEEPS ON SAYING NO?
HA, THEN I'LL KILL HIM...
WITH MY OWN TWO HANDS!

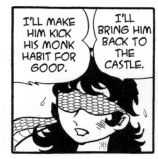

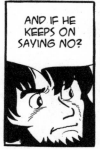

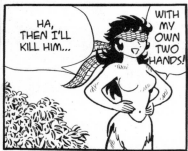

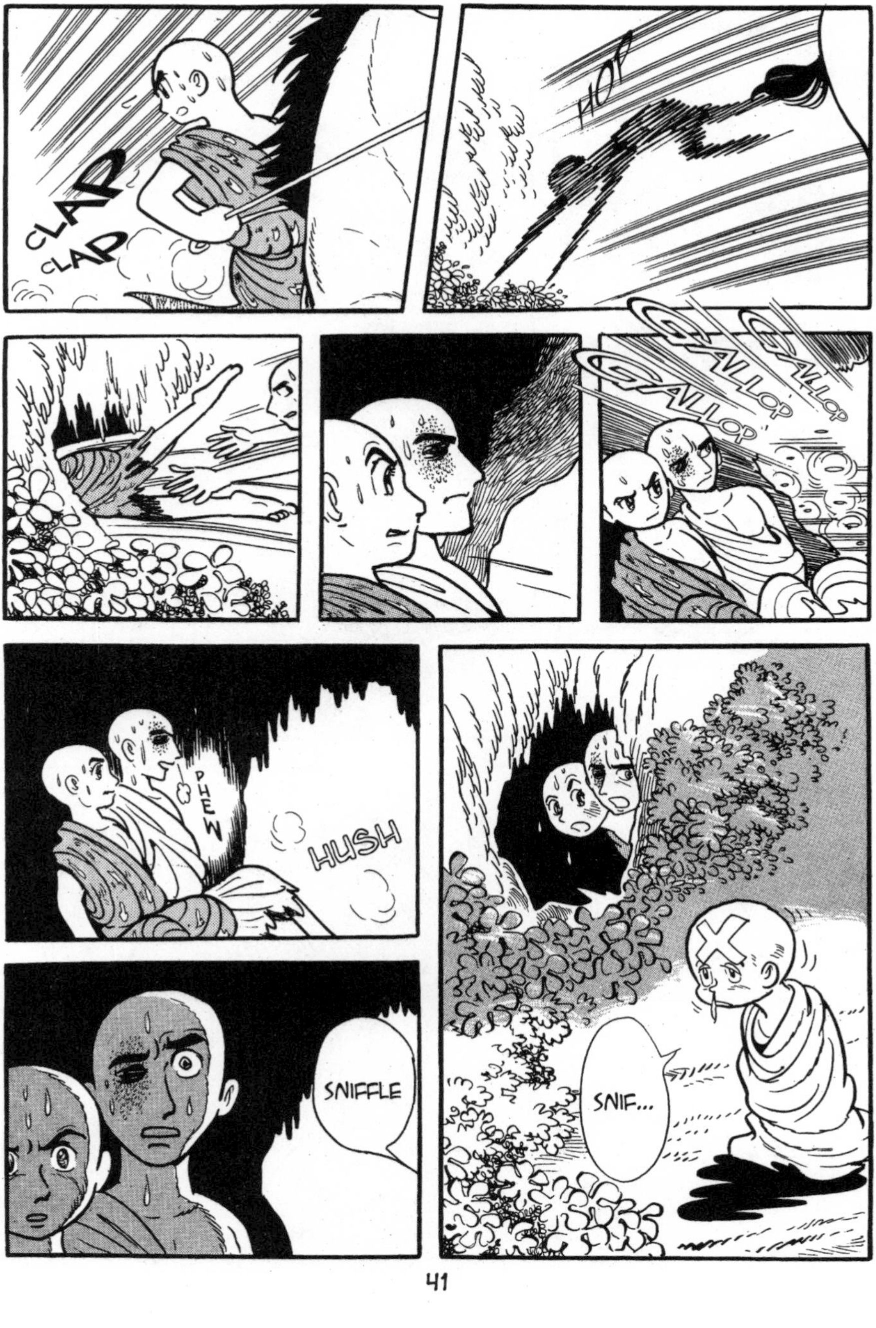
CLAP
CLAP
HOP
GALLOP
GALLOP
GALLOP
PHEW
HUSH
SNIF...
SNIFFLE

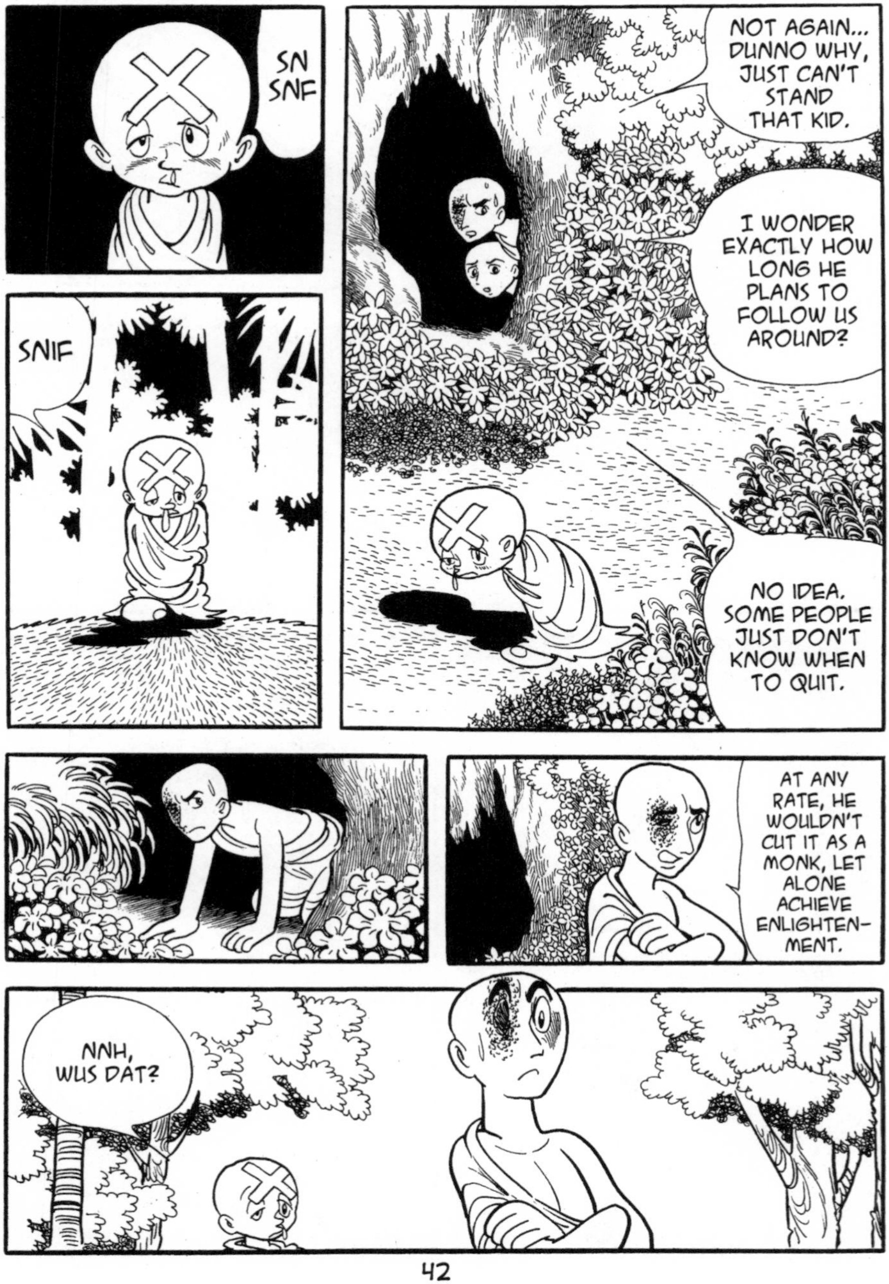
SN SNF
SNIF
NOT AGAIN... DUNNO WHY, JUST CAN'T STAND THAT KID.
I WONDER EXACTLY HOW LONG HE PLANS TO FOLLOW US AROUND?
NO IDEA. SOME PEOPLE JUST DON'T KNOW WHEN TO QUIT.
AT ANY RATE, HE WOULDN'T CUT IT AS A MONK, LET ALONE ACHIEVE ENLIGHTEN-MENT.
NNH, WUS DAT?

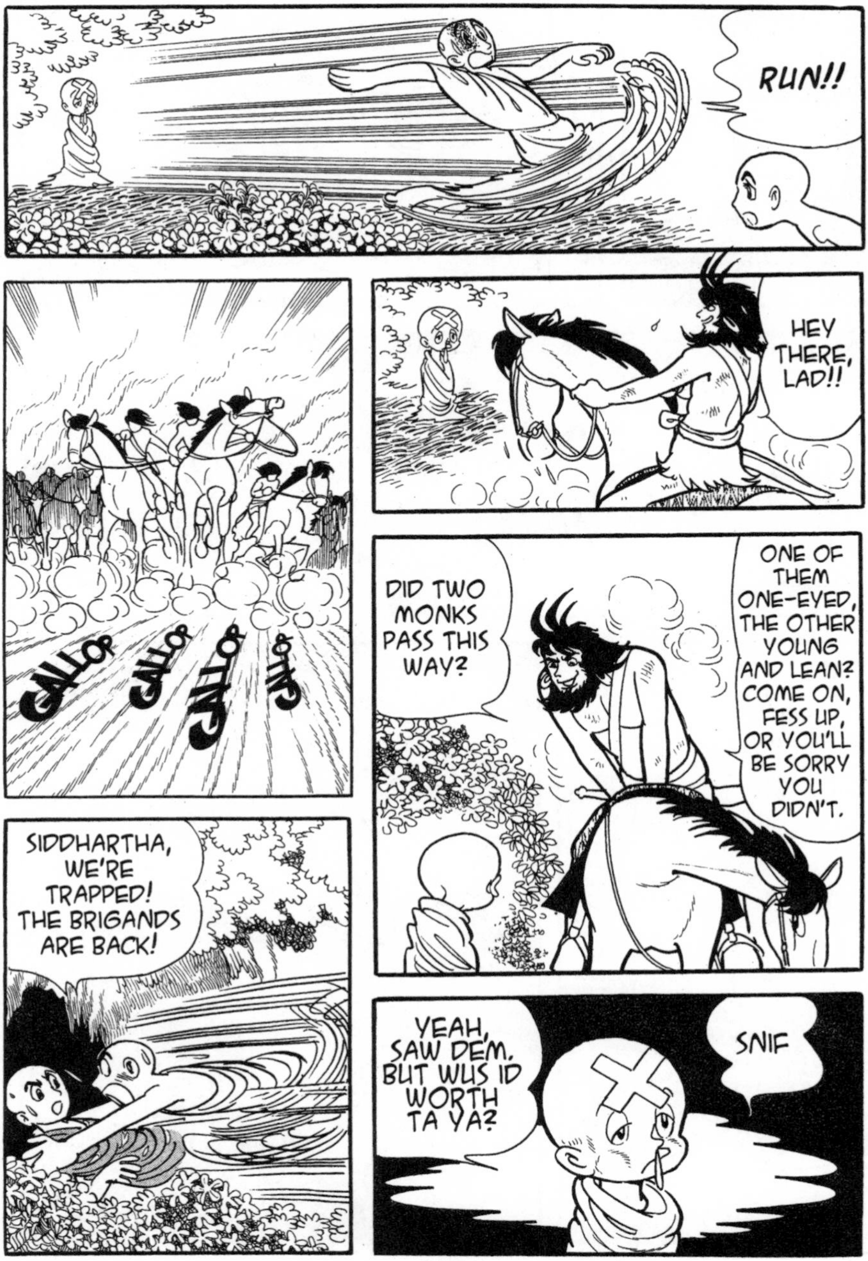
RUN!!
GALLOP GALLOP GALLOP GALLOP
HEY THERE, LAD!!
DID TWO MONKS PASS THIS WAY?
ONE OF THEM ONE-EYED, THE OTHER YOUNG AND LEAN? COME ON, FESS UP, OR YOU'LL BE SORRY YOU DIDN'T.
SIDDHARTHA, WE'RE TRAPPED! THE BRIGANDS ARE BACK!
YEAH, SAW DEM. BUT WUS ID WORTH TA YA?
SNIF

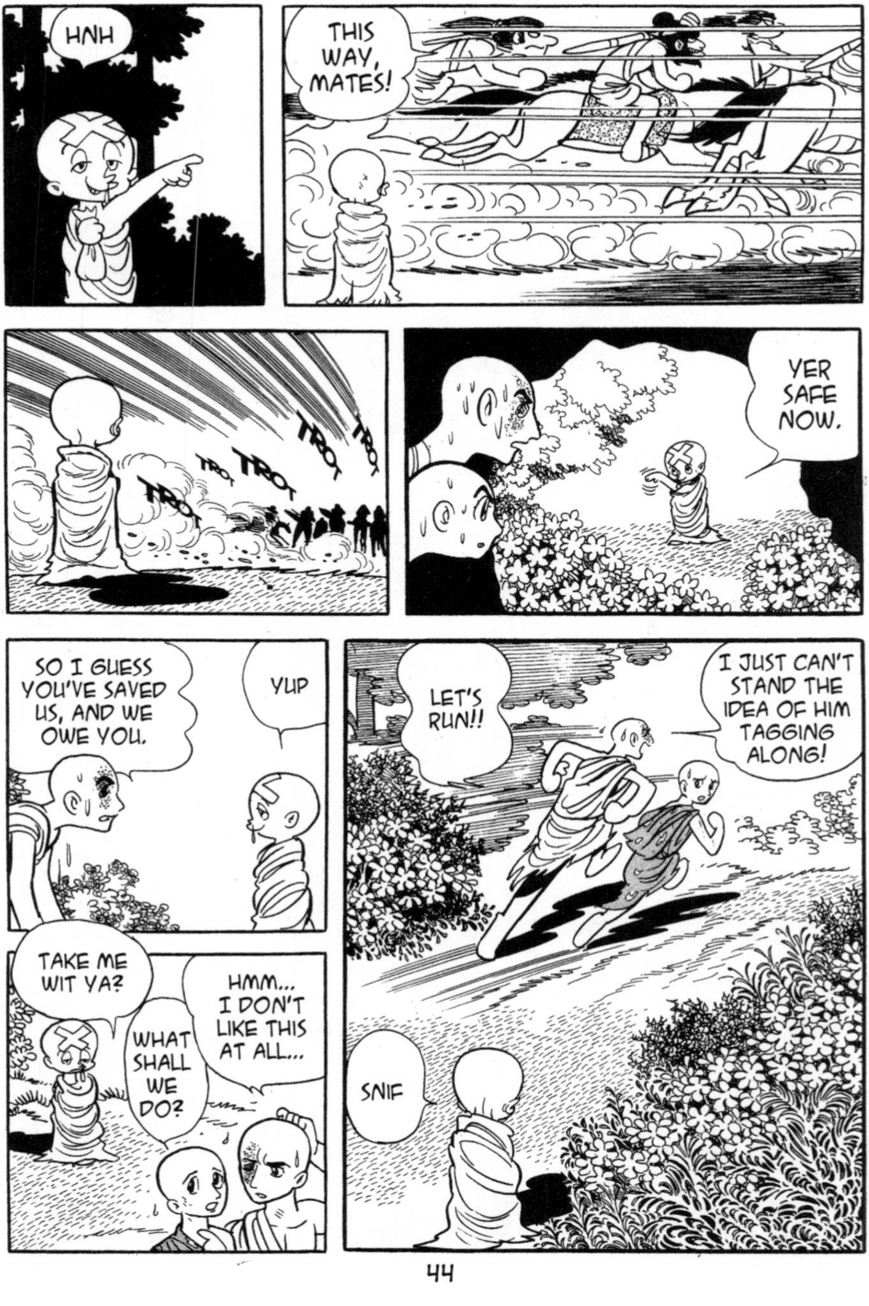
HNH
THIS WAY, MATES!
TROT TROT TROT TROT TROT
YER SAFE NOW.
SO I GUESS YOU'VE SAVED US, AND WE OWE YOU.
YUP
TAKE ME WIT YA?
WHAT SHALL WE DO?
HMM... I DON'T LIKE THIS AT ALL...
LET'S RUN!!
I JUST CAN'T STAND THE IDEA OF HIM TAGGING ALONG!
SNIF

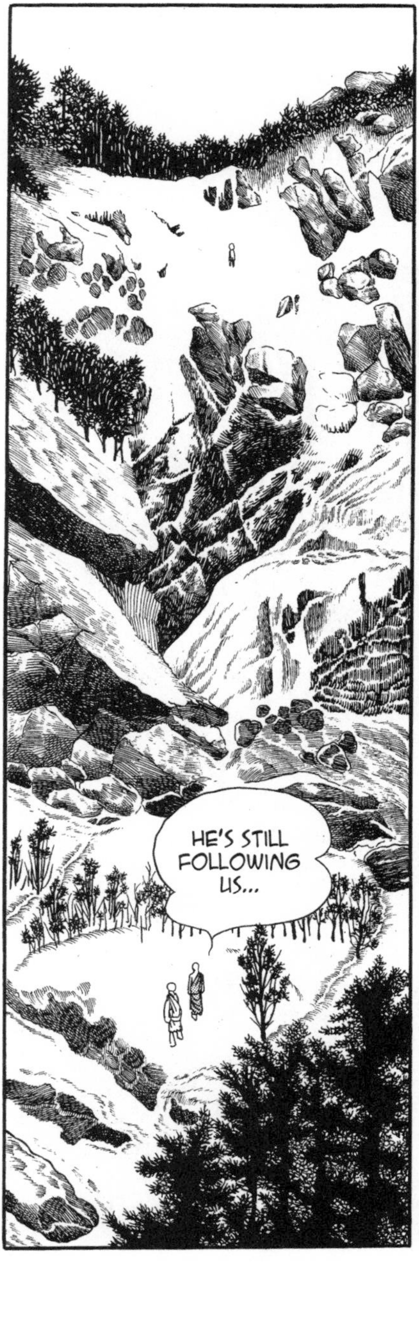
HE'S STILL FOLLOWING US...
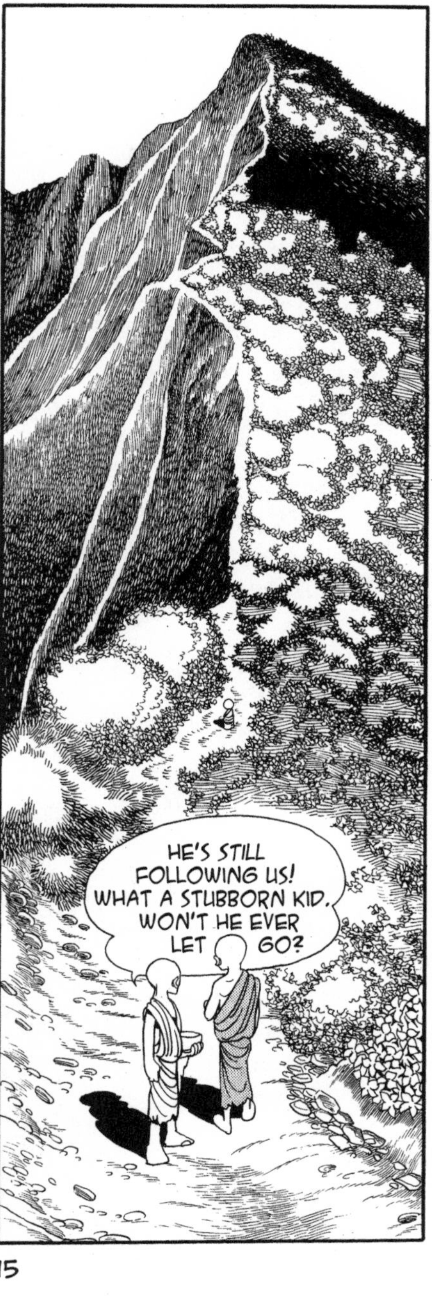
HE'S STILL FOLLOWING US! WHAT A STUBBORN KID. WON'T HE EVER LET GO?

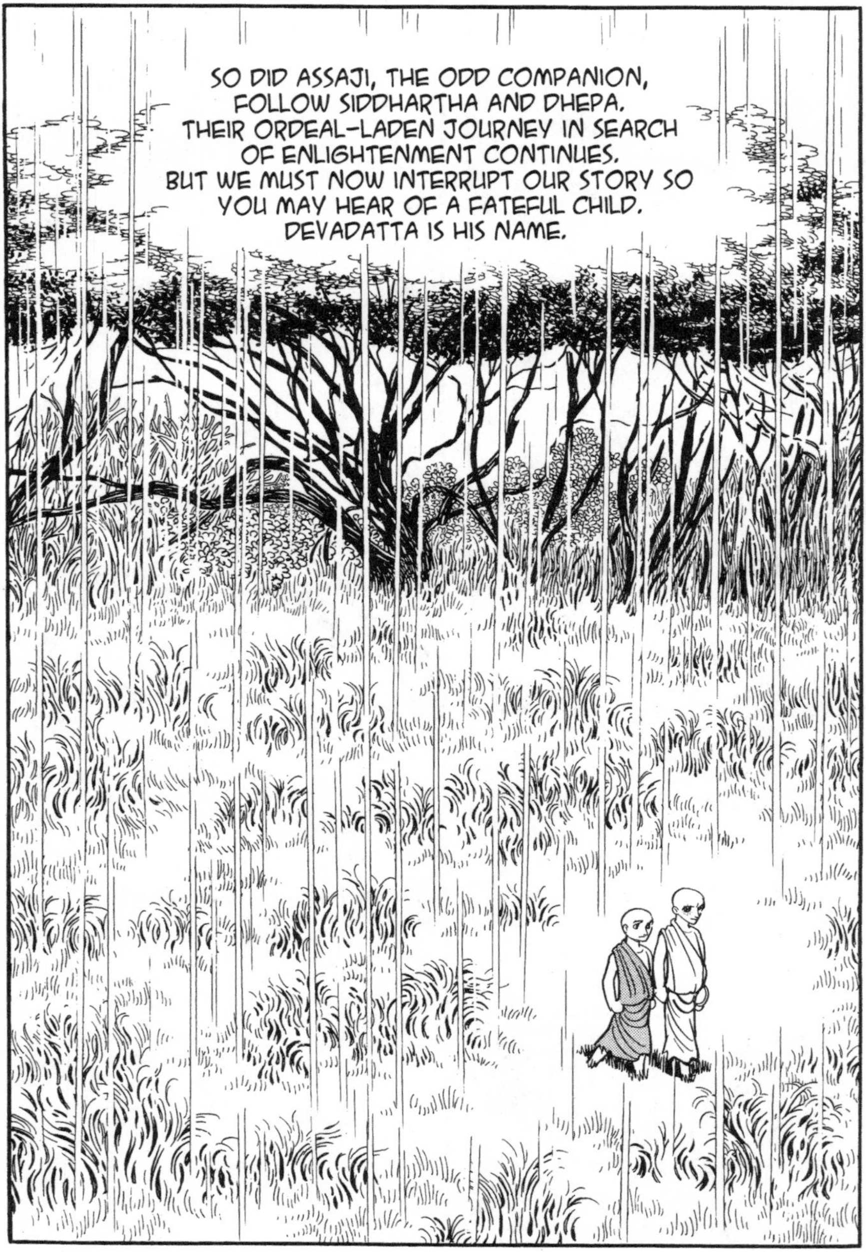
SO DID ASSAJI, THE ODD COMPANION, FOLLOW SIDDHARTHA AND DHEPA. THEIR ORDEAL-LADEN JOURNEY IN SEARCH OF ENLIGHTENMENT CONTINUES. BUT WE MUST NOW INTERRUPT OUR STORY SO YOU MAY HEAR OF A FATEFUL CHILD. DEVADATTA IS HIS NAME.

CHAPTER TWO

SURVIVAL OF THE FITTEST

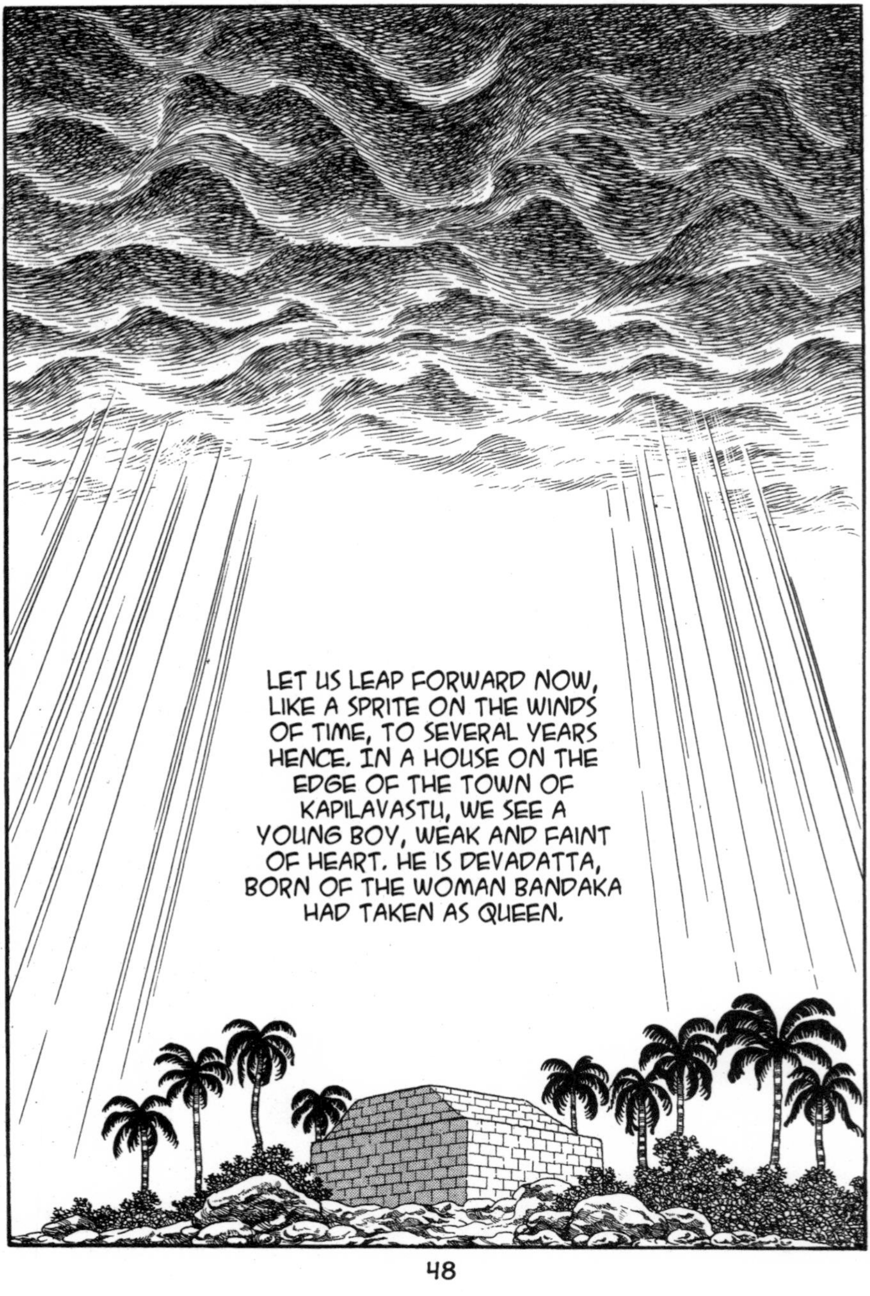
LET US LEAP FORWARD NOW, LIKE A SPRITE ON THE WINDS OF TIME, TO SEVERAL YEARS HENCE. IN A HOUSE ON THE EDGE OF THE TOWN OF KAPILAVASTU, WE SEE A YOUNG BOY, WEAK AND FAINT OF HEART. HE IS DEVADATTA, BORN OF THE WOMAN BANDAKA HAD TAKEN AS QUEEN.

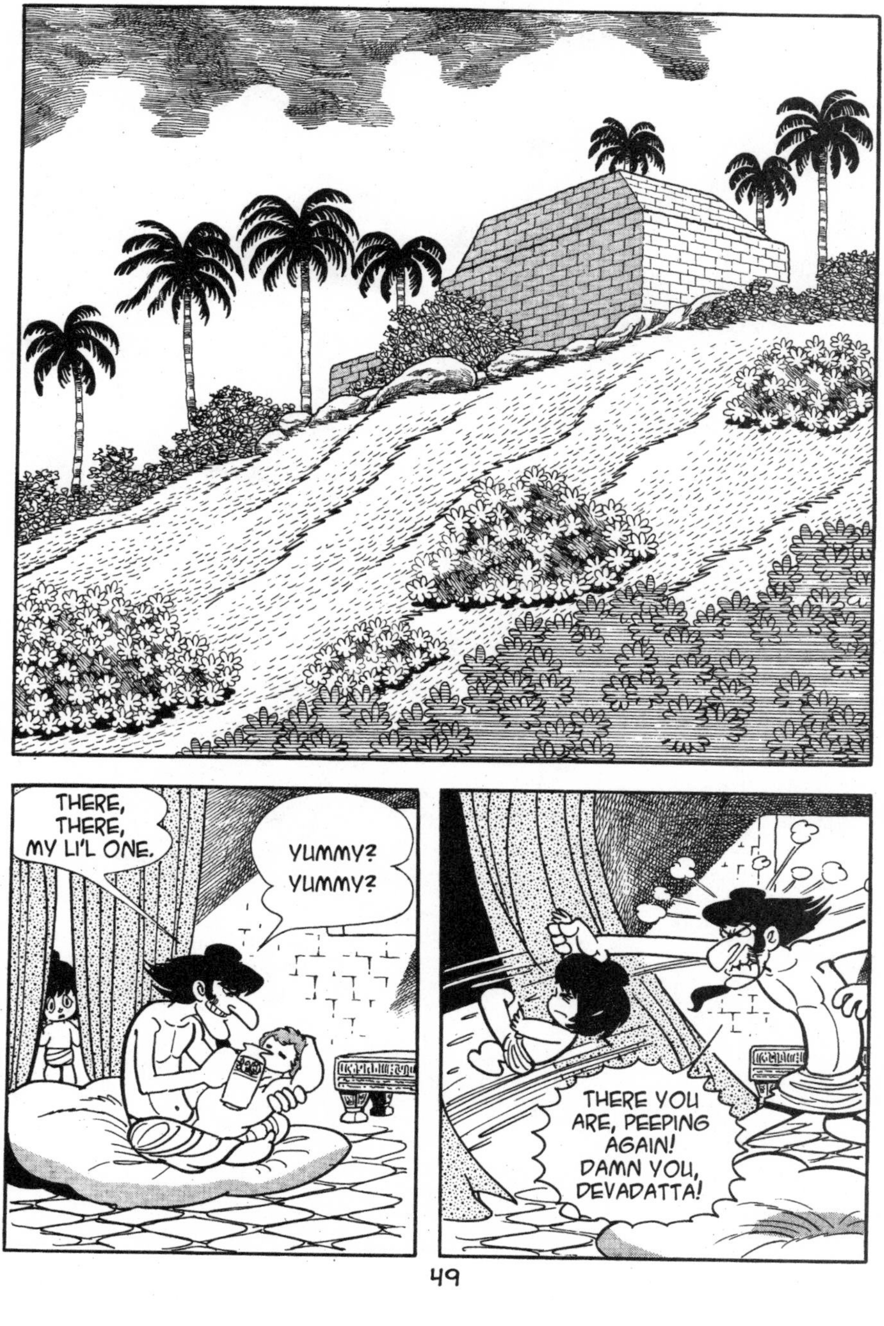
THERE, THERE, MY LI'L ONE.
YUMMY? YUMMY?
THERE YOU ARE, PEEPING AGAIN! DAMN YOU, DEVADATTA!

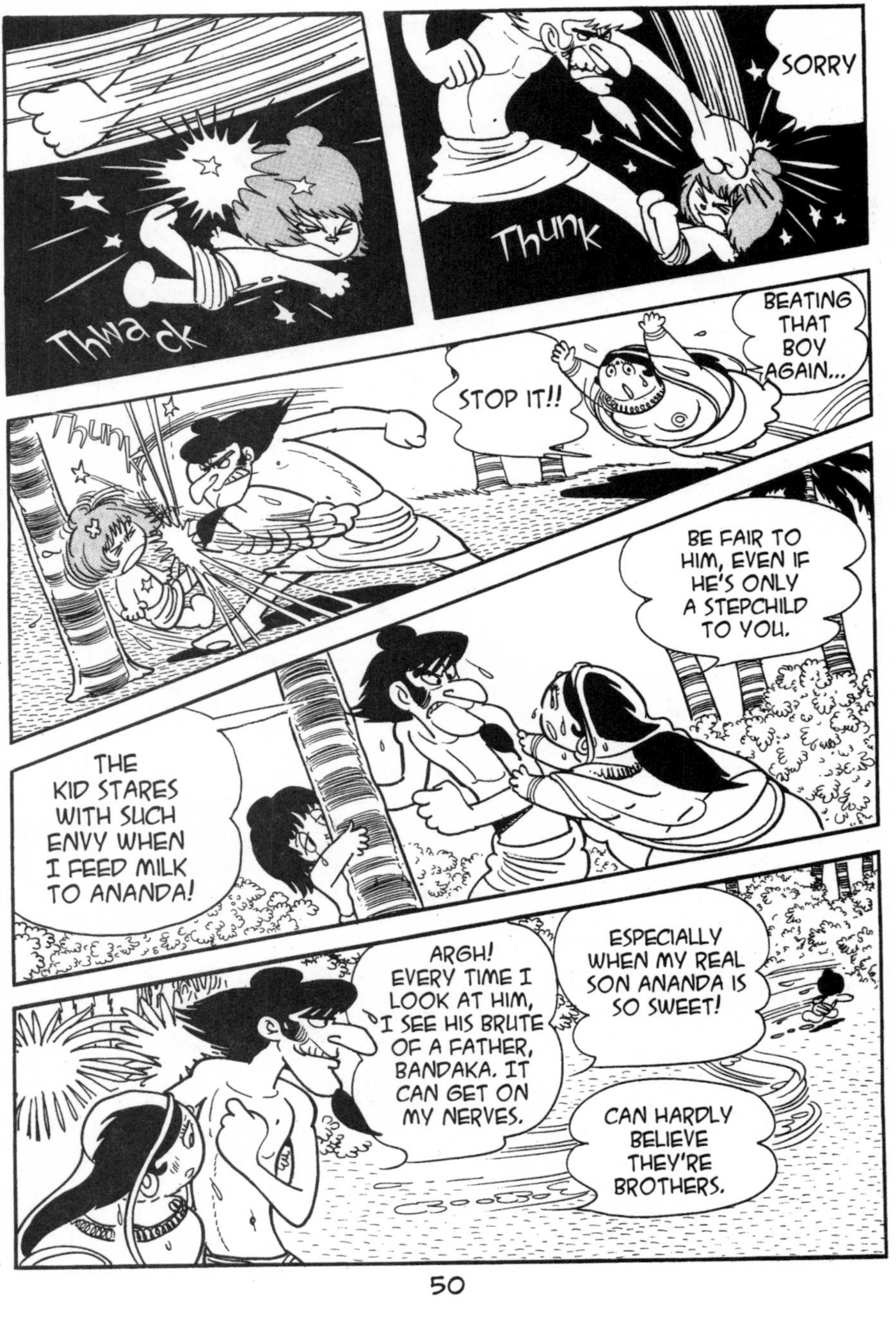
Thwack
SORRY
Thunk
Thunk
STOP IT!!
BEATING THAT BOY AGAIN...
BE FAIR TO HIM, EVEN IF HE'S ONLY A STEPCHILD TO YOU.
THE KID STARES WITH SUCH ENVY WHEN I FEED MILK TO ANANDA!
ARGH! EVERY TIME I LOOK AT HIM, I SEE HIS BRUTE OF A FATHER, BANDAKA. IT CAN GET ON MY NERVES.
ESPECIALLY WHEN MY REAL SON ANANDA IS SO SWEET!
CAN HARDLY BELIEVE THEY'RE BROTHERS.

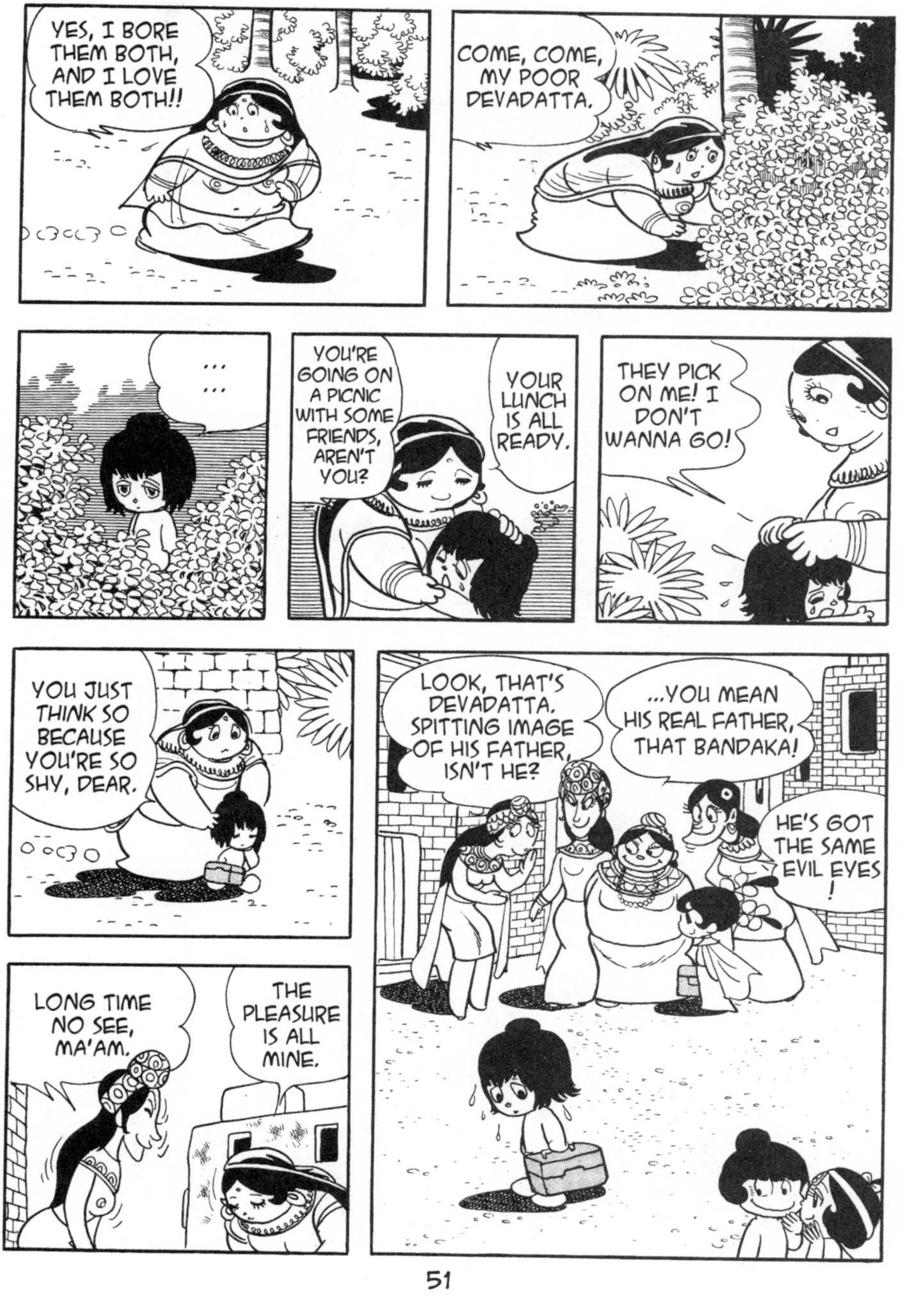
YES, I BORE THEM BOTH, AND I LOVE THEM BOTH!!
COME, COME, MY POOR DEVADATTA.
... ...
YOU'RE GOING ON A PICNIC WITH SOME FRIENDS, AREN'T YOU?
YOUR LUNCH IS ALL READY.
THEY PICK ON ME! I DON'T WANNA GO!
YOU JUST THINK SO BECAUSE YOU'RE SO SHY, DEAR.
LONG TIME NO SEE, MA'AM.
THE PLEASURE IS ALL MINE.
LOOK, THAT'S DEVADATTA. SPITTING IMAGE OF HIS FATHER, ISN'T HE?
...YOU MEAN HIS REAL FATHER, THAT BANDAKA!
HE'S GOT THE SAME EVIL EYES!

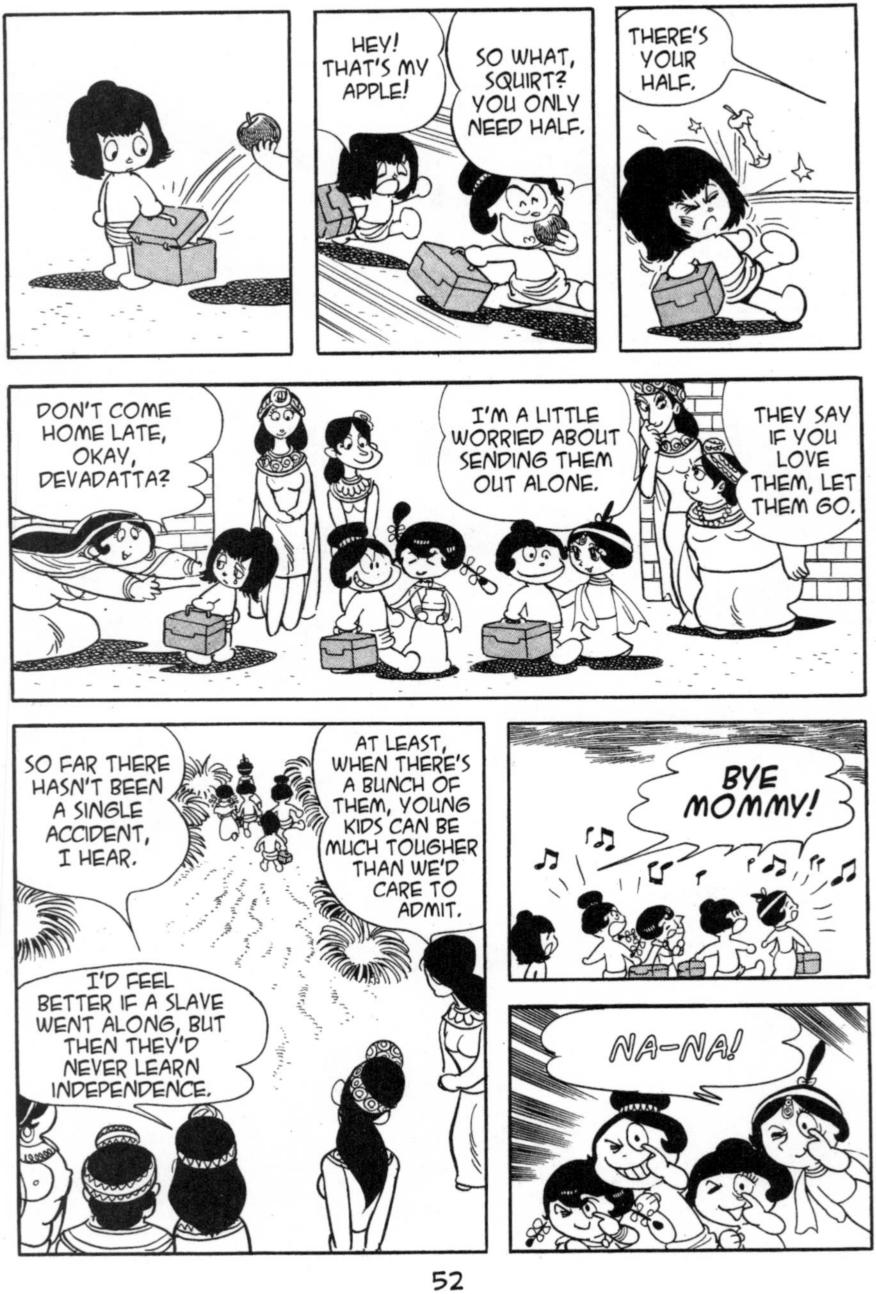
HEY! THAT'S MY APPLE!
SO WHAT, SQUIRT? YOU ONLY NEED HALF.
THERE'S YOUR HALF.
DON'T COME HOME LATE, OKAY, DEVADATTA?
I'M A LITTLE WORRIED ABOUT SENDING THEM OUT ALONE.
THEY SAY IF YOU LOVE THEM, LET THEM GO.
SO FAR THERE HASN'T BEEN A SINGLE ACCIDENT, I HEAR.
AT LEAST, WHEN THERE'S A BUNCH OF THEM, YOUNG KIDS CAN BE MUCH TOUGHER THAN WE'D CARE TO ADMIT.
I'D FEEL BETTER IF A SLAVE WENT ALONG, BUT THEN THEY'D NEVER LEARN INDEPENDENCE.
BYE MOMMY!
NA-NA!

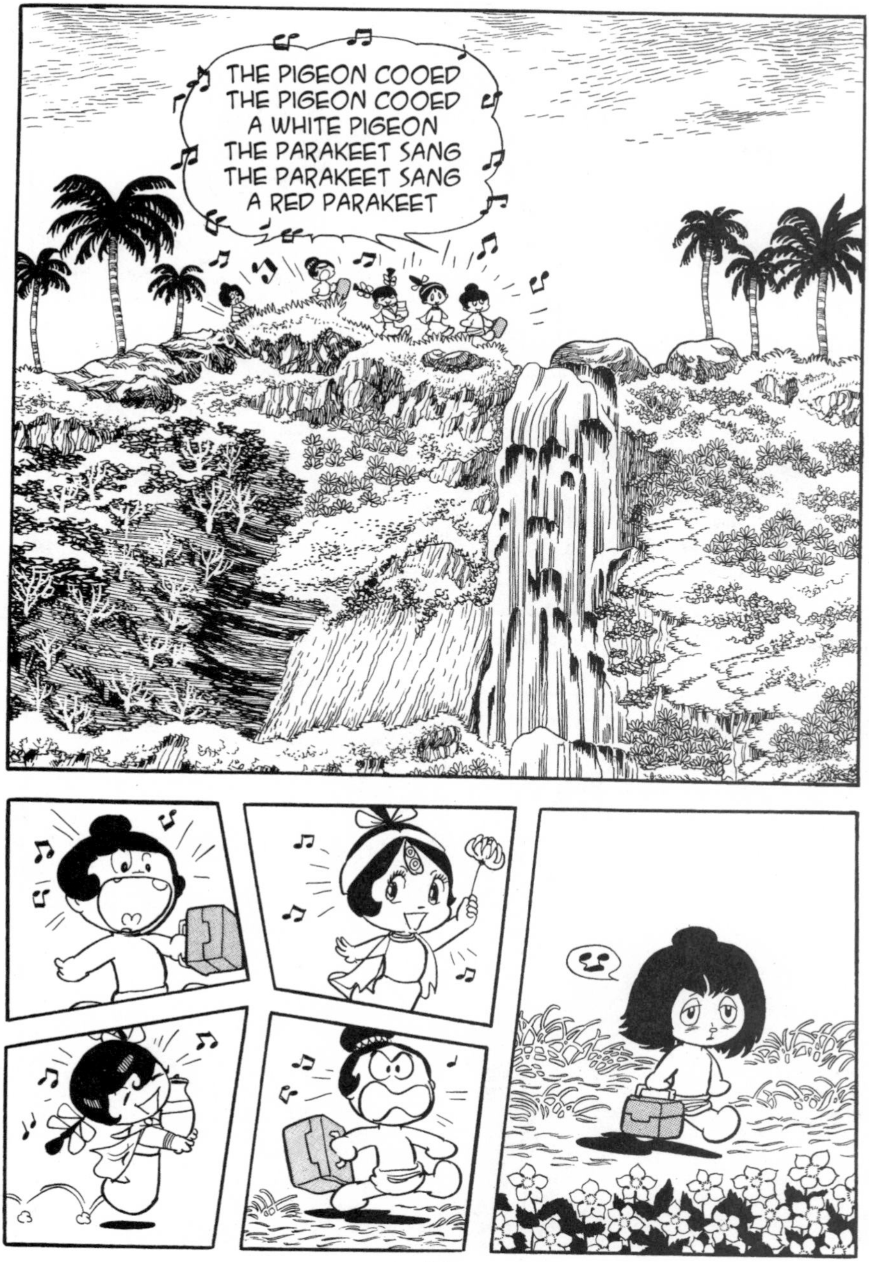
THE PIGEON COOED
THE PIGEON COOED
A WHITE PIGEON
THE PARAKEET SANG
THE PARAKEET SANG
A RED PARAKEET

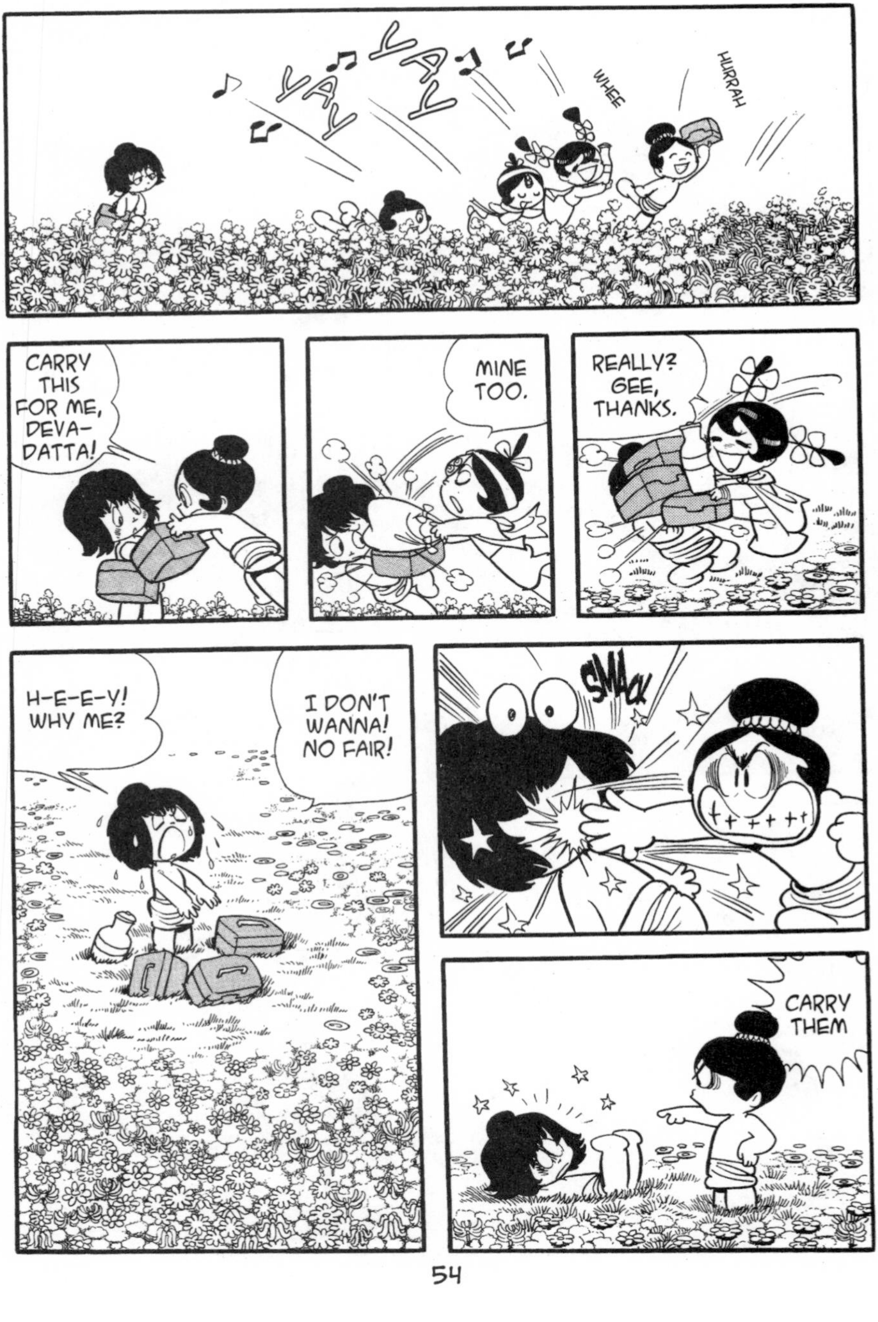
YAY
YAY
YAY
WHEE
HURRAH
CARRY THIS FOR ME, DEVA-DATTA!
MINE TOO.
REALLY? GEE, THANKS.
H-E-E-Y! WHY ME?
I DON'T WANNA! NO FAIR!
SMACK
CARRY THEM

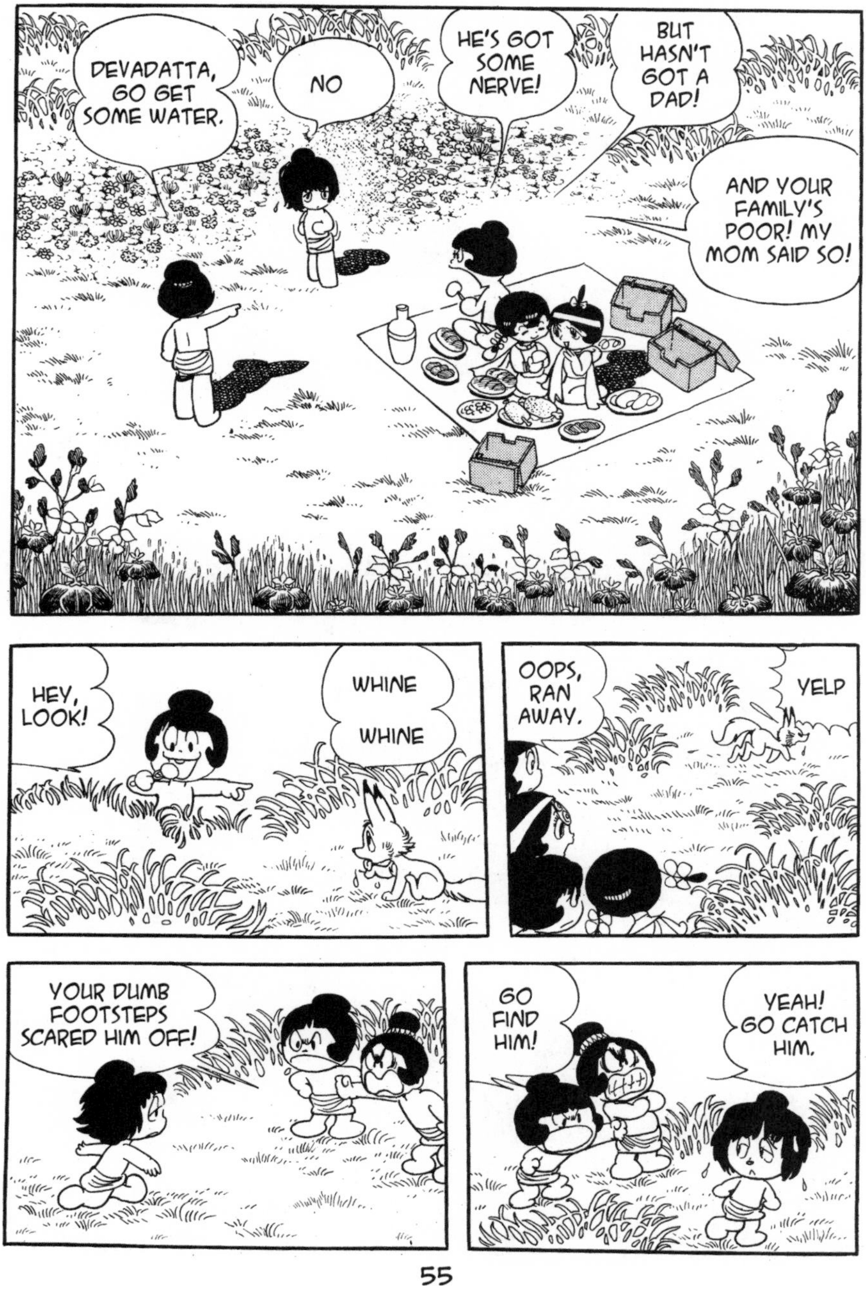
DEVADATTA, GO GET SOME WATER.
NO
HE'S GOT SOME NERVE!
BUT HASN'T GOT A DAD!
AND YOUR FAMILY'S POOR! MY MOM SAID SO!
HEY, LOOK!
WHINE
WHINE
OOPS, RAN AWAY.
YELP
YOUR DUMB FOOTSTEPS SCARED HIM OFF!
GO FIND HIM!
YEAH! GO CATCH HIM.

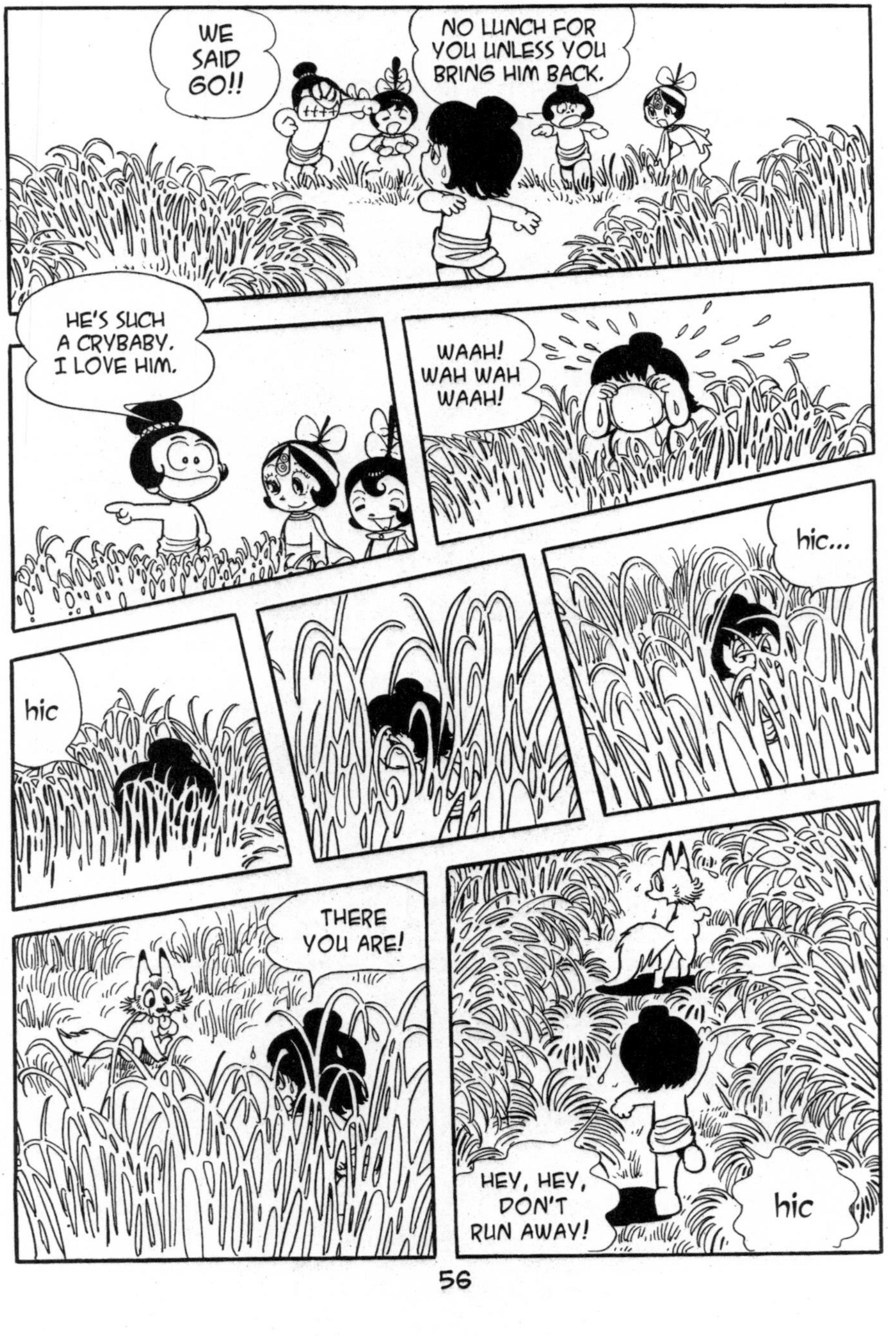
WE SAID GO!!
NO LUNCH FOR YOU UNLESS YOU BRING HIM BACK.
HE'S SUCH A CRYBABY. I LOVE HIM.
WAAH! WAH WAH WAAH!
hic
hic...
THERE YOU ARE!
HEY, HEY, DON'T RUN AWAY!
hic

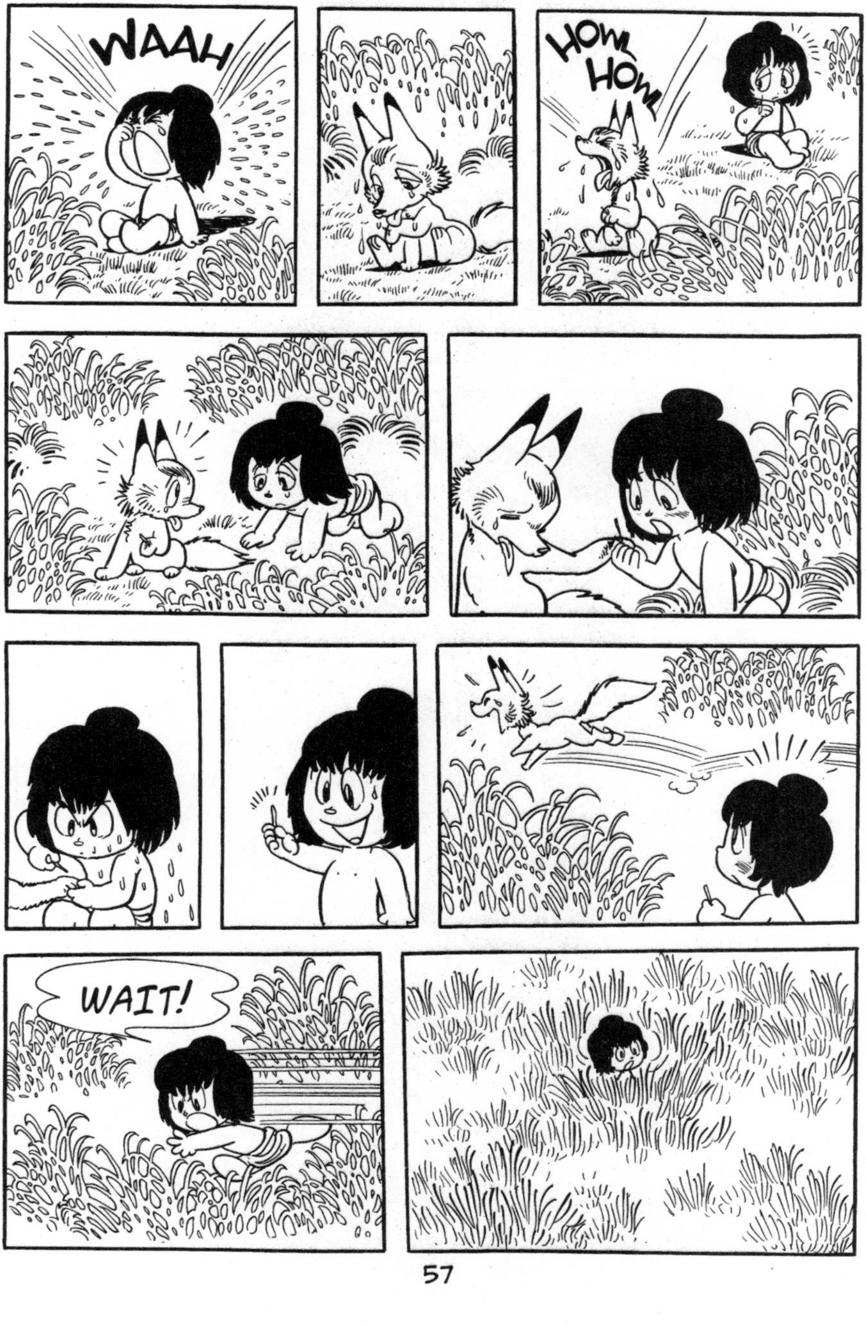
WAAH
HOWL
HOWL
WAIT!

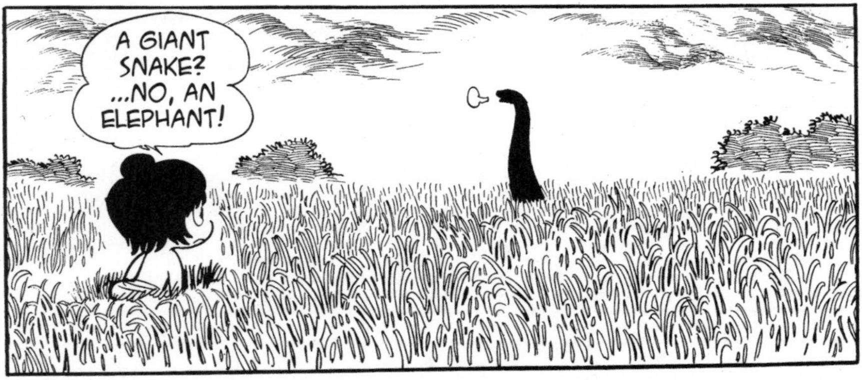
A GIANT SNAKE? ...NO, AN ELEPHANT!

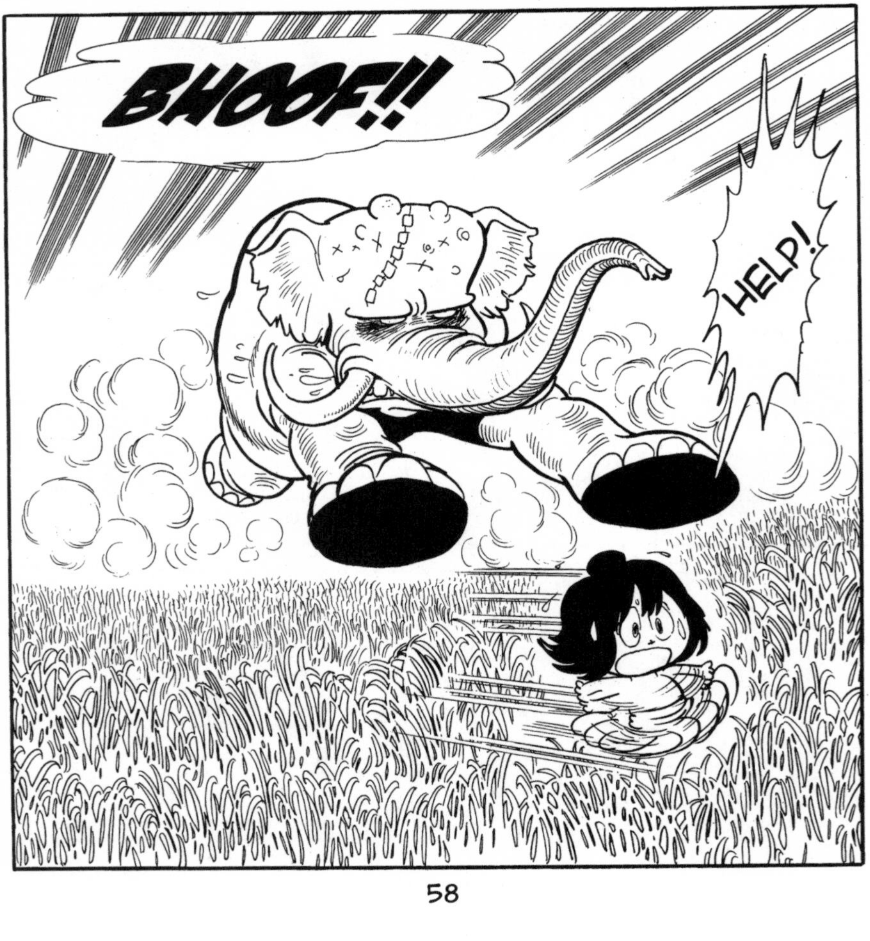
BHOOF!!
HELP!

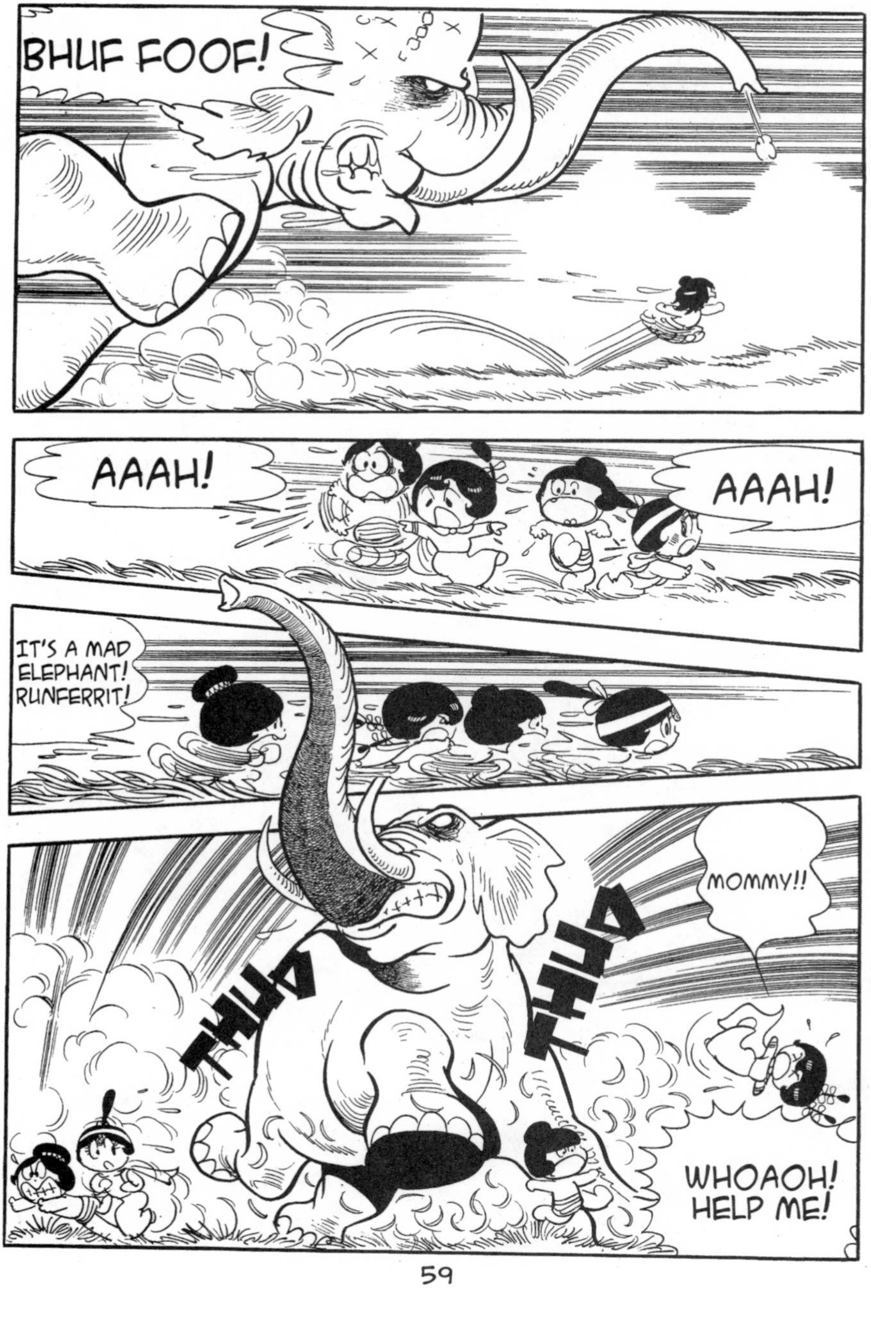
BHUF FOOF!
AAAH!
AAAH!
IT'S A MAD ELEPHANT! RUNFERRIT!
MOMMY!!
THUD
THUD
WHOAOH! HELP ME!

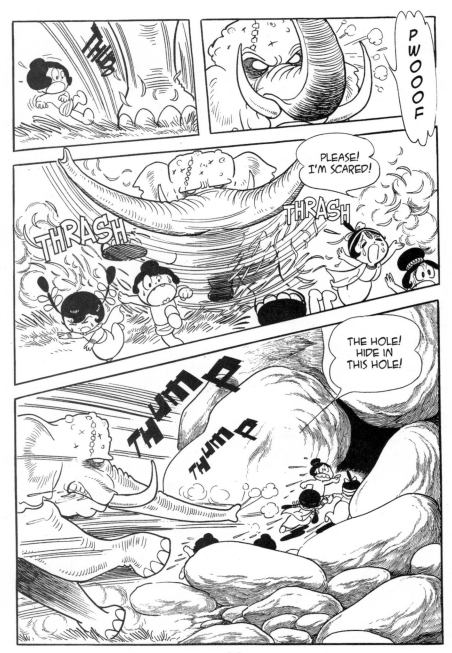

60

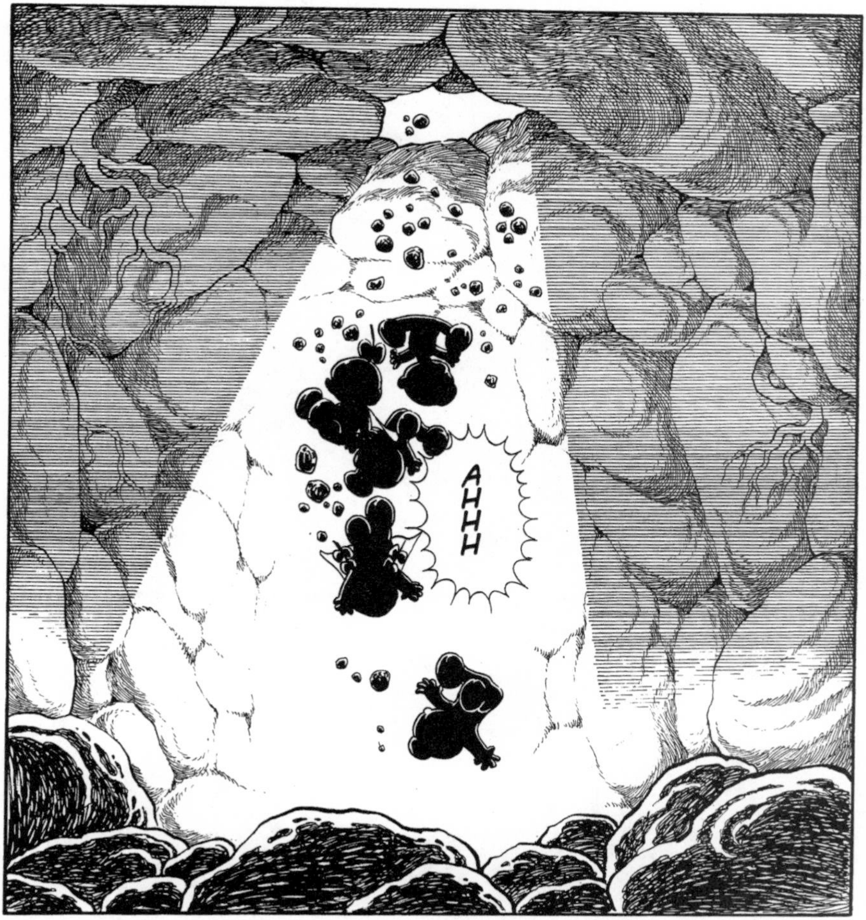
AHHH

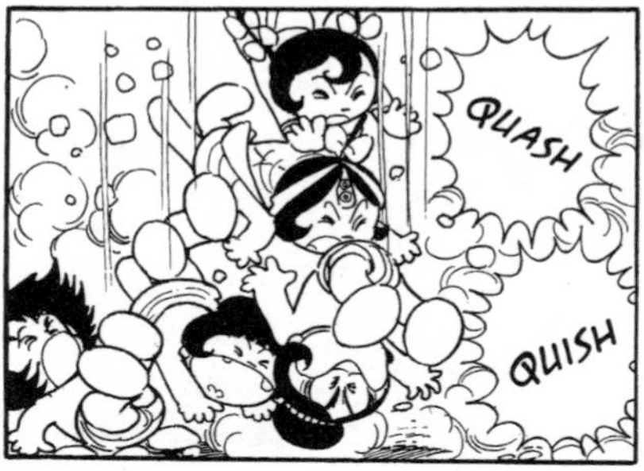
QUASH
QUISH

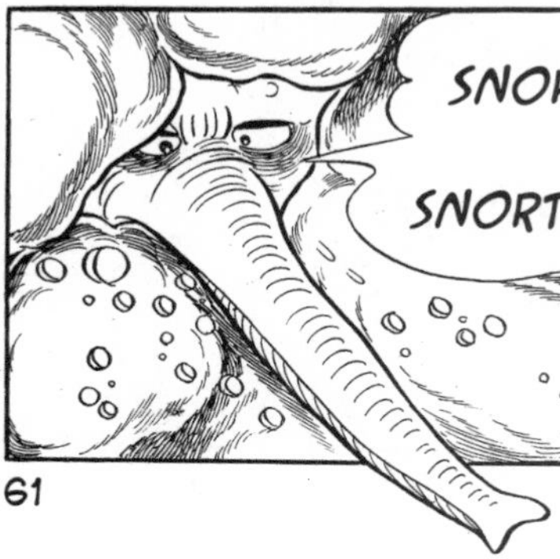
SNORT!!
SNORT!!

...   ...

PHOOF PHOOF

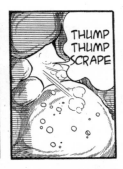

THUMP THUMP SCRAPE

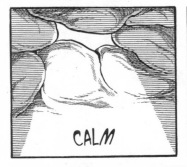

CALM

I THINK HE'S GONE

THAT WAS SCARY

OH NO, I LOST MY DOLLY...

IDIOT!! DID YOU HAVE TO COME RUNNING OUR WAY?!

LET'S GET OUT OF THIS HOLE.

IT'S SO COLD DOWN HERE.

HOW DO WE CLIMB THIS?

WHY DON'T YOU GIVE IT A TRY, DEVA-DATTA?

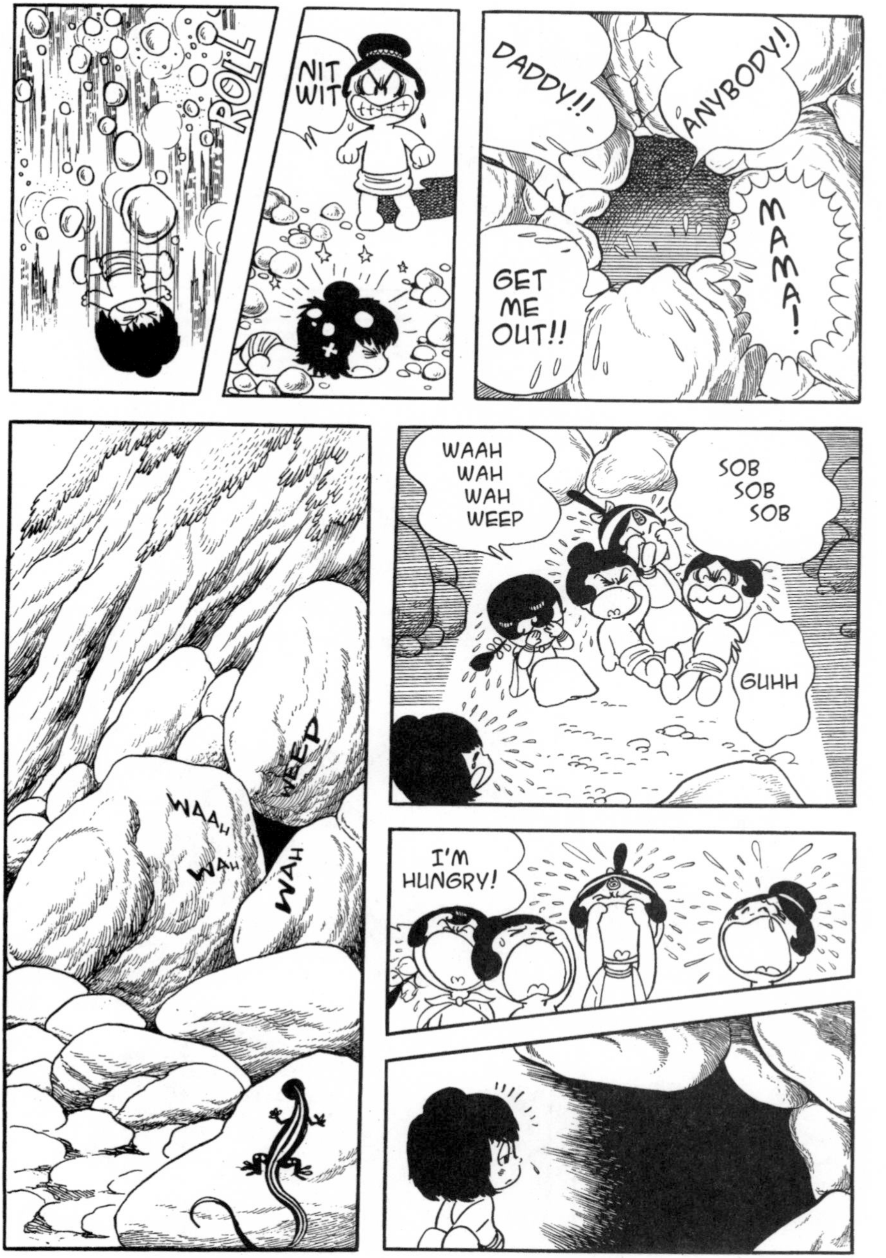
ROLL
NIT WIT
DADDY!!
ANYBODY!
MAMA!
GET ME OUT!!
WAAH WAH
WEEP
WAH
WAAH WAH WAH WEEP
SOB SOB SOB
GUHH
I'M HUNGRY!

64

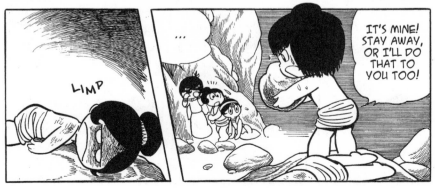

66

GULP...
...GULP...

MASH

SHRIEK

MURDER !!

STOP!

2 WEEKS THEY'VE BEEN MISSING NOW.

2 FULL WEEKS. A LONG TIME TO GO WITHOUT FOOD AND WATER. TOO LONG...

PERHAPS THEY WOUND UP IN ANOTHER VILLAGE AND WERE TAKEN INTO CUSTODY.

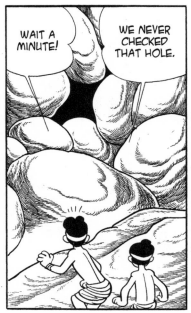

WAIT A MINUTE!

WE NEVER CHECKED THAT HOLE.

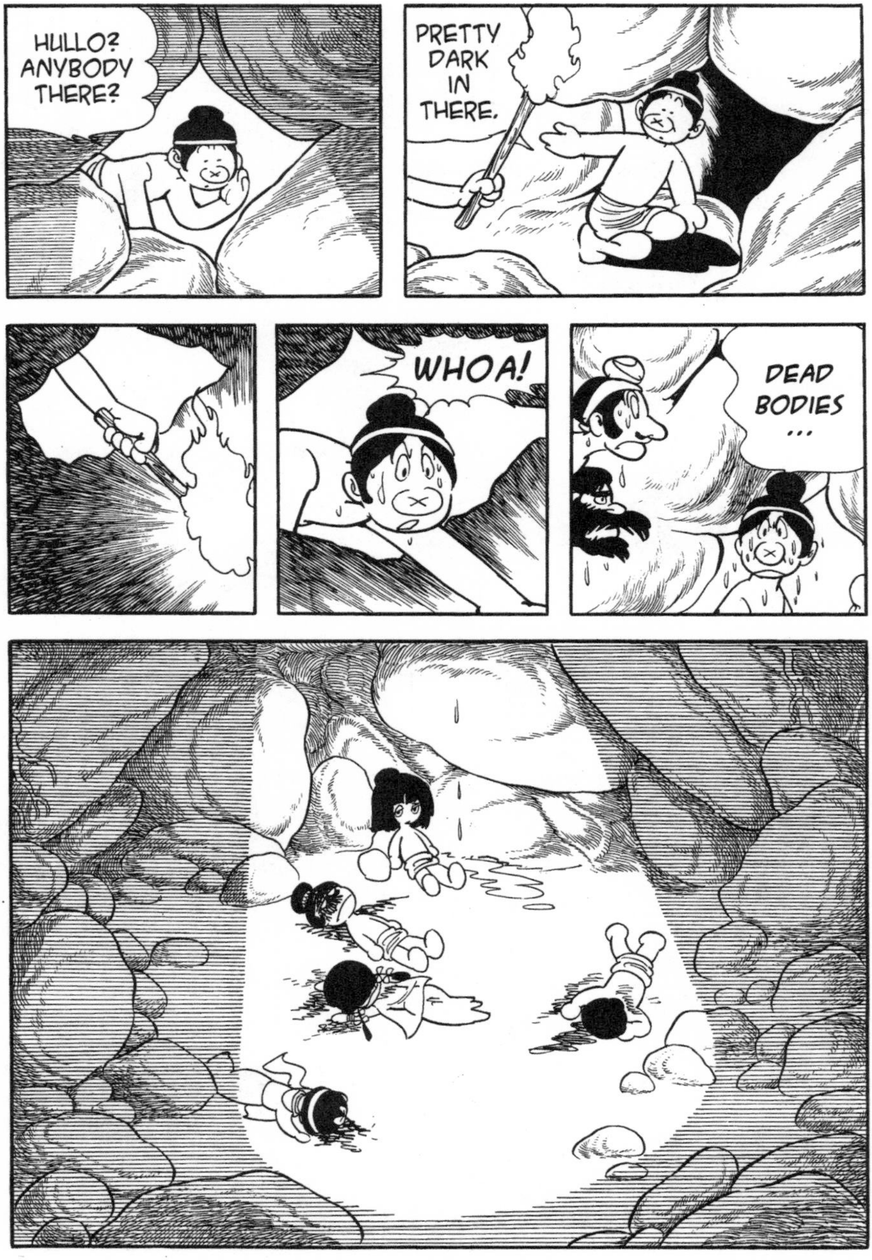
HULLO? ANYBODY THERE?
PRETTY DARK IN THERE.
WHOA!
DEAD BODIES ...

71

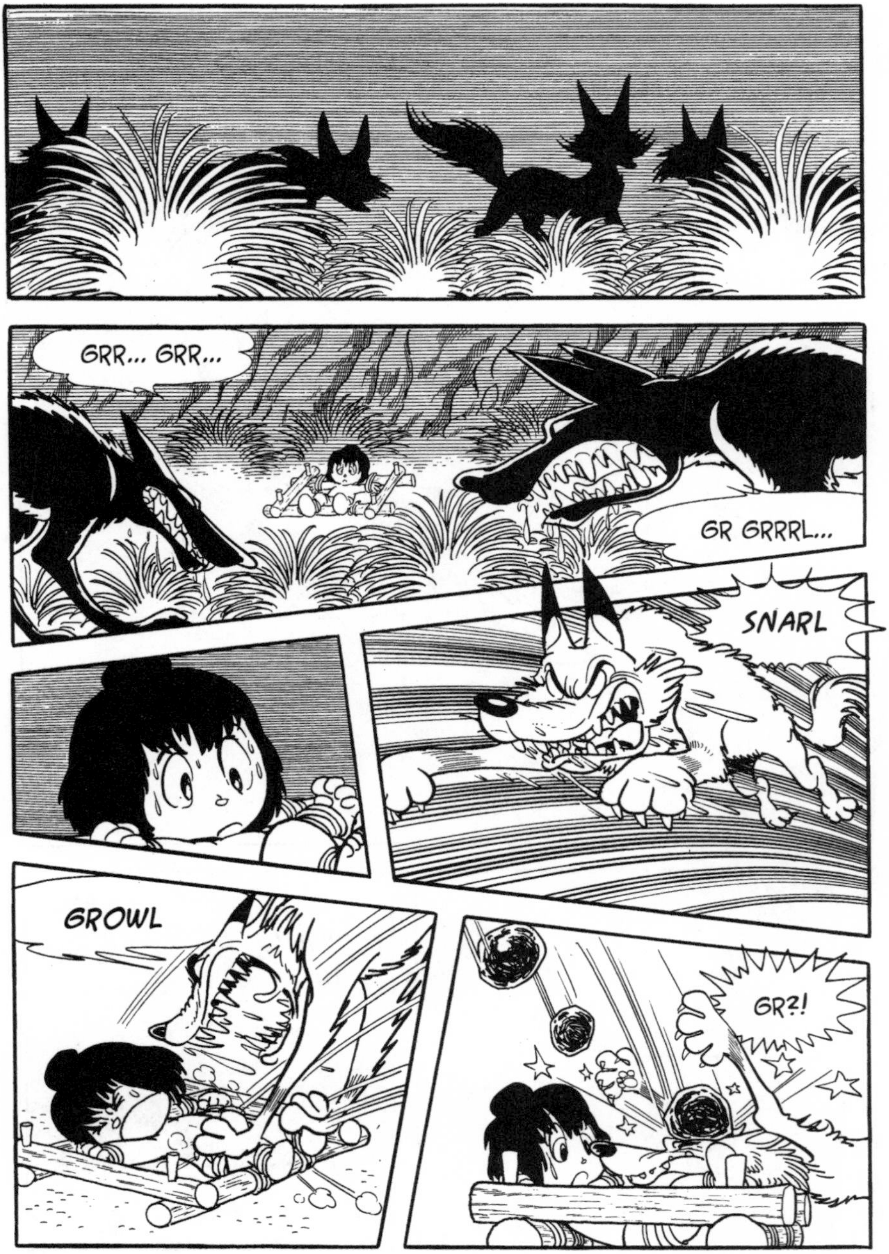
GRR... GRR...
GR GRRRL...
SNARL
GROWL
GR?!

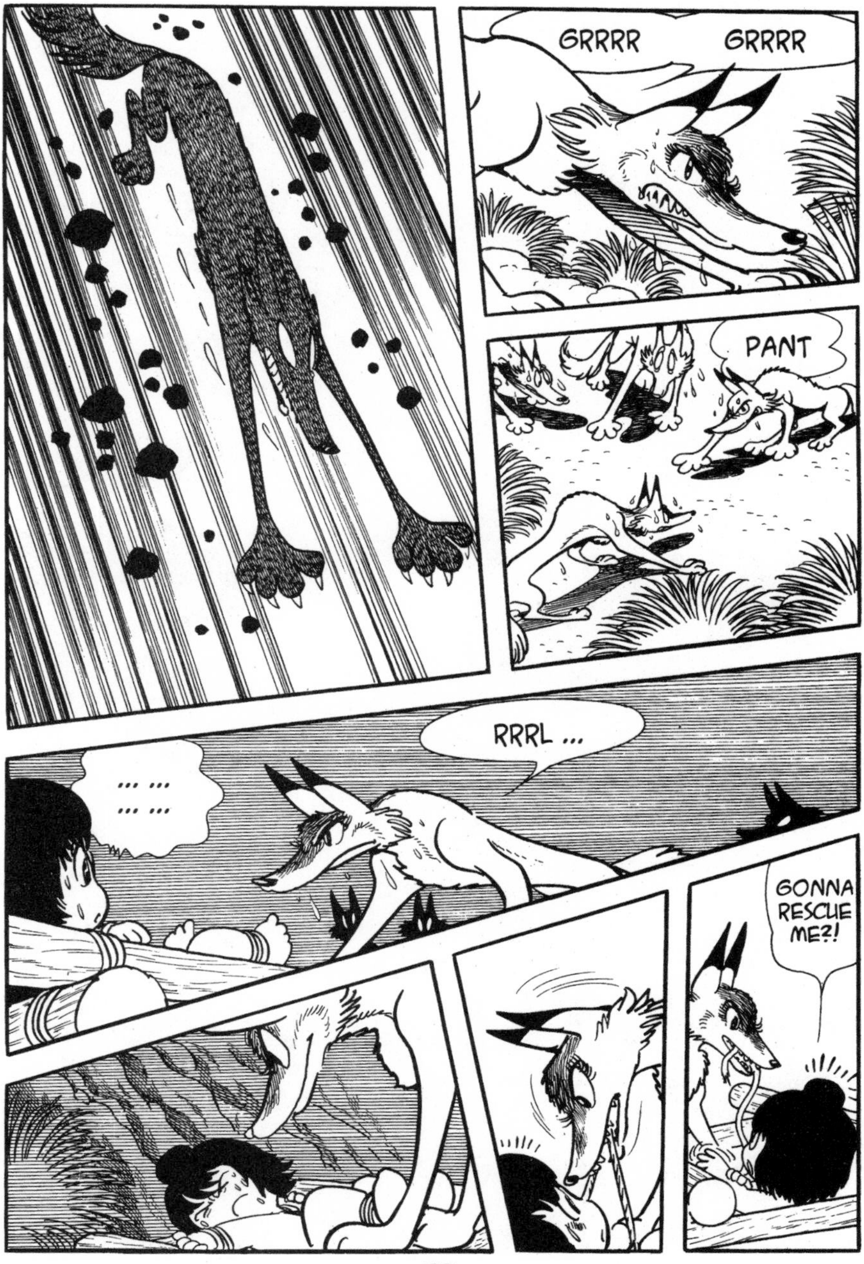
GRRRR GRRRR
PANT
RRRL ...
... ...
... ...
GONNA RESCUE ME?!

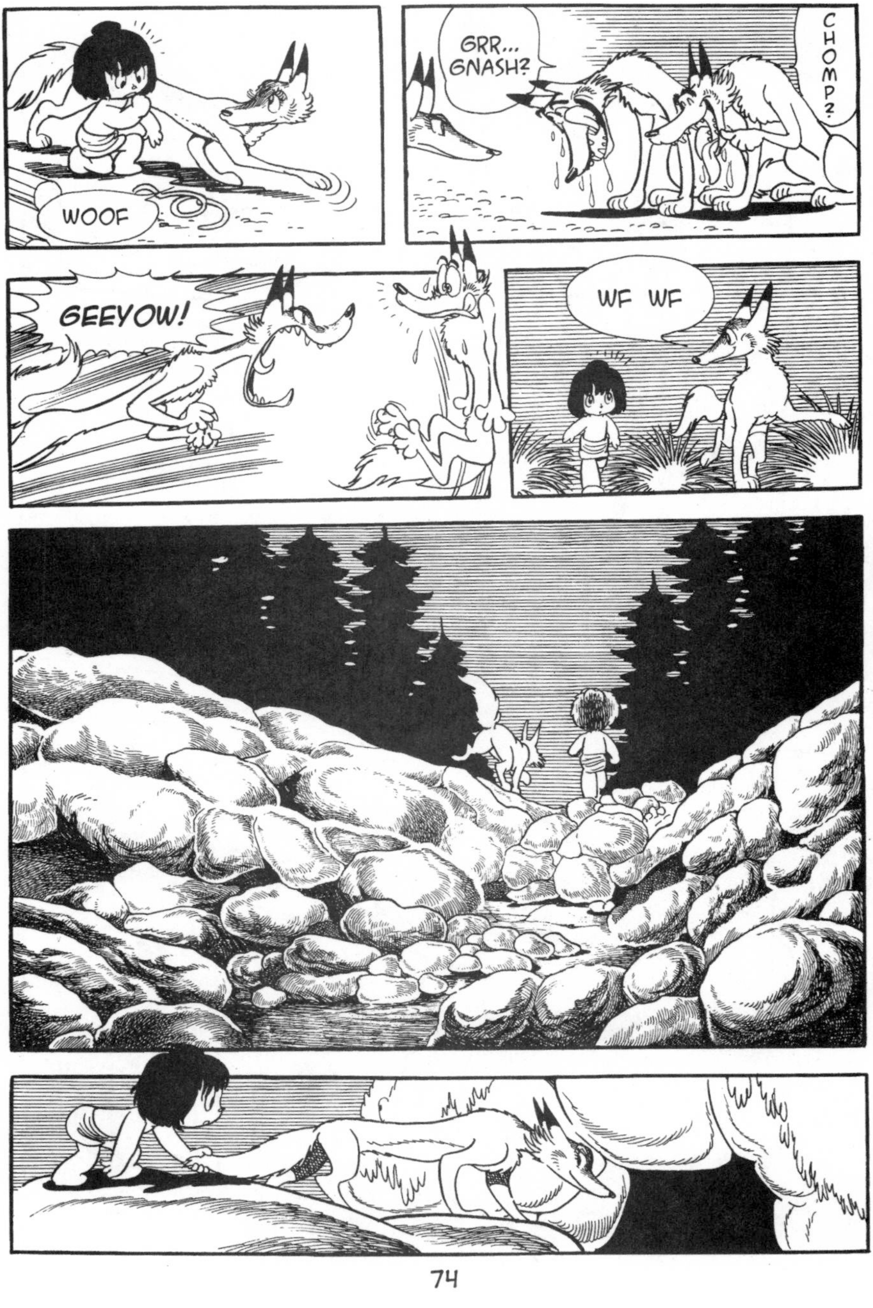
WOOF
GRR... GNASH?
CHOMP?
GEEYOW!
WF WF

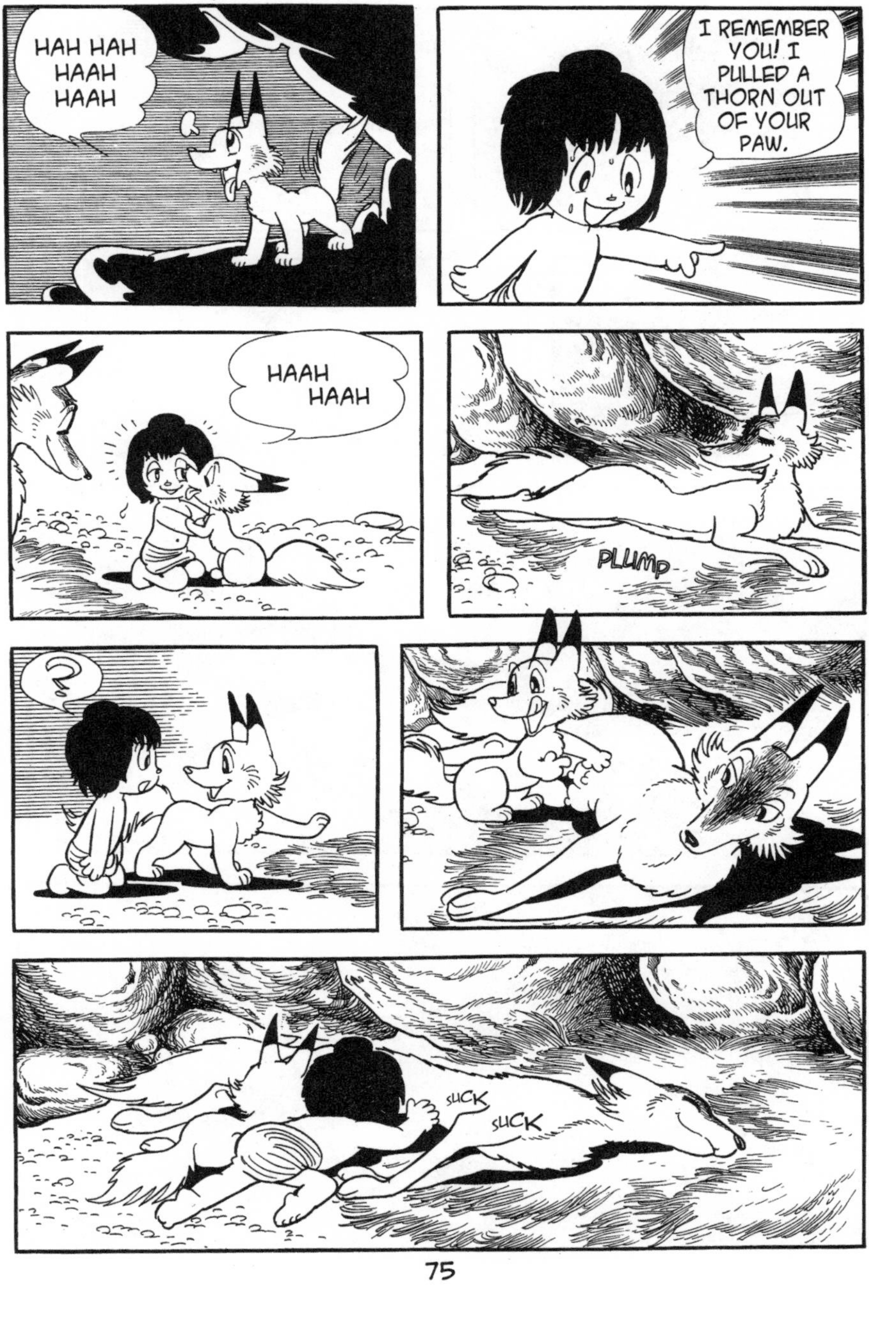
HAH HAH HAAH HAAH
I REMEMBER YOU! I PULLED A THORN OUT OF YOUR PAW.
HAAH HAAH
PLUMP
?
SUCK
SUCK

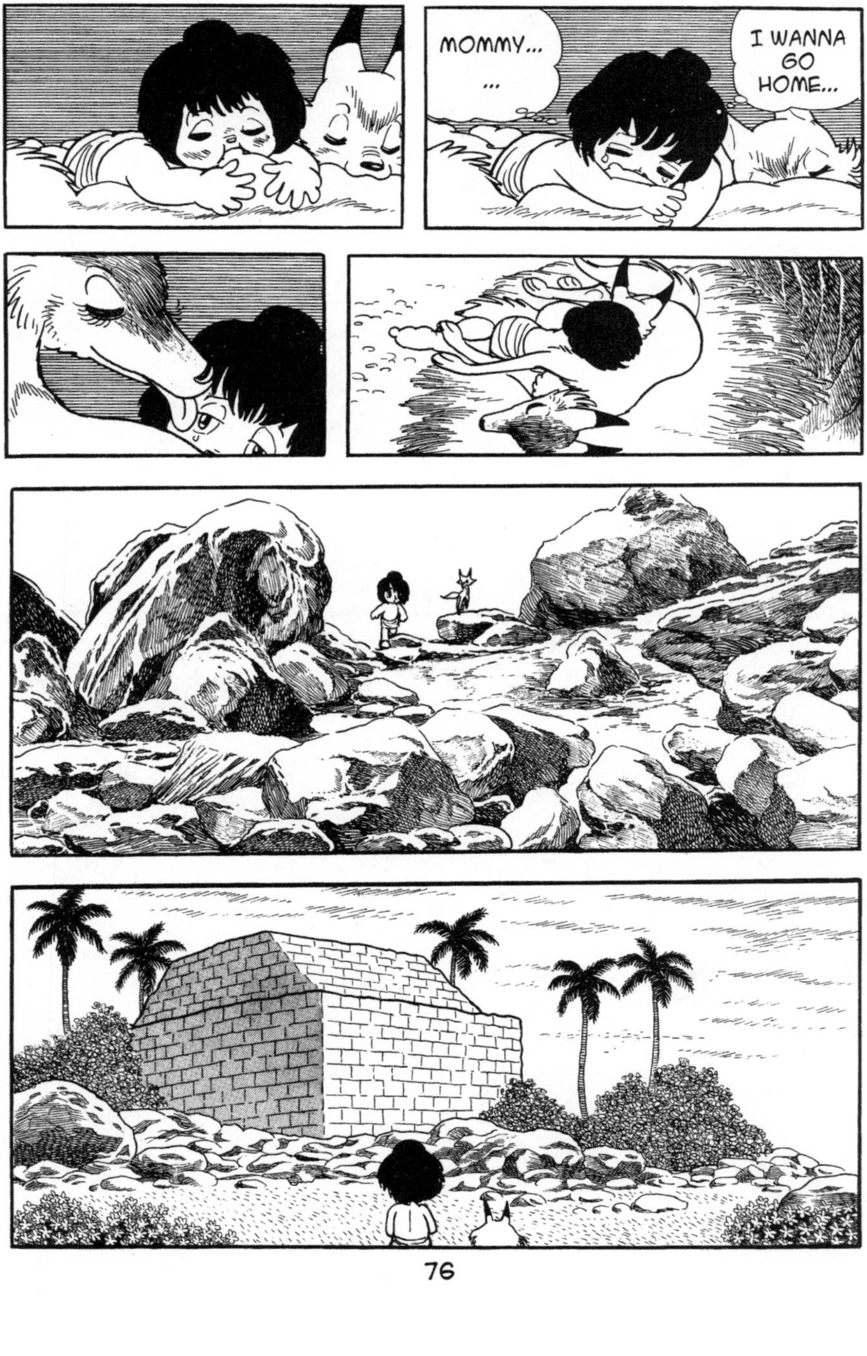
MOMMY...
...
I WANNA GO HOME...

77

78

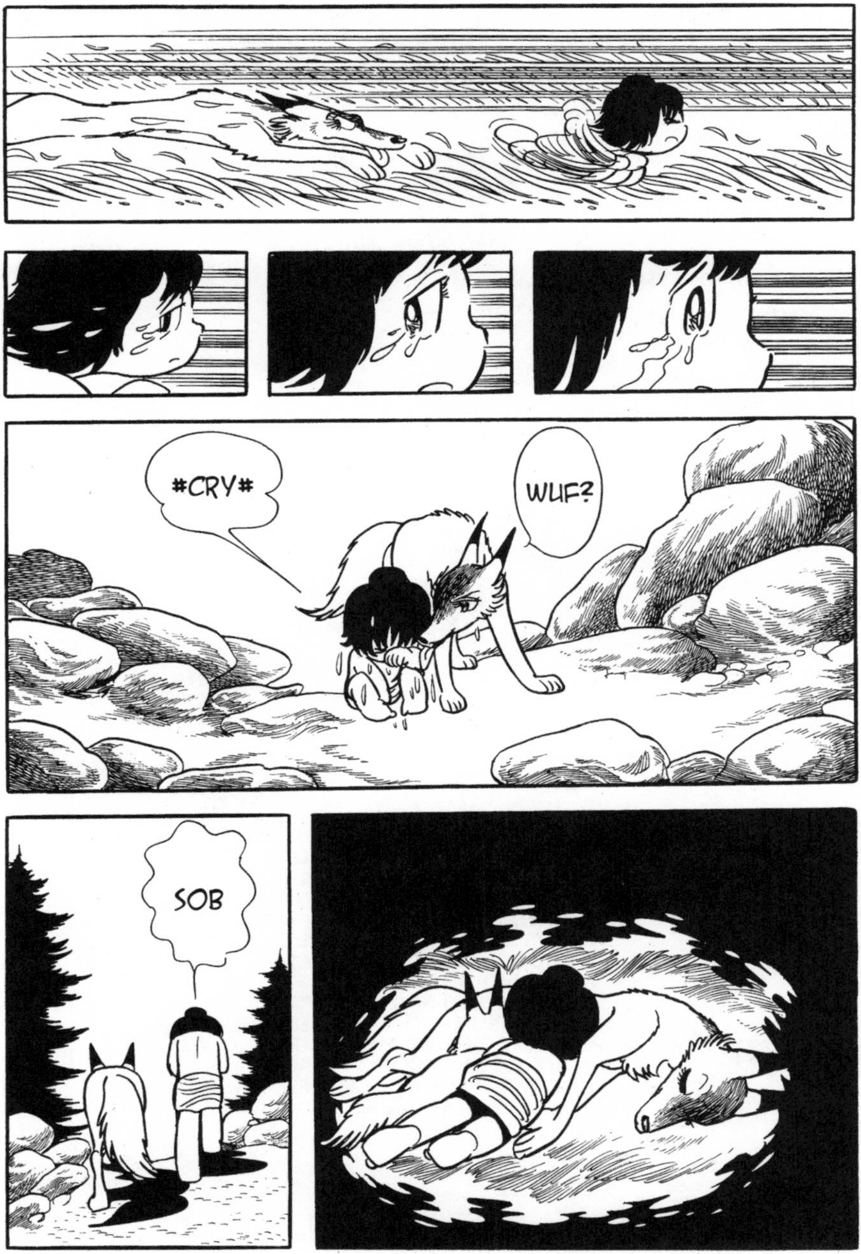

#CRY#
WUF?
SOB

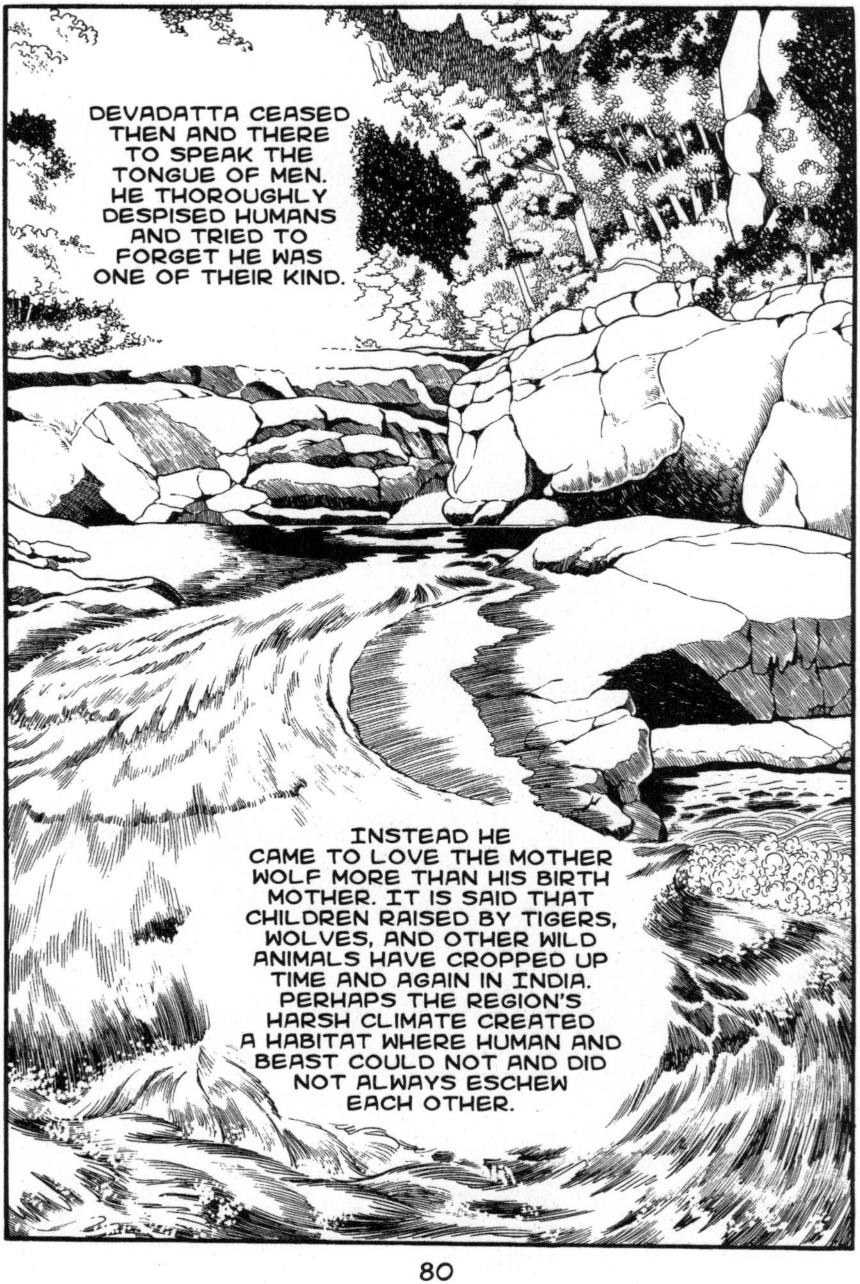
DEVADATTA CEASED THEN AND THERE TO SPEAK THE TONGUE OF MEN. HE THOROUGHLY DESPISED HUMANS AND TRIED TO FORGET HE WAS ONE OF THEIR KIND.
INSTEAD HE CAME TO LOVE THE MOTHER WOLF MORE THAN HIS BIRTH MOTHER. IT IS SAID THAT CHILDREN RAISED BY TIGERS, WOLVES, AND OTHER WILD ANIMALS HAVE CROPPED UP TIME AND AGAIN IN INDIA. PERHAPS THE REGION'S HARSH CLIMATE CREATED A HABITAT WHERE HUMAN AND BEAST COULD NOT AND DID NOT ALWAYS ESCHEW EACH OTHER.

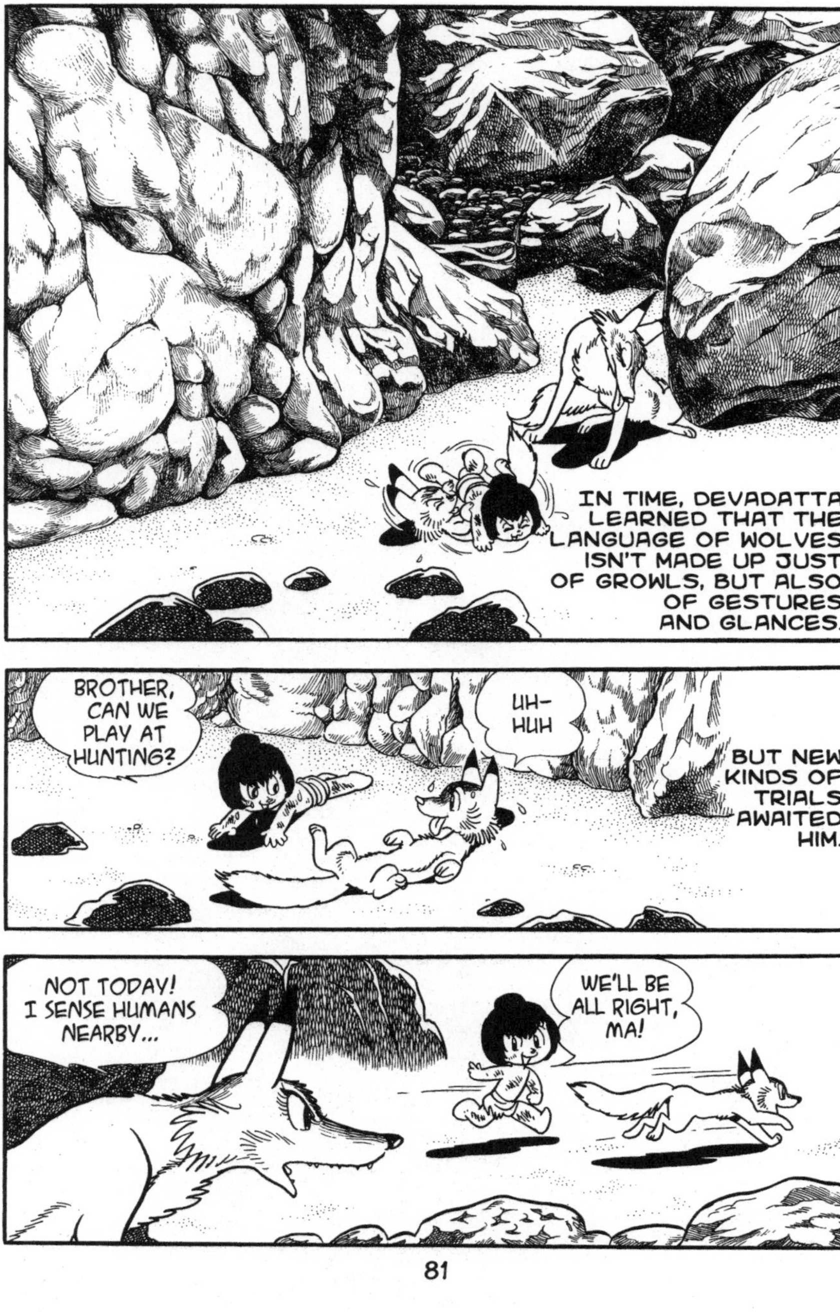
IN TIME, DEVADATTA LEARNED THAT THE LANGUAGE OF WOLVES ISN'T MADE UP JUST OF GROWLS, BUT ALSO OF GESTURES AND GLANCES.
BROTHER, CAN WE PLAY AT HUNTING?
UH-HUH
BUT NEW KINDS OF TRIALS AWAITED HIM.
NOT TODAY! I SENSE HUMANS NEARBY...
WE'LL BE ALL RIGHT, MA!

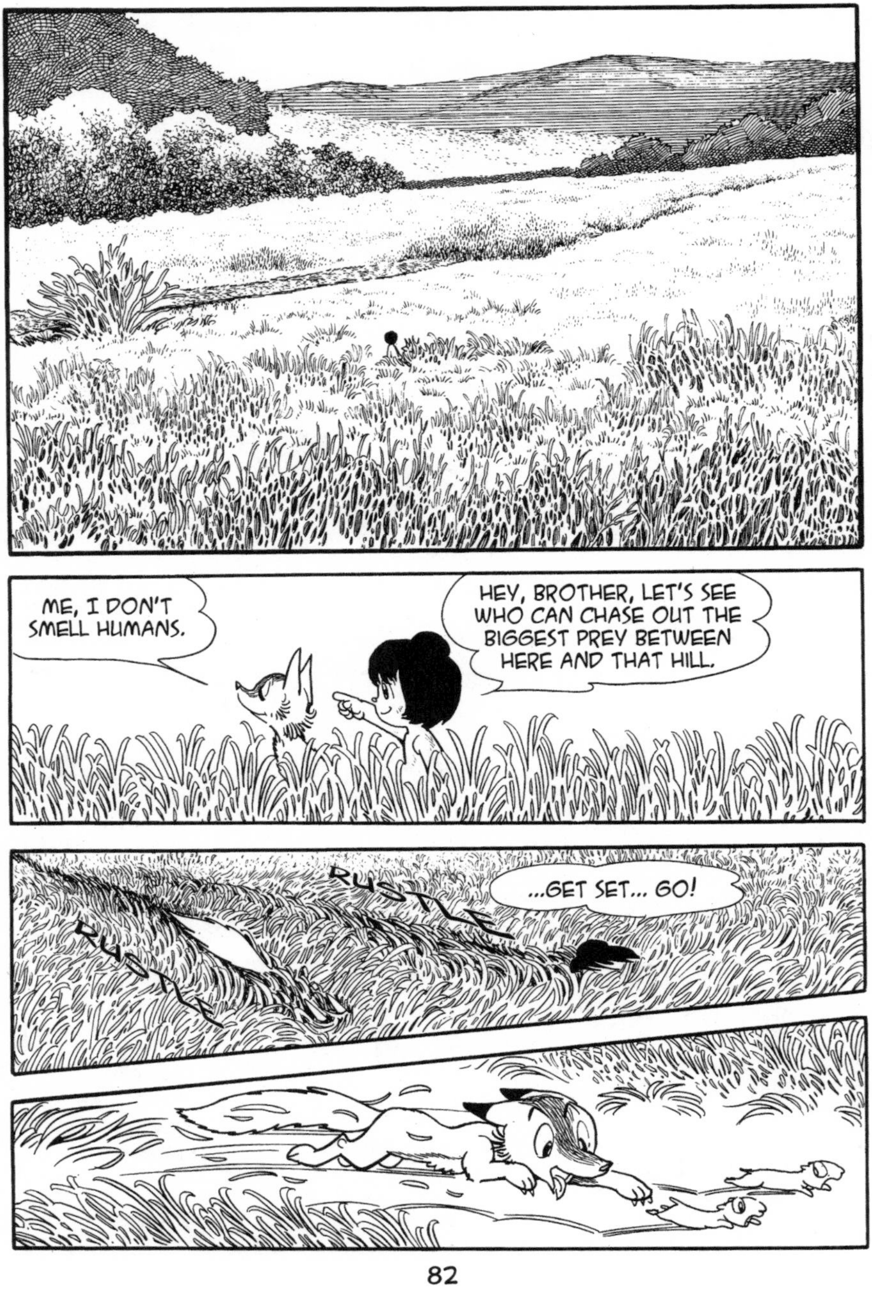
ME, I DON'T SMELL HUMANS.
HEY, BROTHER, LET'S SEE WHO CAN CHASE OUT THE BIGGEST PREY BETWEEN HERE AND THAT HILL.
RUSTLE
RUSTLE
...GET SET... GO!

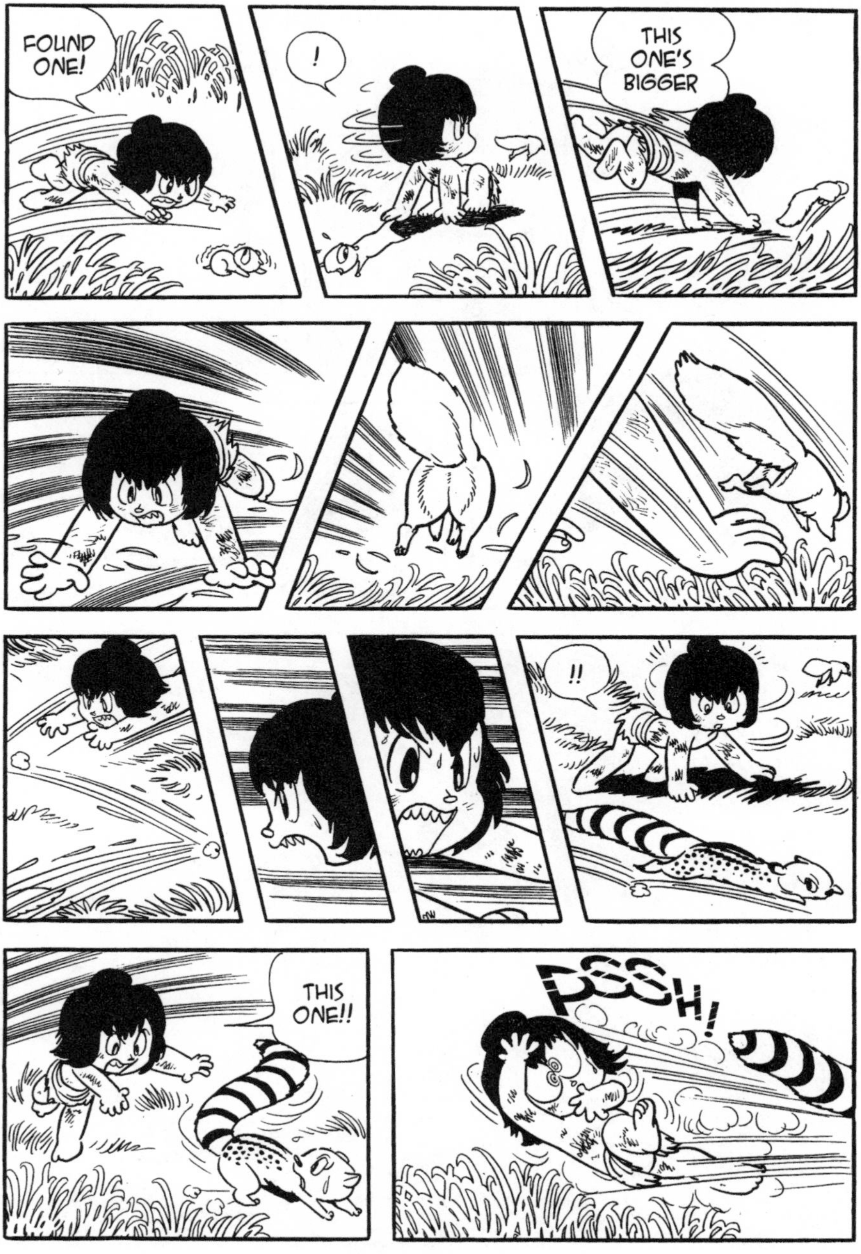
FOUND ONE!
!
THIS ONE'S BIGGER
!!
THIS ONE!!
PSSSH!

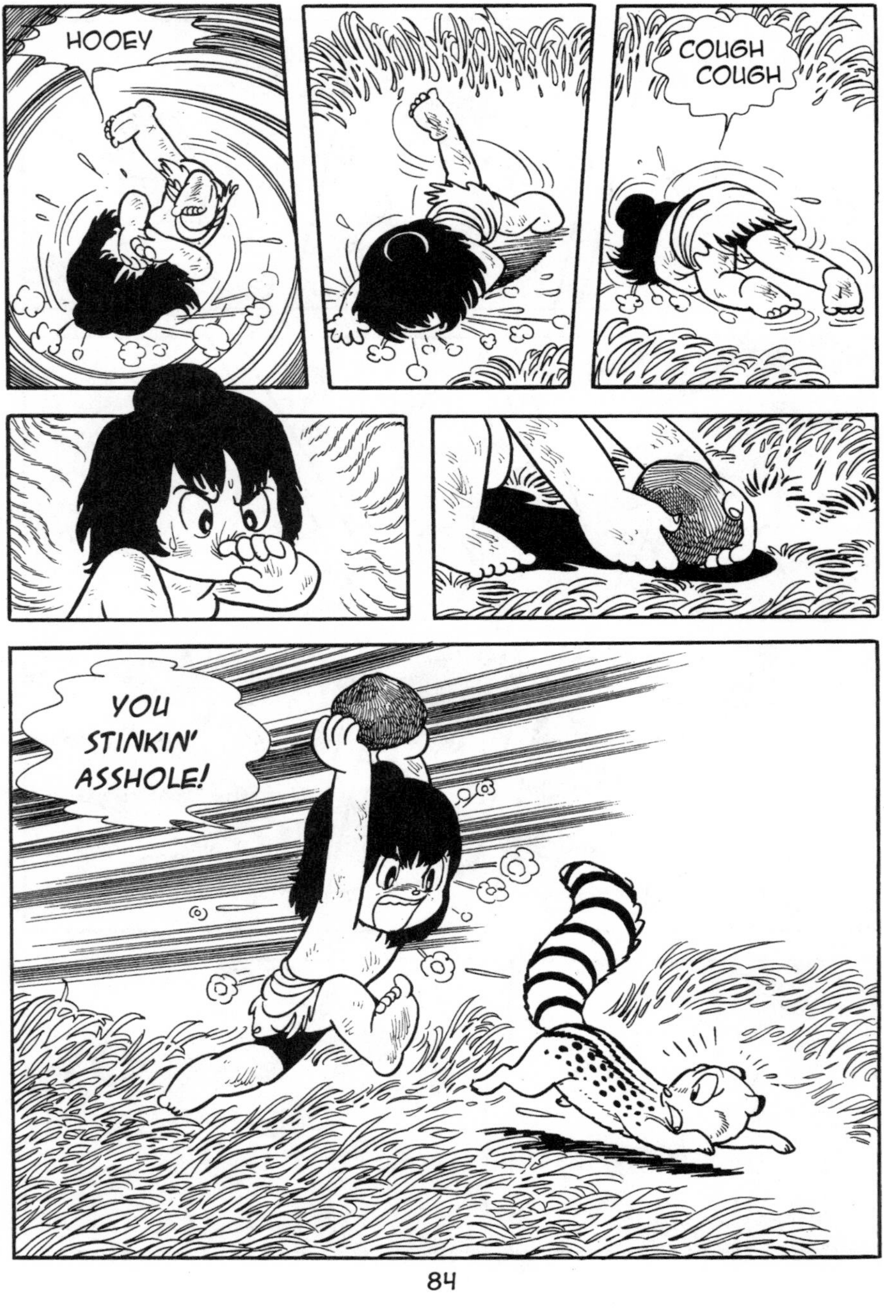
HOOEY
COUGH COUGH
YOU STINKIN' ASSHOLE!

86

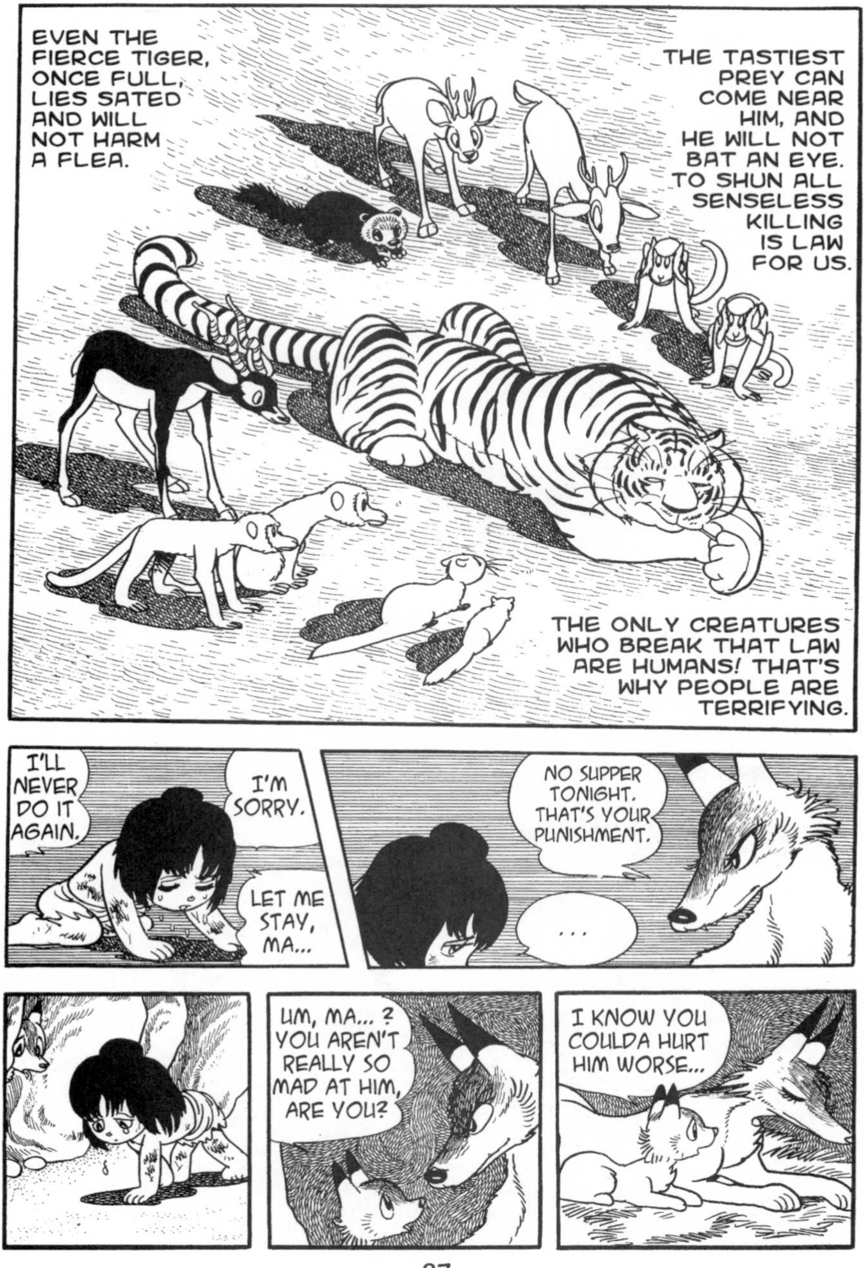
EVEN THE FIERCE TIGER, ONCE FULL, LIES SATED AND WILL NOT HARM A FLEA.
THE TASTIEST PREY CAN COME NEAR HIM, AND HE WILL NOT BAT AN EYE. TO SHUN ALL SENSELESS KILLING IS LAW FOR US.
THE ONLY CREATURES WHO BREAK THAT LAW ARE HUMANS! THAT'S WHY PEOPLE ARE TERRIFYING.
I'LL NEVER DO IT AGAIN.
I'M SORRY.
LET ME STAY, MA...
NO SUPPER TONIGHT. THAT'S YOUR PUNISHMENT.
...
UM, MA... ? YOU AREN'T REALLY SO MAD AT HIM, ARE YOU?
I KNOW YOU COULDA HURT HIM WORSE...

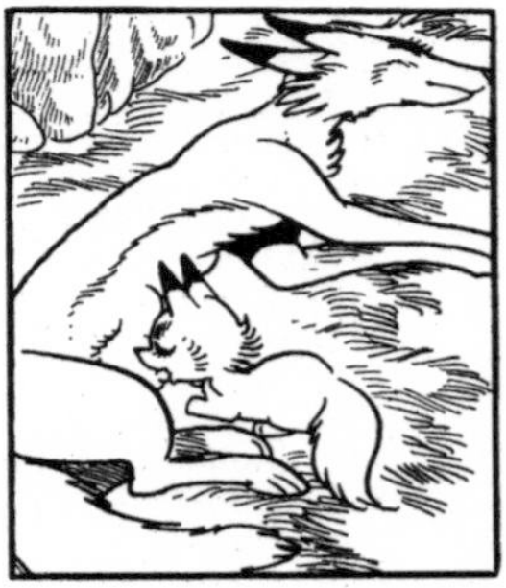
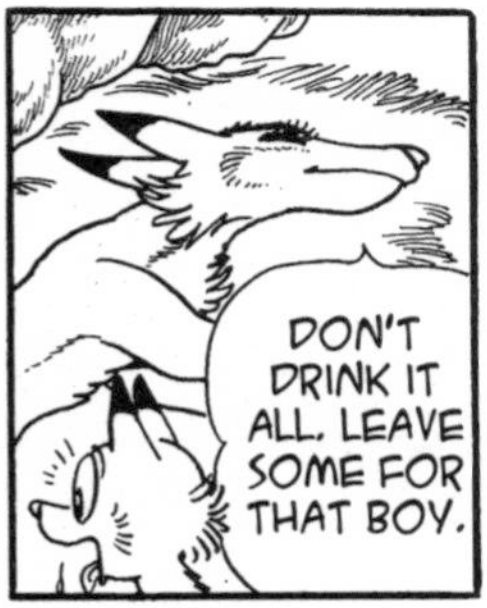
DON'T DRINK IT ALL. LEAVE SOME FOR THAT BOY.
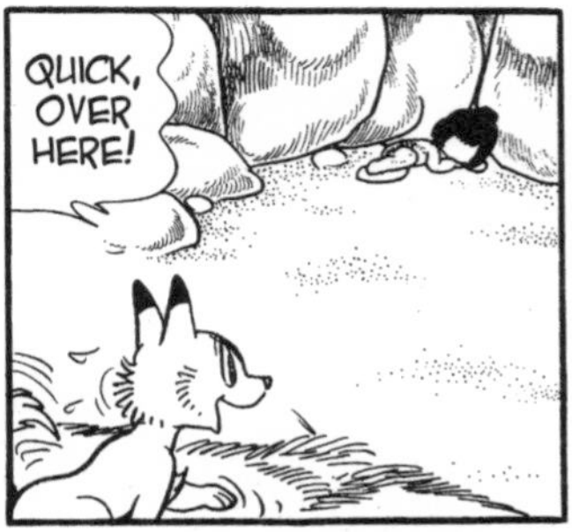
QUICK, OVER HERE!
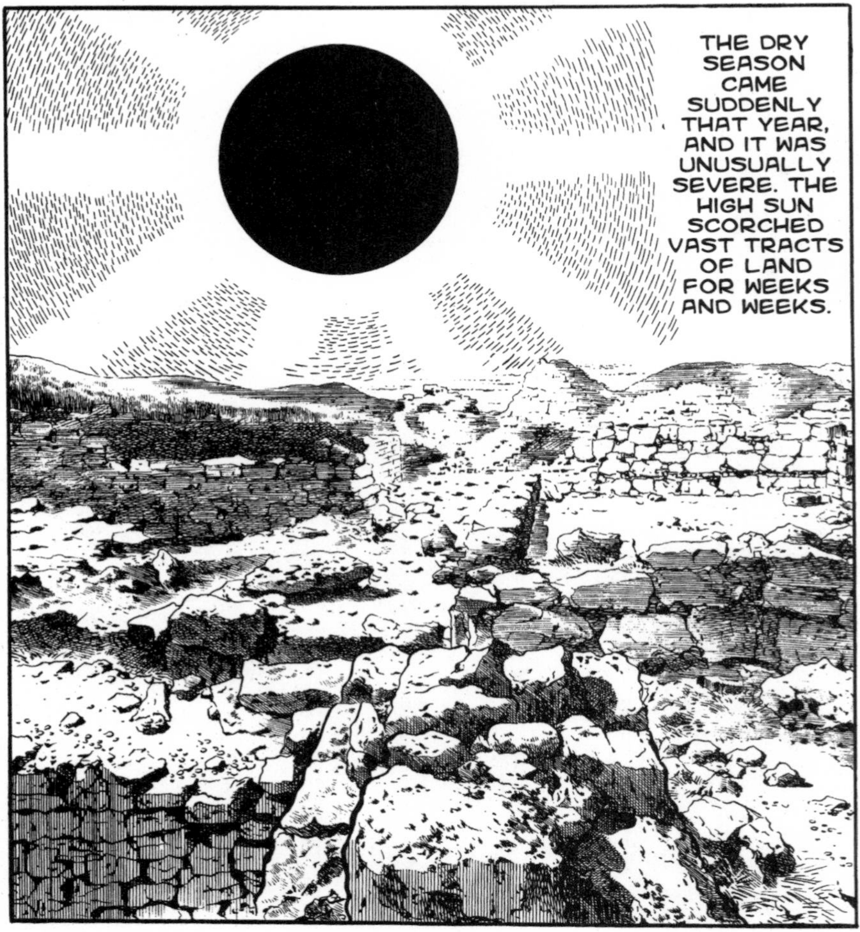
THE DRY SEASON CAME SUDDENLY THAT YEAR, AND IT WAS UNUSUALLY SEVERE. THE HIGH SUN SCORCHED VAST TRACTS OF LAND FOR WEEKS AND WEEKS.

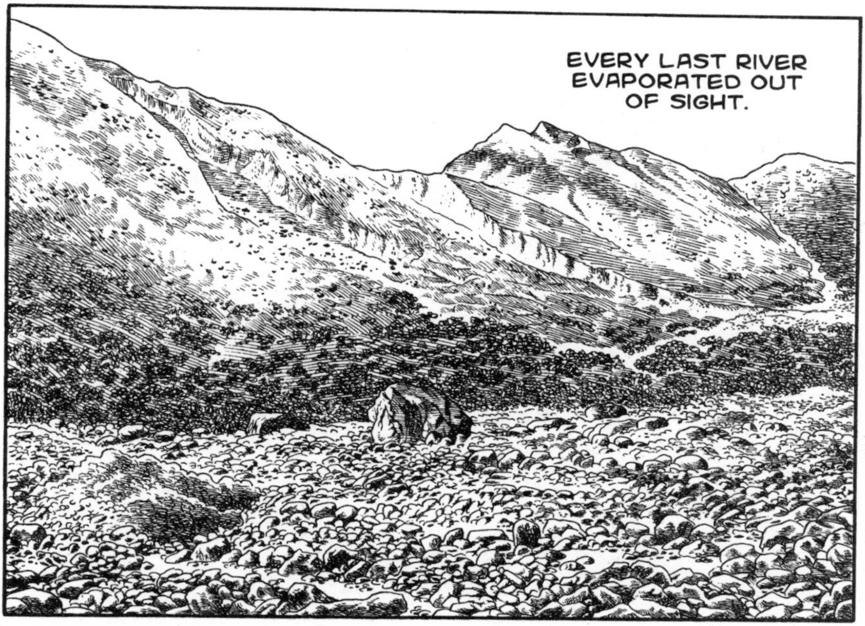
EVERY LAST RIVER EVAPORATED OUT OF SIGHT.

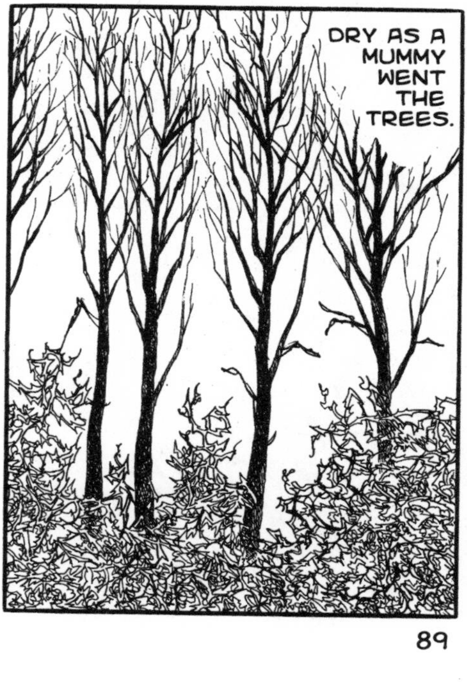
DRY AS A MUMMY WENT THE TREES.

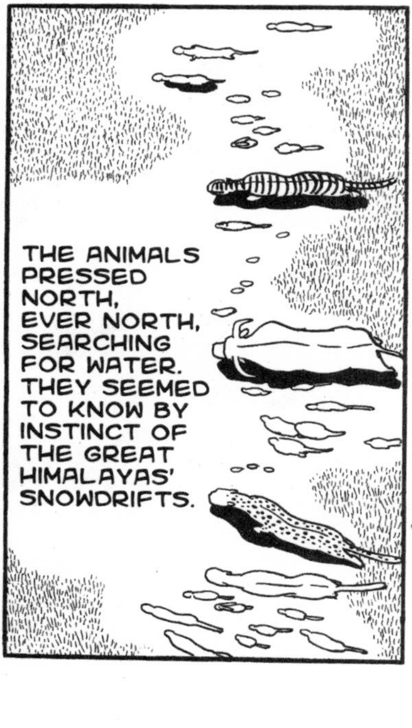
THE ANIMALS PRESSED NORTH, EVER NORTH, SEARCHING FOR WATER. THEY SEEMED TO KNOW BY INSTINCT OF THE GREAT HIMALAYAS' SNOWDRIFTS.

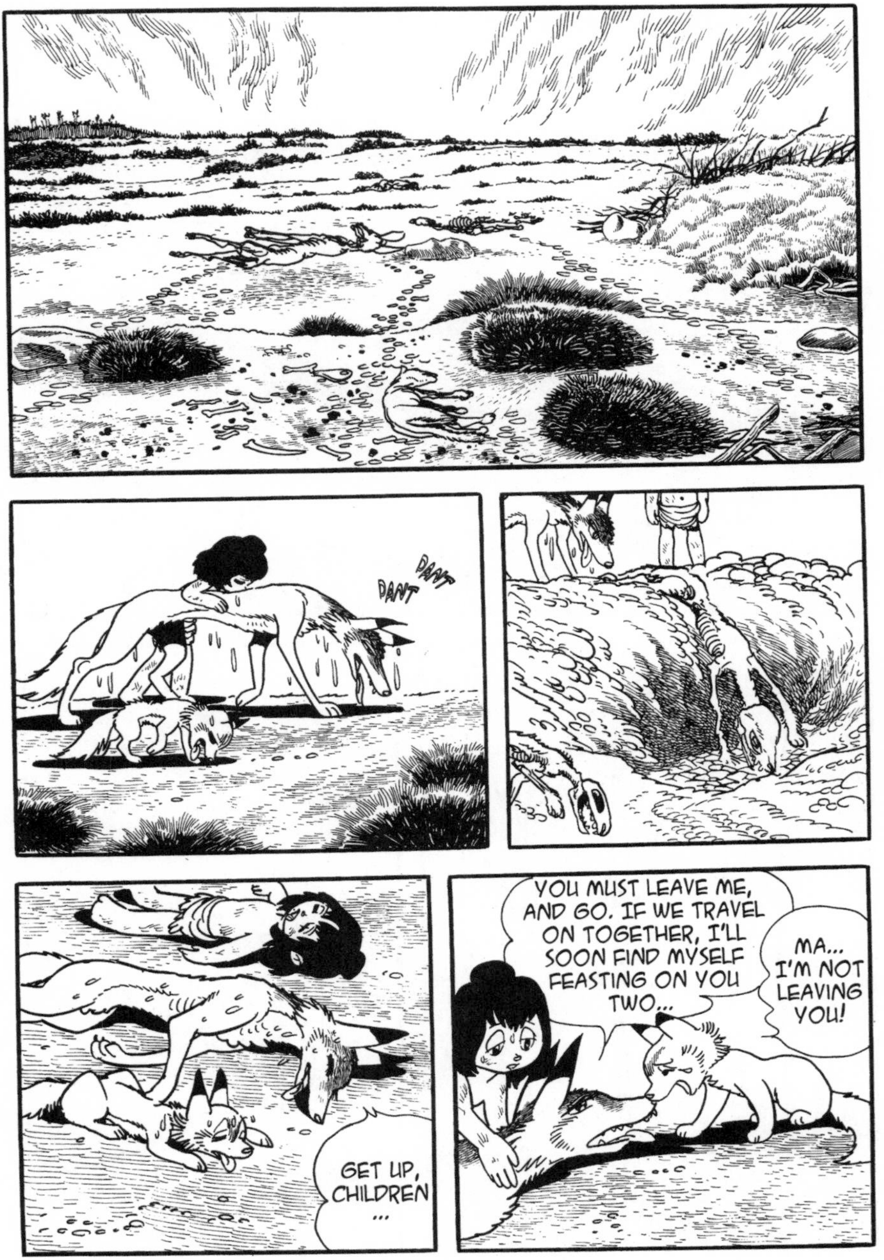
PANT
PANT
GET UP, CHILDREN ...
YOU MUST LEAVE ME, AND GO. IF WE TRAVEL ON TOGETHER, I'LL SOON FIND MYSELF FEASTING ON YOU TWO...
MA... I'M NOT LEAVING YOU!

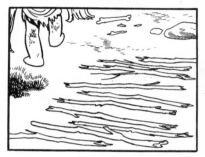

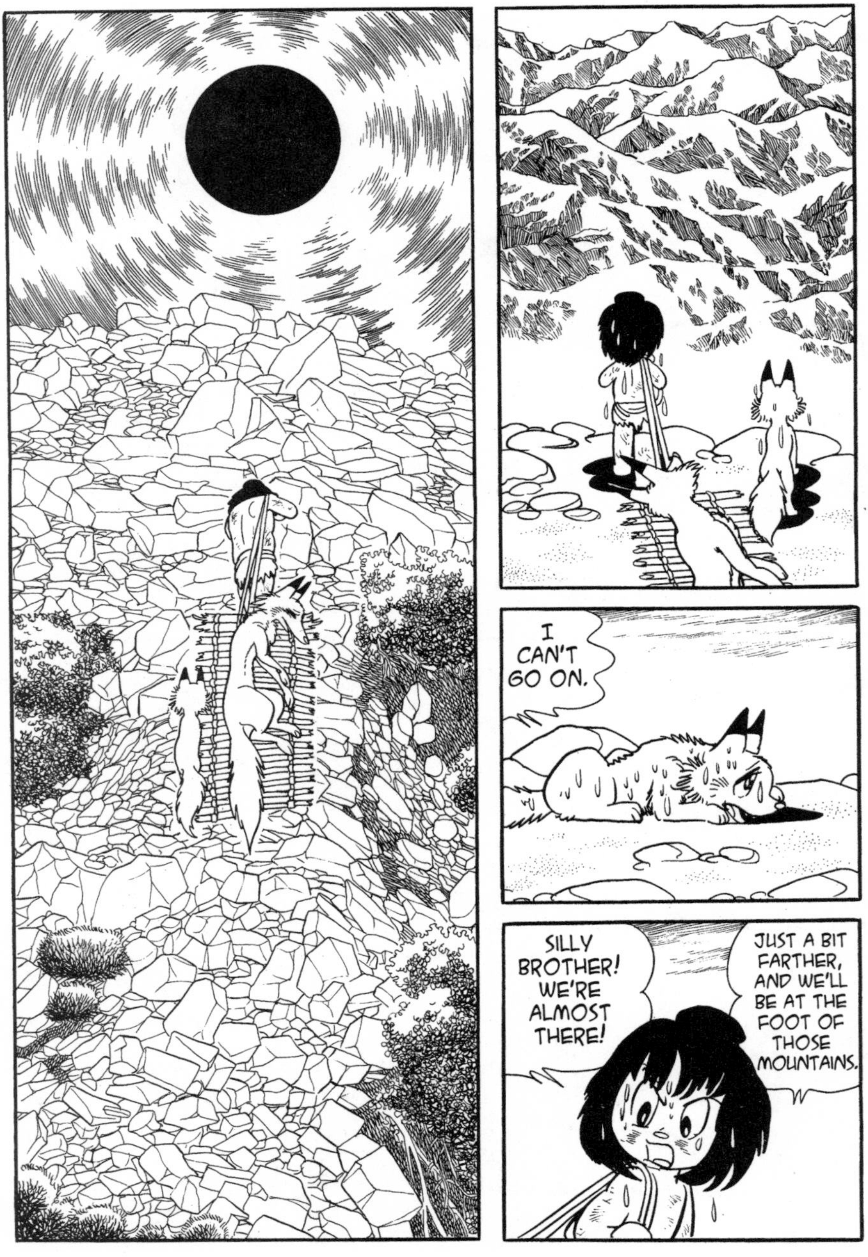
I CAN'T GO ON.
SILLY BROTHER! WE'RE ALMOST THERE!
JUST A BIT FARTHER, AND WE'LL BE AT THE FOOT OF THOSE MOUNTAINS.

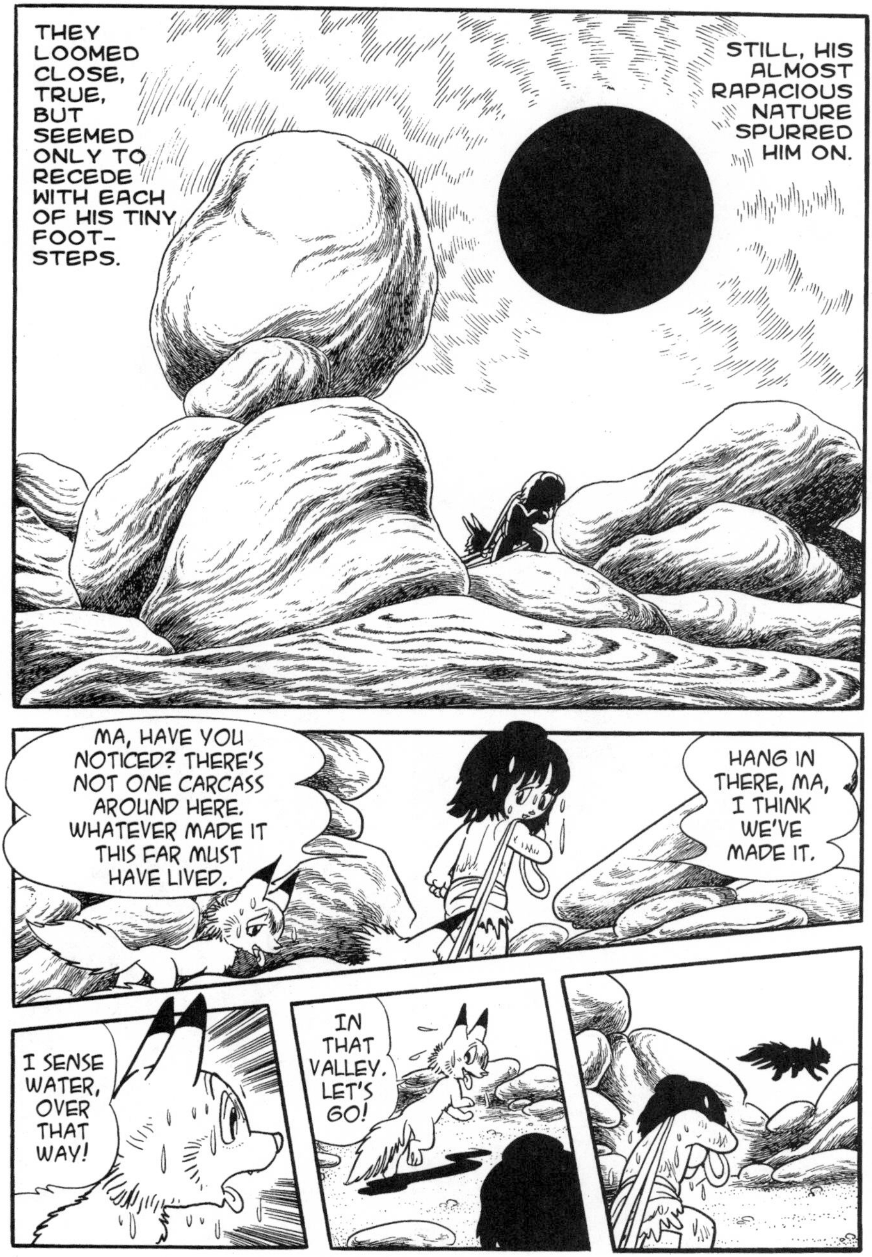
THEY LOOMED CLOSE, TRUE, BUT SEEMED ONLY TO RECEDE WITH EACH OF HIS TINY FOOT-STEPS.
STILL, HIS ALMOST RAPACIOUS NATURE SPURRED HIM ON.
MA, HAVE YOU NOTICED? THERE'S NOT ONE CARCASS AROUND HERE. WHATEVER MADE IT THIS FAR MUST HAVE LIVED.
HANG IN THERE, MA, I THINK WE'VE MADE IT.
I SENSE WATER, OVER THAT WAY!
IN THAT VALLEY. LET'S GO!

94

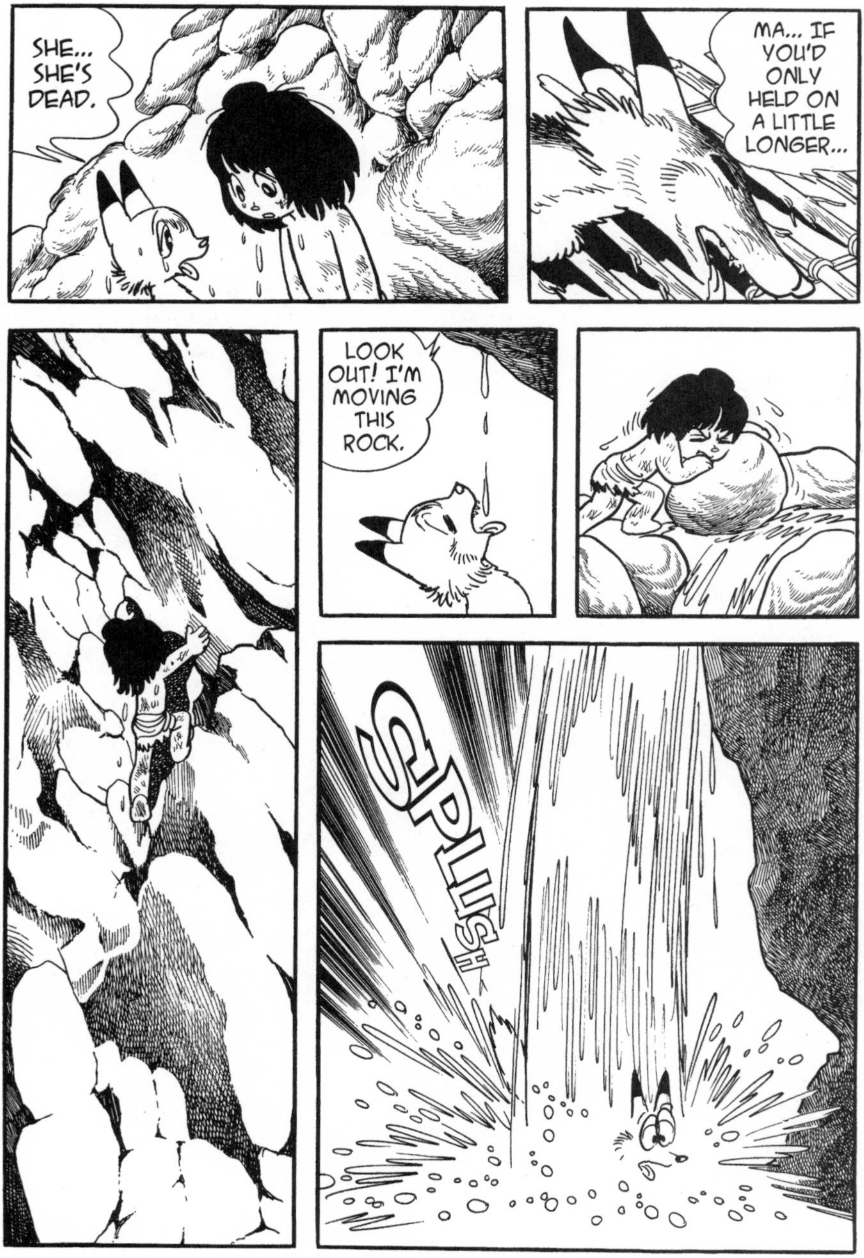
SHE... SHE'S DEAD.
MA... IF YOU'D ONLY HELD ON A LITTLE LONGER...
LOOK OUT! I'M MOVING THIS ROCK.
SPLUSH

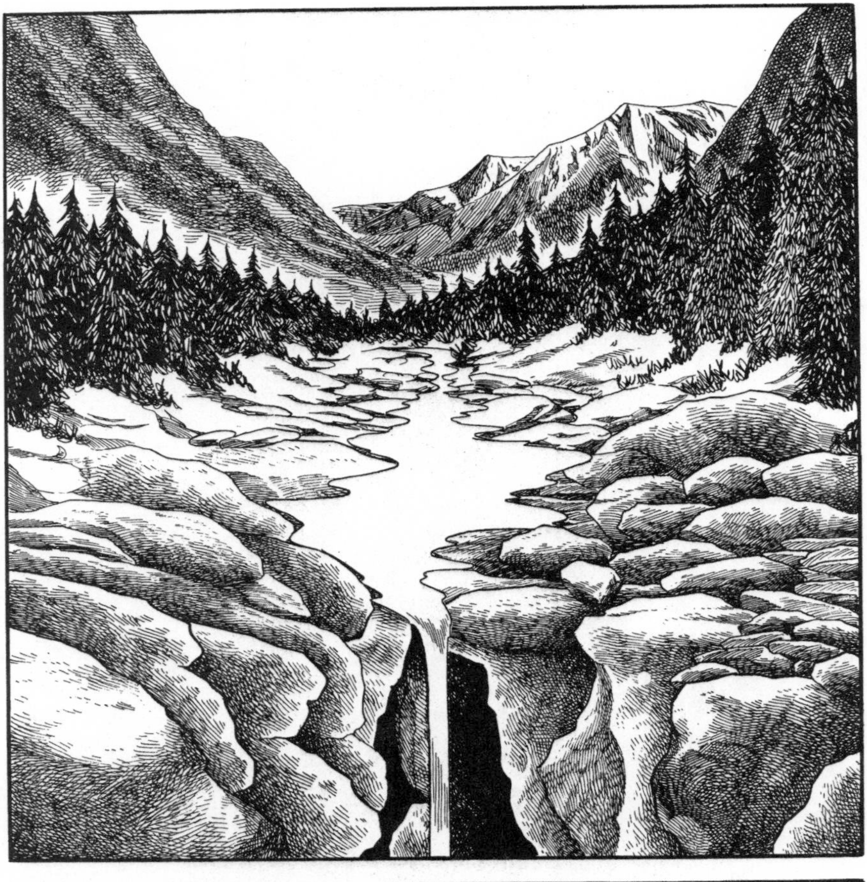

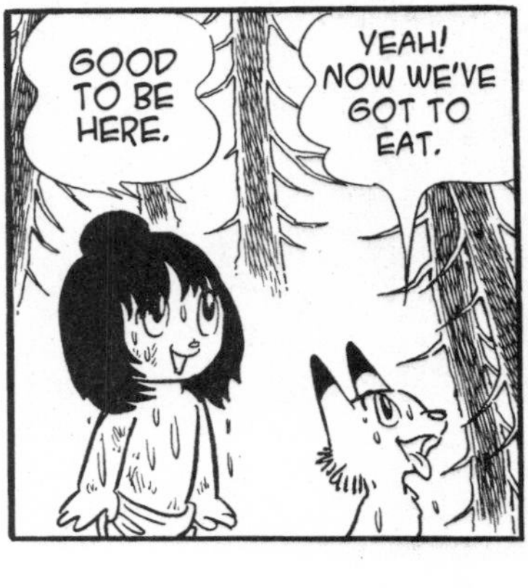
GOOD TO BE HERE.
YEAH! NOW WE'VE GOT TO EAT.

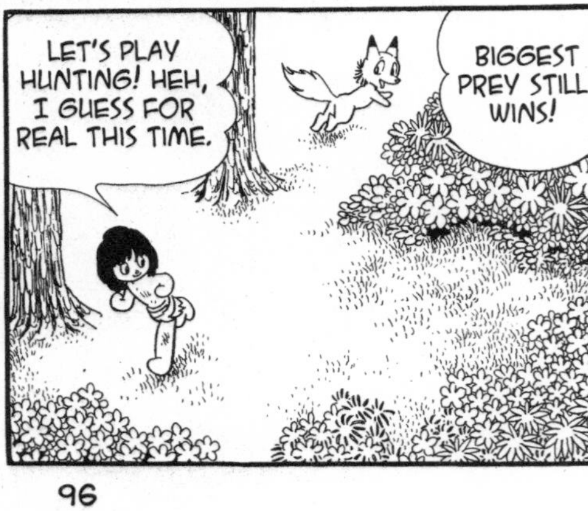
LET'S PLAY HUNTING! HEH, I GUESS FOR REAL THIS TIME.
BIGGEST PREY STILL WINS!

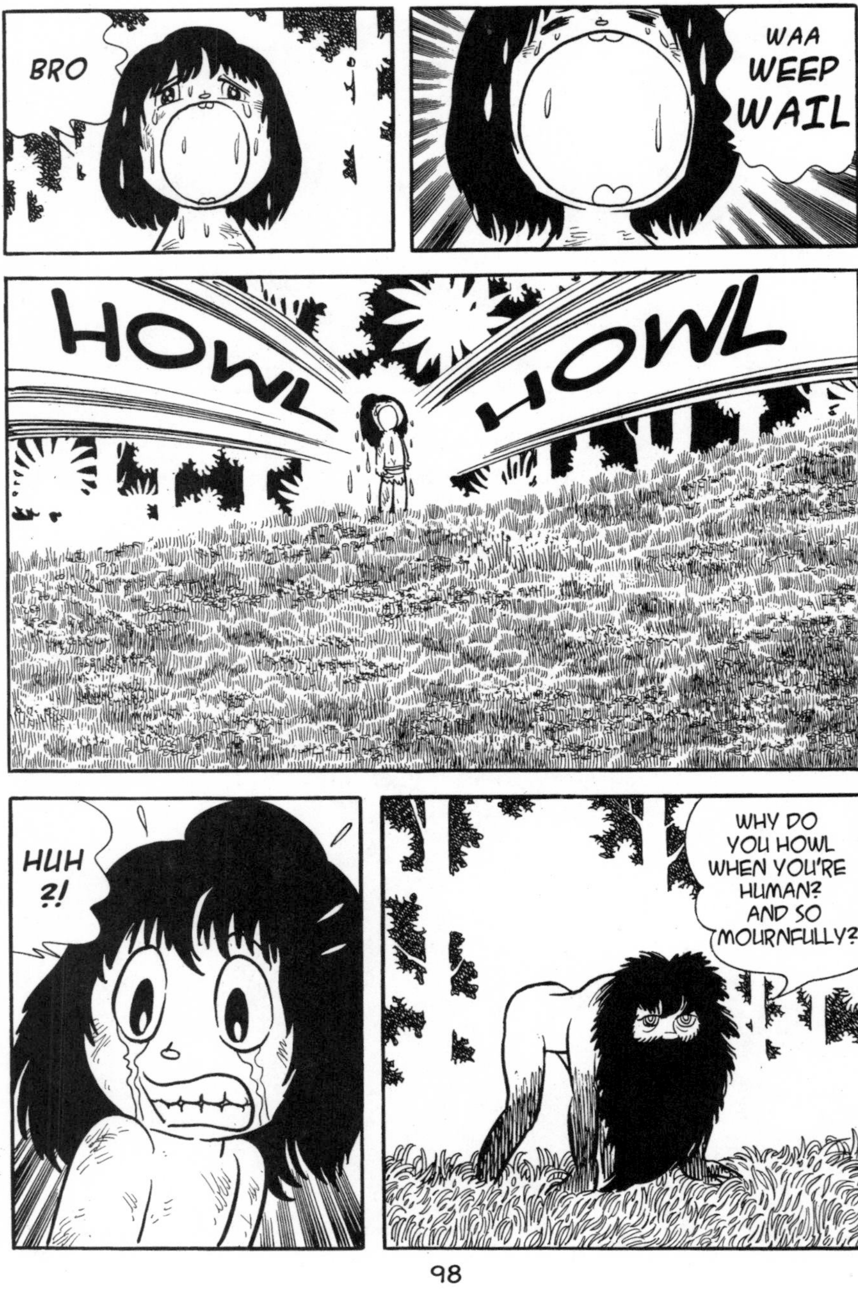

BRO
WAA WEEP WAIL
HOWL HOWL
HUH ?!
WHY DO YOU HOWL WHEN YOU'RE HUMAN? AND SO MOURNFULLY?

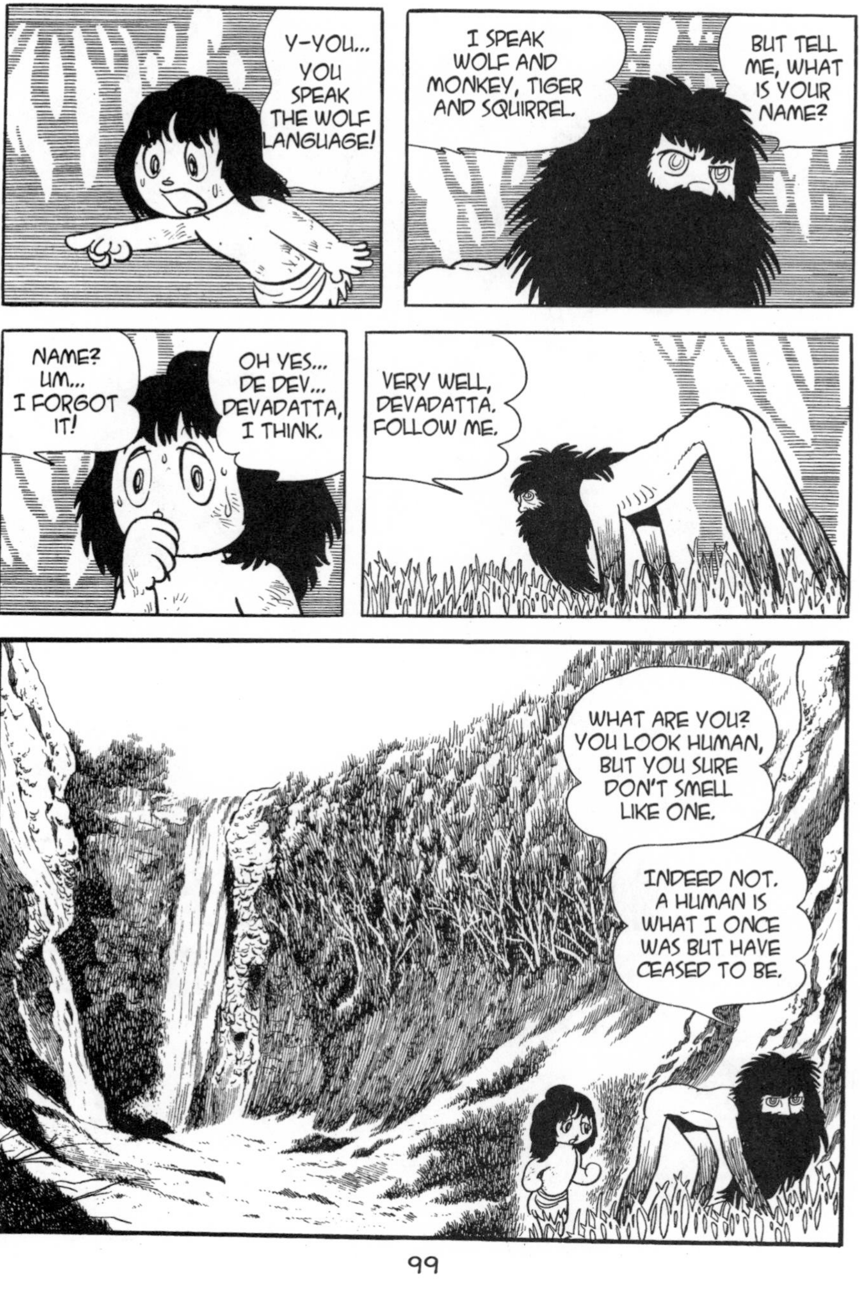
Y-YOU... YOU SPEAK THE WOLF LANGUAGE!
I SPEAK WOLF AND MONKEY, TIGER AND SQUIRREL.
BUT TELL ME, WHAT IS YOUR NAME?
NAME? UM... I FORGOT IT!
OH YES... DE DEV... DEVADATTA, I THINK.
VERY WELL, DEVADATTA. FOLLOW ME.
WHAT ARE YOU? YOU LOOK HUMAN, BUT YOU SURE DON'T SMELL LIKE ONE.
INDEED NOT. A HUMAN IS WHAT I ONCE WAS BUT HAVE CEASED TO BE.

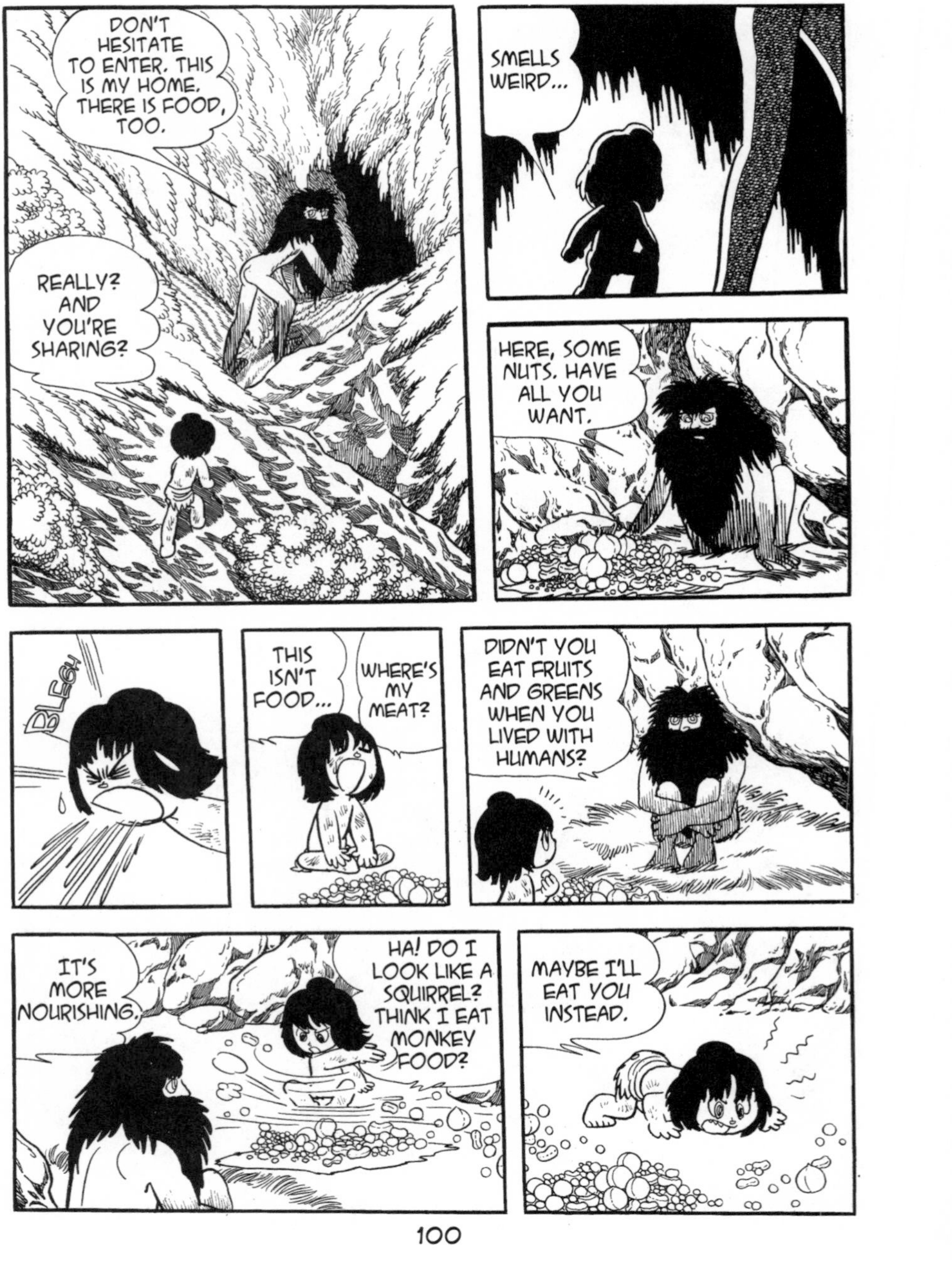
DON'T HESITATE TO ENTER. THIS IS MY HOME. THERE IS FOOD, TOO.
REALLY? AND YOU'RE SHARING?
SMELLS WEIRD...
HERE, SOME NUTS. HAVE ALL YOU WANT.
BLEGH
THIS ISN'T FOOD...
WHERE'S MY MEAT?
DIDN'T YOU EAT FRUITS AND GREENS WHEN YOU LIVED WITH HUMANS?
IT'S MORE NOURISHING.
HA! DO I LOOK LIKE A SQUIRREL? THINK I EAT MONKEY FOOD?
MAYBE I'LL EAT YOU INSTEAD.

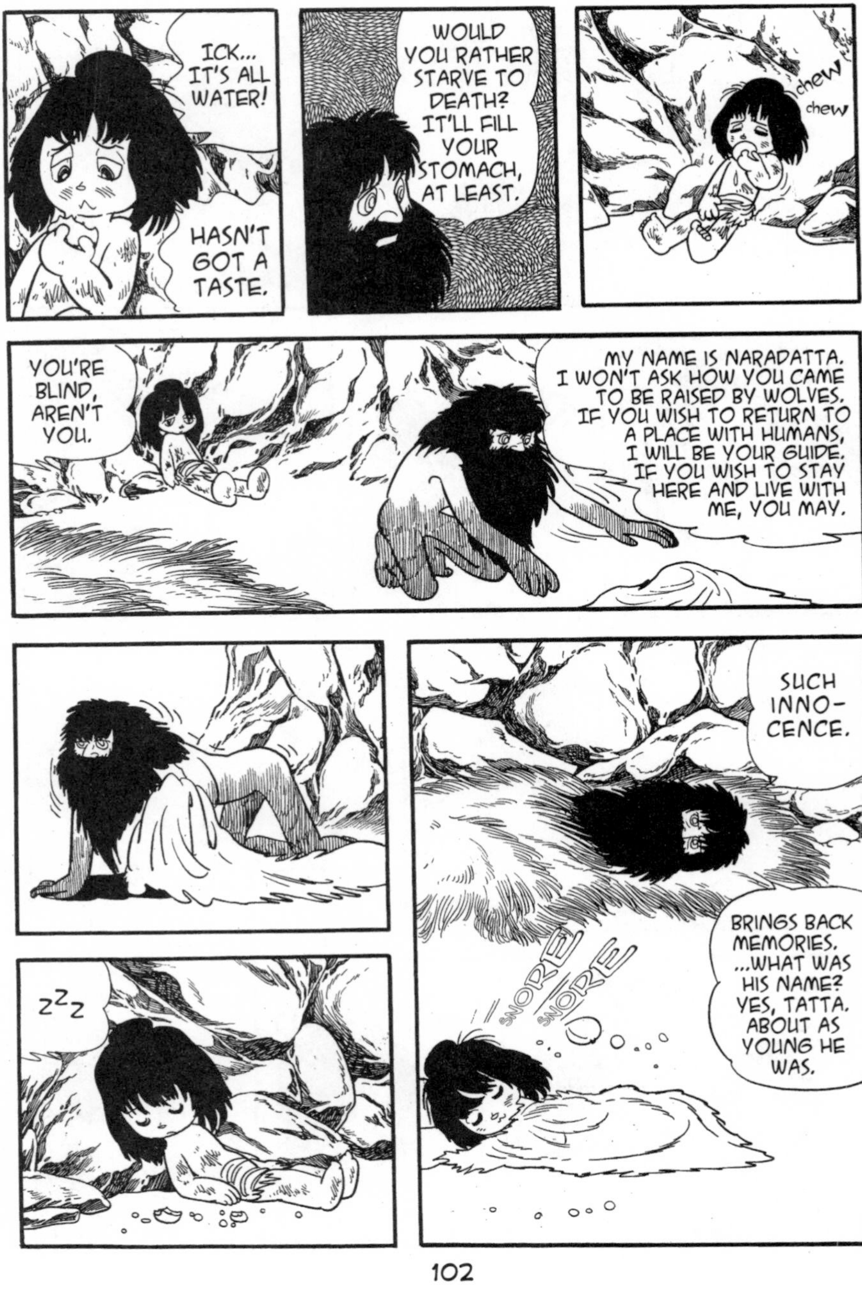
ICK... IT'S ALL WATER!
HASN'T GOT A TASTE.
WOULD YOU RATHER STARVE TO DEATH? IT'LL FILL YOUR STOMACH, AT LEAST.
chew chew
YOU'RE BLIND, AREN'T YOU.
MY NAME IS NARADATTA. I WON'T ASK HOW YOU CAME TO BE RAISED BY WOLVES. IF YOU WISH TO RETURN TO A PLACE WITH HUMANS, I WILL BE YOUR GUIDE. IF YOU WISH TO STAY HERE AND LIVE WITH ME, YOU MAY.
SUCH INNO-CENCE.
BRINGS BACK MEMORIES. ...WHAT WAS HIS NAME? YES, TATTA. ABOUT AS YOUNG HE WAS.
SNORE SNORE
ZZZ

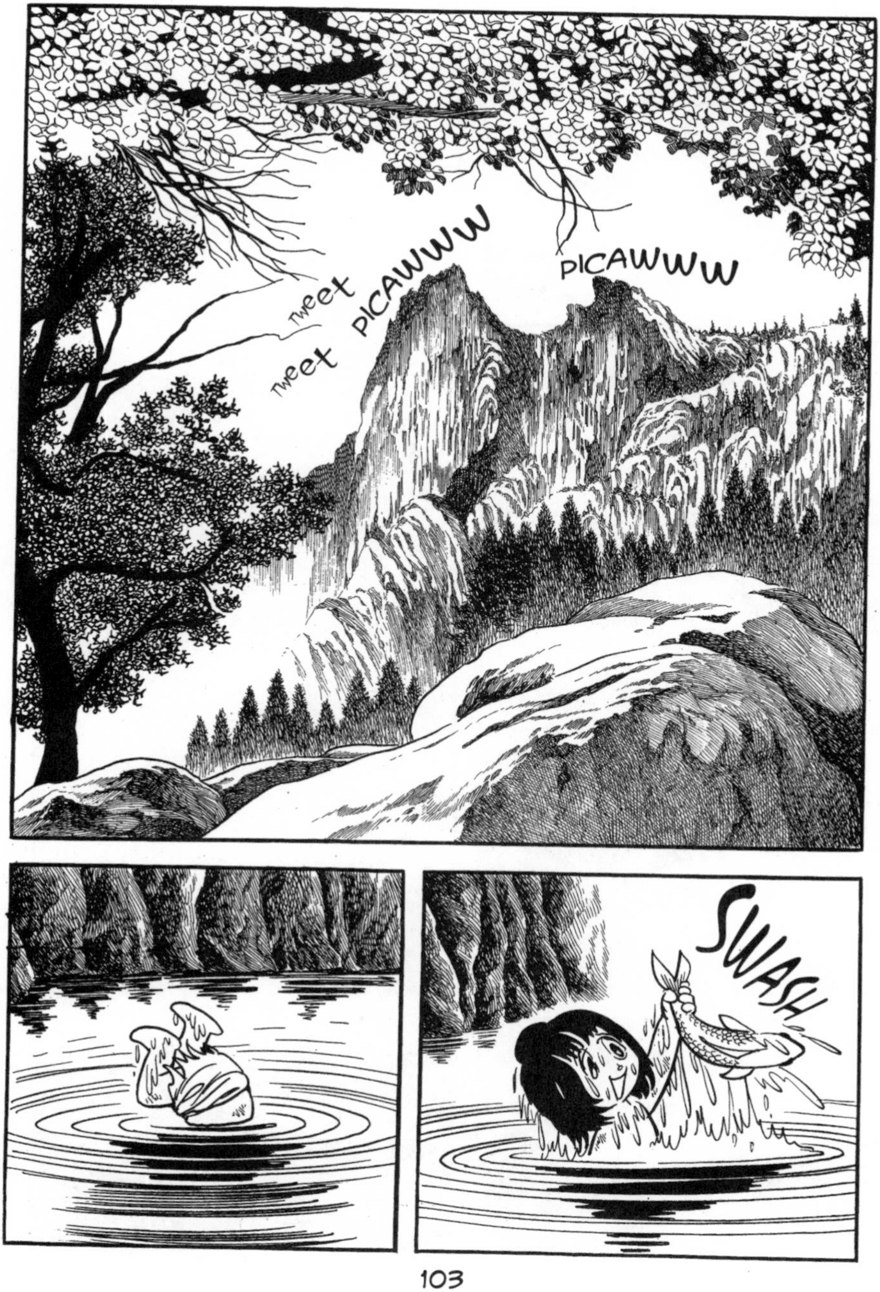
TWEET TWEET
PICAWWW
PICAWWW
SWASH

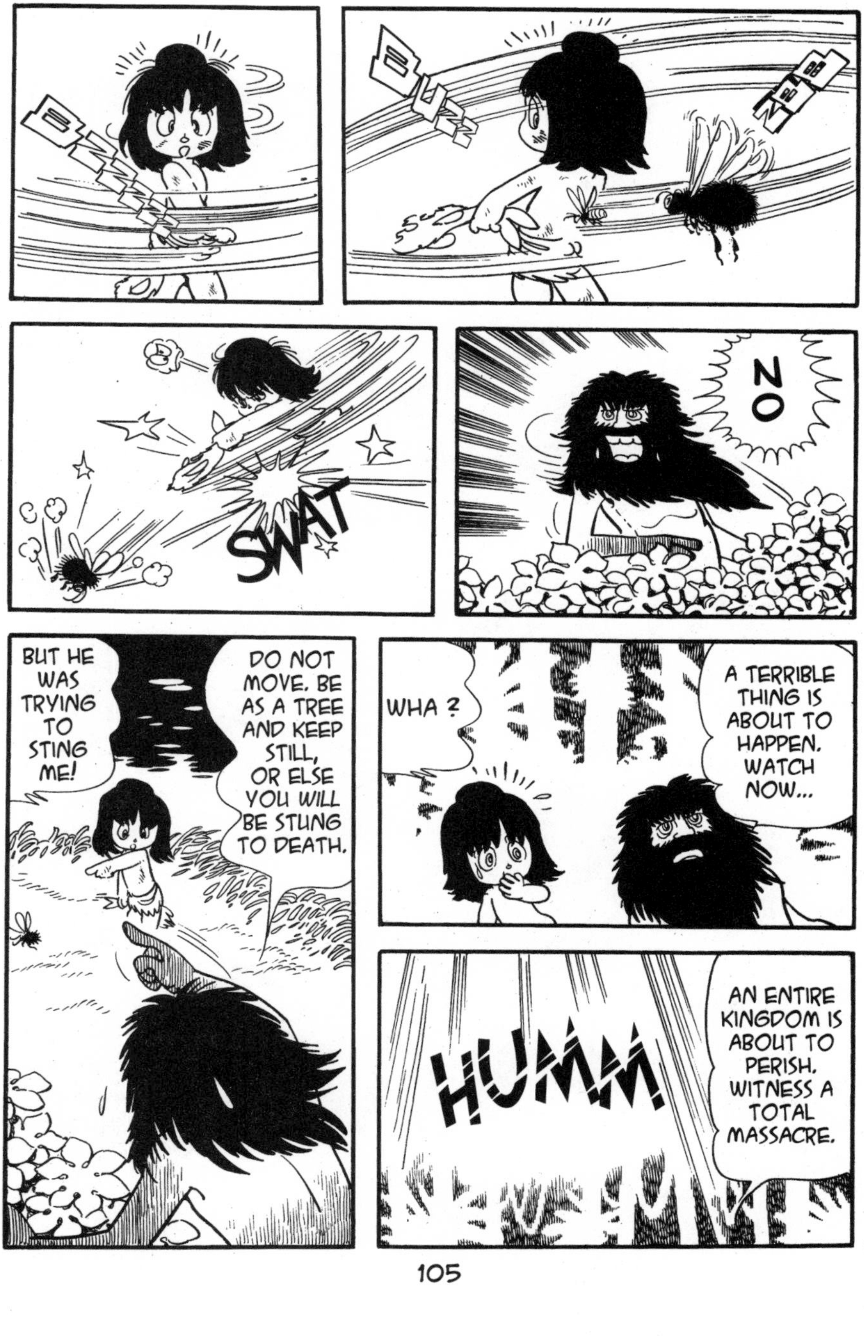
SWAT
NO
BUT HE WAS TRYING TO STING ME!
DO NOT MOVE. BE AS A TREE AND KEEP STILL, OR ELSE YOU WILL BE STUNG TO DEATH.
WHA ?
A TERRIBLE THING IS ABOUT TO HAPPEN. WATCH NOW...
HUMM
AN ENTIRE KINGDOM IS ABOUT TO PERISH. WITNESS A TOTAL MASSACRE.

SMALLER BEES ARE FIGHTING BIGGER BEES!

TWO TRIBES BUILT COLONIES NEXT TO EACH OTHER. THERE WASN'T ENOUGH FOOD TO SUPPORT BOTH.

UNLESS ONE KINGDOM FALLS, BOTH ARE DOOMED. THEY RESORT TO WAR TO DECIDE THEIR FATE.

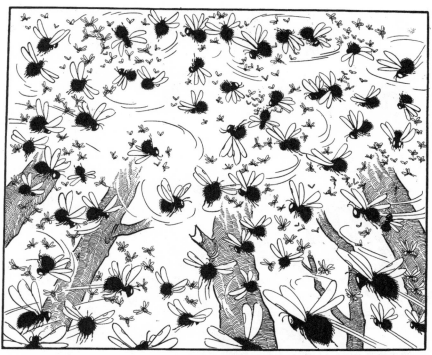

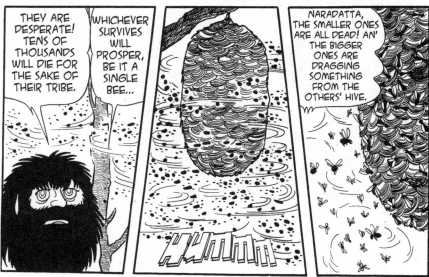

THEY ARE DESPERATE! TENS OF THOUSANDS WILL DIE FOR THE SAKE OF THEIR TRIBE.

WHICHEVER SURVIVES WILL PROSPER, BE IT A SINGLE BEE...

NARADATTA, THE SMALLER ONES ARE ALL DEAD! AN' THE BIGGER ONES ARE DRAGGING SOMETHING FROM THE OTHERS' HIVE.

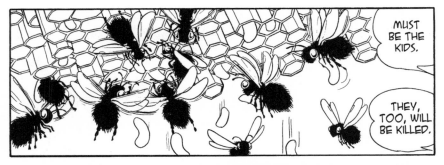

MUST BE THE KIDS.

THEY, TOO, WILL BE KILLED.

BUT THEY DIDN'T DO ANYTHING WRONG...

HEY! NOW THEY'VE FOUND ONE WITH A BIG BELLY!

THAT'S SURELY THE QUEEN.

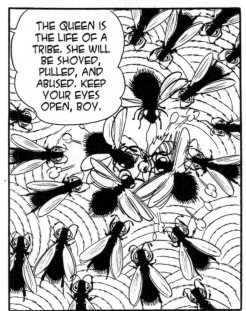

THE QUEEN IS THE LIFE OF A TRIBE. SHE WILL BE SHOVED, PULLED, AND ABUSED. KEEP YOUR EYES OPEN, BOY.

108

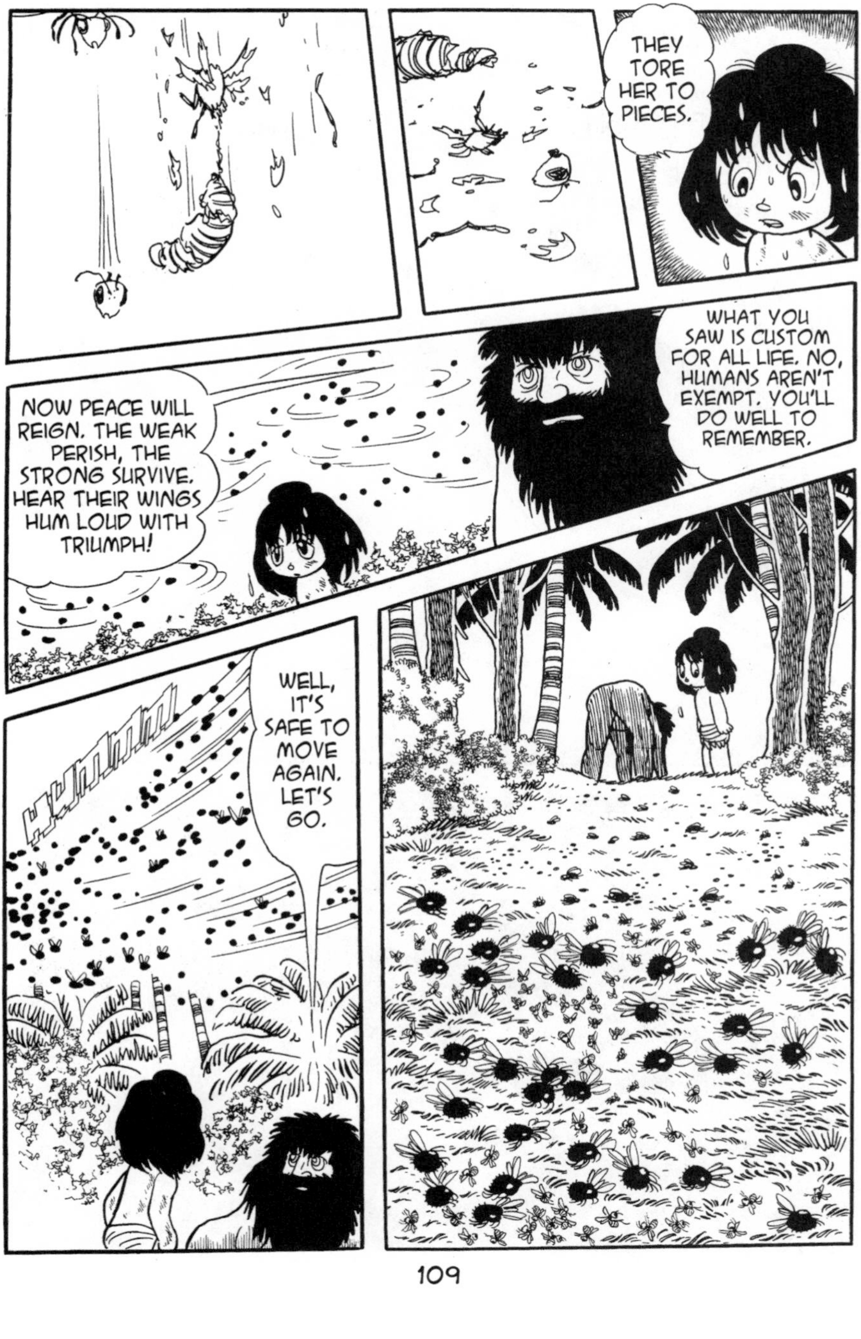
THEY TORE HER TO PIECES.
NOW PEACE WILL REIGN. THE WEAK PERISH, THE STRONG SURVIVE. HEAR THEIR WINGS HUM LOUD WITH TRIUMPH!
WHAT YOU SAW IS CUSTOM FOR ALL LIFE. NO, HUMANS AREN'T EXEMPT. YOU'LL DO WELL TO REMEMBER.
WELL, IT'S SAFE TO MOVE AGAIN. LET'S GO.

CHAPTER THREE

THE HAG AND THE WAIF

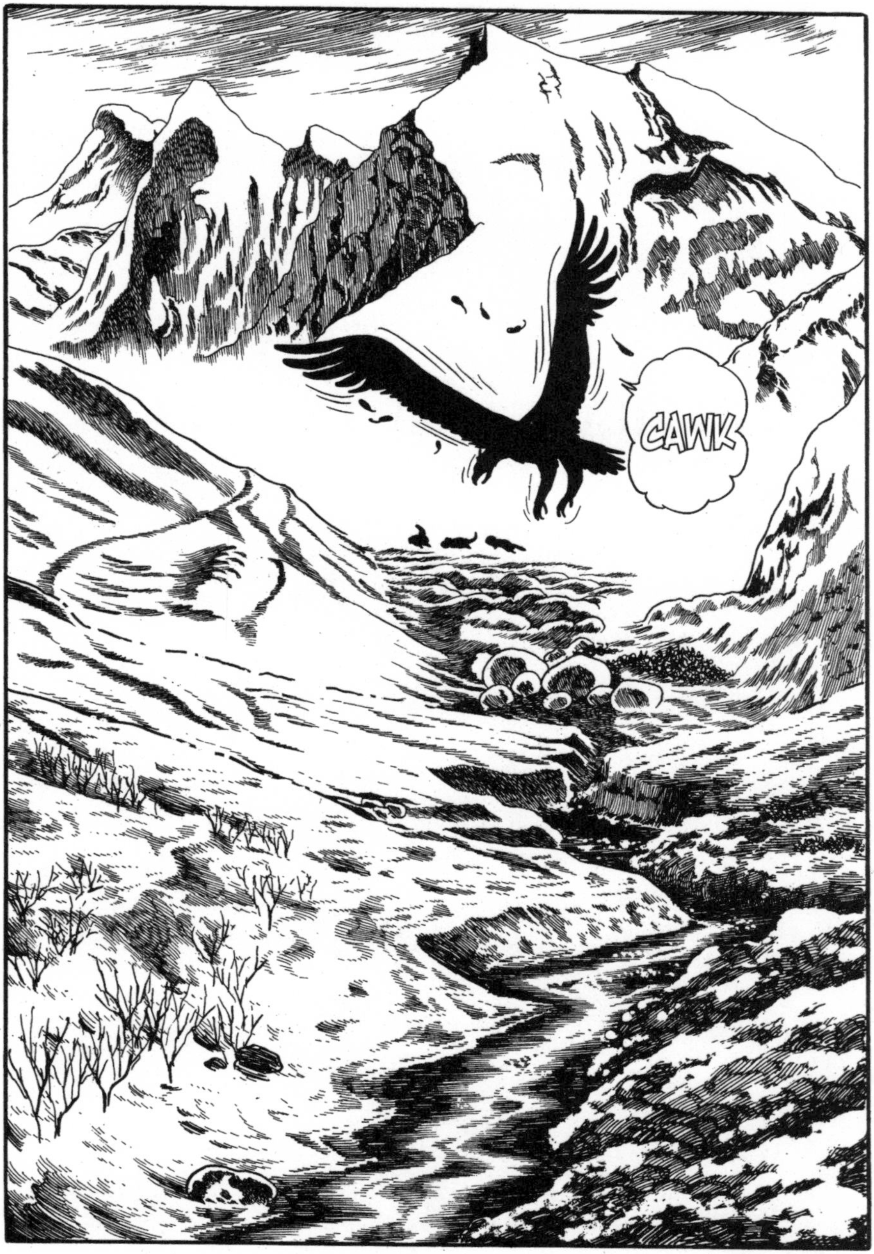
CAWK

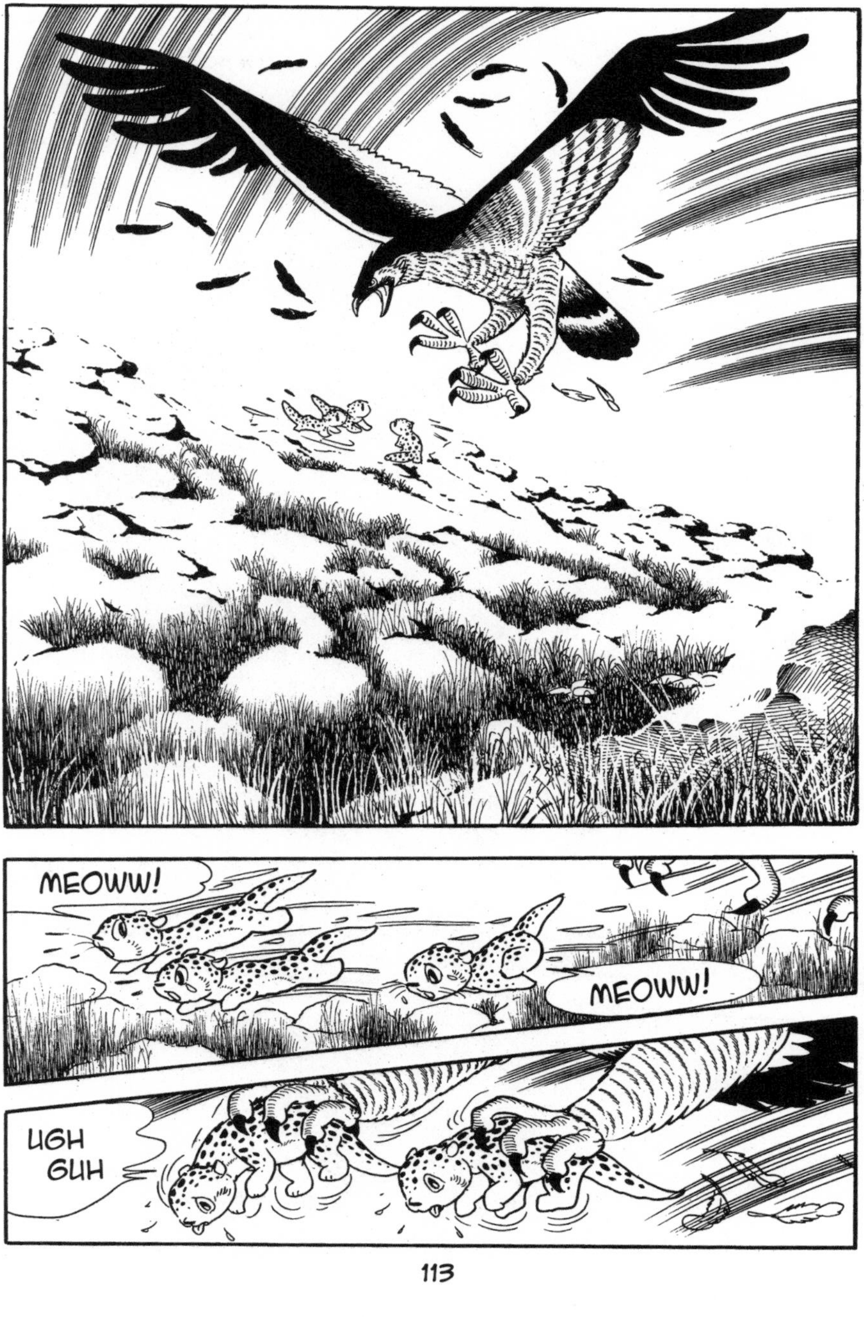
MEOWW!
MEOWW!
UGH GUH

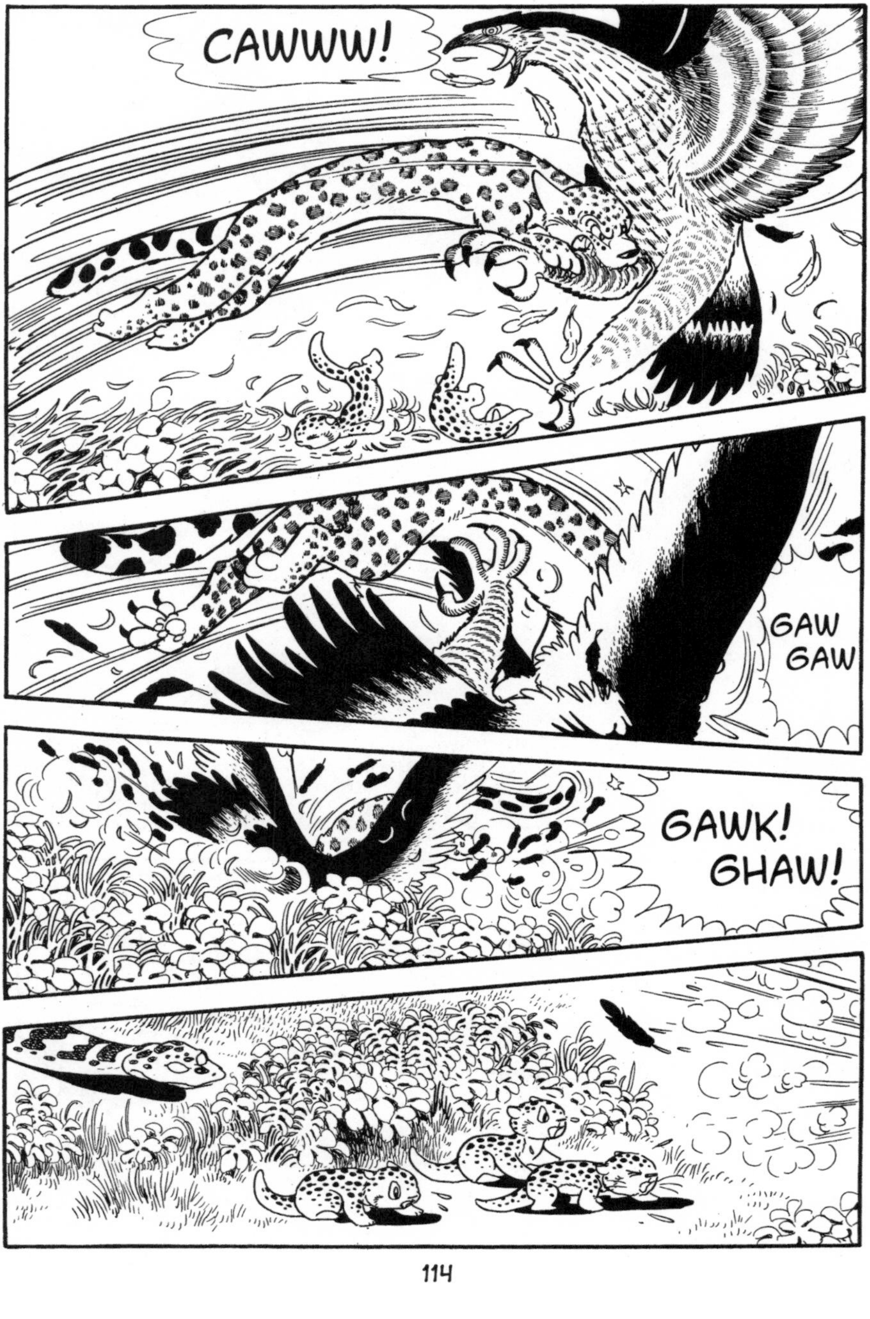
CAWWW!
GAW GAW
GAWK! GHAW!

HISS
WRAP
CRUNCH
CHOKE
GAG
GAWK
GHAK

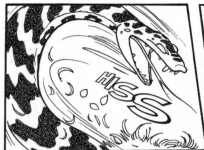

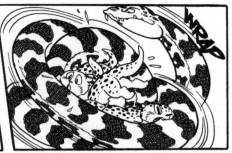

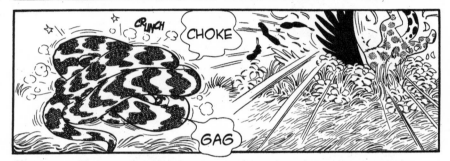

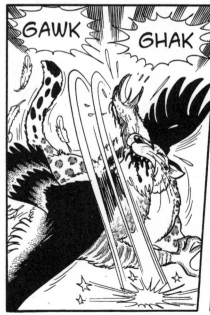

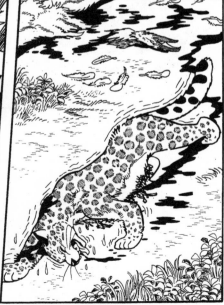

URR...

THUD

TWITCH
TWITCH

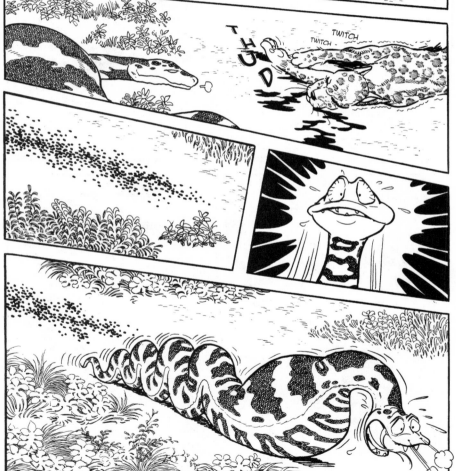

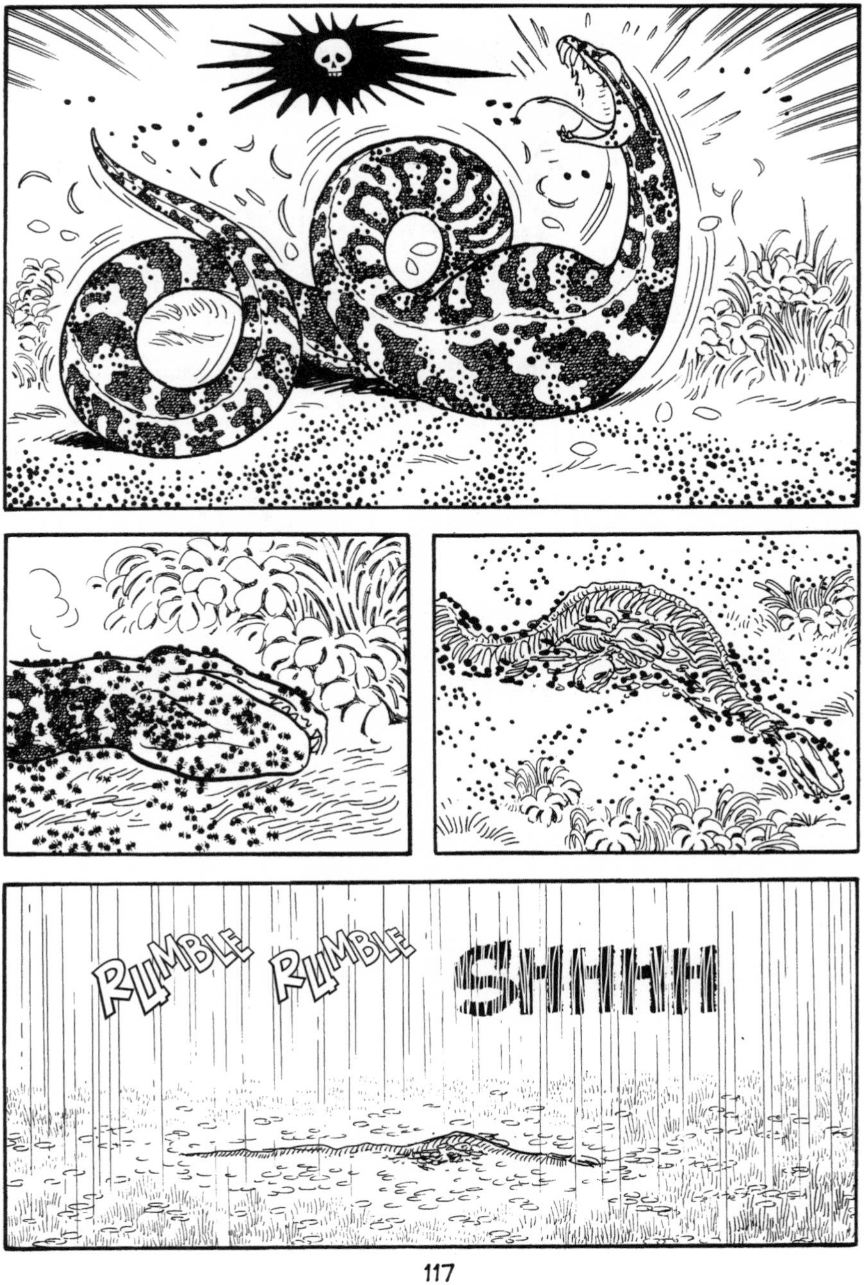
RUMBLE RUMBLE
SHHHH

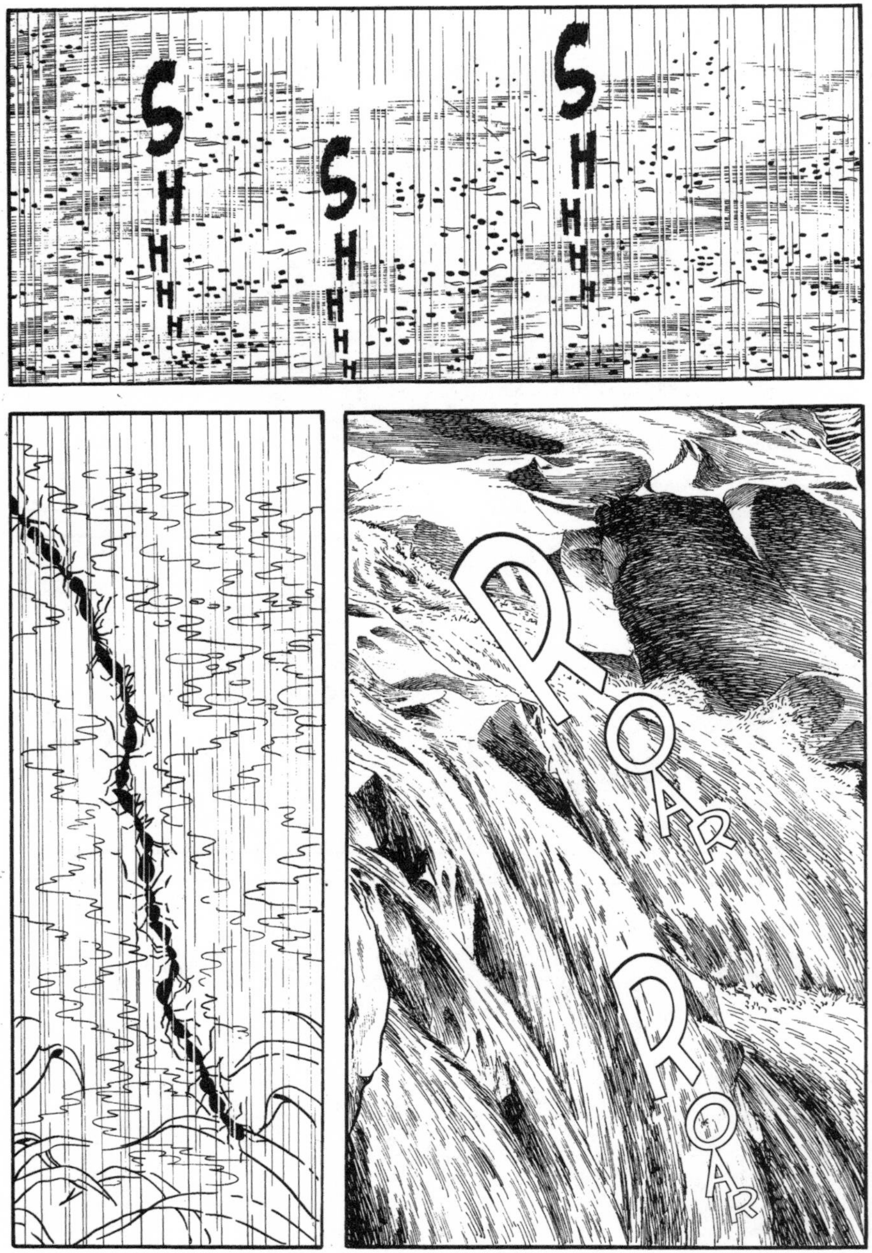
SHHHH
SHHHH
SHHHH
ROAR
ROAR

SHHHH
SHHHH
SHHHH
SPLASH

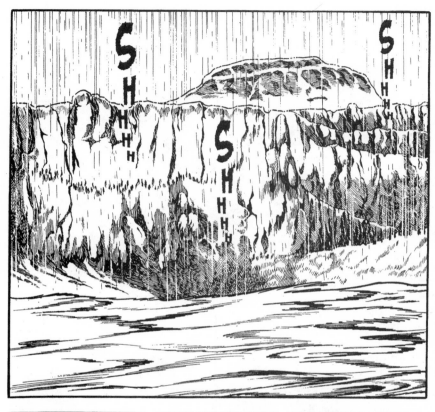

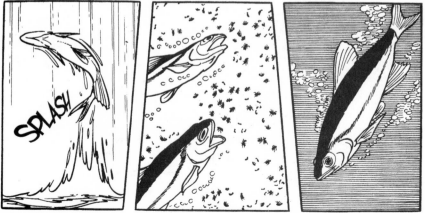

NO NEED TO HIDE IT. I KNOW YOU COME HERE IN SECRET TO HUNT AND EAT FISH.

A CHILD OF YOUR AGE IS ALWAYS HUNGRY.

DON'T YOU GET HUNGRY, LIVING ON JUST FRUITS AND NUTS?

I HAVE SWORN NOT TO KILL, NOT EVEN A BUG.

YOU KNEW?

BUT DIDN'T YOU SAY THAT THE STRONG SURVIVE AND THE WEAK PERISH? ISN'T THAT THE LAW OF NATURE?

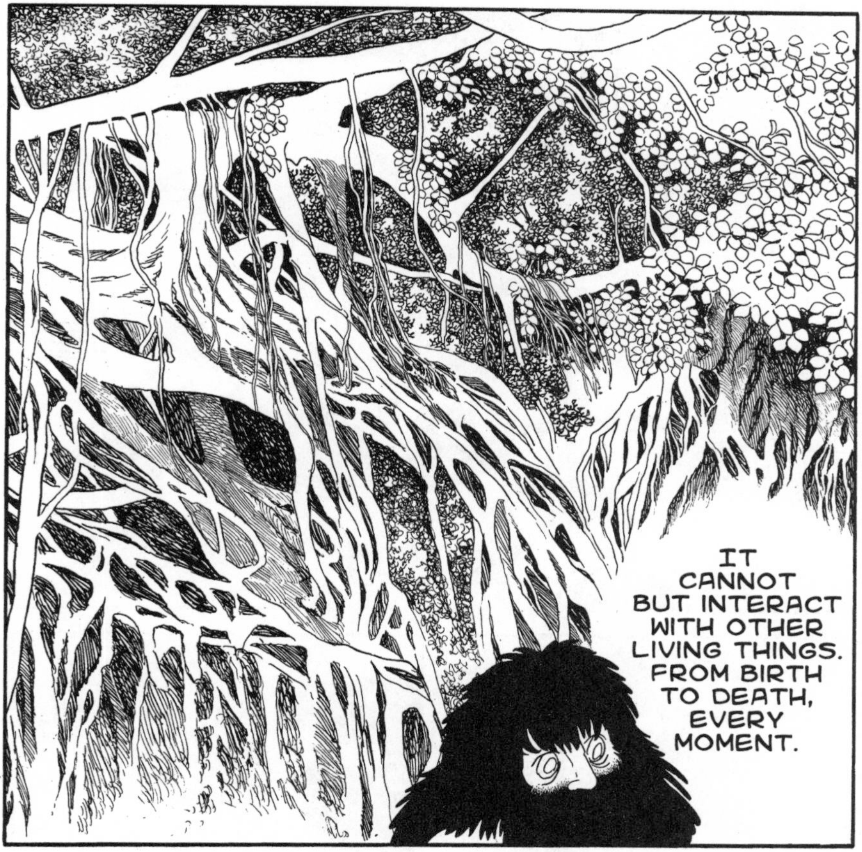
IT CANNOT BUT INTERACT WITH OTHER LIVING THINGS. FROM BIRTH TO DEATH, EVERY MOMENT.
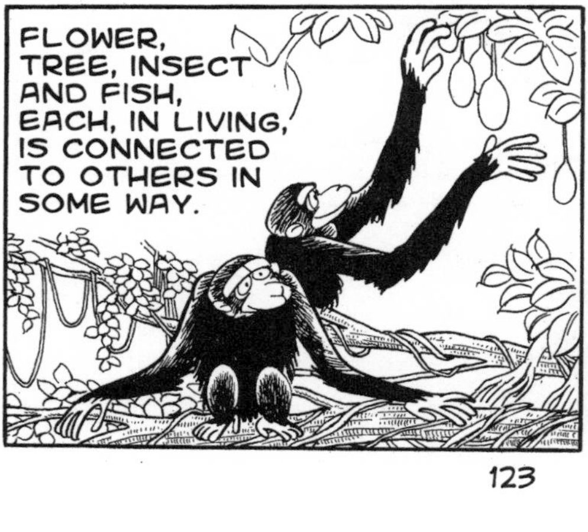
FLOWER, TREE, INSECT AND FISH, EACH, IN LIVING, IS CONNECTED TO OTHERS IN SOME WAY.
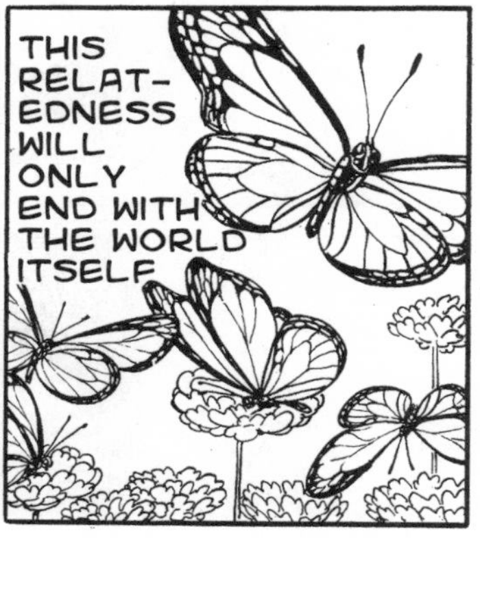
THIS RELAT-EDNESS WILL ONLY END WITH THE WORLD ITSELF

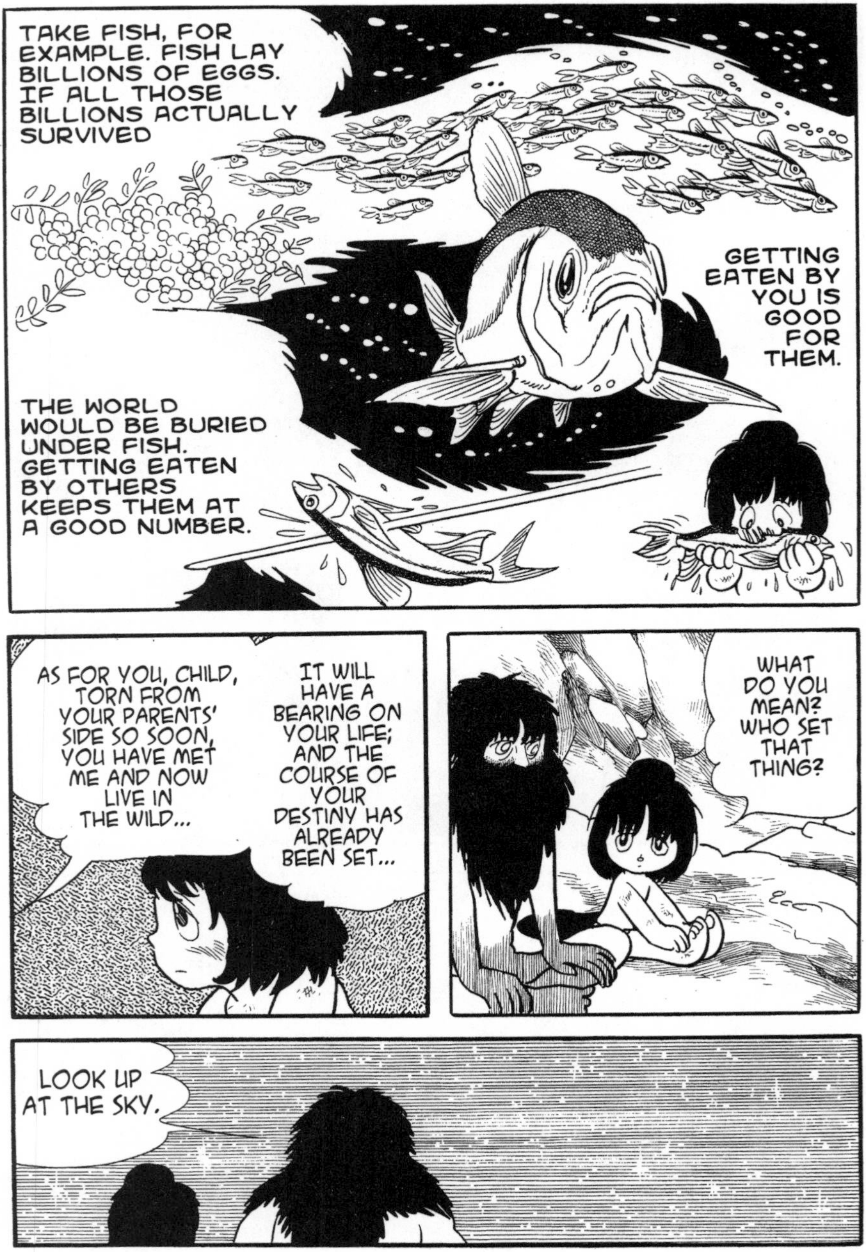
TAKE FISH, FOR EXAMPLE. FISH LAY BILLIONS OF EGGS. IF ALL THOSE BILLIONS ACTUALLY SURVIVED
THE WORLD WOULD BE BURIED UNDER FISH. GETTING EATEN BY OTHERS KEEPS THEM AT A GOOD NUMBER.
GETTING EATEN BY YOU IS GOOD FOR THEM.
AS FOR YOU, CHILD, TORN FROM YOUR PARENTS' SIDE SO SOON, YOU HAVE MET ME AND NOW LIVE IN THE WILD...
IT WILL HAVE A BEARING ON YOUR LIFE; AND THE COURSE OF YOUR DESTINY HAS ALREADY BEEN SET...
WHAT DO YOU MEAN? WHO SET THAT THING?
LOOK UP AT THE SKY.

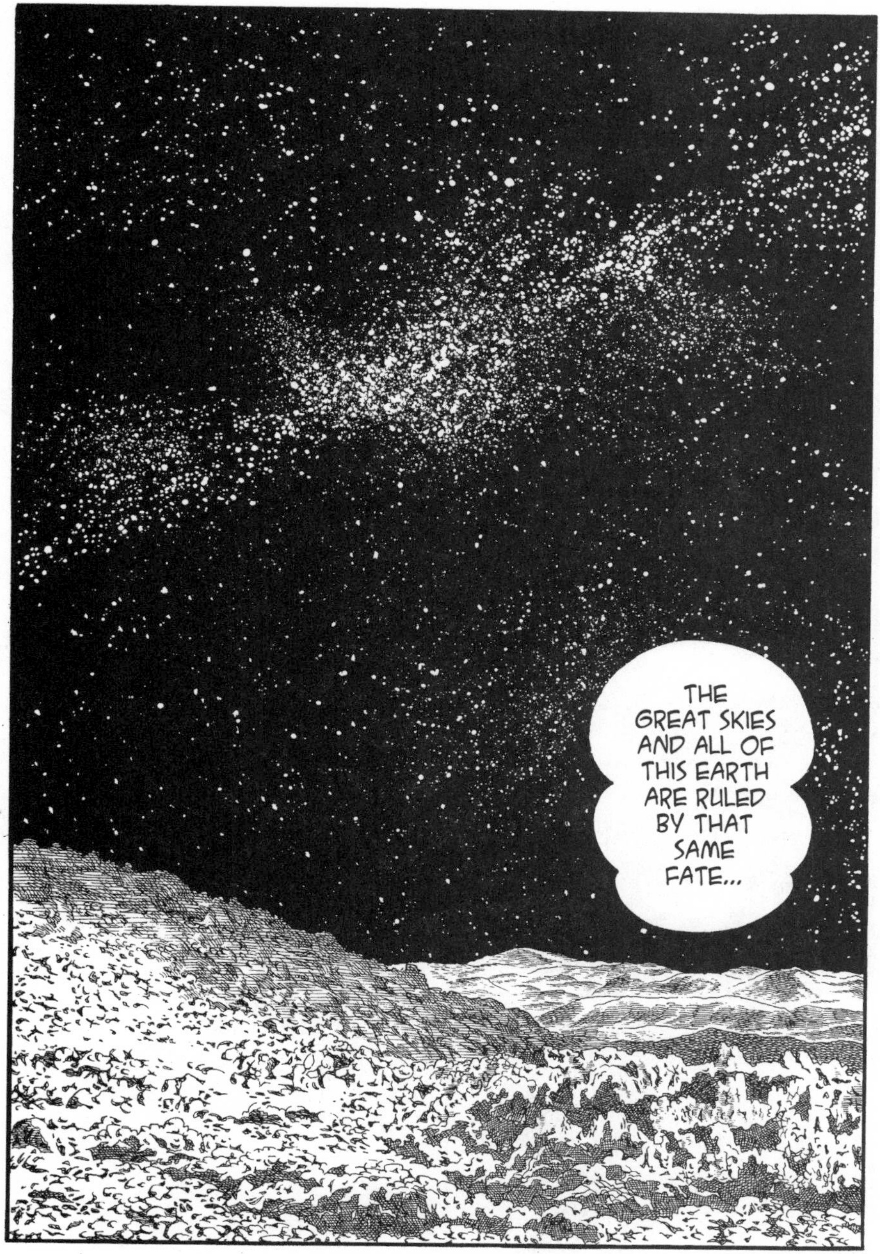
THE GREAT SKIES AND ALL OF THIS EARTH ARE RULED BY THAT SAME FATE...

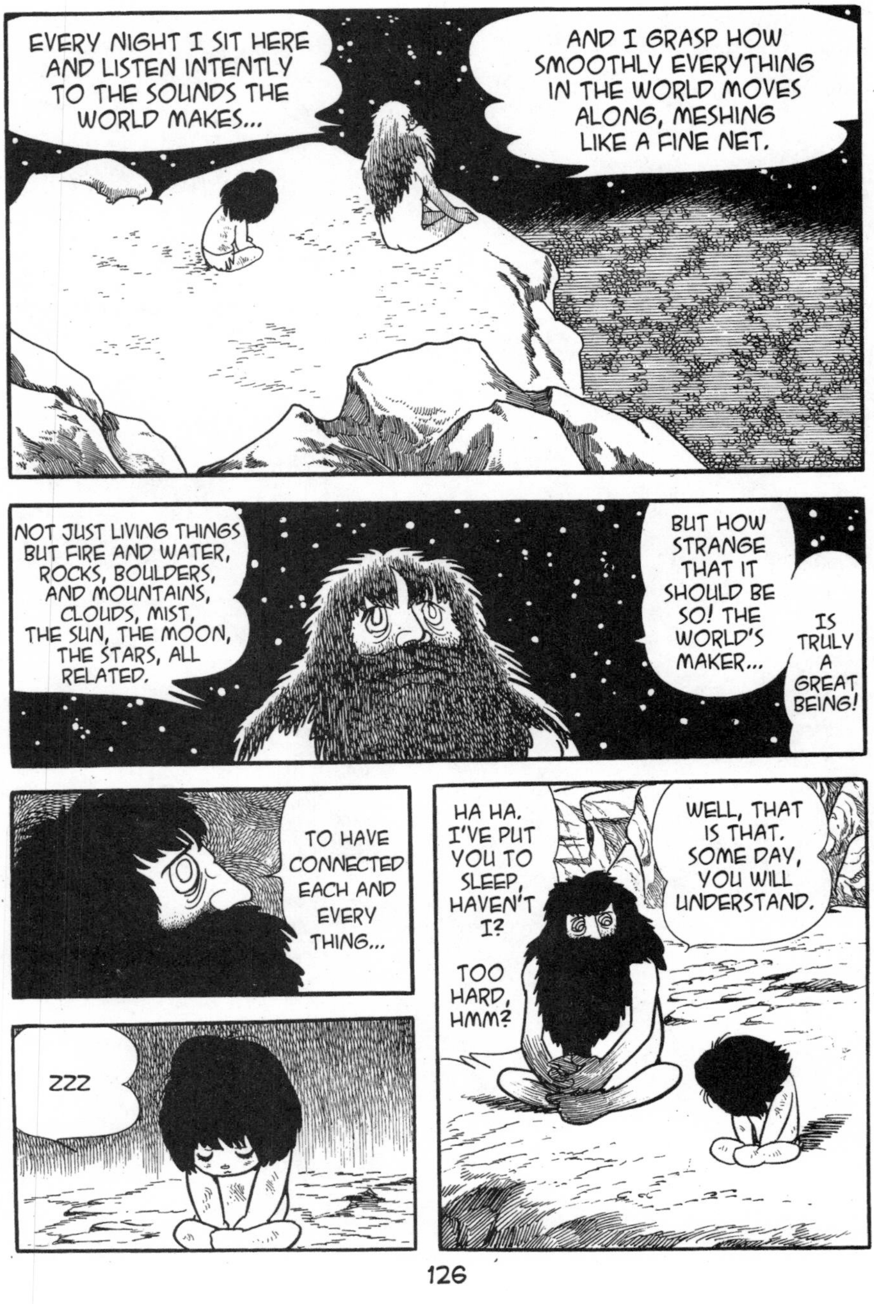
EVERY NIGHT I SIT HERE AND LISTEN INTENTLY TO THE SOUNDS THE WORLD MAKES...
AND I GRASP HOW SMOOTHLY EVERYTHING IN THE WORLD MOVES ALONG, MESHING LIKE A FINE NET.
NOT JUST LIVING THINGS BUT FIRE AND WATER, ROCKS, BOULDERS, AND MOUNTAINS, CLOUDS, MIST, THE SUN, THE MOON, THE STARS, ALL RELATED.
BUT HOW STRANGE THAT IT SHOULD BE SO! THE WORLD'S MAKER...
IS TRULY A GREAT BEING!
TO HAVE CONNECTED EACH AND EVERY THING...
ZZZ
HA HA. I'VE PUT YOU TO SLEEP, HAVEN'T I?
TOO HARD, HMM?
WELL, THAT IS THAT. SOME DAY, YOU WILL UNDERSTAND.

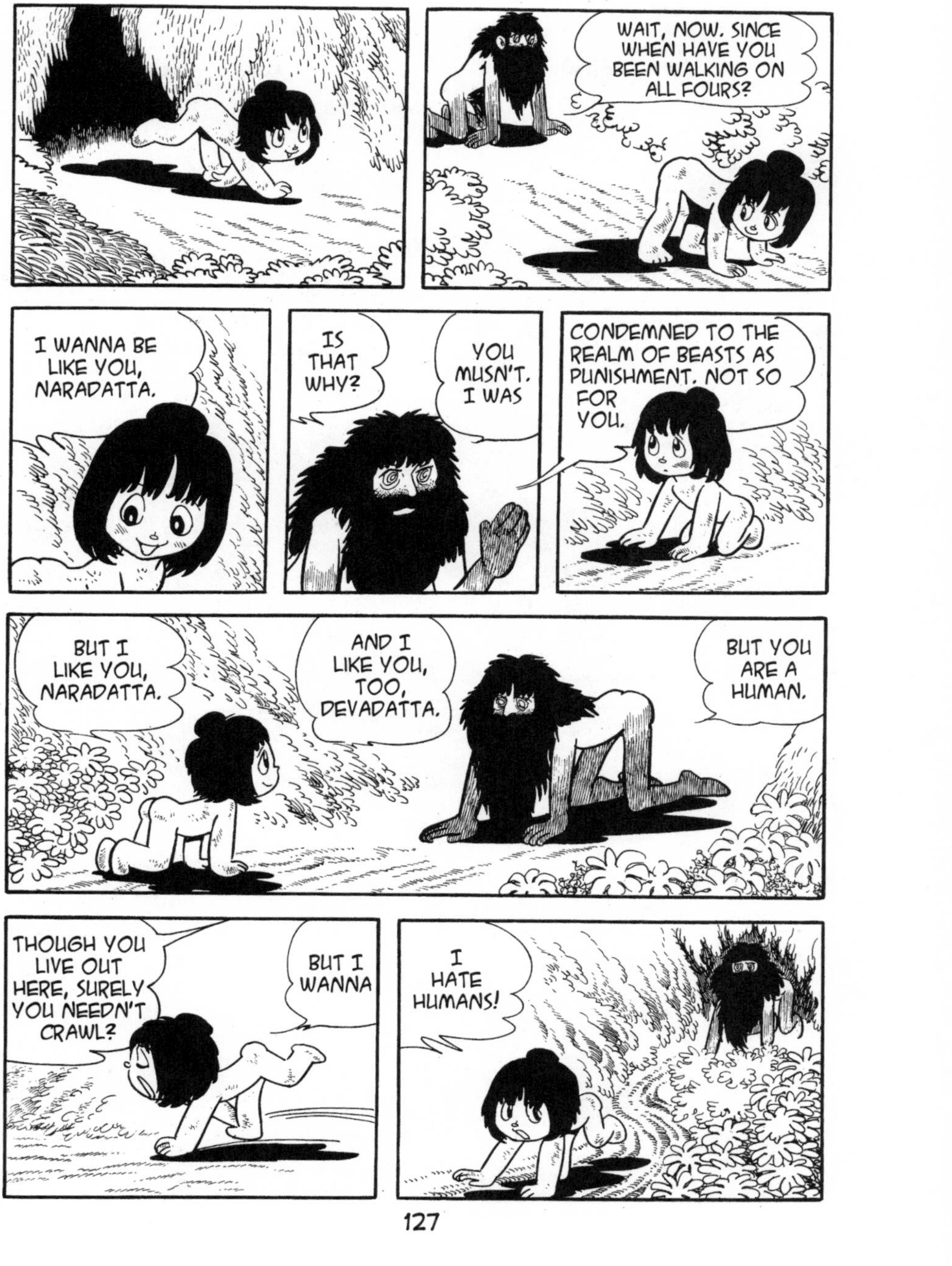
WAIT, NOW. SINCE WHEN HAVE YOU BEEN WALKING ON ALL FOURS?
I WANNA BE LIKE YOU, NARADATTA.
IS THAT WHY?
YOU MUSN'T. I WAS
CONDEMNED TO THE REALM OF BEASTS AS PUNISHMENT. NOT SO FOR YOU.
BUT I LIKE YOU, NARADATTA.
AND I LIKE YOU, TOO, DEVADATTA.
BUT YOU ARE A HUMAN.
THOUGH YOU LIVE OUT HERE, SURELY YOU NEEDN'T CRAWL?
BUT I WANNA
I HATE HUMANS!

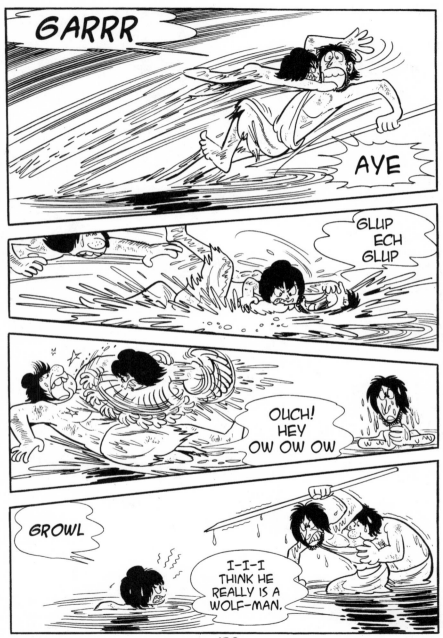

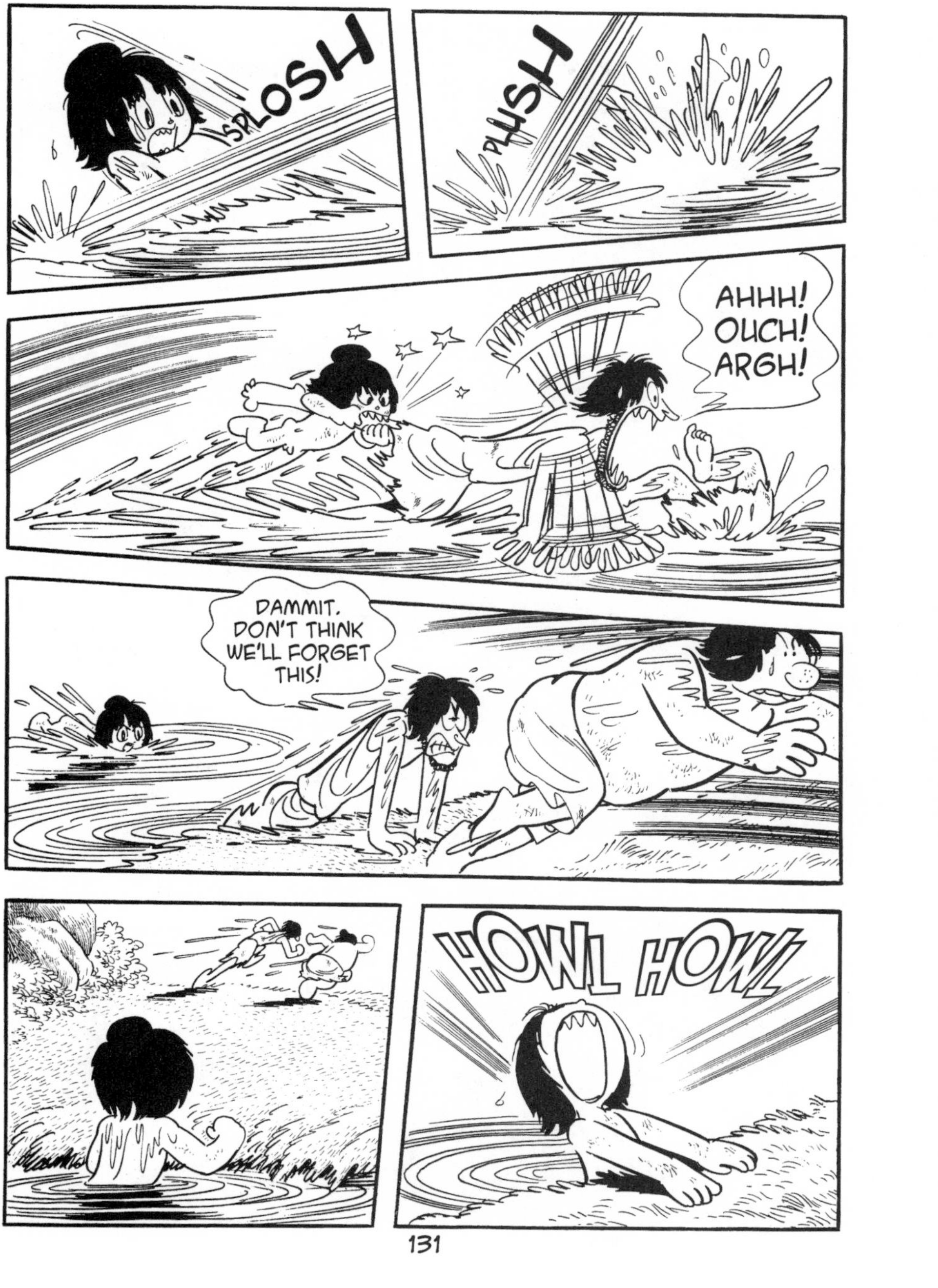
SPLOSH
PLUSH
AHHH! OUCH! ARGH!
DAMMIT. DON'T THINK WE'LL FORGET THIS!
HOWL HOWL

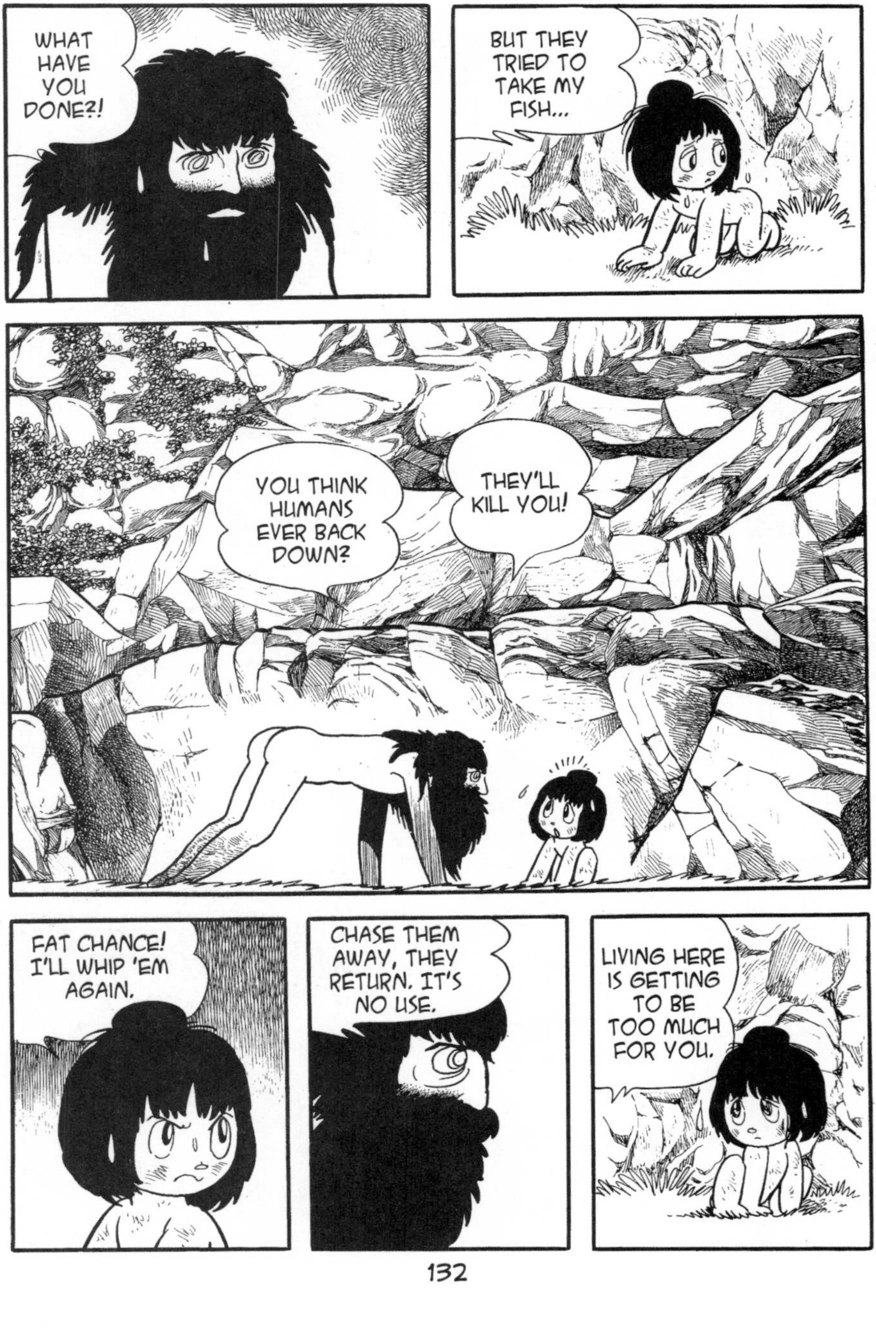
WHAT HAVE YOU DONE?!
BUT THEY TRIED TO TAKE MY FISH...
YOU THINK HUMANS EVER BACK DOWN?
THEY'LL KILL YOU!
FAT CHANCE! I'LL WHIP 'EM AGAIN.
CHASE THEM AWAY, THEY RETURN. IT'S NO USE.
LIVING HERE IS GETTING TO BE TOO MUCH FOR YOU.

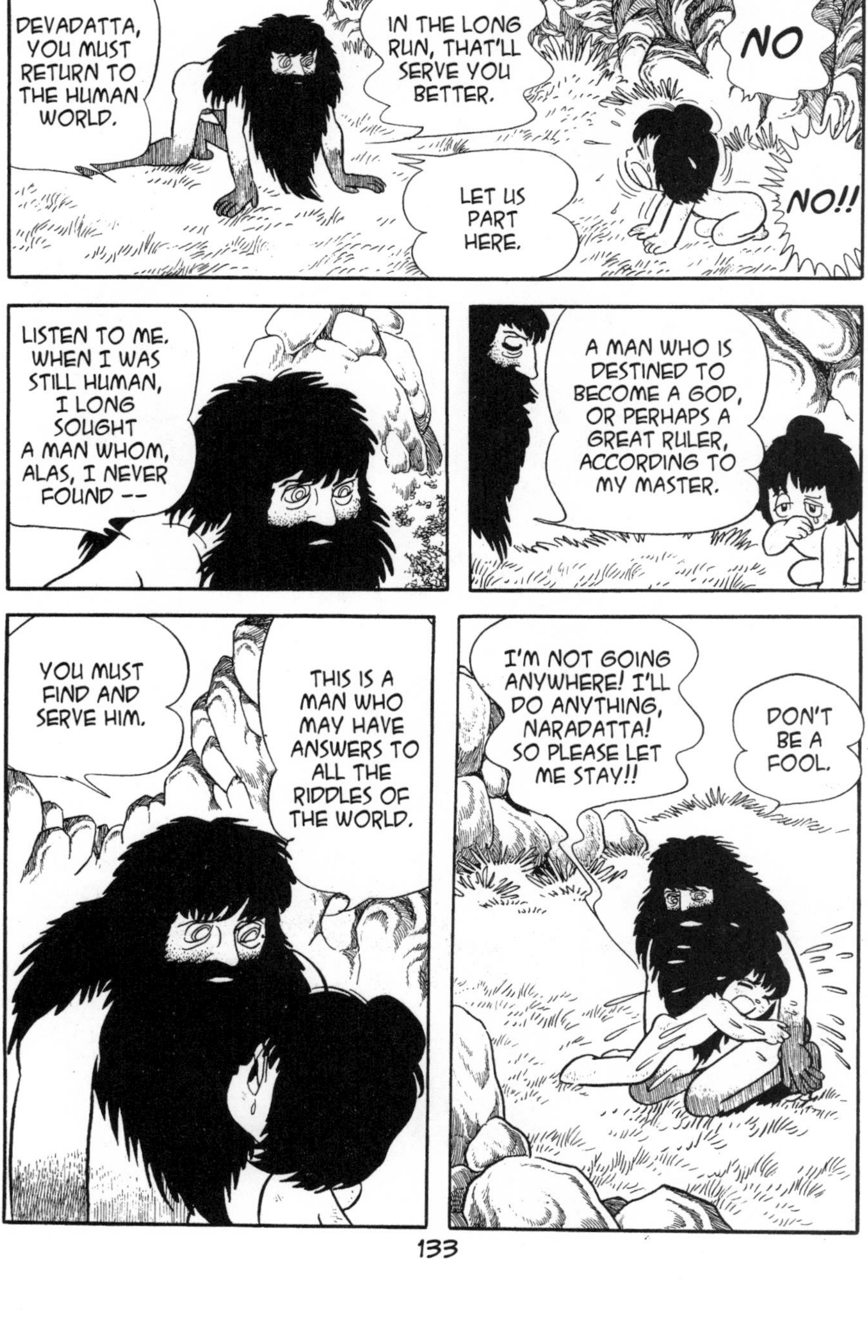
DEVADATTA, YOU MUST RETURN TO THE HUMAN WORLD.
IN THE LONG RUN, THAT'LL SERVE YOU BETTER.
LET US PART HERE.
NO
NO!!
LISTEN TO ME. WHEN I WAS STILL HUMAN, I LONG SOUGHT A MAN WHOM, ALAS, I NEVER FOUND --
A MAN WHO IS DESTINED TO BECOME A GOD, OR PERHAPS A GREAT RULER, ACCORDING TO MY MASTER.
YOU MUST FIND AND SERVE HIM.
THIS IS A MAN WHO MAY HAVE ANSWERS TO ALL THE RIDDLES OF THE WORLD.
I'M NOT GOING ANYWHERE! I'LL DO ANYTHING, NARADATTA! SO PLEASE LET ME STAY!!
DON'T BE A FOOL.

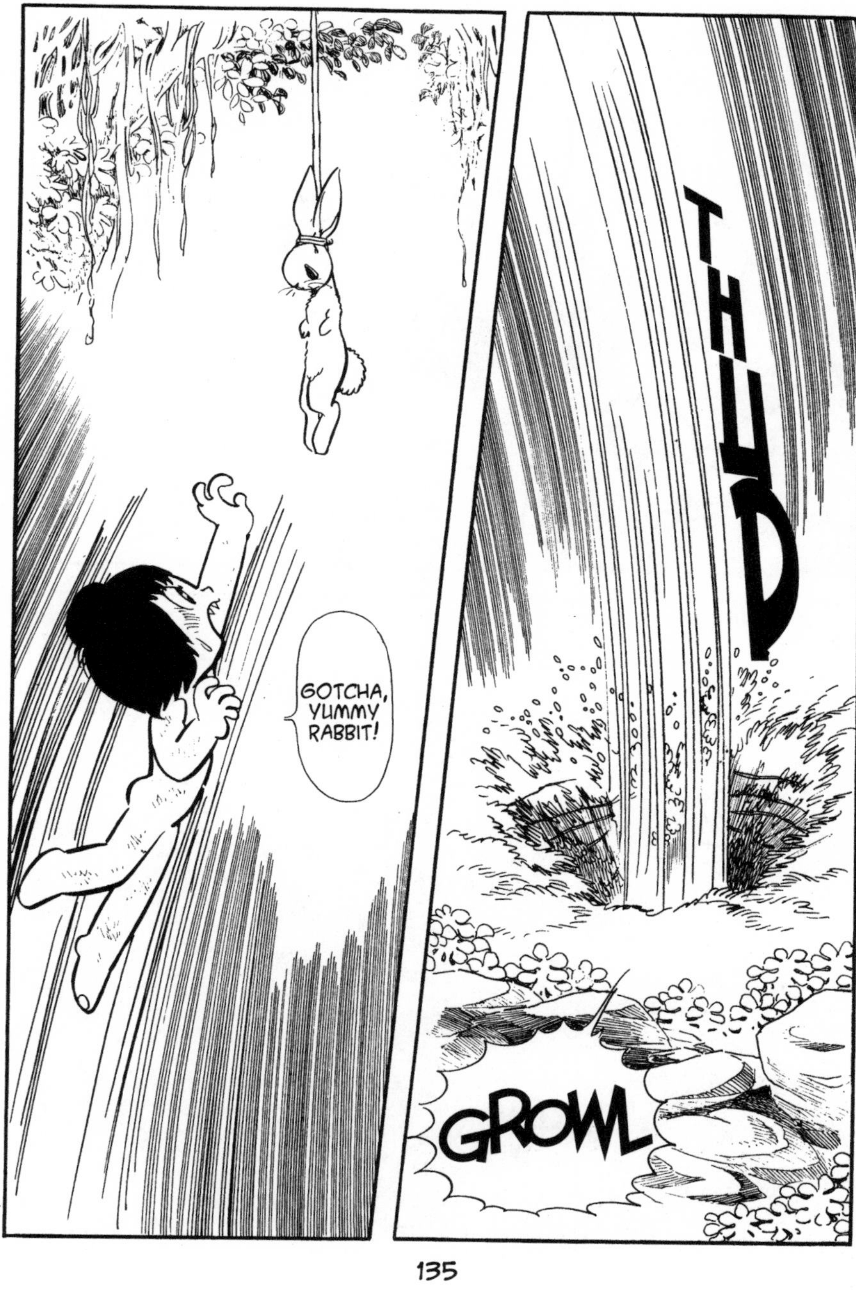
GOTCHA, YUMMY RABBIT!
THUD
GROWL

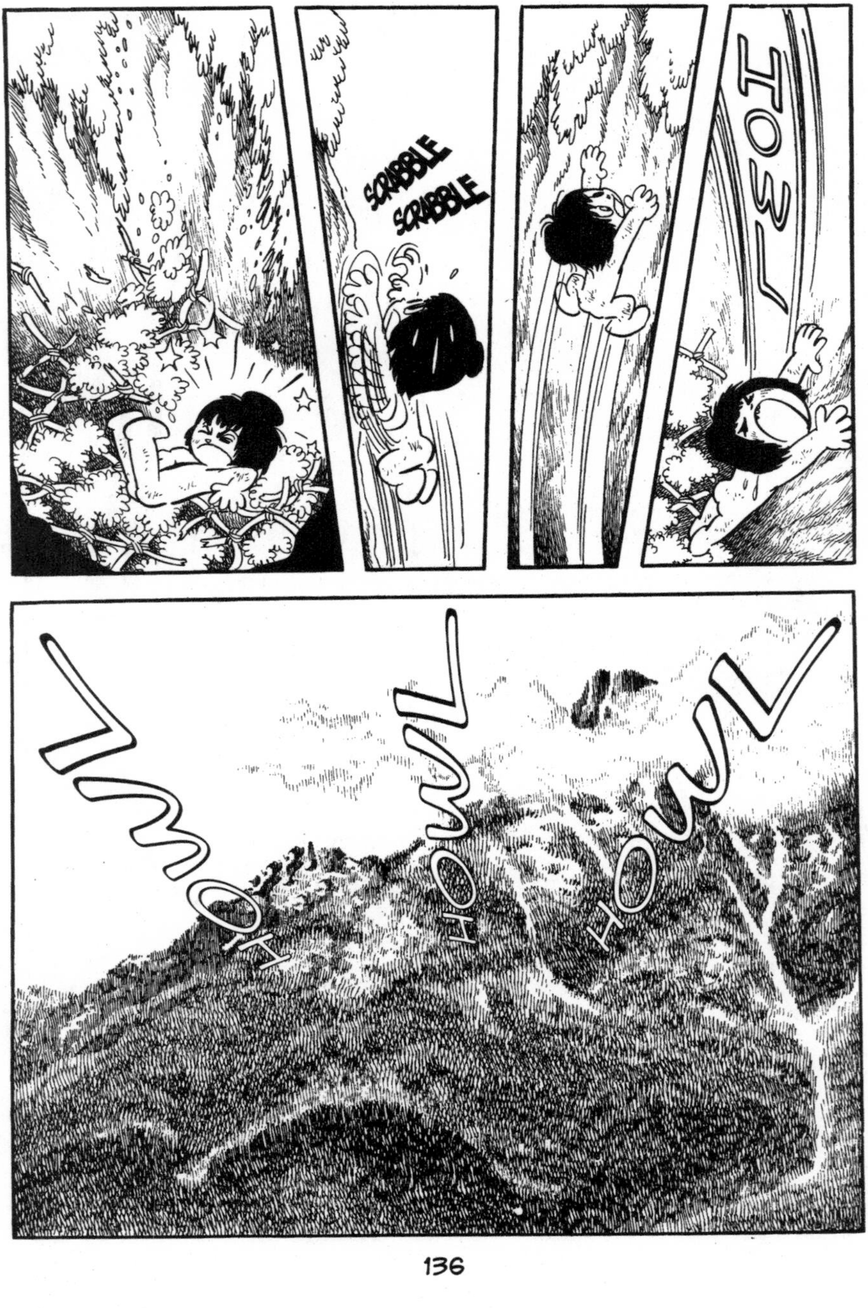
SCRABBLE
SCRABBLE
HOWL
HOWL
HOWL
HOWL

137

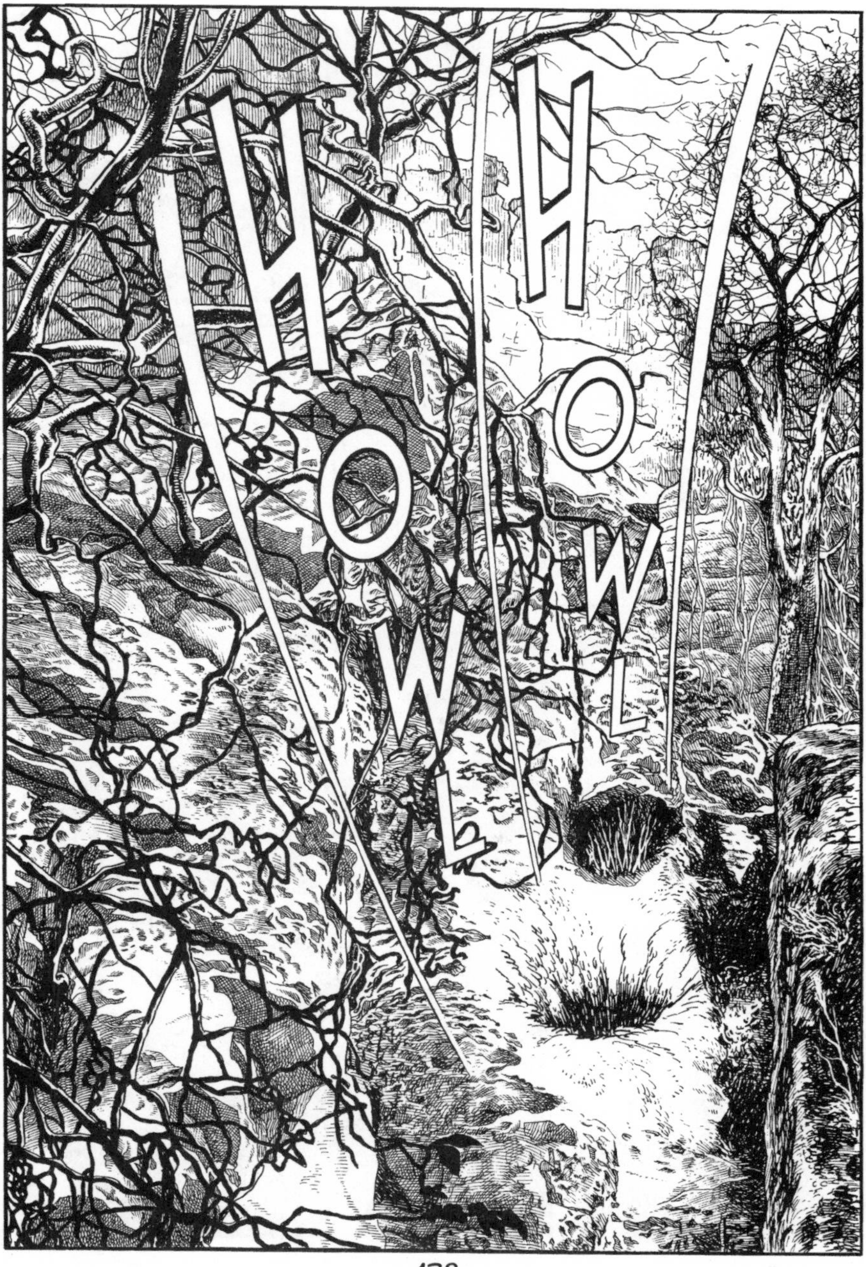
HOWL
HOWL

139

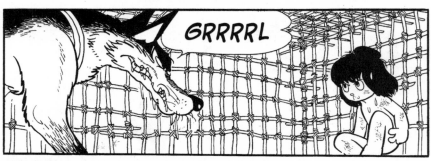

140

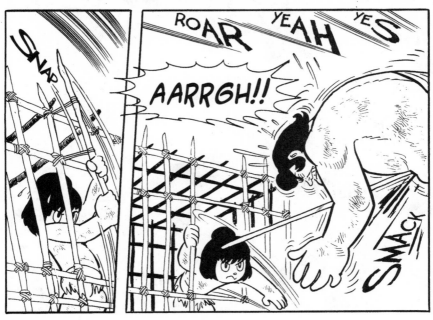

141

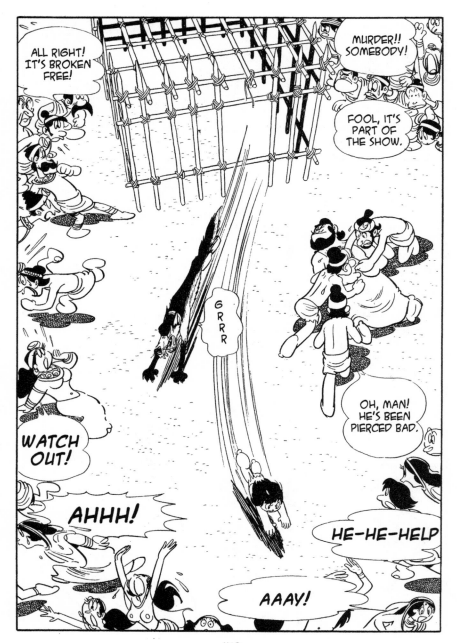

142

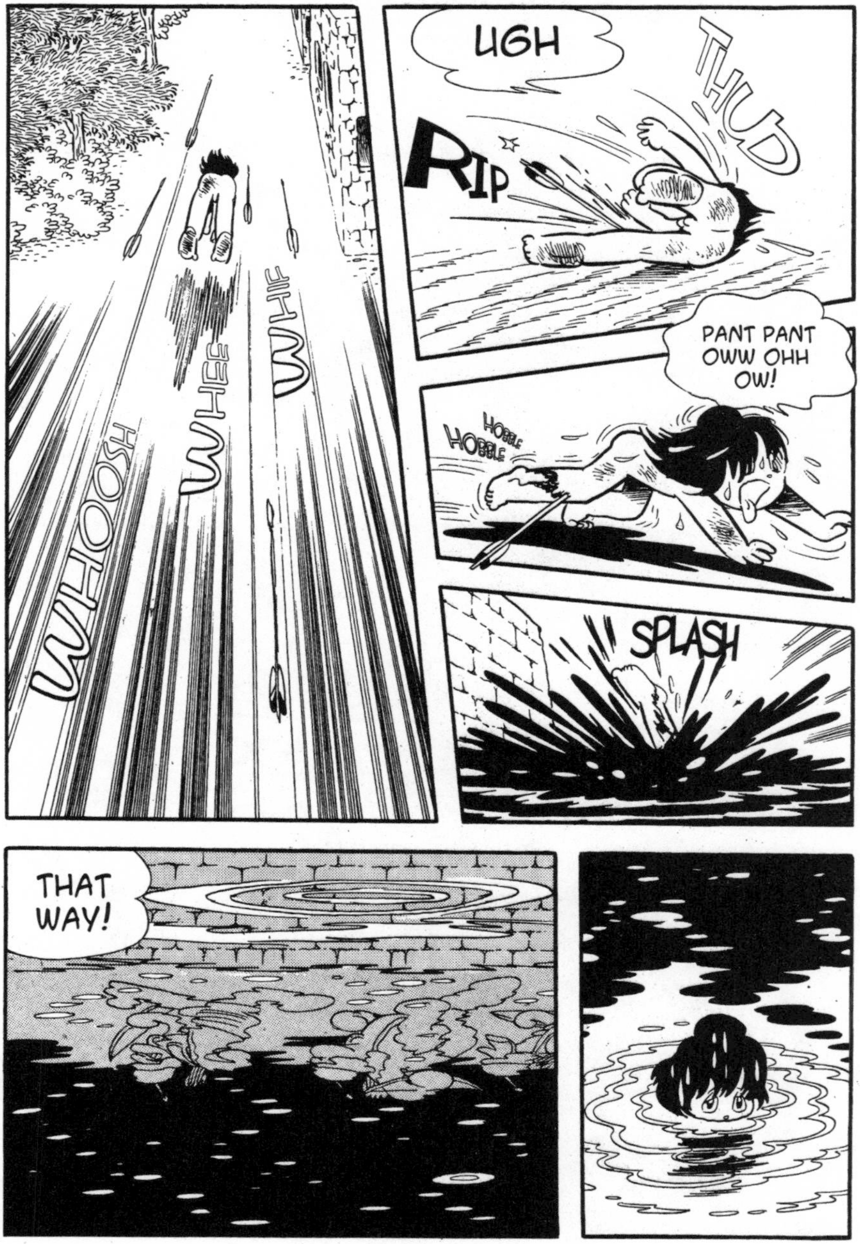
WHOOSH
WHEE
WHIF
UGH
THUD
RIP
PANT PANT OWW OHH OW!
HOBBLE HOBBLE
SPLASH
THAT WAY!

146

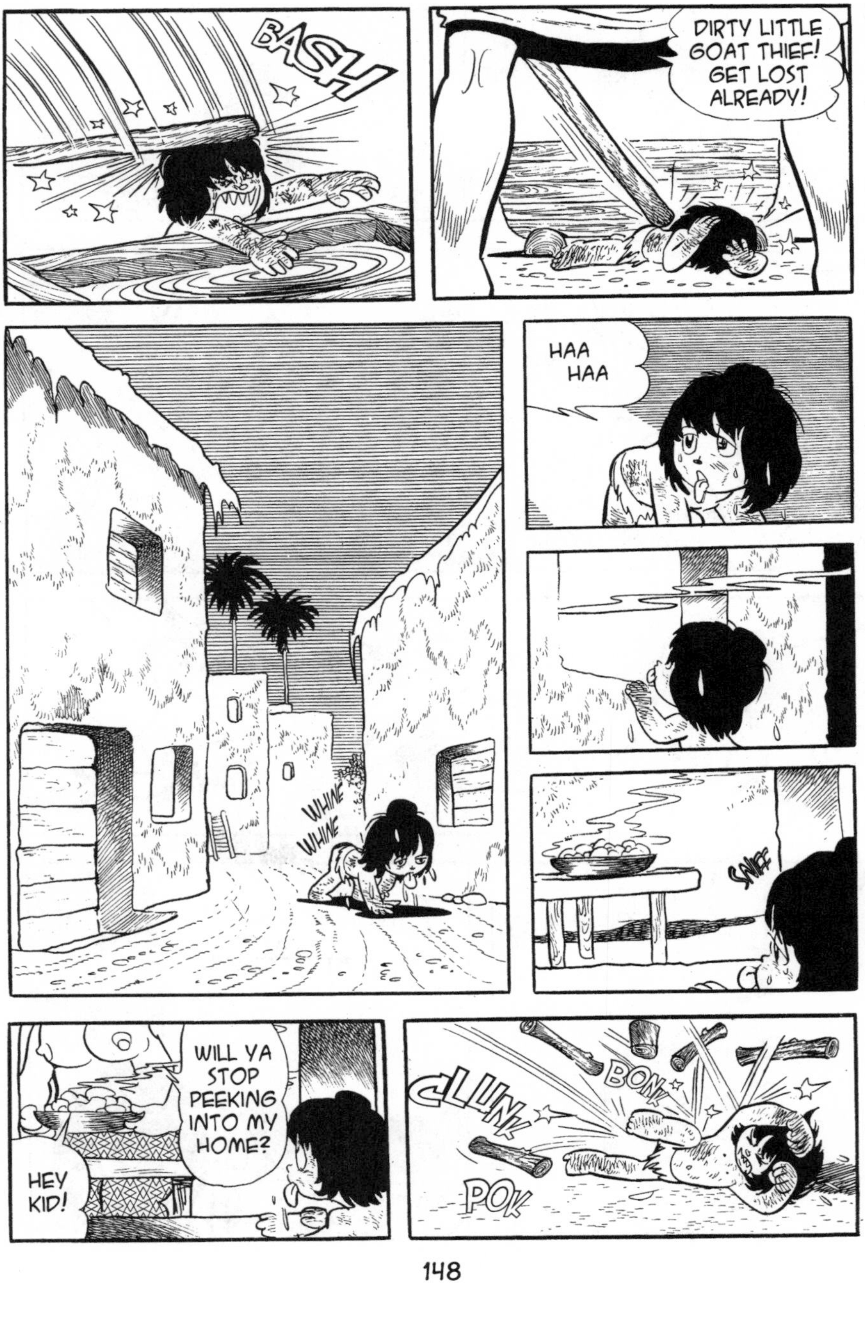
BASH
DIRTY LITTLE GOAT THIEF! GET LOST ALREADY!
WHINE WHINE
HAA HAA
SNIFF
HEY KID!
WILL YA STOP PEEKING INTO MY HOME?
CLUNK
BONK
POK

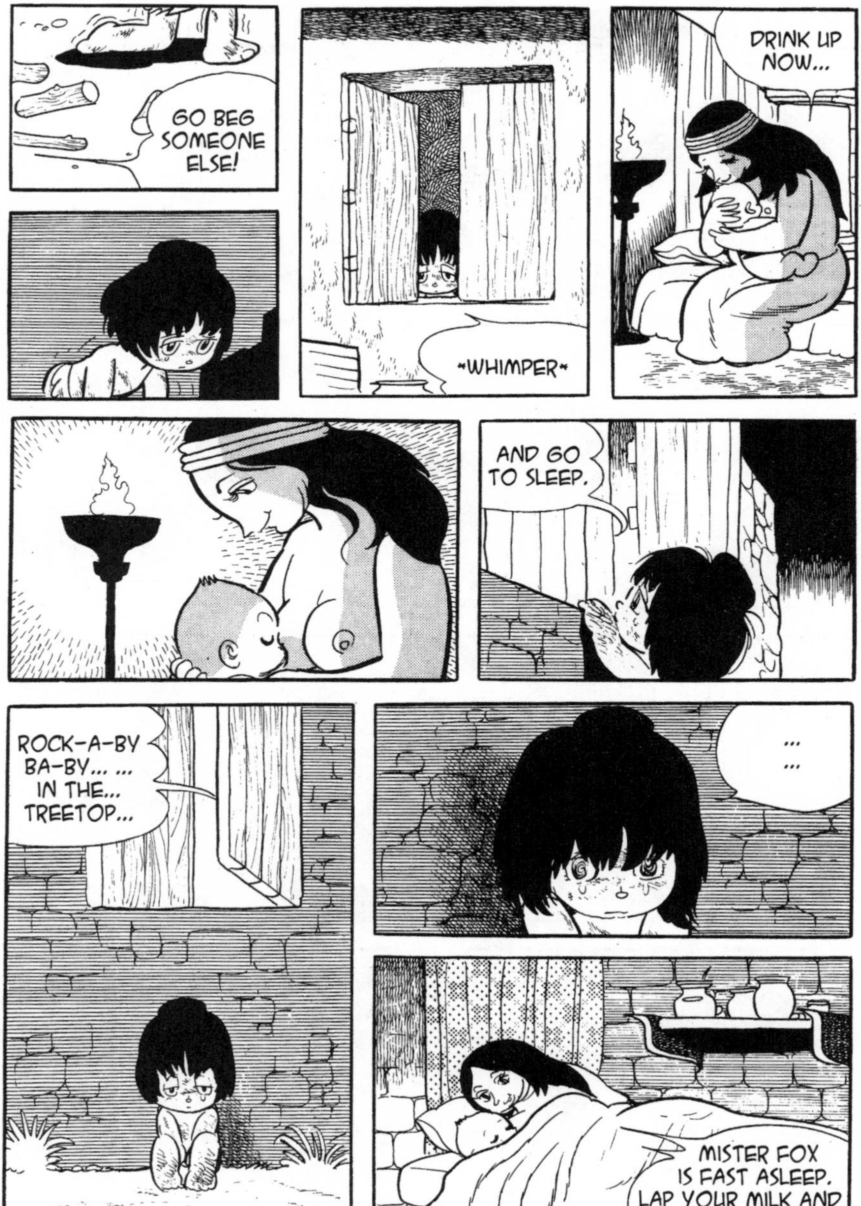
GO BEG SOMEONE ELSE!
WHIMPER
DRINK UP NOW...
AND GO TO SLEEP.
ROCK-A-BY BA-BY... ... IN THE... TREETOP...
... ...
MISTER FOX IS FAST ASLEEP. LAP YOUR MILK AND GET SOME SLEEP.

150

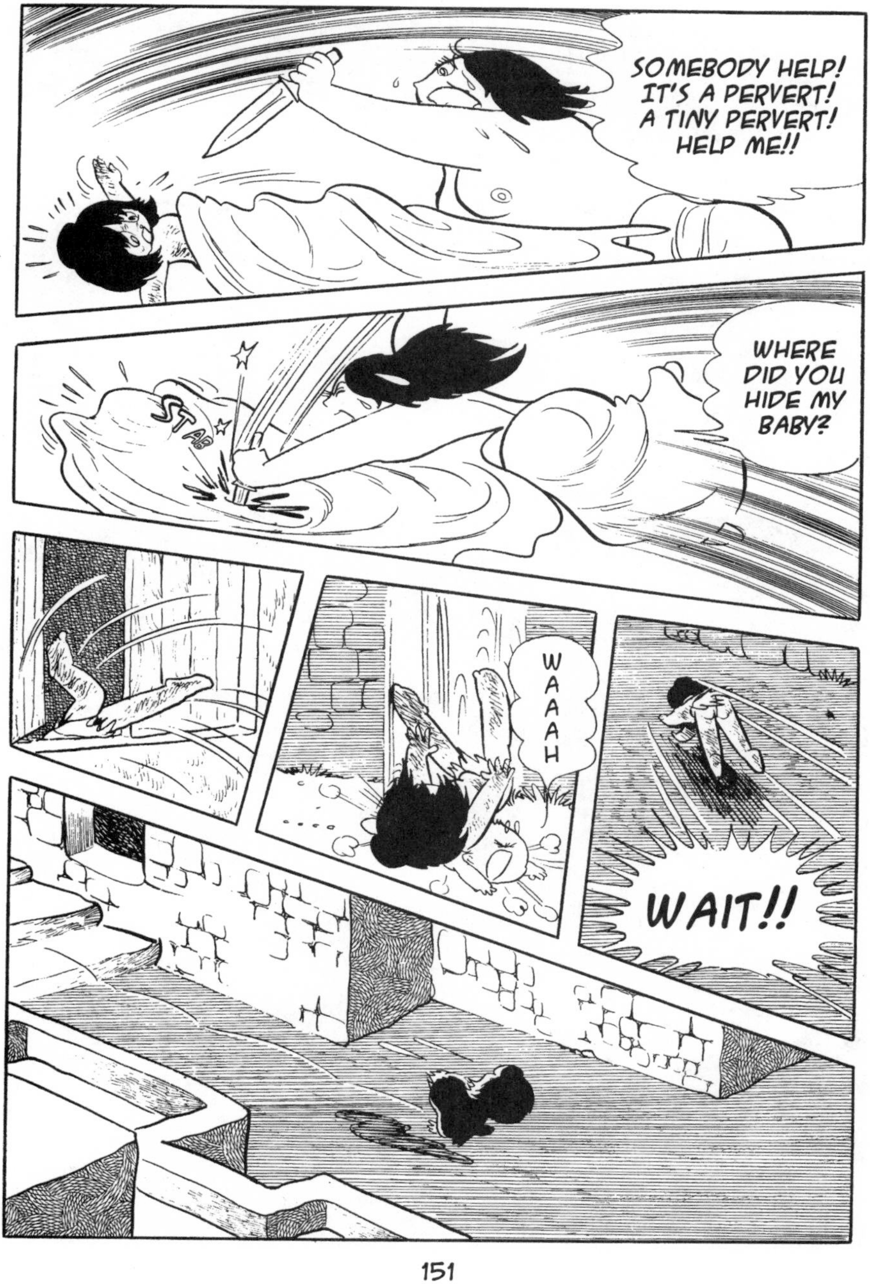
SOMEBODY HELP! IT'S A PERVERT! A TINY PERVERT! HELP ME!!
WHERE DID YOU HIDE MY BABY?
STAB
WAAAAH
WAIT!!

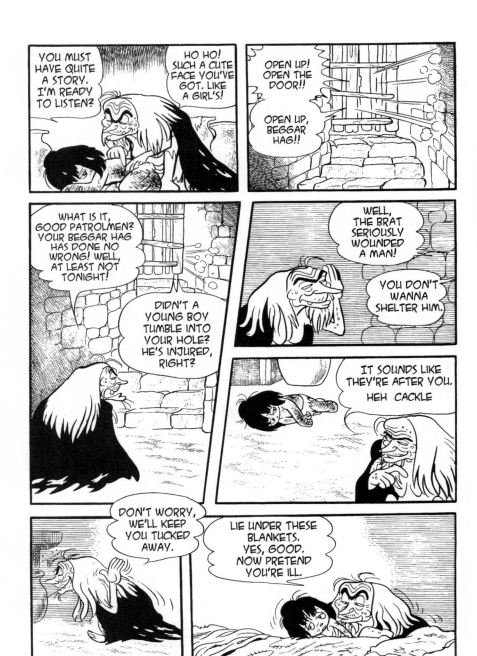

154

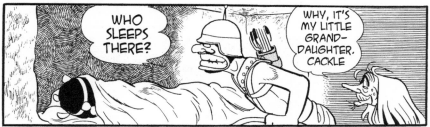

155

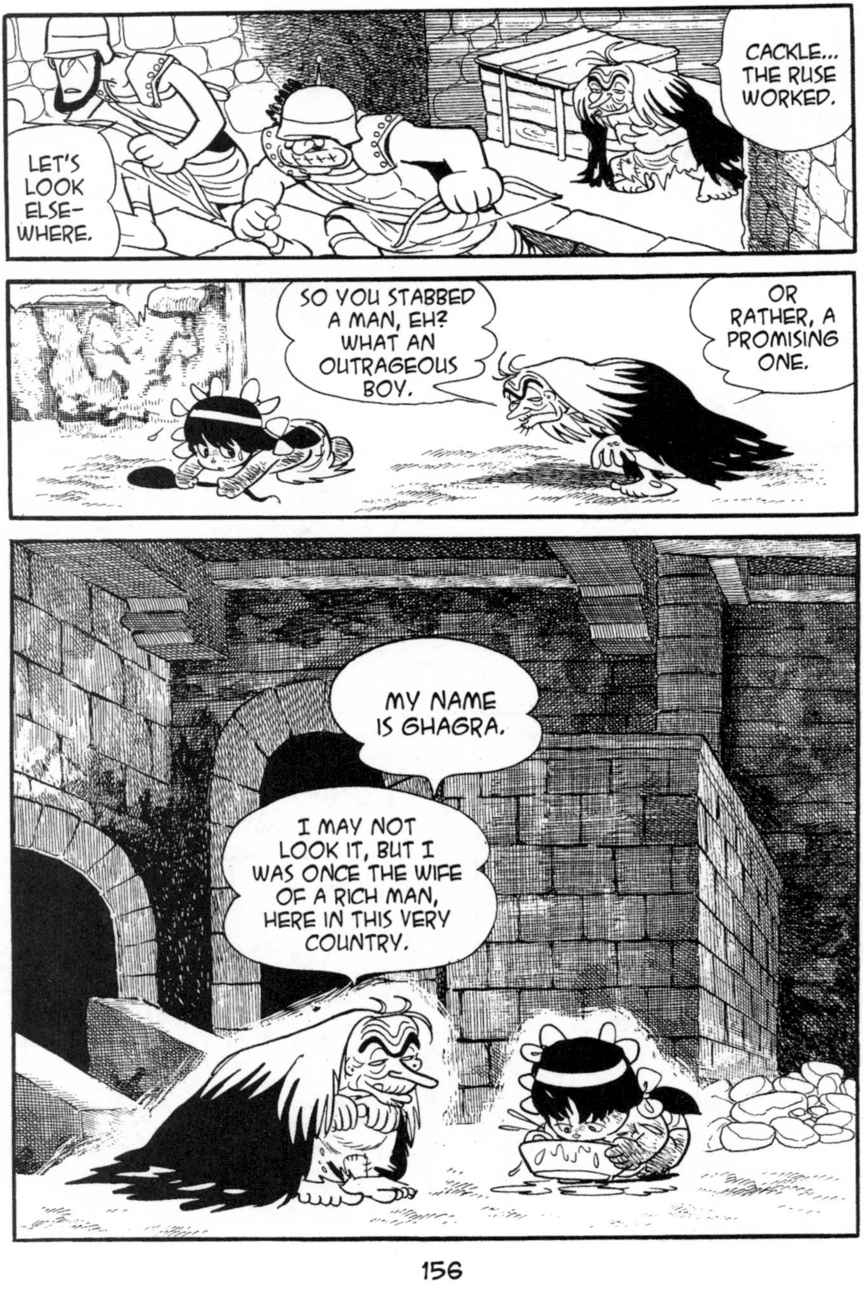
LET'S LOOK ELSE-WHERE.
CACKLE... THE RUSE WORKED.
SO YOU STABBED A MAN, EH? WHAT AN OUTRAGEOUS BOY.
OR RATHER, A PROMISING ONE.
MY NAME IS GHAGRA.
I MAY NOT LOOK IT, BUT I WAS ONCE THE WIFE OF A RICH MAN, HERE IN THIS VERY COUNTRY.

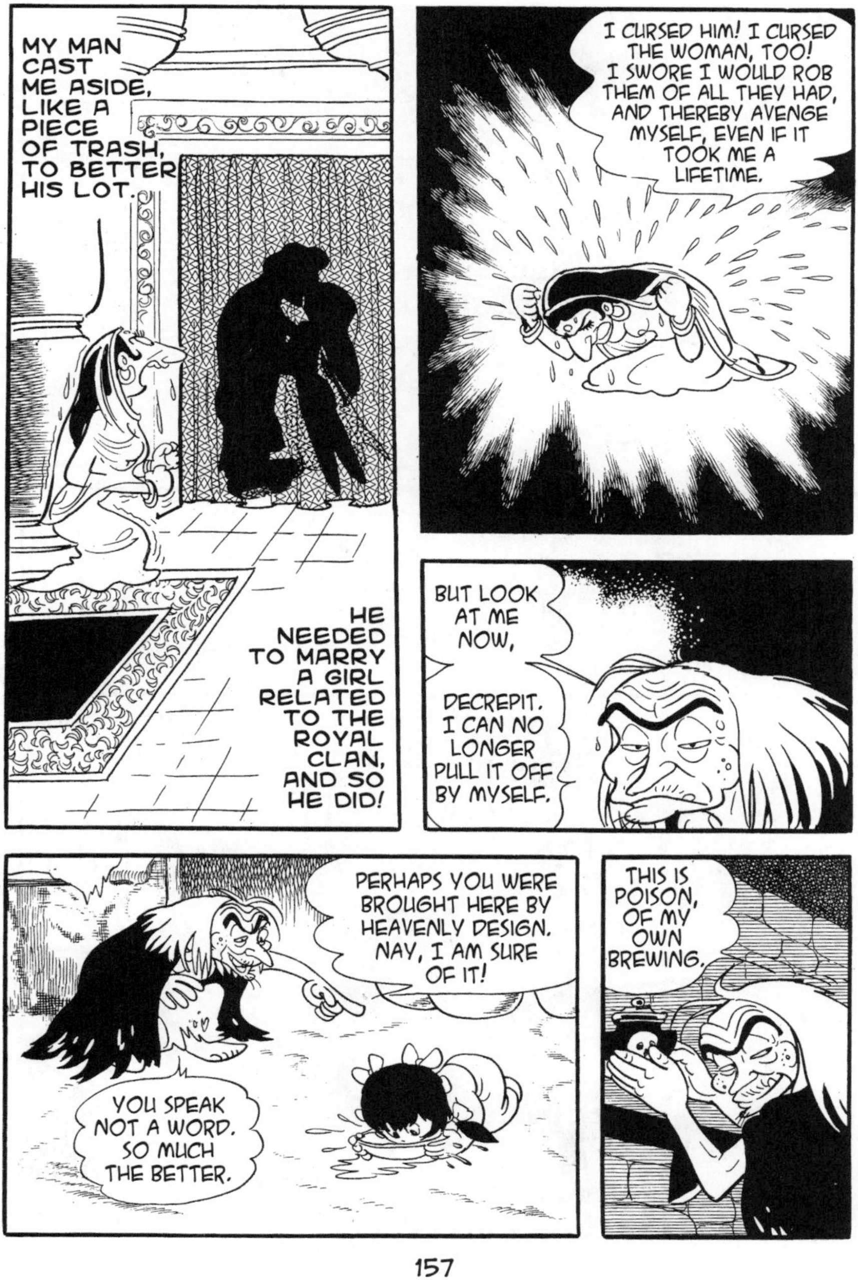
MY MAN CAST ME ASIDE, LIKE A PIECE OF TRASH, TO BETTER HIS LOT.
HE NEEDED TO MARRY A GIRL RELATED TO THE ROYAL CLAN, AND SO HE DID!
I CURSED HIM! I CURSED THE WOMAN, TOO! I SWORE I WOULD ROB THEM OF ALL THEY HAD, AND THEREBY AVENGE MYSELF, EVEN IF IT TOOK ME A LIFETIME.
BUT LOOK AT ME NOW,
DECREPIT. I CAN NO LONGER PULL IT OFF BY MYSELF.
PERHAPS YOU WERE BROUGHT HERE BY HEAVENLY DESIGN. NAY, I AM SURE OF IT!
YOU SPEAK NOT A WORD. SO MUCH THE BETTER.
THIS IS POISON, OF MY OWN BREWING.

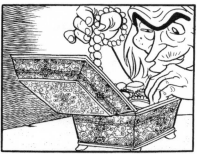

HO! HO HO! A BEAUTY! WHAT A FETCHING MAIDEN!

RISE AND BEHOLD YOURSELF IN THE MIRROR. CHARMING, EHH?

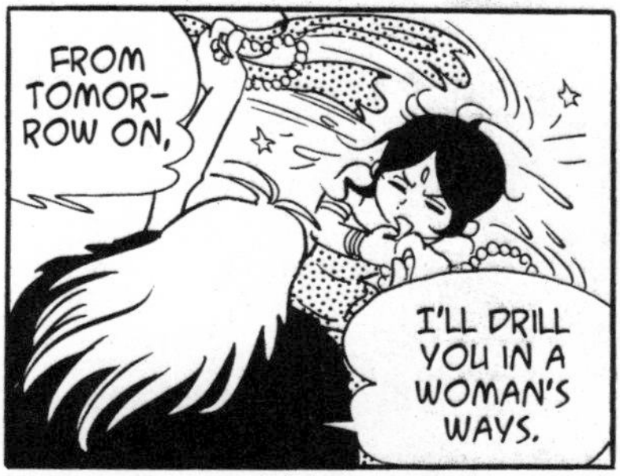
FROM TOMOR-ROW ON,
I'LL DRILL YOU IN A WOMAN'S WAYS.

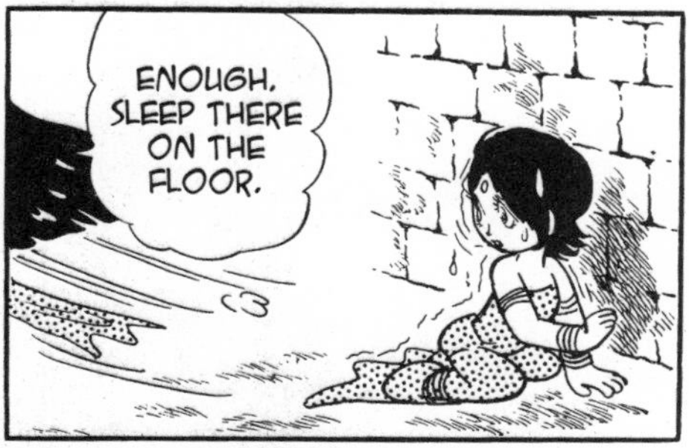
ENOUGH. SLEEP THERE ON THE FLOOR.

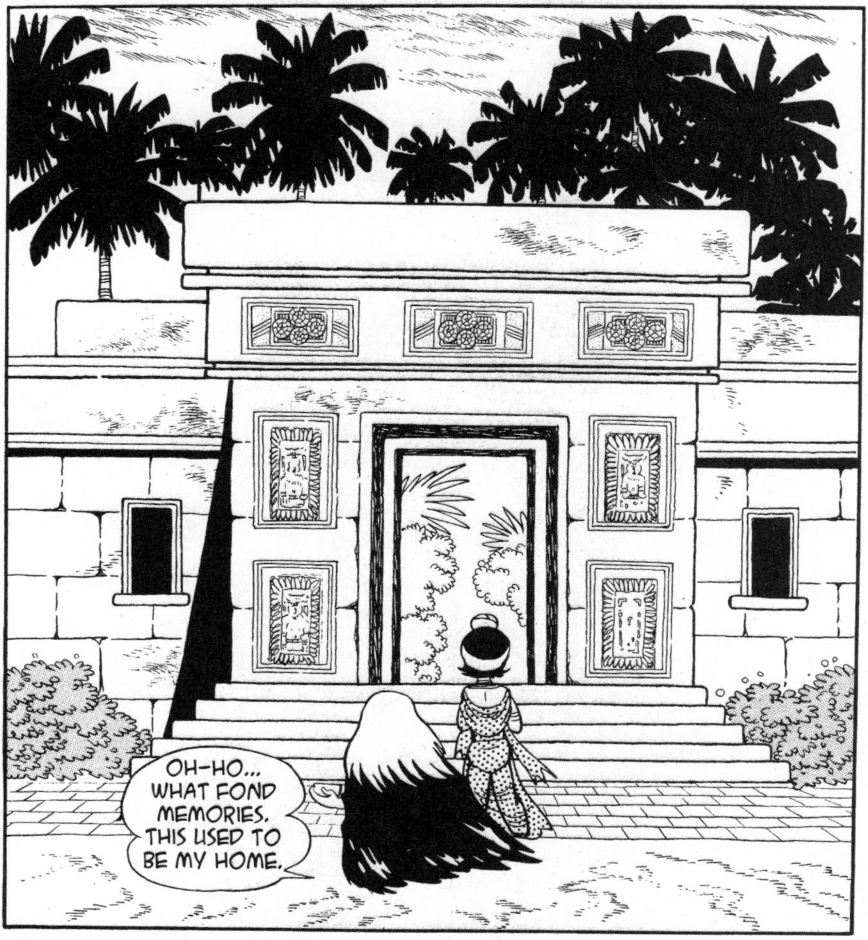
OH-HO... WHAT FOND MEMORIES. THIS USED TO BE MY HOME.

163

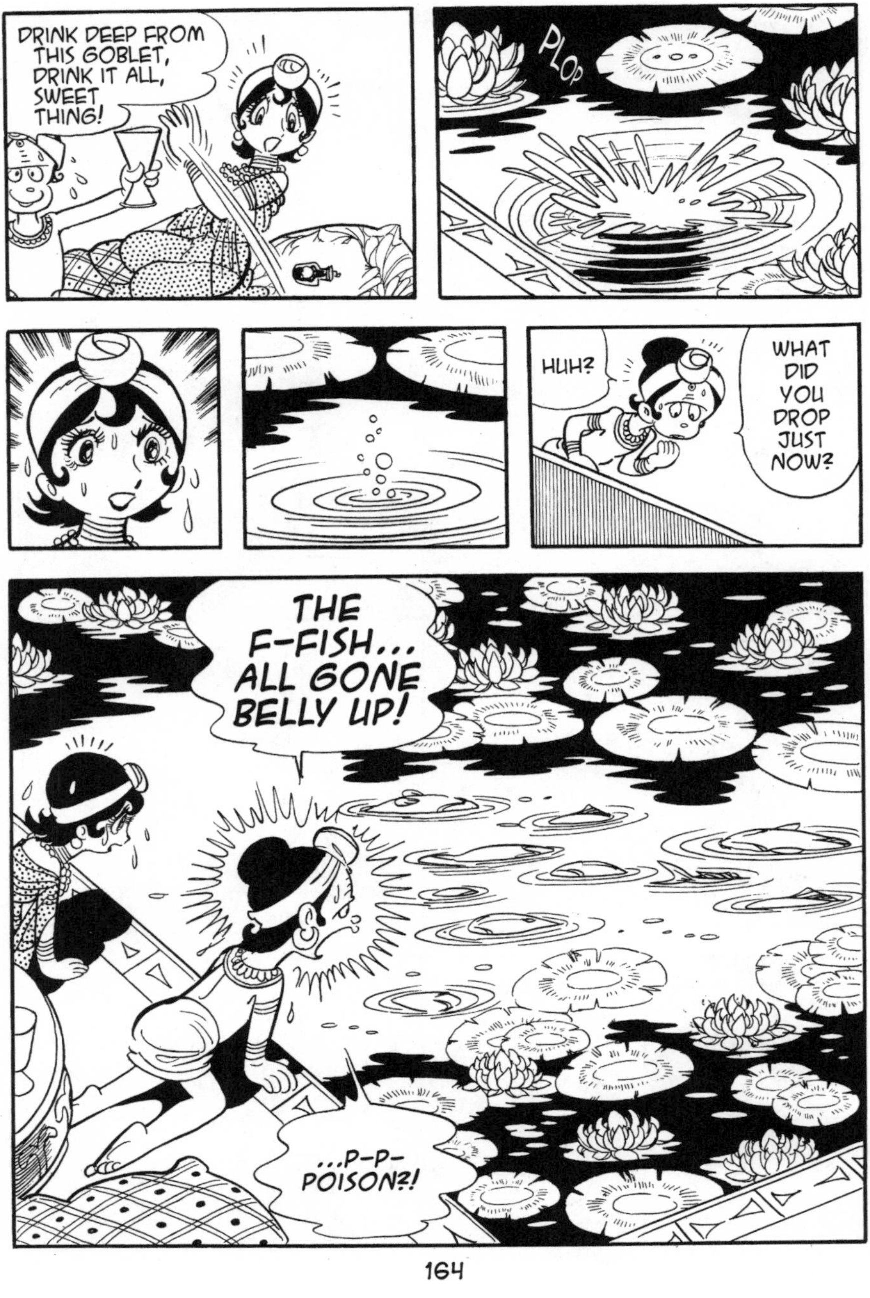
DRINK DEEP FROM THIS GOBLET, DRINK IT ALL, SWEET THING!
PLOP
HUH?
WHAT DID YOU DROP JUST NOW?
THE F-FISH... ALL GONE BELLY UP!
...P-P-POISON?!

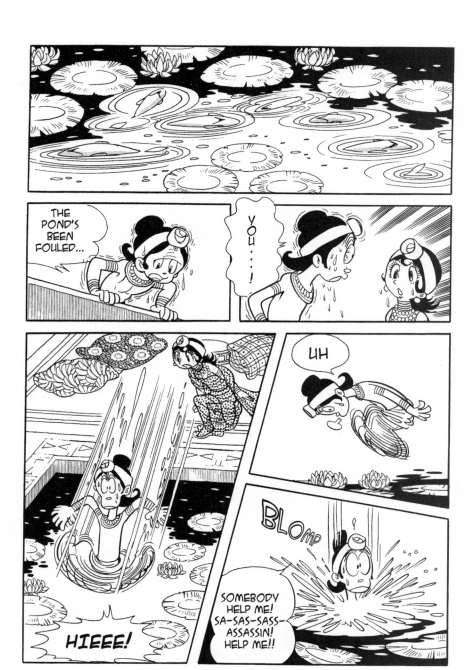

165

167

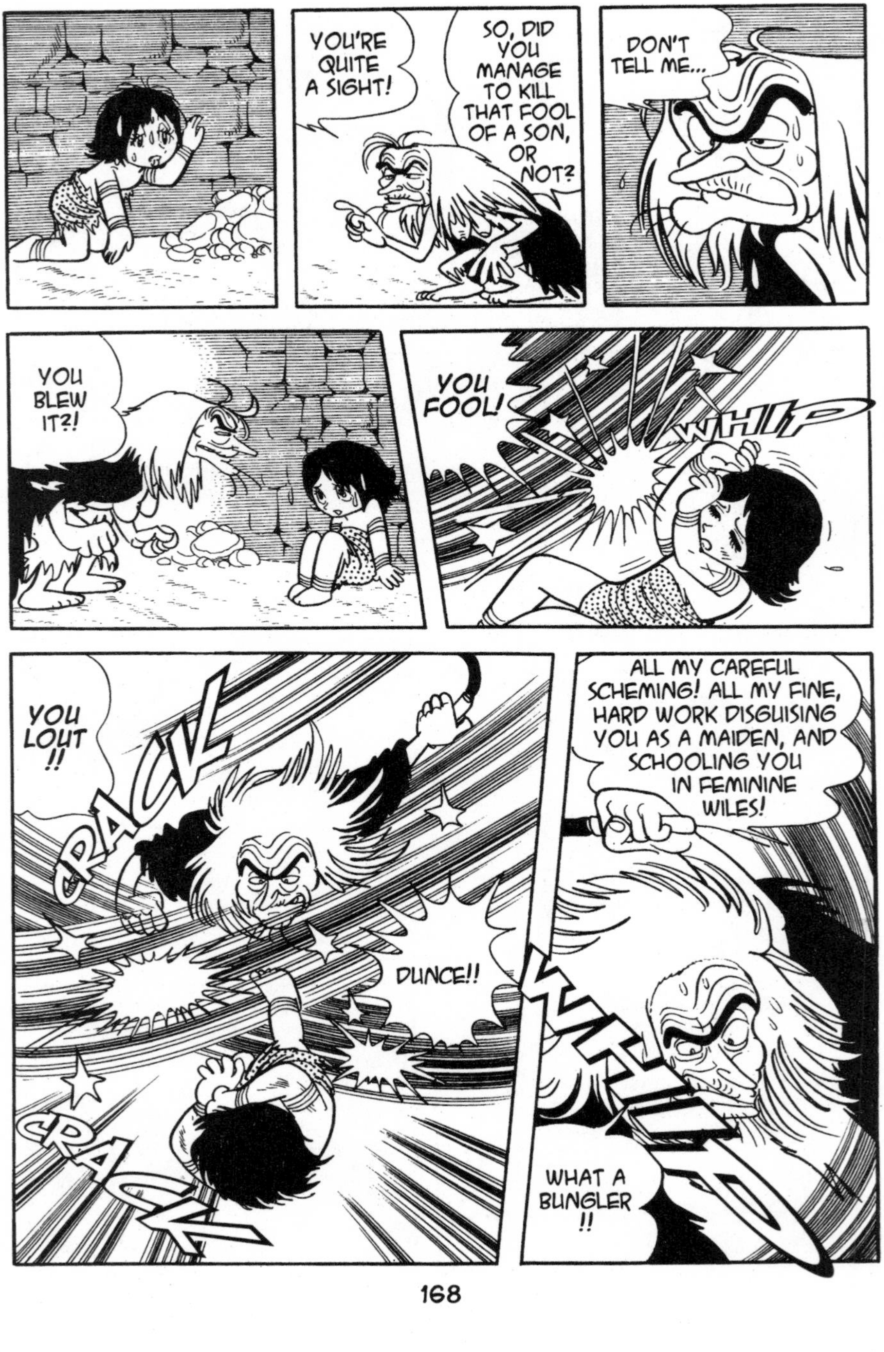
YOU'RE QUITE A SIGHT!
SO, DID YOU MANAGE TO KILL THAT FOOL OF A SON, OR NOT?
DON'T TELL ME...
YOU BLEW IT?!
YOU FOOL!
WHIP
YOU LOUT !!
CRACK
DUNCE!!
CRACK
ALL MY CAREFUL SCHEMING! ALL MY FINE, HARD WORK DISGUISING YOU AS A MAIDEN, AND SCHOOLING YOU IN FEMININE WILES!
WHIP
WHAT A BUNGLER !!

169

DEVADATTA'S EYES OPENED WIDE WITH ASTONISHMENT; EAGER FOR A CLUE, HE STARED AND STARED AT THE OLD HAG. JUST WHAT HAD MADE HER SO DELIRIOUSLY HAPPY?

IT WAS THOSE TINY STONES THAT HAD ENCHANTED HER! AND SO DID YOUNG DEVADATTA LEARN OF THE MAGICAL POWER OF GEMS.

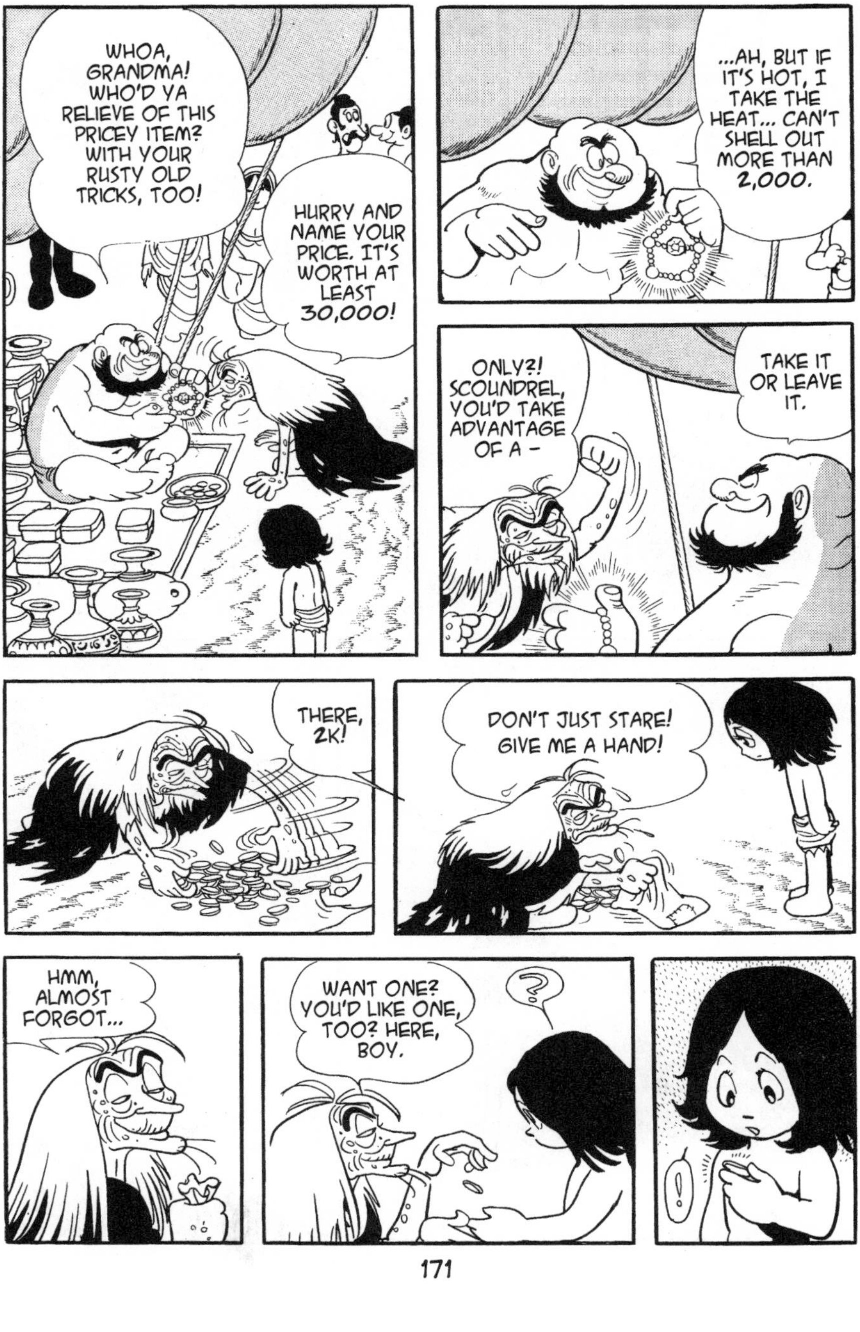
WHOA, GRANDMA! WHO'D YA RELIEVE OF THIS PRICEY ITEM? WITH YOUR RUSTY OLD TRICKS, TOO!
HURRY AND NAME YOUR PRICE. IT'S WORTH AT LEAST 30,000!
...AH, BUT IF IT'S HOT, I TAKE THE HEAT... CAN'T SHELL OUT MORE THAN 2,000.
ONLY?! SCOUNDREL, YOU'D TAKE ADVANTAGE OF A –
TAKE IT OR LEAVE IT.
THERE, 2K!
DON'T JUST STARE! GIVE ME A HAND!
HMM, ALMOST FORGOT...
WANT ONE? YOU'D LIKE ONE, TOO? HERE, BOY.
?
!

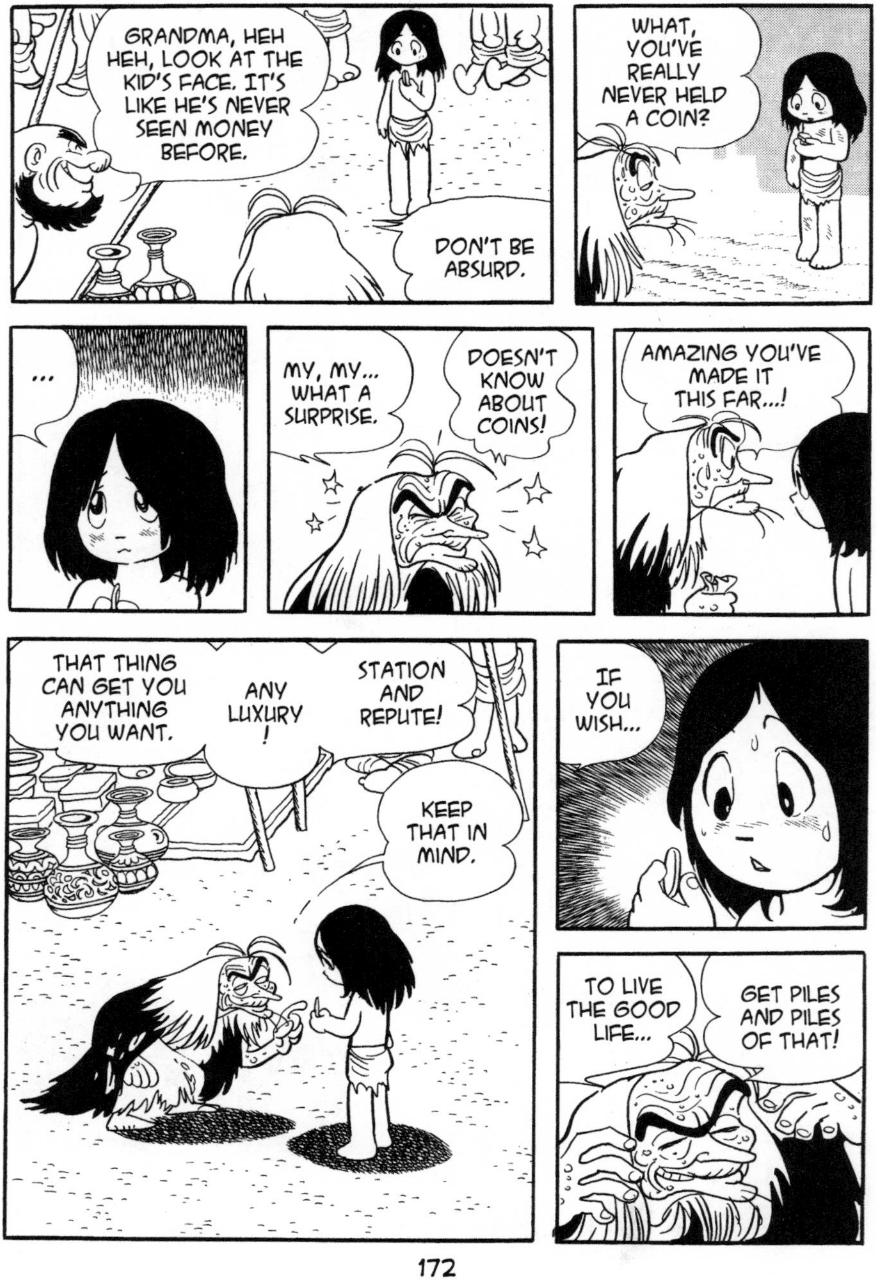
GRANDMA, HEH HEH, LOOK AT THE KID'S FACE. IT'S LIKE HE'S NEVER SEEN MONEY BEFORE.
DON'T BE ABSURD.
WHAT, YOU'VE REALLY NEVER HELD A COIN?
...
MY, MY... WHAT A SURPRISE.
DOESN'T KNOW ABOUT COINS!
AMAZING YOU'VE MADE IT THIS FAR...!
THAT THING CAN GET YOU ANYTHING YOU WANT.
ANY LUXURY!
STATION AND REPUTE!
KEEP THAT IN MIND.
IF YOU WISH...
TO LIVE THE GOOD LIFE...
GET PILES AND PILES OF THAT!

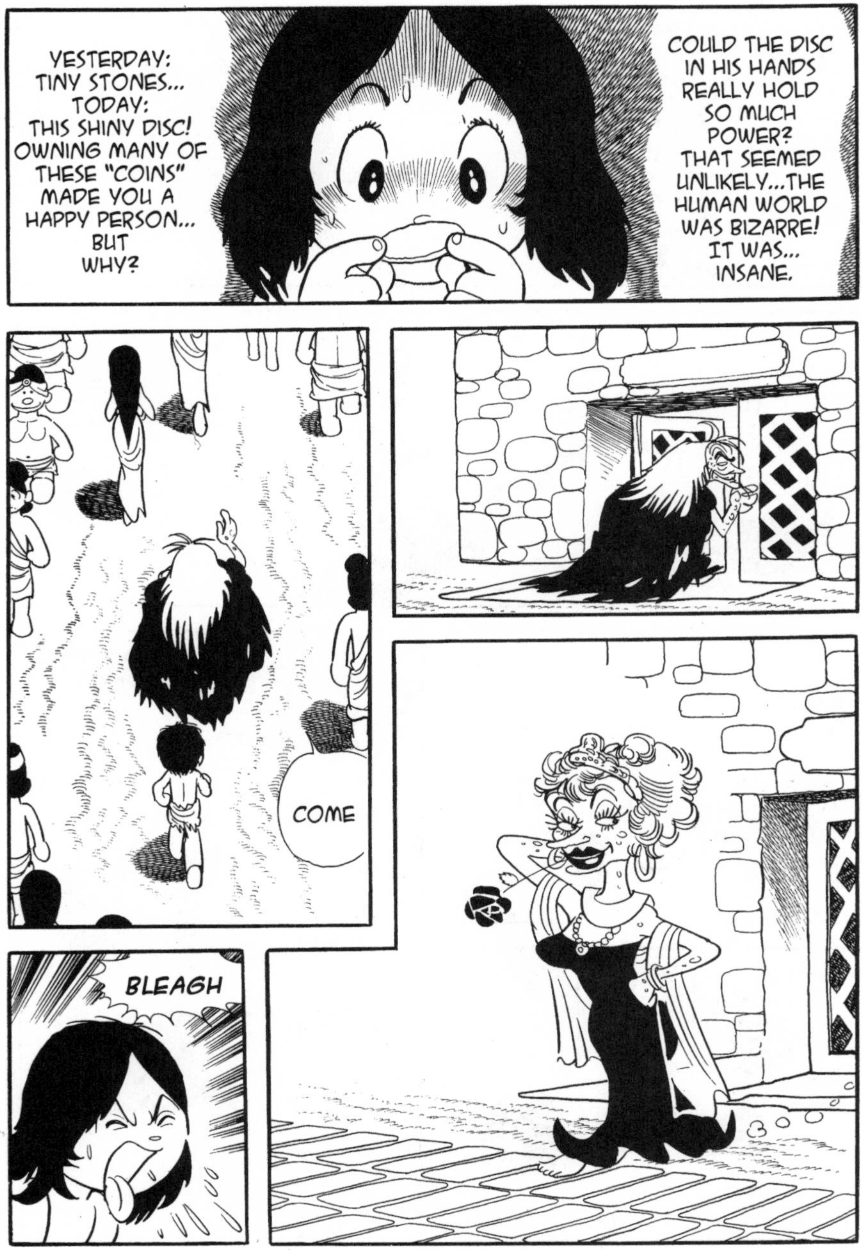

YESTERDAY: TINY STONES... TODAY: THIS SHINY DISC! OWNING MANY OF THESE "COINS" MADE YOU A HAPPY PERSON... BUT WHY?
COULD THE DISC IN HIS HANDS REALLY HOLD SO MUCH POWER? THAT SEEMED UNLIKELY...THE HUMAN WORLD WAS BIZARRE! IT WAS... INSANE.
COME
BLEAGH

174

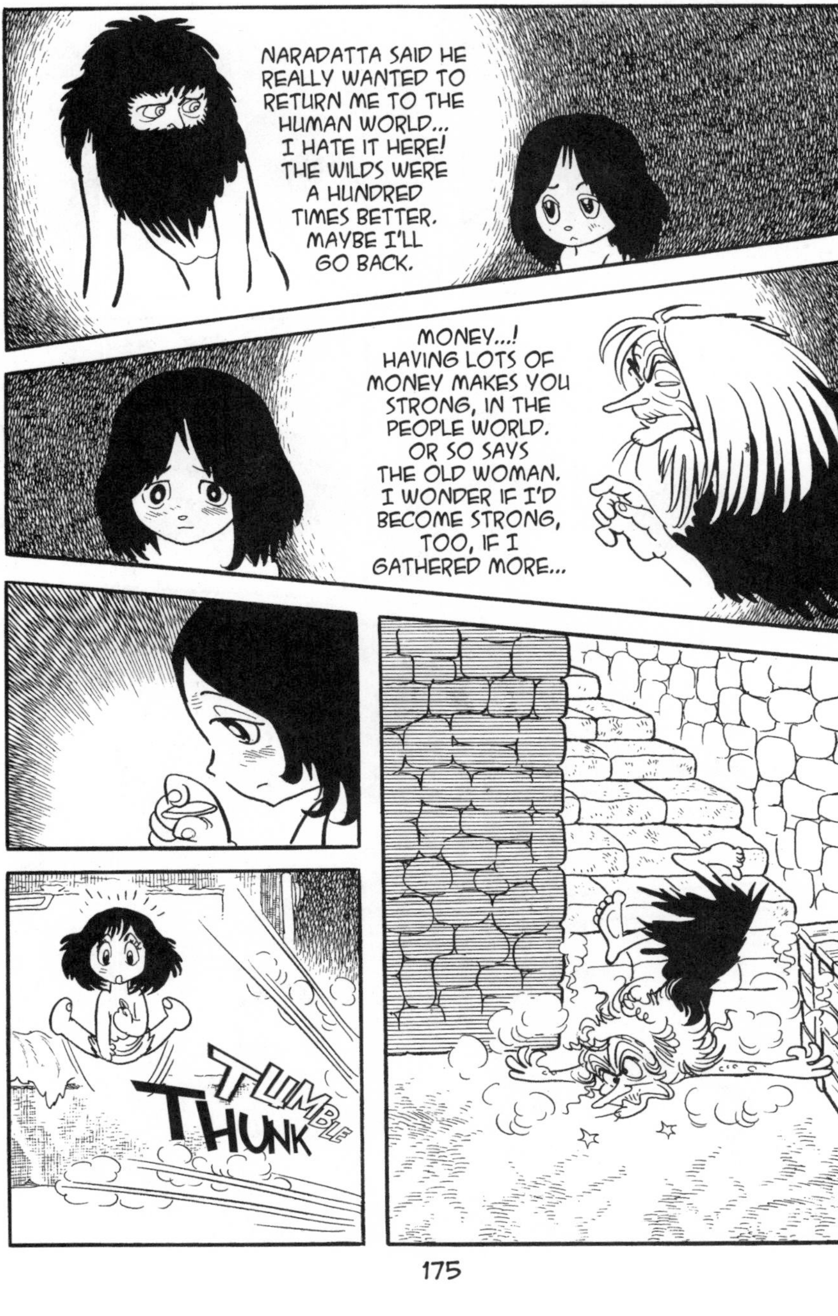
NARADATTA SAID HE REALLY WANTED TO RETURN ME TO THE HUMAN WORLD... I HATE IT HERE! THE WILDS WERE A HUNDRED TIMES BETTER. MAYBE I'LL GO BACK.
MONEY...! HAVING LOTS OF MONEY MAKES YOU STRONG, IN THE PEOPLE WORLD. OR SO SAYS THE OLD WOMAN. I WONDER IF I'D BECOME STRONG, TOO, IF I GATHERED MORE...
TUMBLE
THUNK

176

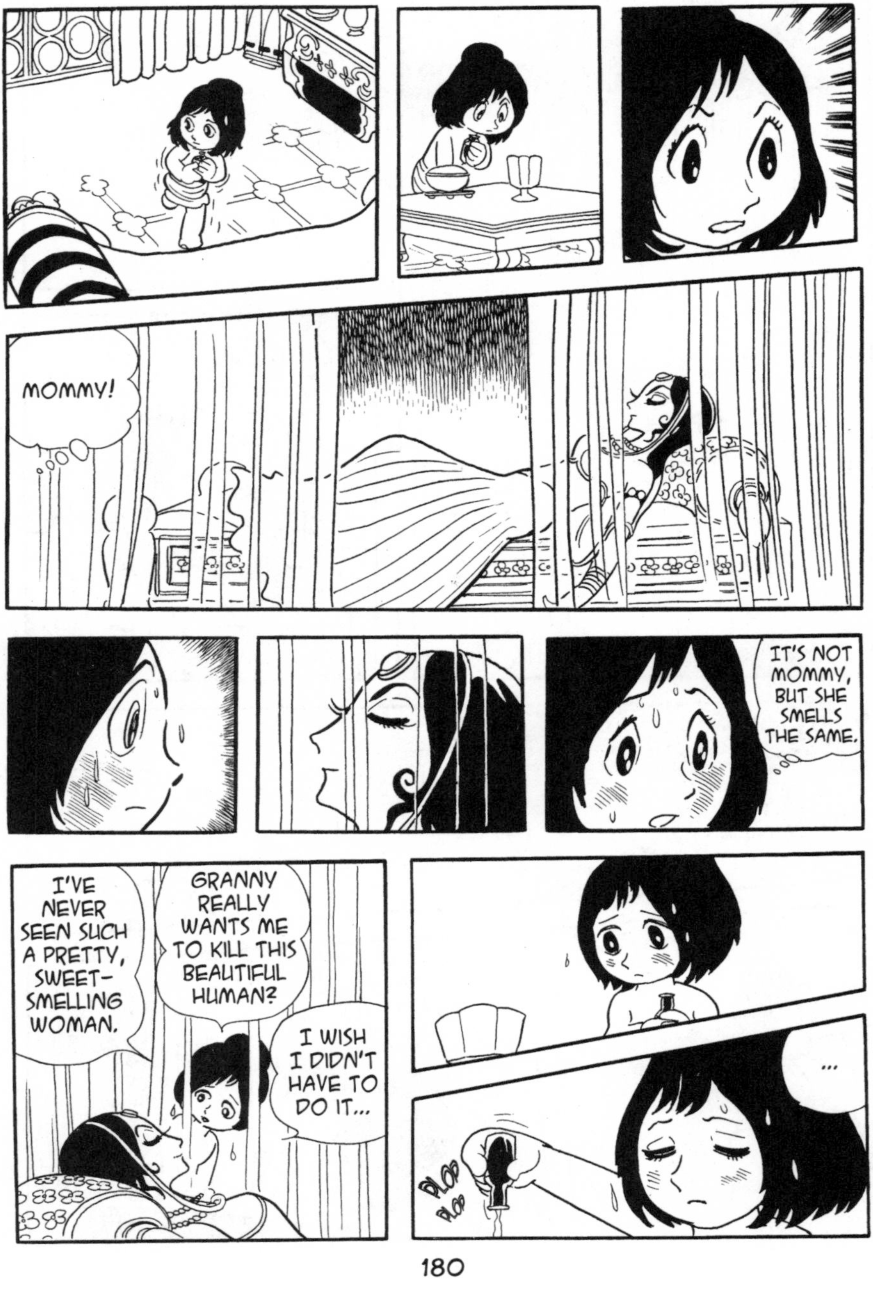
MOMMY!
IT'S NOT MOMMY, BUT SHE SMELLS THE SAME.
I'VE NEVER SEEN SUCH A PRETTY, SWEET-SMELLING WOMAN.
GRANNY REALLY WANTS ME TO KILL THIS BEAUTIFUL HUMAN?
I WISH I DIDN'T HAVE TO DO IT...
...
PLOP PLOP

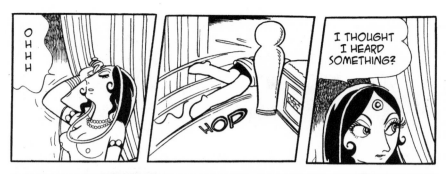

181

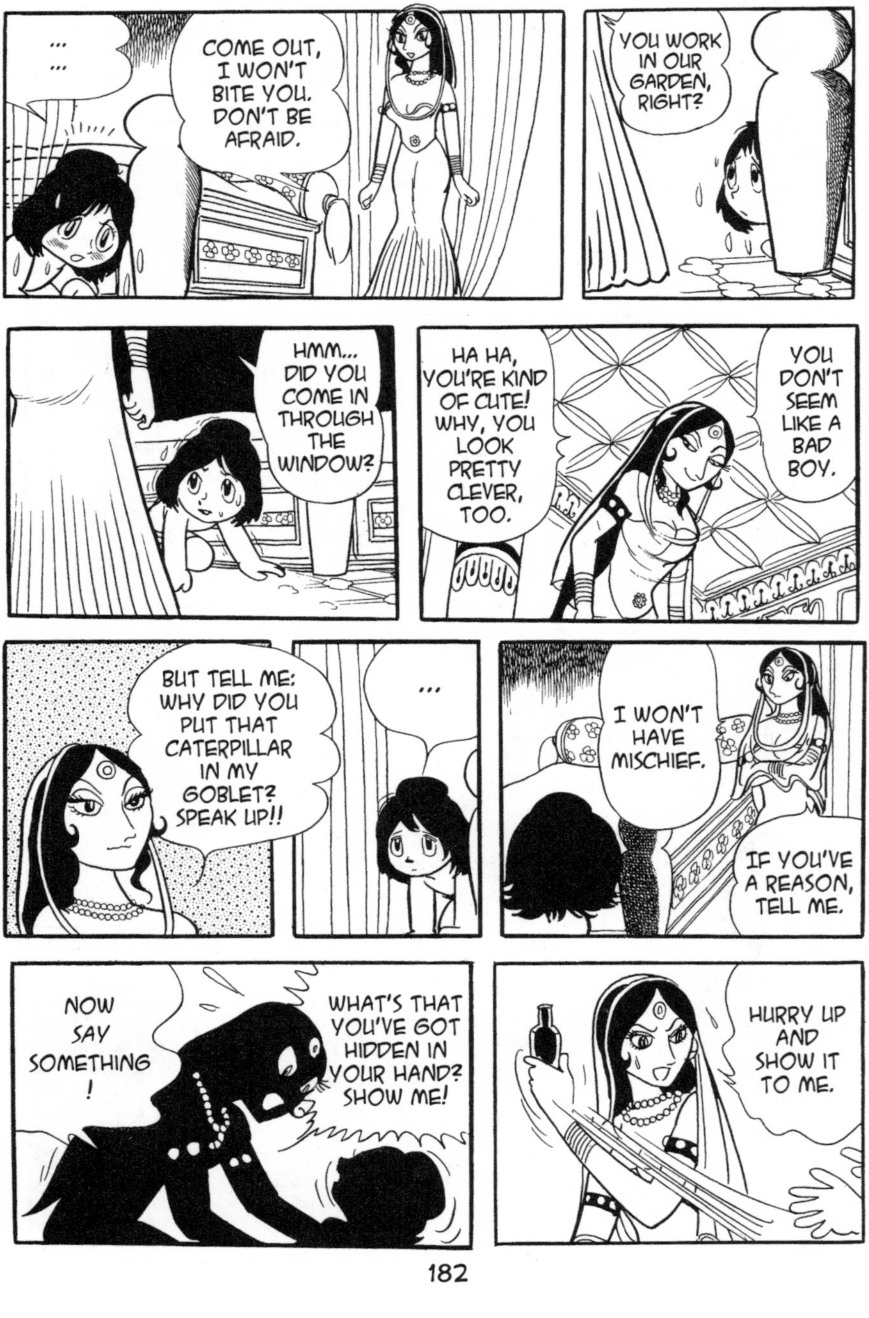
...
...
COME OUT, I WON'T BITE YOU. DON'T BE AFRAID.
YOU WORK IN OUR GARDEN, RIGHT?
HMM... DID YOU COME IN THROUGH THE WINDOW?
HA HA, YOU'RE KIND OF CUTE! WHY, YOU LOOK PRETTY CLEVER, TOO.
YOU DON'T SEEM LIKE A BAD BOY.
BUT TELL ME: WHY DID YOU PUT THAT CATERPILLAR IN MY GOBLET? SPEAK UP!!
...
I WON'T HAVE MISCHIEF.
IF YOU'VE A REASON, TELL ME.
NOW SAY SOMETHING!
WHAT'S THAT YOU'VE GOT HIDDEN IN YOUR HAND? SHOW ME!
HURRY UP AND SHOW IT TO ME.

POISON

WHY... WHAT IS THIS?

WHY WON'T YOU SPEAK? ARE YOU DUMB?

HAVE YOU COME TO KILL ME?

HOW... HORRIBLE!

BUT WHY THE CATER-PILLAR?

...AND NOT THE POISON?

M...MOMMY

"MOMMY" DID YOU SAY?

LIKE MOMMY...

I SEE!

YOU COULDN'T KILL ME BECAUSE I REMINDED YOU OF YOUR MOTHER.

183

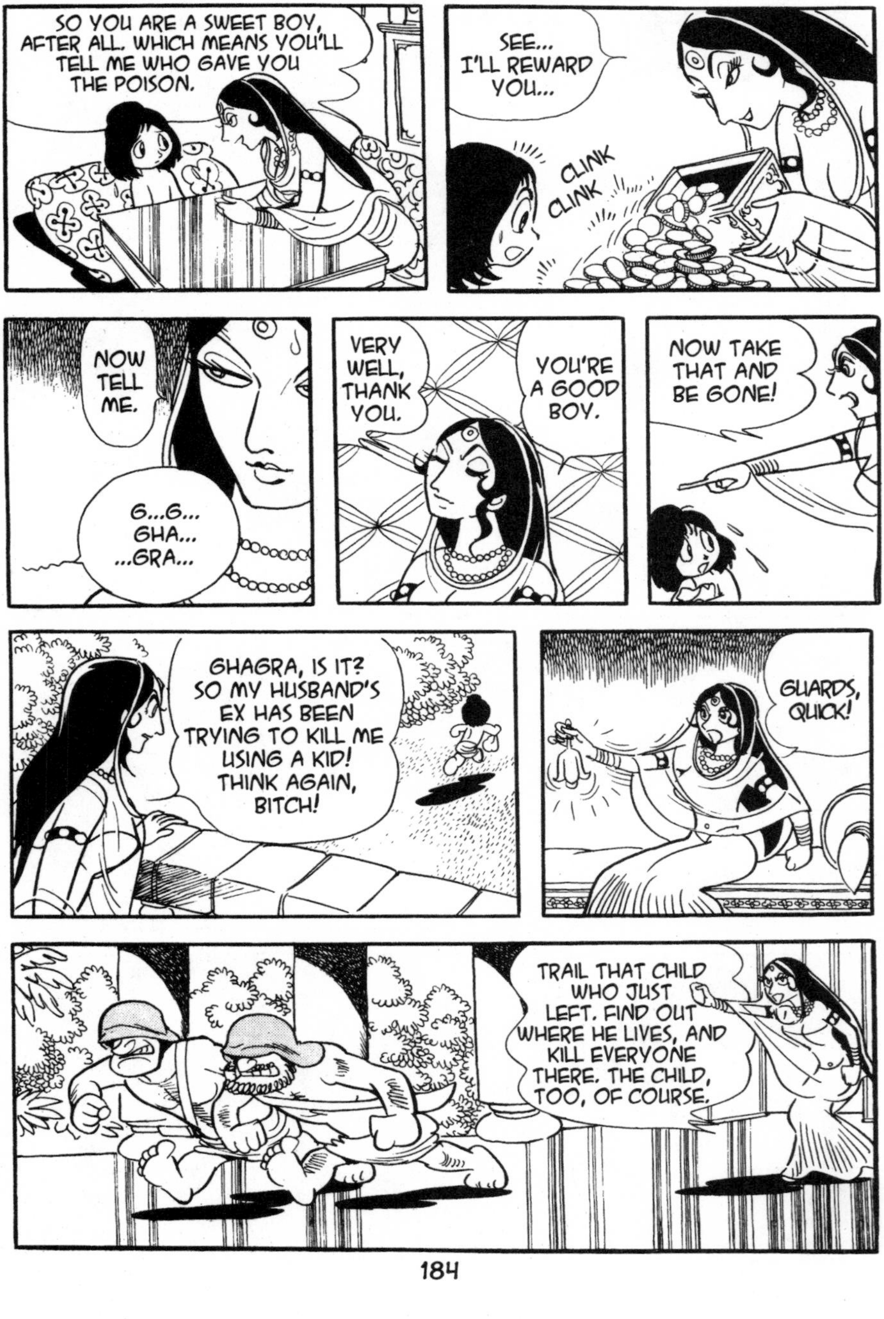
SO YOU ARE A SWEET BOY, AFTER ALL. WHICH MEANS YOU'LL TELL ME WHO GAVE YOU THE POISON.
SEE... I'LL REWARD YOU...
CLINK
CLINK
NOW TELL ME.
G...G... GHA... ...GRA...
VERY WELL, THANK YOU.
YOU'RE A GOOD BOY.
NOW TAKE THAT AND BE GONE!
GHAGRA, IS IT? SO MY HUSBAND'S EX HAS BEEN TRYING TO KILL ME USING A KID! THINK AGAIN, BITCH!
GUARDS, QUICK!
TRAIL THAT CHILD WHO JUST LEFT. FIND OUT WHERE HE LIVES, AND KILL EVERYONE THERE. THE CHILD, TOO, OF COURSE.

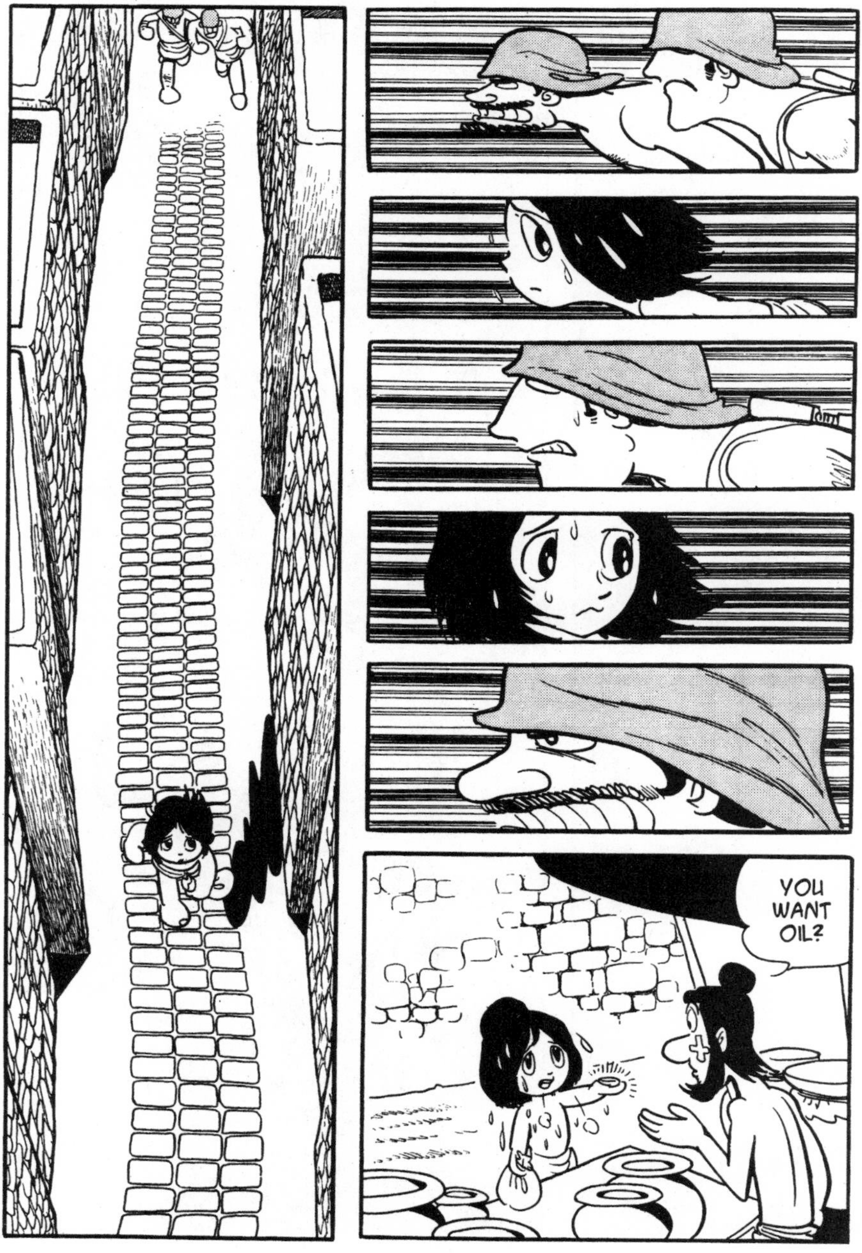
YOU WANT OIL?

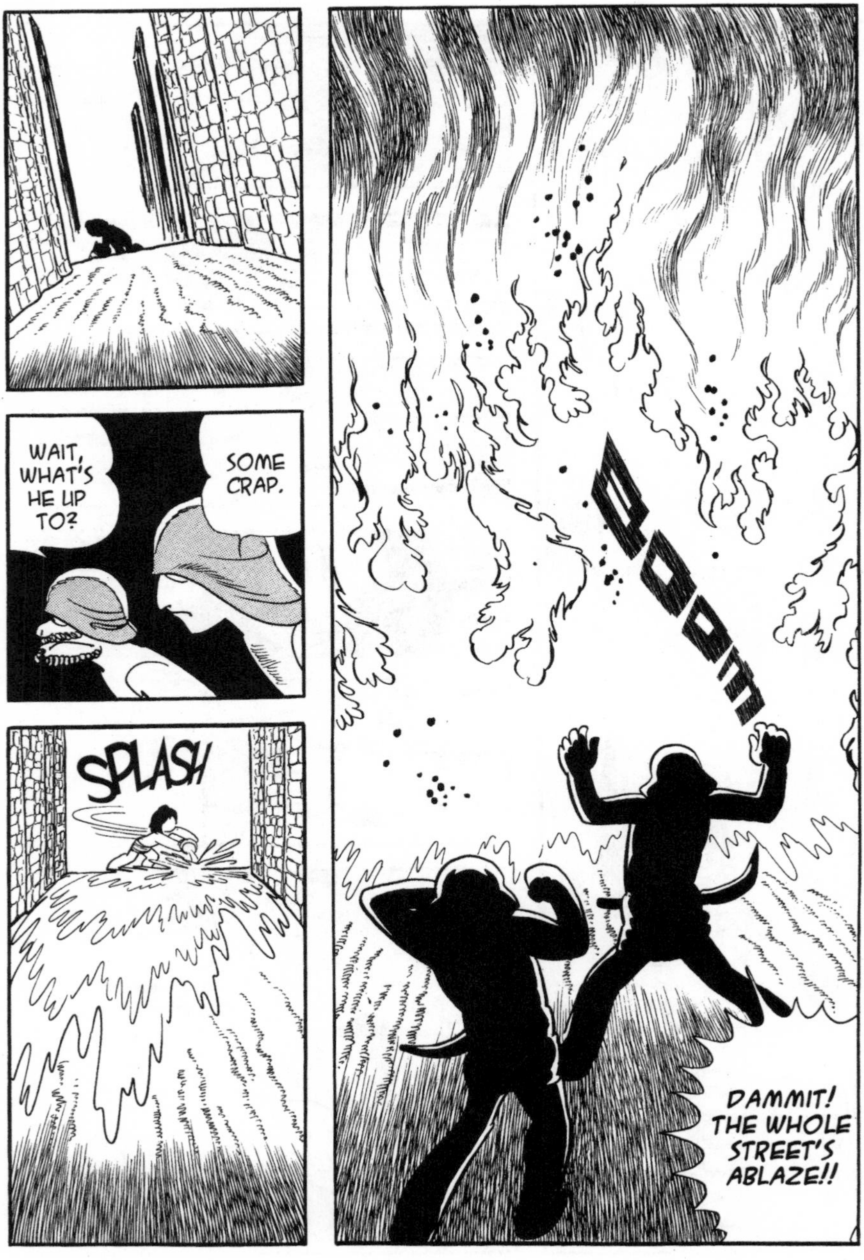
WAIT, WHAT'S HE UP TO?
SOME CRAP.
SPLASH
BOOM
DAMMIT! THE WHOLE STREET'S ABLAZE!!

HUH?

GHA...GRA...K-KILL COMING!...NOW!!

WHAAAAT?

BUNGLED IT AGAIN, DID YOU, NINCOMPOOP! AND NOW THEY'RE AFTER YOU, IS THAT IT?

TELL ME IN WORDS! WHAT NOW?

I I I'M TOO OLD TOO OLD TO BE RUN-RUNNING LIKE THIS!

WHEEZ

WHEEZ

RUN NOW... FAST

WHAT A FIASCO !!

188

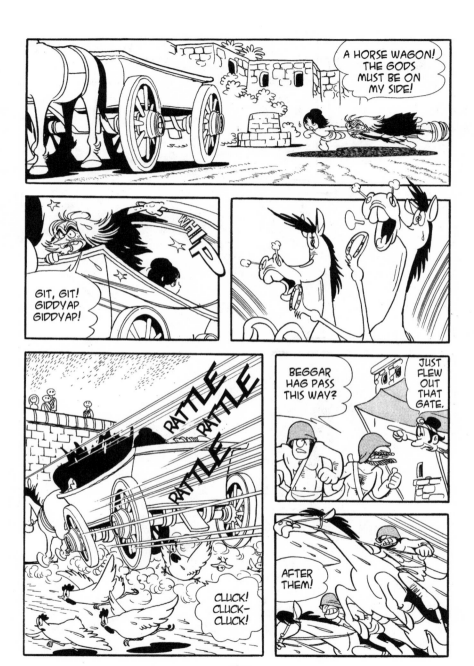

GALLOP
GALLOP
...
WUF OOOF
UH...
SLITHER
WHINE
WHINE
WHINE

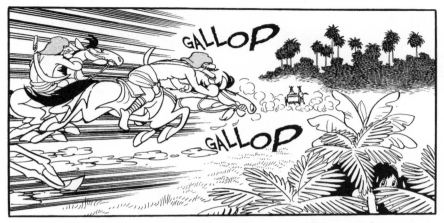

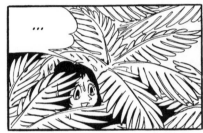

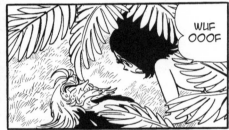

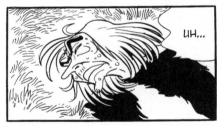

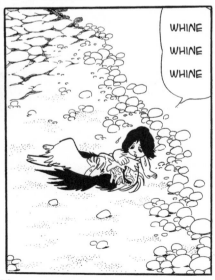

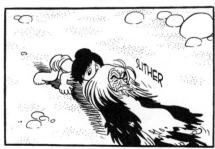

LOOKS LIKE IT'S OVER FOR ME.

CAN'T EVEN MUSTER THE WILL TO STAND. D'RATHER REST... FOREVER.

'TIS THE ONLY THING

THAT NO PILE OF GOLD'S EVER FIXED.

YOU'RE STILL YOUNG, LAD... WHEN YOU GROW UP, YOU'LL SEE HOW LIFE MAKES YOU VILE. VILE.

IN THE END WE ALL MUST DIE.

NO USE WAILING ABOUT THAT...

192

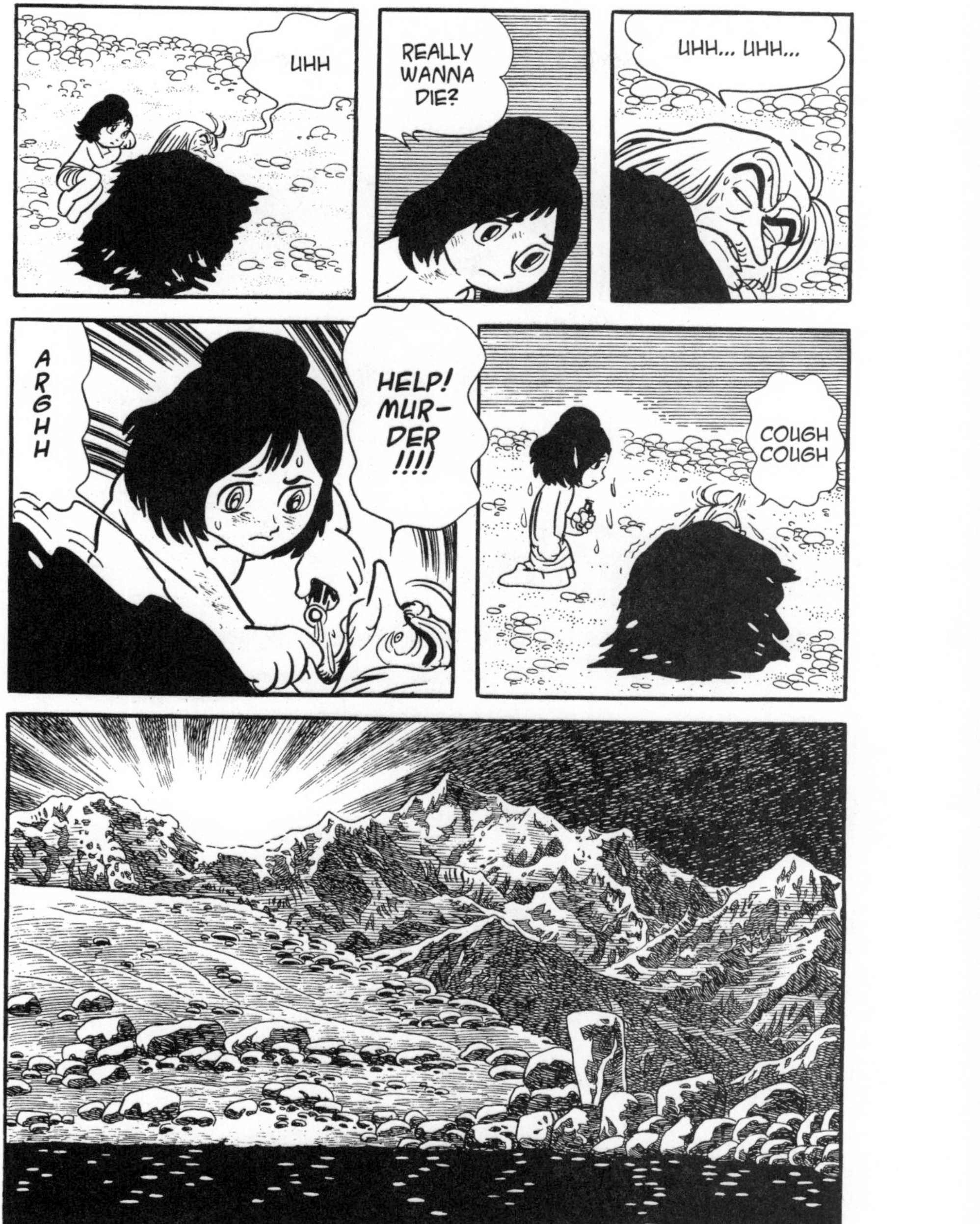
UHH
REALLY WANNA DIE?
UHH... UHH...
ARGHH
HELP! MURDER!!!!
COUGH COUGH

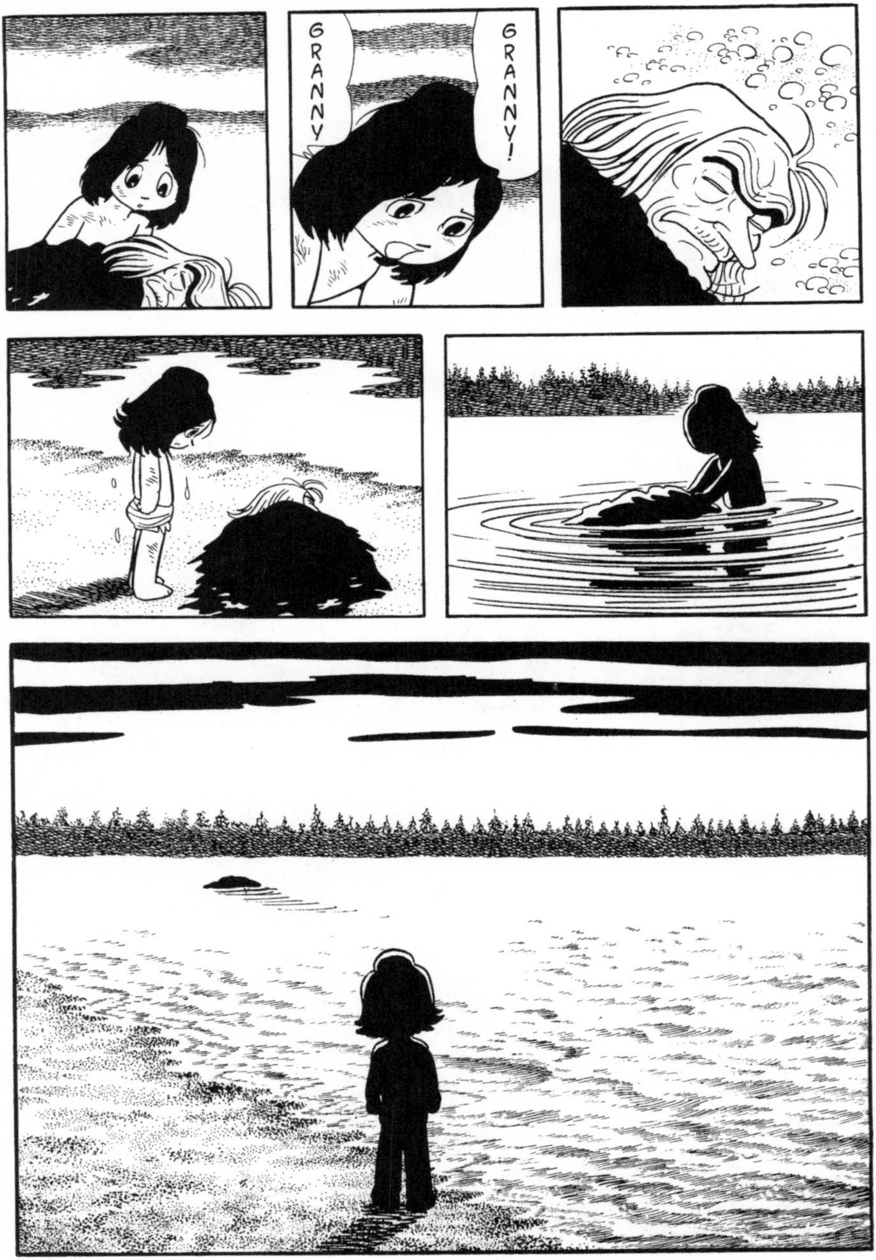
GRANNY
GRANNY!

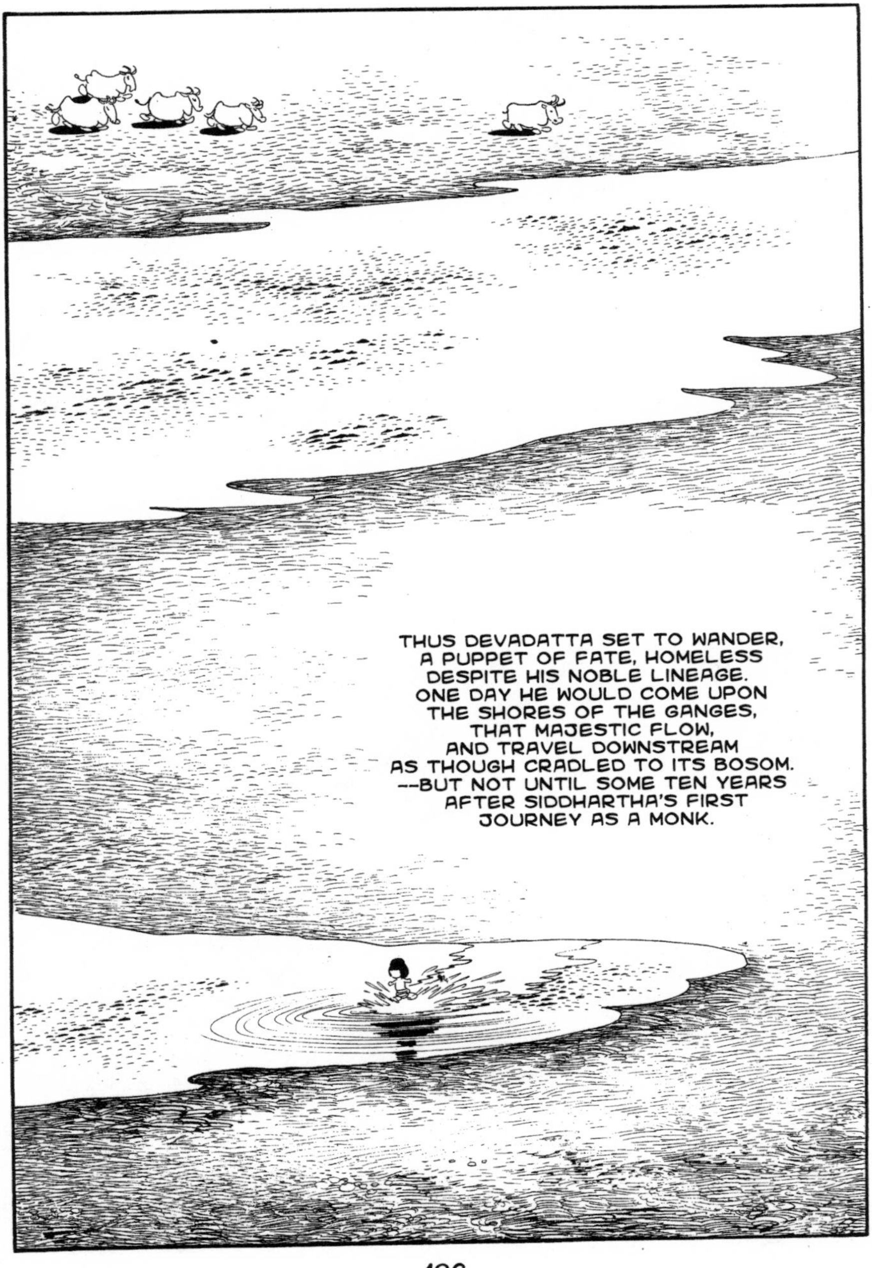
THUS DEVADATTA SET TO WANDER, A PUPPET OF FATE, HOMELESS DESPITE HIS NOBLE LINEAGE. ONE DAY HE WOULD COME UPON THE SHORES OF THE GANGES, THAT MAJESTIC FLOW, AND TRAVEL DOWNSTREAM AS THOUGH CRADLED TO ITS BOSOM. --BUT NOT UNTIL SOME TEN YEARS AFTER SIDDHARTHA'S FIRST JOURNEY AS A MONK.

CHAPTER FOUR

SUKANDA THE KNIGHT

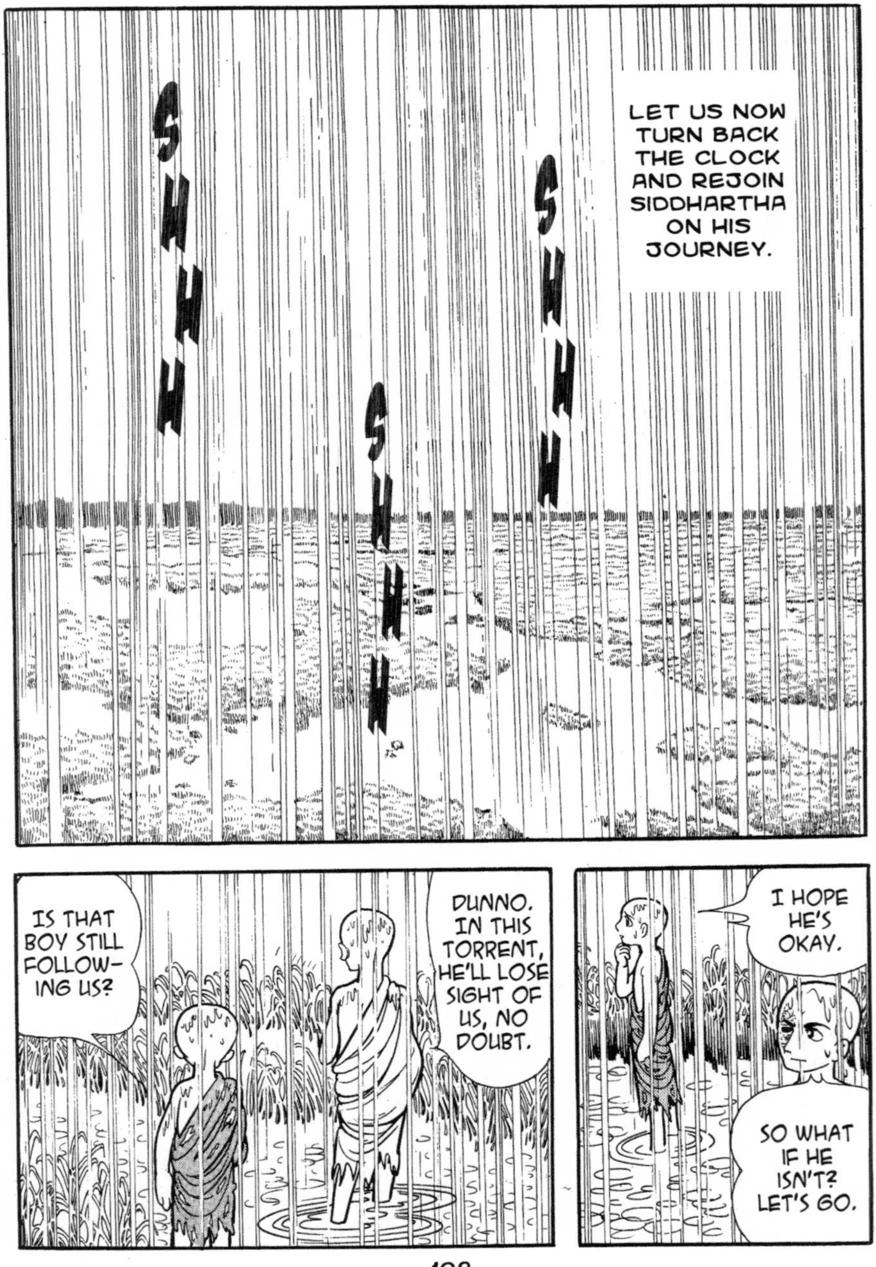
LET US NOW TURN BACK THE CLOCK AND REJOIN SIDDHARTHA ON HIS JOURNEY.
SHHH
SHHH
SHHH
IS THAT BOY STILL FOLLOW-ING US?
DUNNO. IN THIS TORRENT, HE'LL LOSE SIGHT OF US, NO DOUBT.
I HOPE HE'S OKAY.
SO WHAT IF HE ISN'T? LET'S GO.

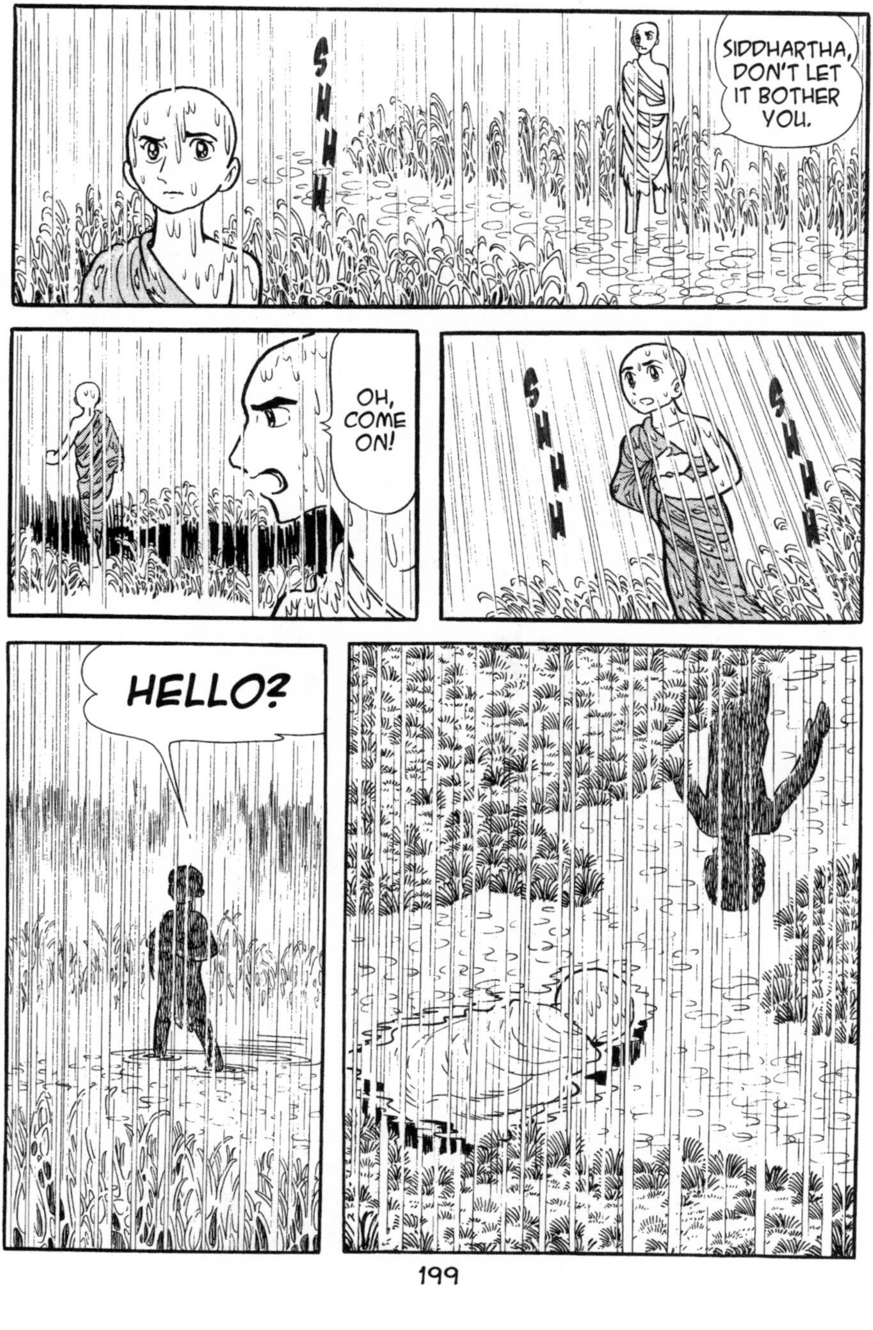
SHHH
SIDDHARTHA, DON'T LET IT BOTHER YOU.
OH, COME ON!
SHHH
SHHH
HELLO?

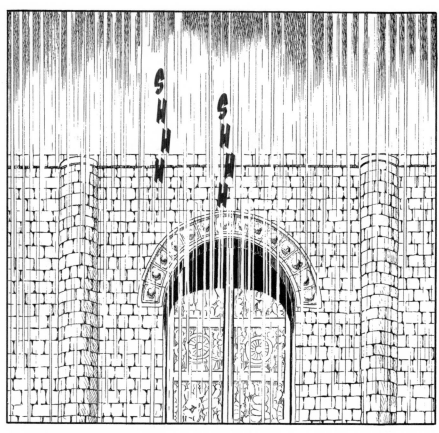

WE ARE SAMANNA. PLEASE OPEN THE GATES AND GRANT US SHELTER.

WE HAD TO CROSS A SEA OF MUD, AND THE CHILD IS ILL.

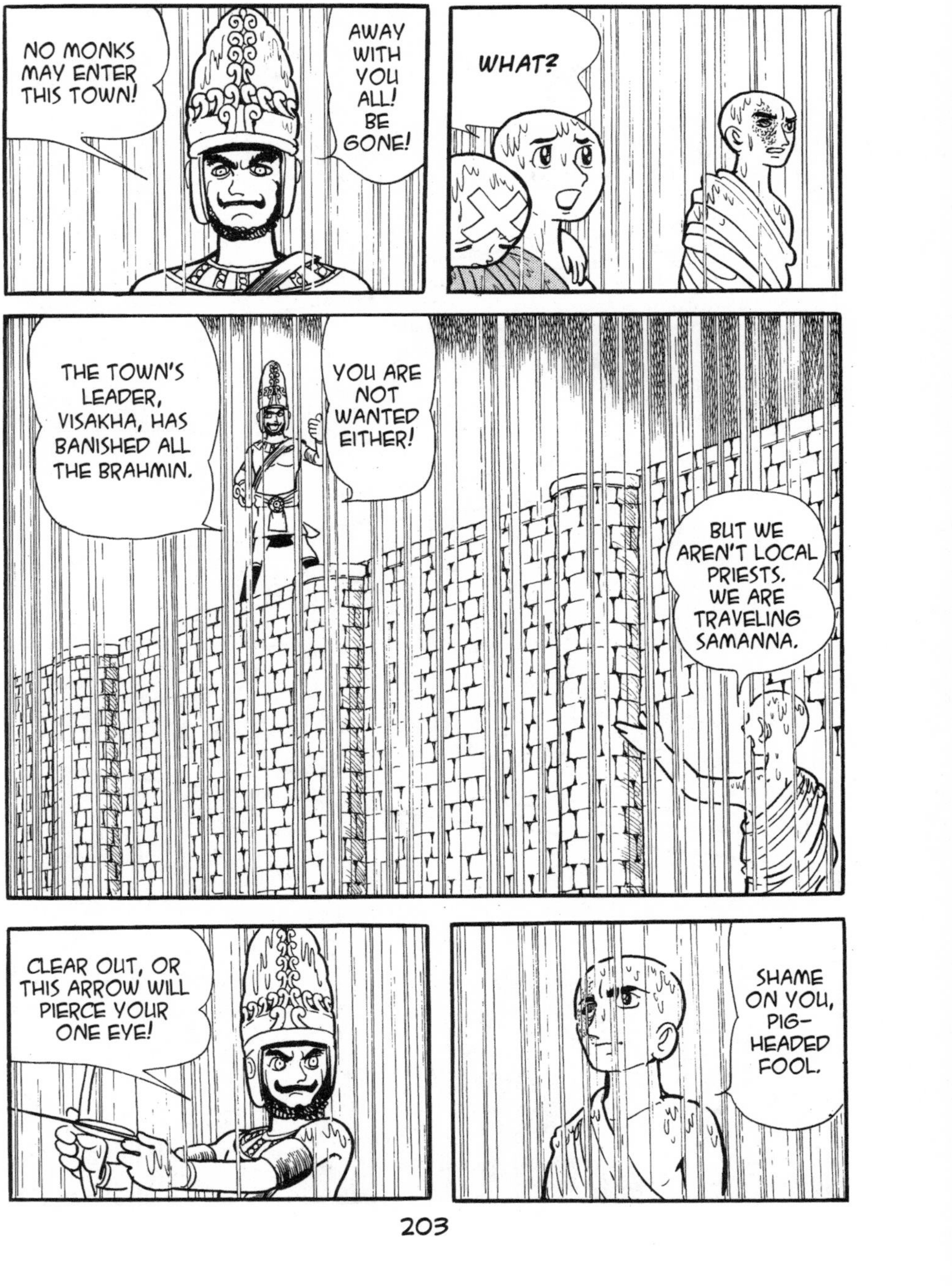
NO MONKS MAY ENTER THIS TOWN!
AWAY WITH YOU ALL! BE GONE!
WHAT?
THE TOWN'S LEADER, VISAKHA, HAS BANISHED ALL THE BRAHMIN.
YOU ARE NOT WANTED EITHER!
BUT WE AREN'T LOCAL PRIESTS. WE ARE TRAVELING SAMANNA.
CLEAR OUT, OR THIS ARROW WILL PIERCE YOUR ONE EYE!
SHAME ON YOU, PIG-HEADED FOOL.

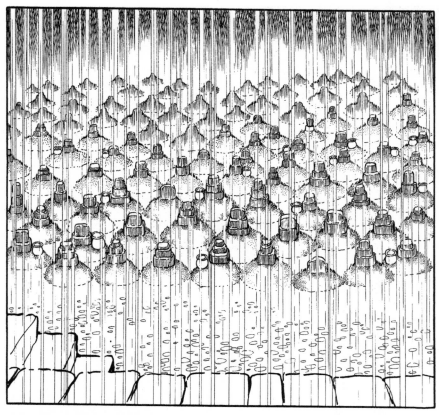

THESE ARE ALL GRAVES!

SOME-THING HAPPEN-ED HERE.

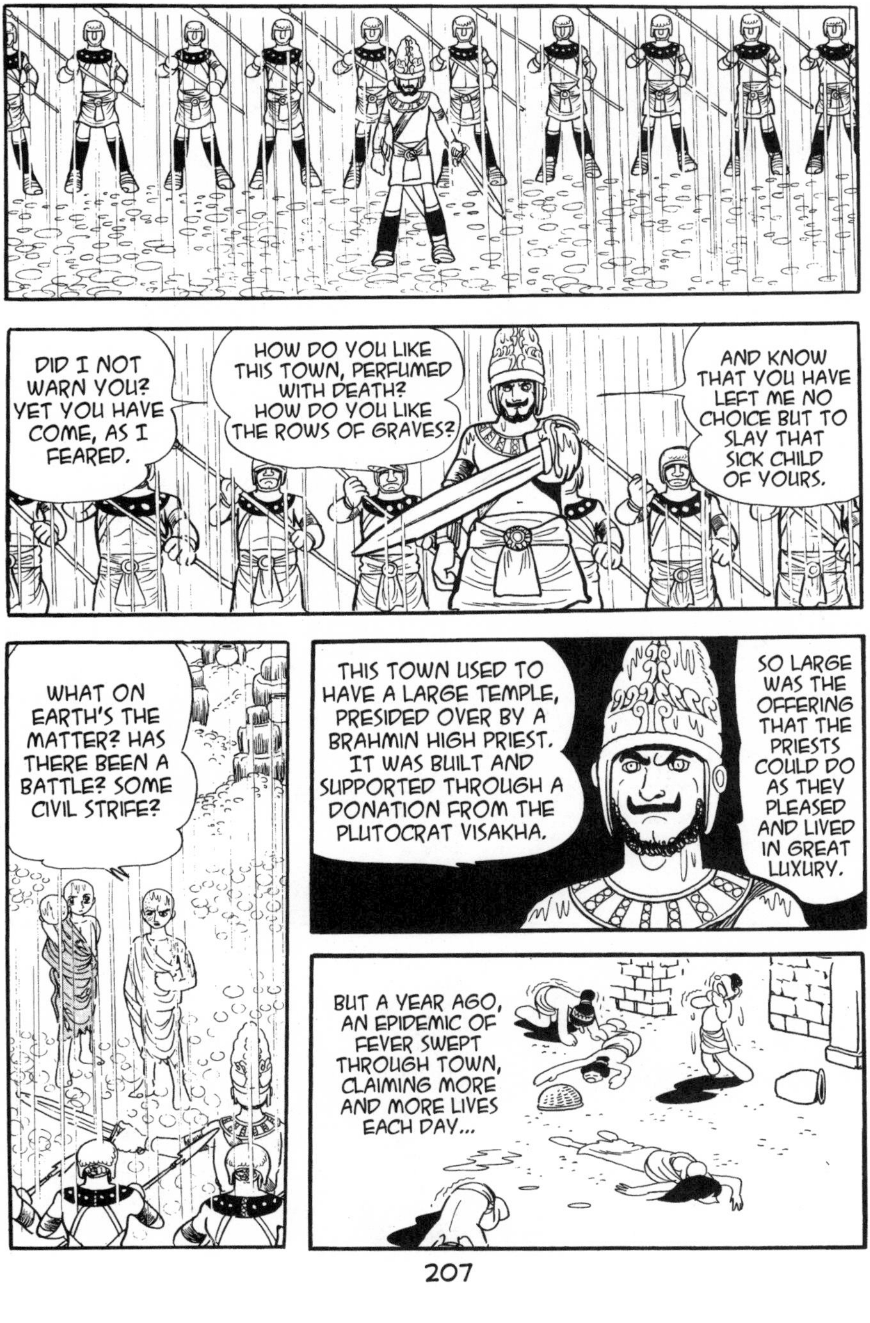
DID I NOT WARN YOU? YET YOU HAVE COME, AS I FEARED.
HOW DO YOU LIKE THIS TOWN, PERFUMED WITH DEATH? HOW DO YOU LIKE THE ROWS OF GRAVES?
AND KNOW THAT YOU HAVE LEFT ME NO CHOICE BUT TO SLAY THAT SICK CHILD OF YOURS.
WHAT ON EARTH'S THE MATTER? HAS THERE BEEN A BATTLE? SOME CIVIL STRIFE?
THIS TOWN USED TO HAVE A LARGE TEMPLE, PRESIDED OVER BY A BRAHMIN HIGH PRIEST. IT WAS BUILT AND SUPPORTED THROUGH A DONATION FROM THE PLUTOCRAT VISAKHA.
SO LARGE WAS THE OFFERING THAT THE PRIESTS COULD DO AS THEY PLEASED AND LIVED IN GREAT LUXURY.
BUT A YEAR AGO, AN EPIDEMIC OF FEVER SWEPT THROUGH TOWN, CLAIMING MORE AND MORE LIVES EACH DAY...

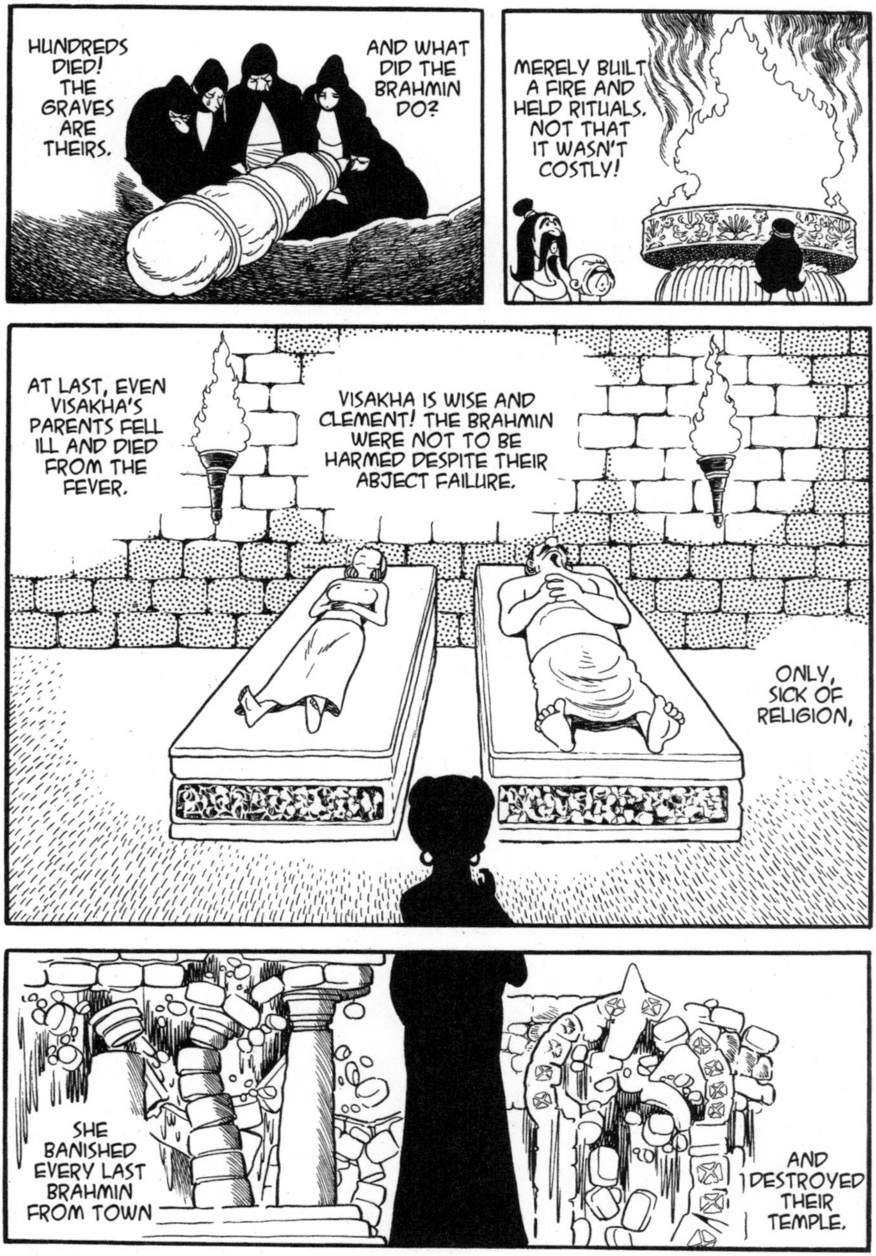
HUNDREDS DIED! THE GRAVES ARE THEIRS.
AND WHAT DID THE BRAHMIN DO?
MERELY BUILT A FIRE AND HELD RITUALS. NOT THAT IT WASN'T COSTLY!
AT LAST, EVEN VISAKHA'S PARENTS FELL ILL AND DIED FROM THE FEVER.
VISAKHA IS WISE AND CLEMENT! THE BRAHMIN WERE NOT TO BE HARMED DESPITE THEIR ABJECT FAILURE.
ONLY, SICK OF RELIGION,
SHE BANISHED EVERY LAST BRAHMIN FROM TOWN
AND DESTROYED THEIR TEMPLE.

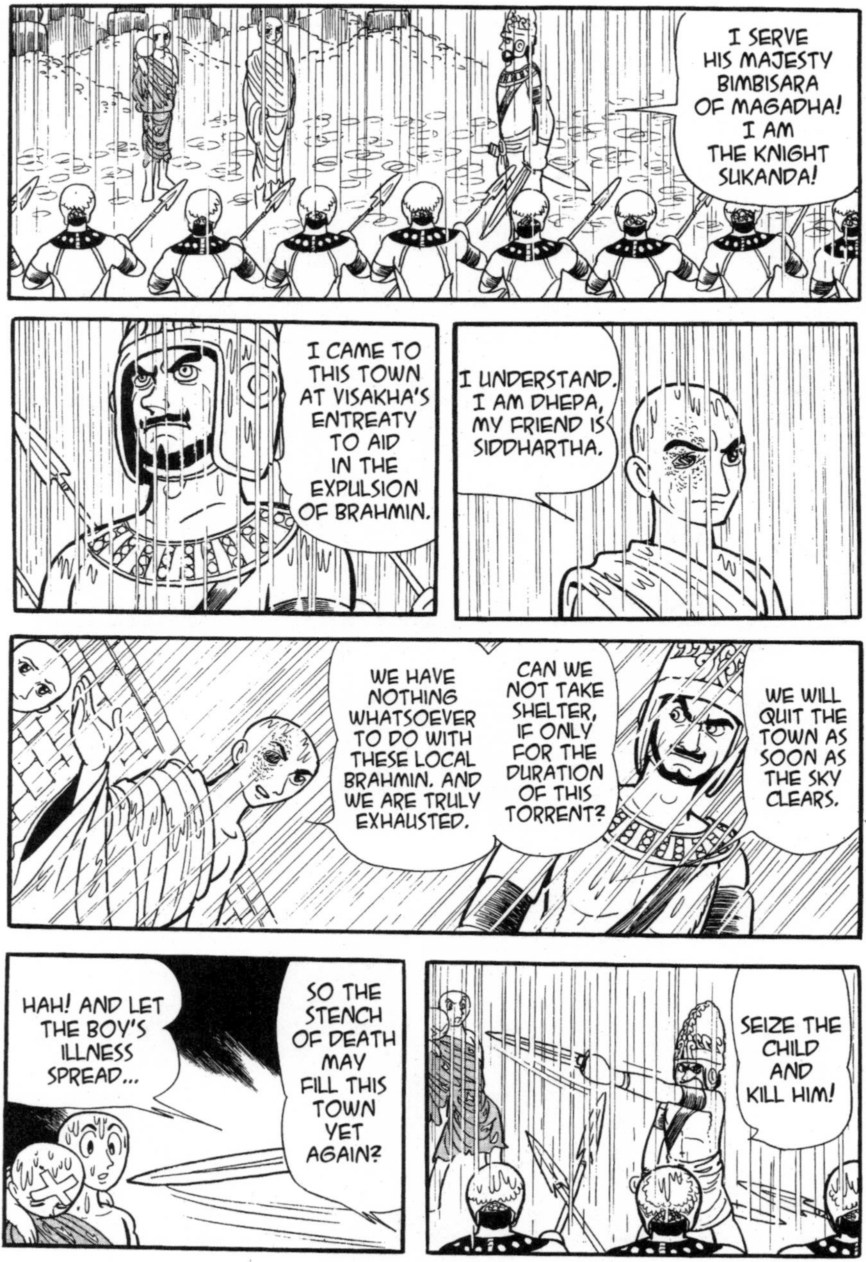
I SERVE HIS MAJESTY BIMBISARA OF MAGADHA! I AM THE KNIGHT SUKANDA!
I CAME TO THIS TOWN AT VISAKHA'S ENTREATY TO AID IN THE EXPULSION OF BRAHMIN.
I UNDERSTAND. I AM DHEPA, MY FRIEND IS SIDDHARTHA.
WE HAVE NOTHING WHATSOEVER TO DO WITH THESE LOCAL BRAHMIN. AND WE ARE TRULY EXHAUSTED.
CAN WE NOT TAKE SHELTER, IF ONLY FOR THE DURATION OF THIS TORRENT?
WE WILL QUIT THE TOWN AS SOON AS THE SKY CLEARS.
HAH! AND LET THE BOY'S ILLNESS SPREAD...
SO THE STENCH OF DEATH MAY FILL THIS TOWN YET AGAIN?
SEIZE THE CHILD AND KILL HIM!

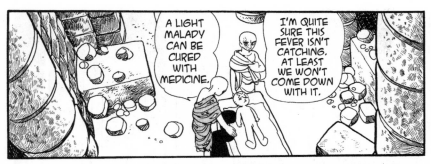

A LIGHT MALADY CAN BE CURED WITH MEDICINE.

I'M QUITE SURE THIS FEVER ISN'T CATCHING. AT LEAST WE WON'T COME DOWN WITH IT.

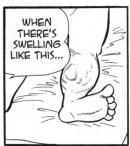

WHEN THERE'S SWELLING LIKE THIS...

THE PUS HAS TO BE DRAWN OUT, AND THE WOUND SEARED WITH HOT IRON. EATING BLUE MOLD HELPS, TOO.

DHEPA, COULD YOU GET A FIRE GOING AT THAT HEARTH?

YOU BETTER KNOW WHAT YOU'RE TALKING ABOUT. THAT GUY MEANT IT ABOUT KILLING YOU.

CAN YOU GET THOSE? I'LL COLLECT THE MOLD.

I NEED A BROKEN SPEAR, A LARGE POT, AND SOME CLOTHS.

213

214

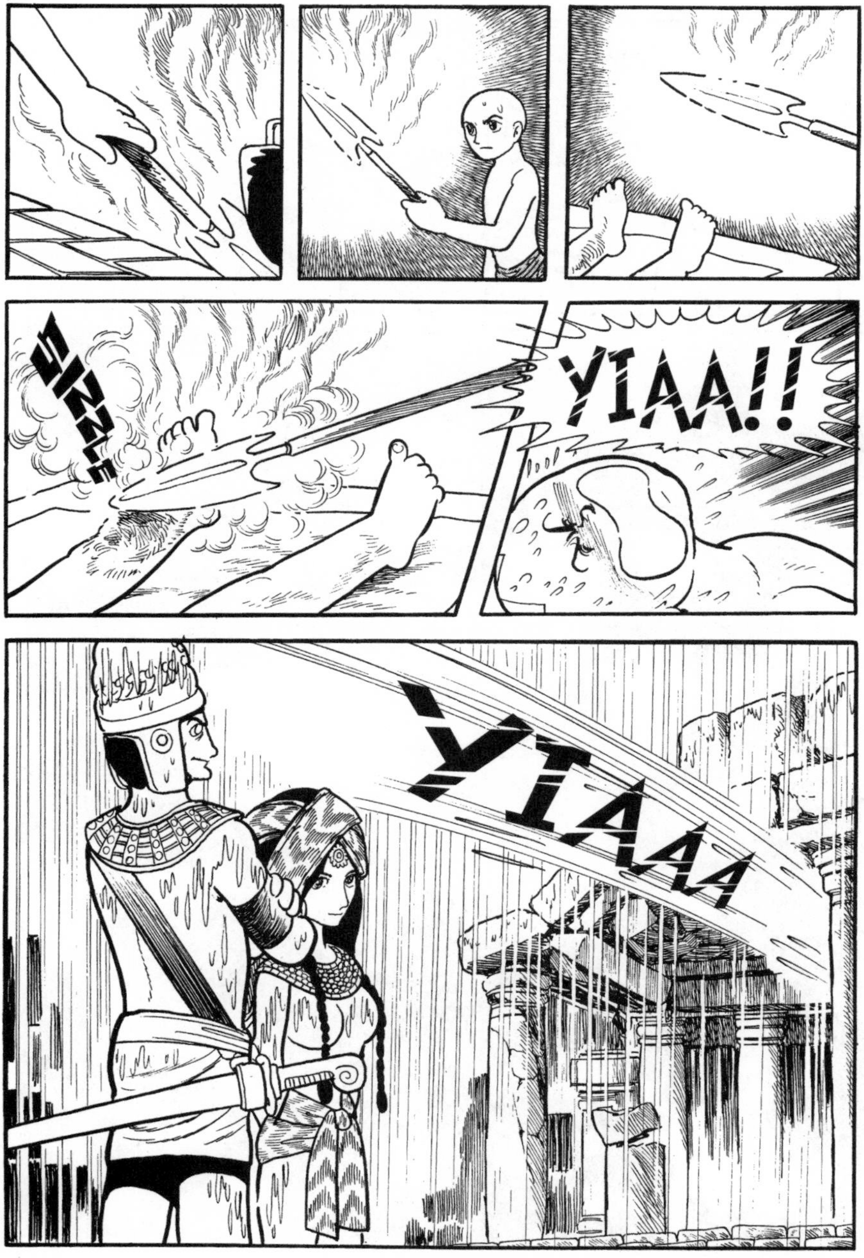
SIZZLE
YIAA!!
YIAAA

218

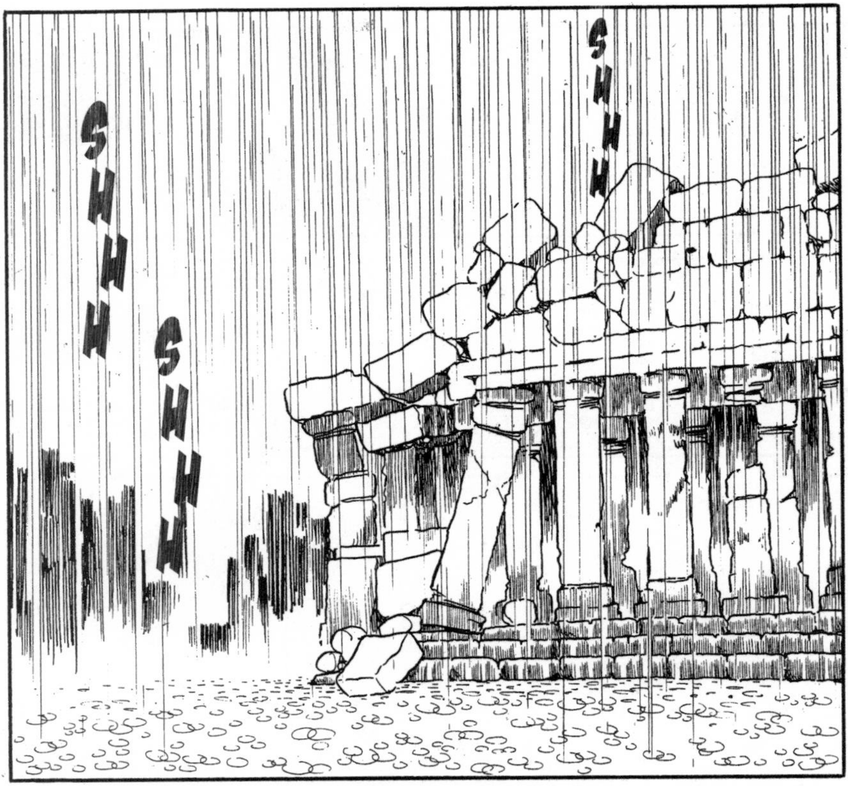
SHHHH
SHHHH
SHHH
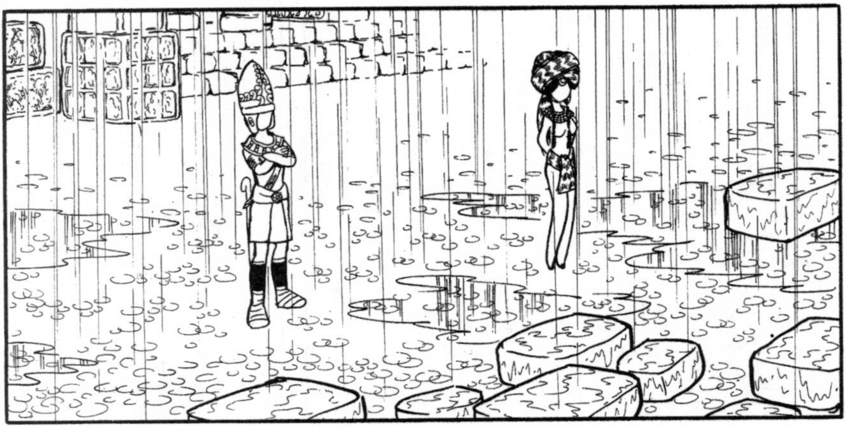

DO YOU THINK THAT MONK SIDDHARTHA CAN CURE THE SICK?

SHHH

HE SEEMS TO THINK HE CAN.

SHHH

VISAKHA, YOU CANNOT STAND HERE ALL NIGHT IN THIS RAIN. YOU'LL FALL ILL!

OH? BUT I WORRY FOR THE YOUNG MONK. YOUR CONCERN IS UNWARRANTED.

YOU JEST!!

MY, HOW SCARY YOU LOOK.

SIR,

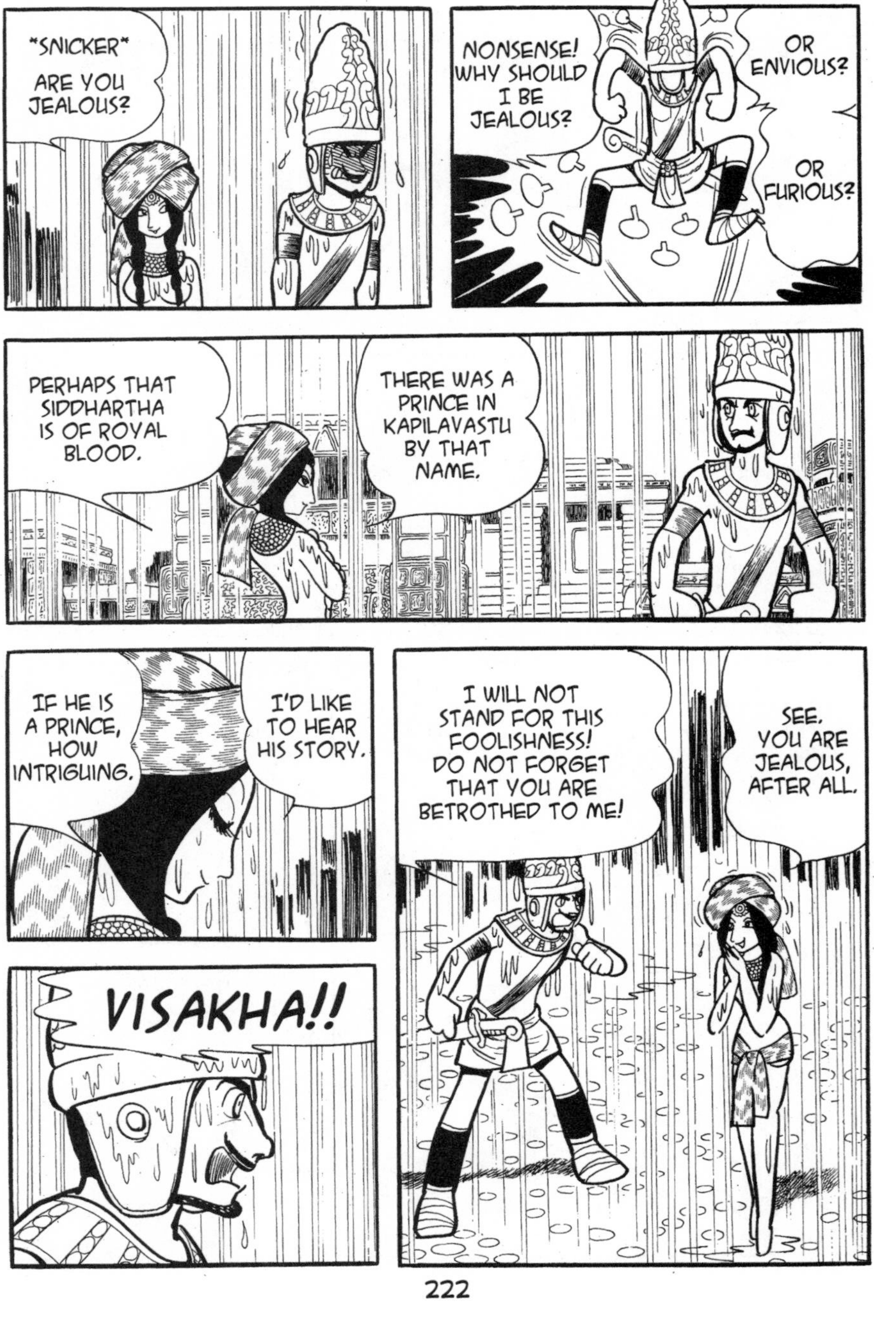
SNICKER
ARE YOU JEALOUS?
NONSENSE! WHY SHOULD I BE JEALOUS?
OR ENVIOUS?
OR FURIOUS?
PERHAPS THAT SIDDHARTHA IS OF ROYAL BLOOD.
THERE WAS A PRINCE IN KAPILAVASTU BY THAT NAME.
IF HE IS A PRINCE, HOW INTRIGUING.
I'D LIKE TO HEAR HIS STORY.
VISAKHA!!
I WILL NOT STAND FOR THIS FOOLISHNESS! DO NOT FORGET THAT YOU ARE BETROTHED TO ME!
SEE. YOU ARE JEALOUS, AFTER ALL.

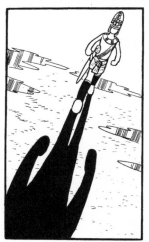

DAY HAS BROKEN, SIDDHARTHA. STEP FORTH!

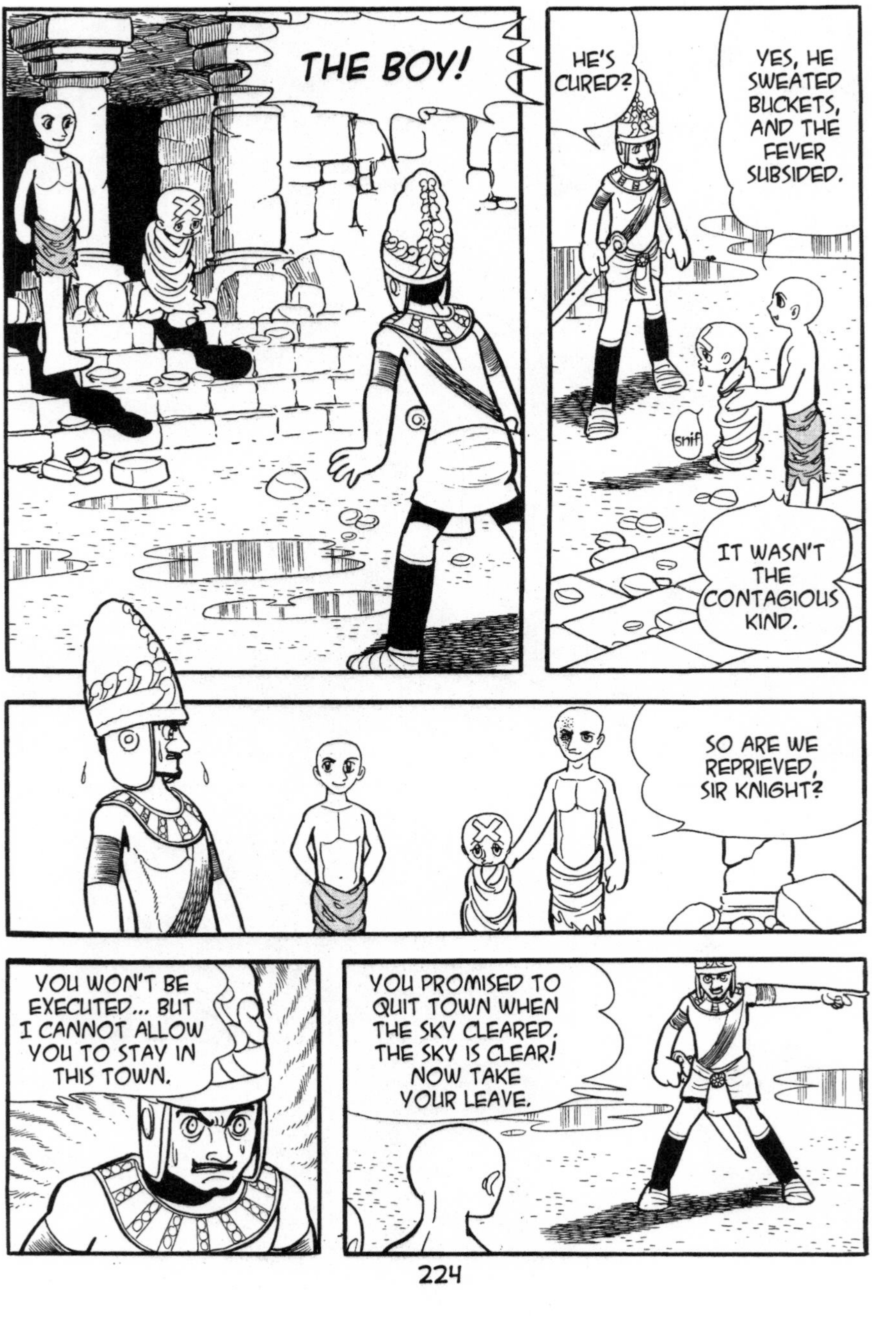
THE BOY!
HE'S CURED?
YES, HE SWEATED BUCKETS, AND THE FEVER SUBSIDED.
snif
IT WASN'T THE CONTAGIOUS KIND.
SO ARE WE REPRIEVED, SIR KNIGHT?
YOU WON'T BE EXECUTED... BUT I CANNOT ALLOW YOU TO STAY IN THIS TOWN.
YOU PROMISED TO QUIT TOWN WHEN THE SKY CLEARED. THE SKY IS CLEAR! NOW TAKE YOUR LEAVE.

WHAT ARE YOU WAITING FOR? I SAID GO!

BUT WE BARELY SLEPT LAST NIGHT! GIVE US SOME TIME TO REST!

B-BUT VISAKHA...

YOU ARE VERY KIND.

WHY DRIVE THEM AWAY LIKE THAT, SUKANDA?

TRAVELERS, I WELCOME YOU ALL TO MY MANSION. HOW ABOUT SOME BREAKFAST?

COME IN. MY NAME IS VISAKHA.

MINE IS THE WEALTHIEST HOUSE IN PANDAWA.

THE KNIGHT HAS TOLD US OF YOU.

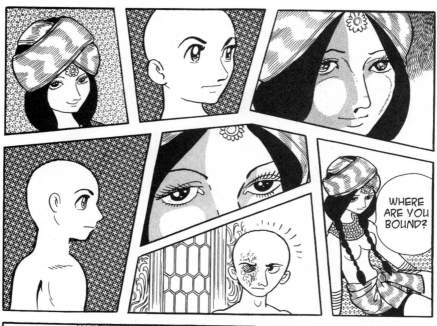

WHERE ARE YOU BOUND?

WE MAKE FOR THE CAPITAL, RAJGRIHA, OF THE KINGDOM OF MAGADHA.

AH, RAJGRIHA. YOU WILL FIND MANY FAMOUS BRAHMIN, AND SAMANNA AND SCHOLARS THERE.

PERHAPS THERE WE WILL FIND WHAT WE SEEK.

AND WHAT DO YOU SEEK?

227

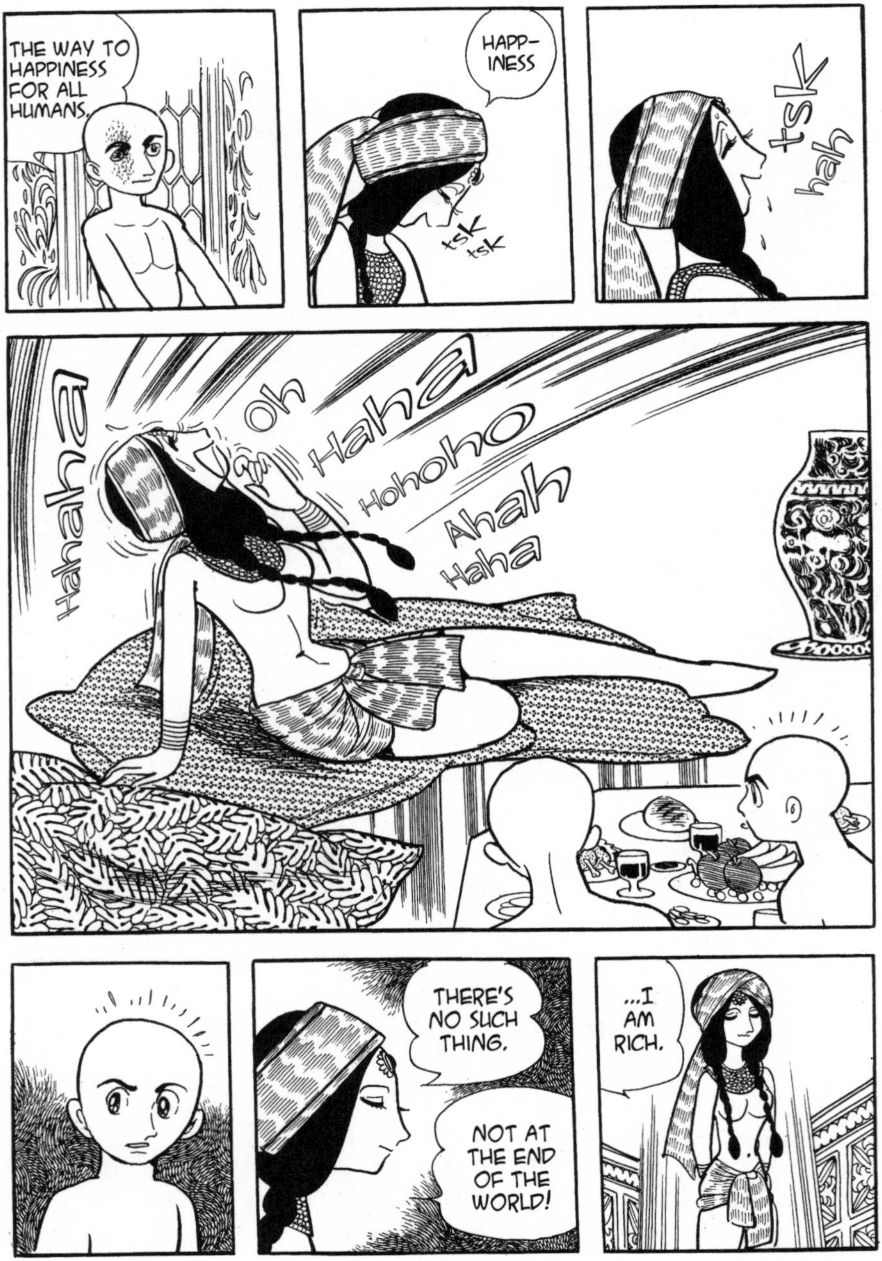

THE WAY TO HAPPINESS FOR ALL HUMANS.
HAPP-INESS
tsk tsk
tsk
hah
Hahaha
Oh
Haha
Hohoho
Ahah
Haha
THERE'S NO SUCH THING.
NOT AT THE END OF THE WORLD!
...I AM RICH.

229

THEN A FAREWELL TOAST.

I DO NOT DRINK!

HOW VERY UPRIGHT! IT'S JUST FRUIT WINE!

MARCH!

LEFT LEFT

LEFT

WHAT IS IT WITH THE SACK?

RIGHT

LEFTOVERS. LUNCH FOR A WEEK.

LEFT

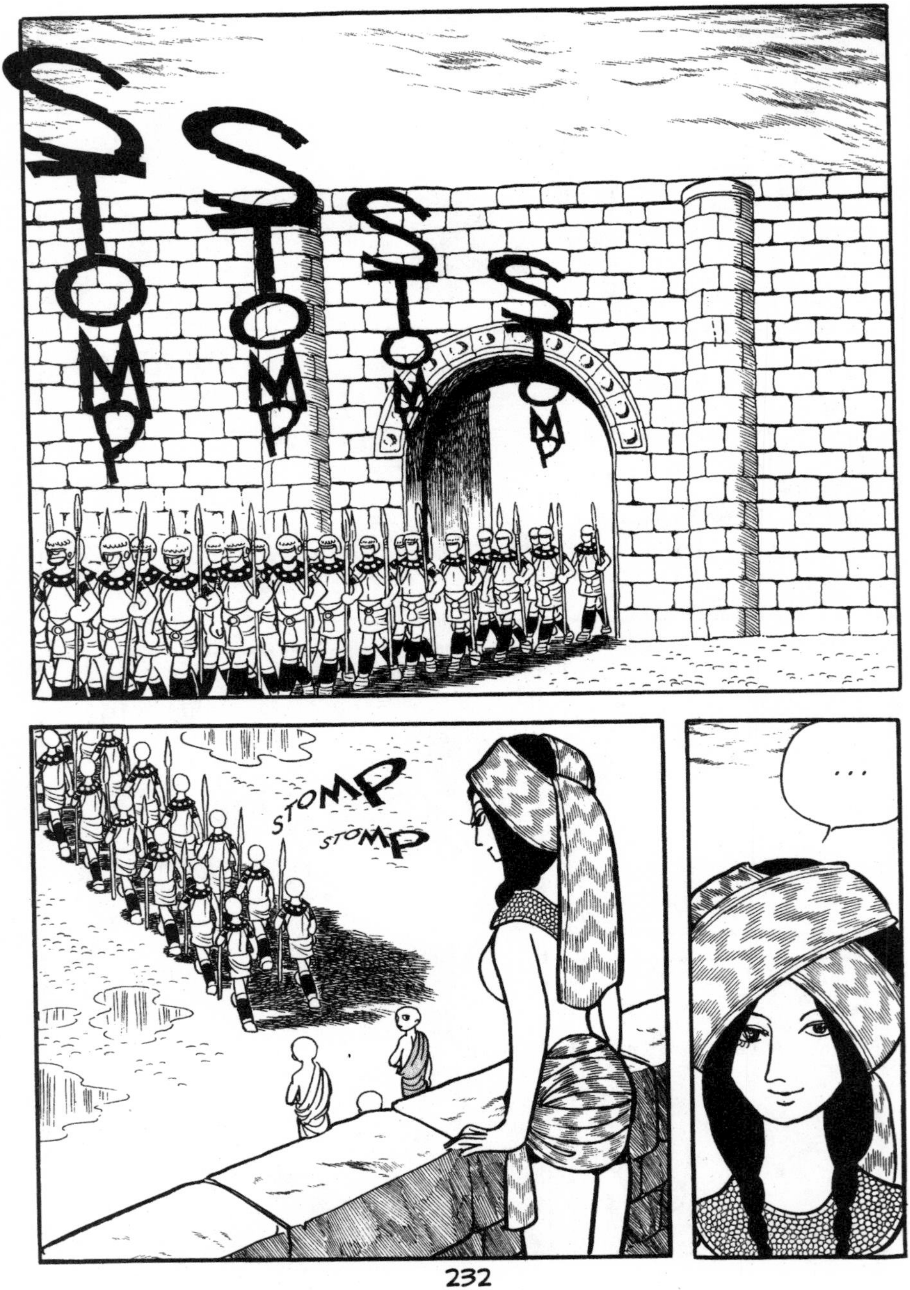
STOMP
STOMP
STOMP
STOMP
STOMP
STOMP
...

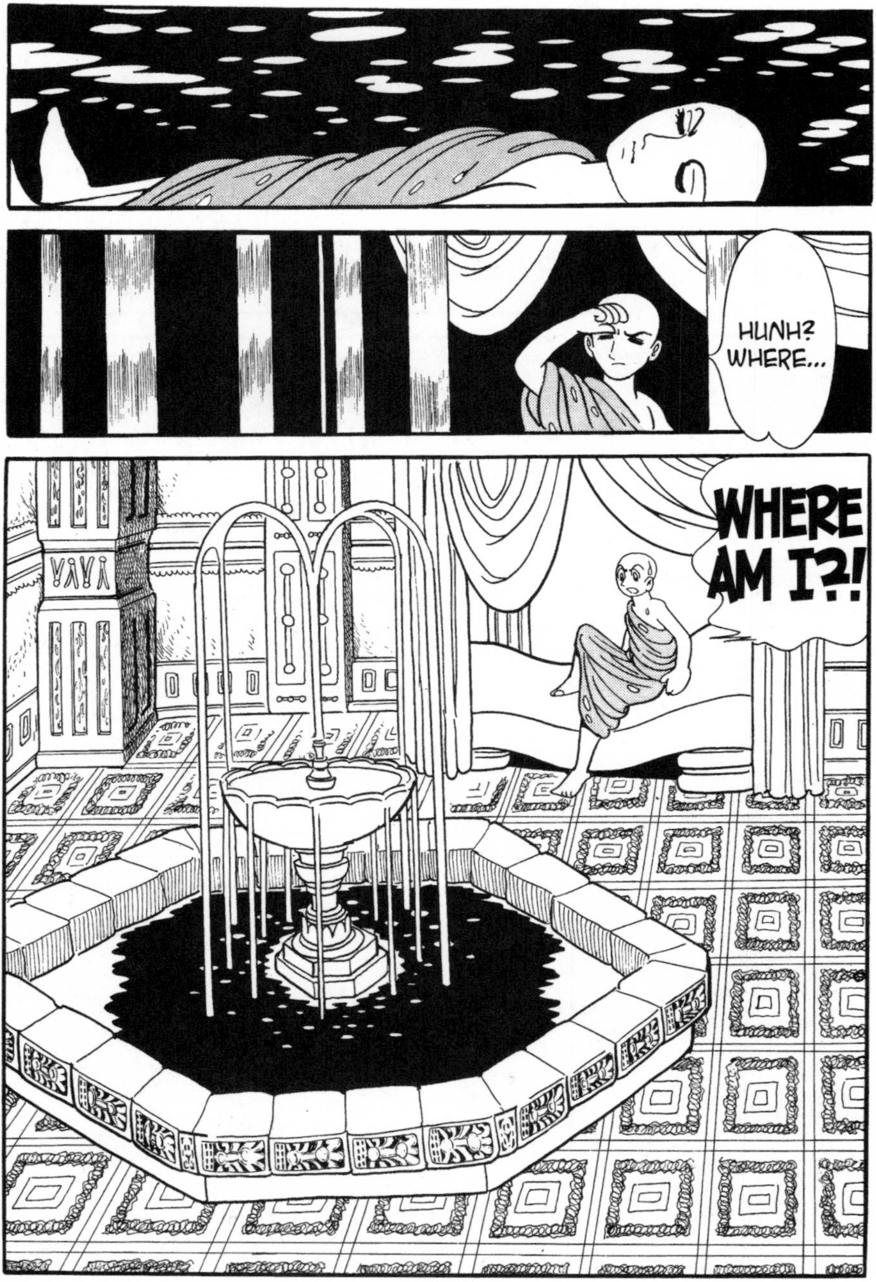
HUNH? WHERE...
WHERE AM I?!

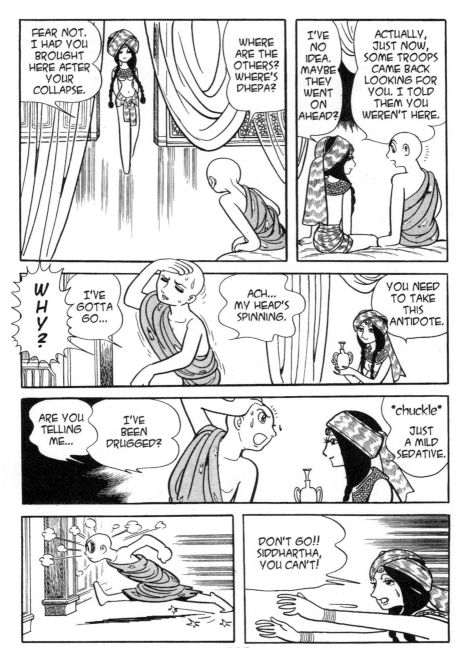

235

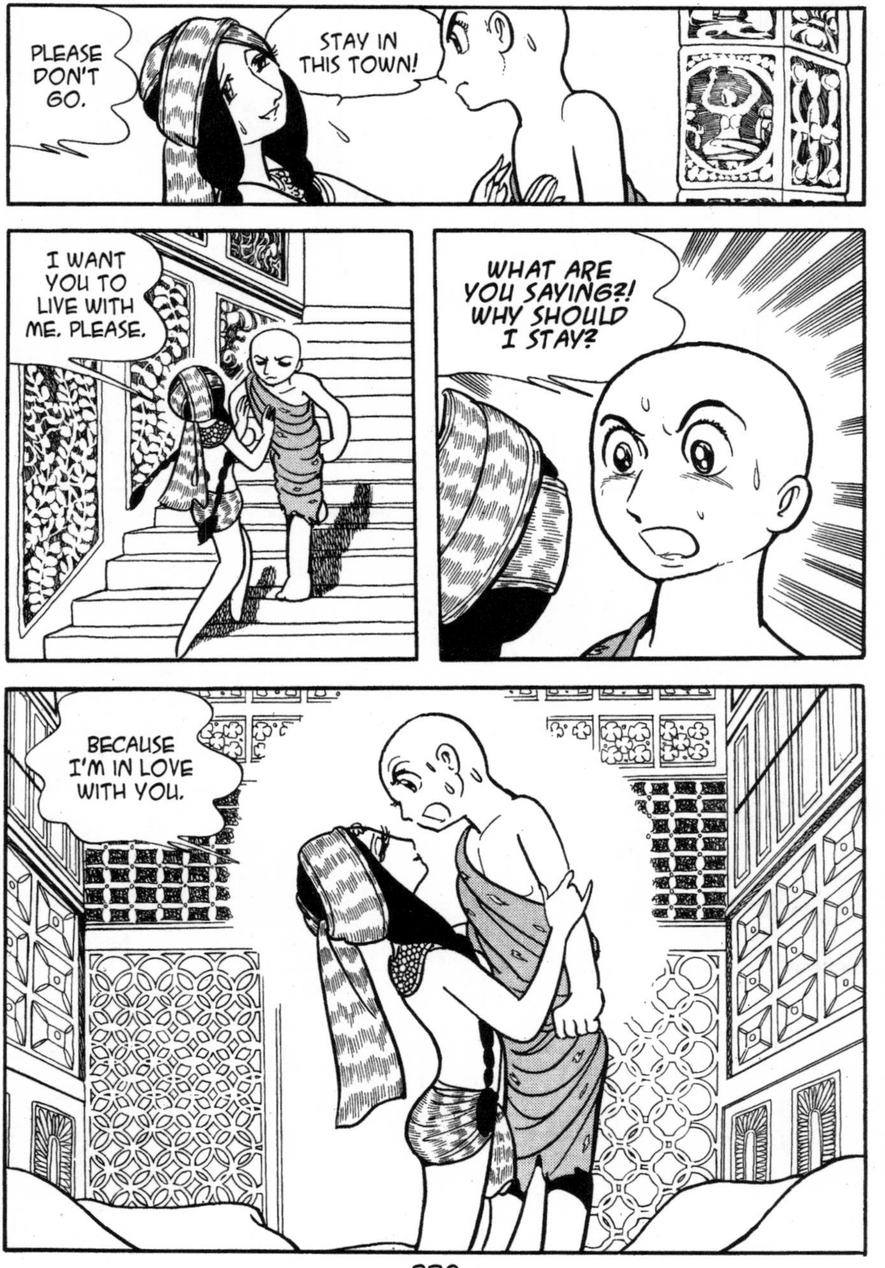
PLEASE DON'T GO.
STAY IN THIS TOWN!
I WANT YOU TO LIVE WITH ME. PLEASE.
WHAT ARE YOU SAYING?! WHY SHOULD I STAY?
BECAUSE I'M IN LOVE WITH YOU.

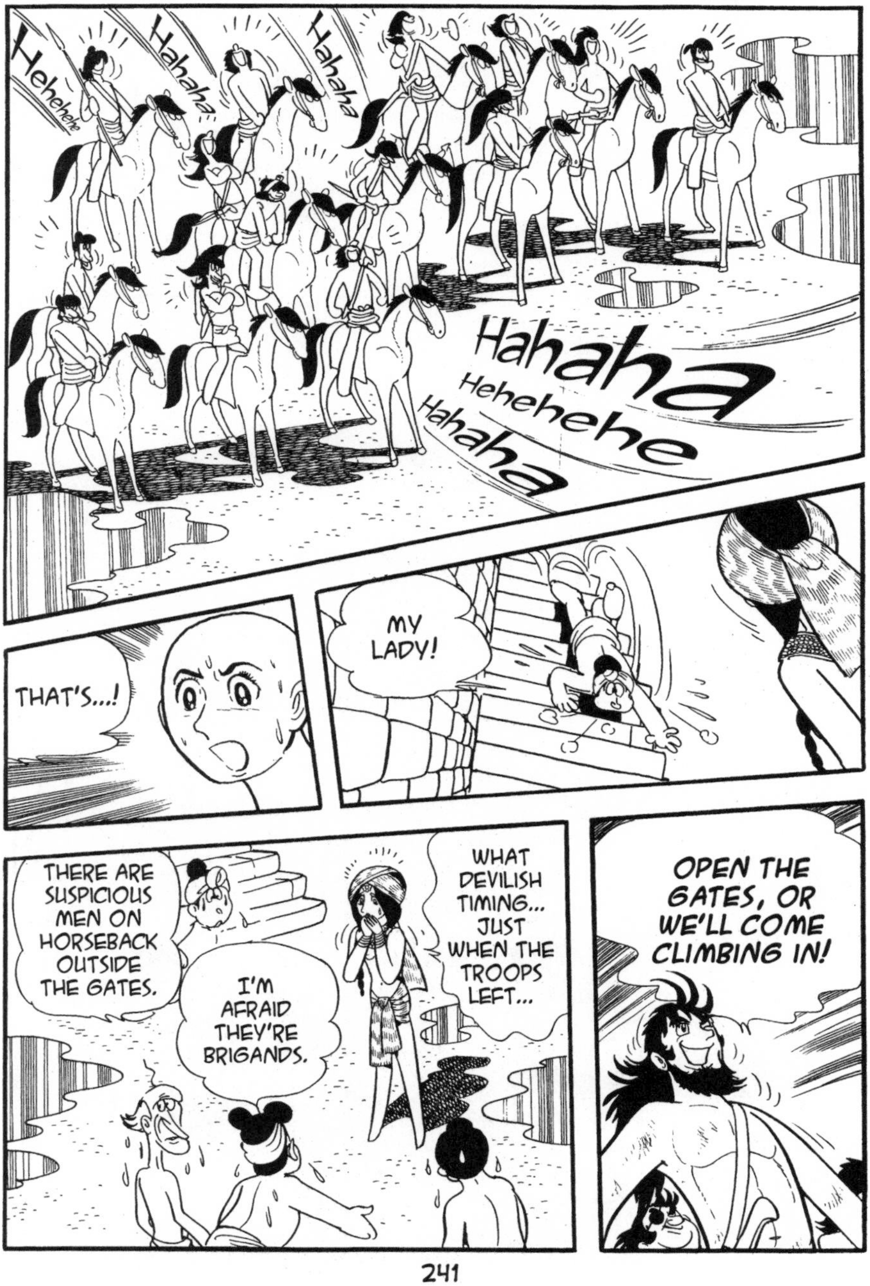
Hehehehe
Hahaha
Hahaha
Hahaha
Hehehehe
Hahaha
THAT'S...!
MY LADY!
THERE ARE SUSPICIOUS MEN ON HORSEBACK OUTSIDE THE GATES.
I'M AFRAID THEY'RE BRIGANDS.
WHAT DEVILISH TIMING... JUST WHEN THE TROOPS LEFT...
OPEN THE GATES, OR WE'LL COME CLIMBING IN!

I KNOW THIS BUNCH.

THEY'RE BANDITS WHO'VE BEEN PURSUING ME.

THEY'LL WREAK HAVOC IF YOU LET THEM IN.

IF I GO WITH THEM, YOUR TOWN WILL BE SPARED.

SO I GO.

NO, YOU DON'T!

I WILL NOT LET YOU LEAVE.

THEN THEY'LL REDUCE THE TOWN TO RUINS.

HUM HO

HUM HO

ROAR

ROAR

YAAA

THEY'RE USING THE STONE STEPS WE BUILT. HERE THEY COME! HIDE!

HIDE, VISAKHA!

YAAA

CLANGE

245

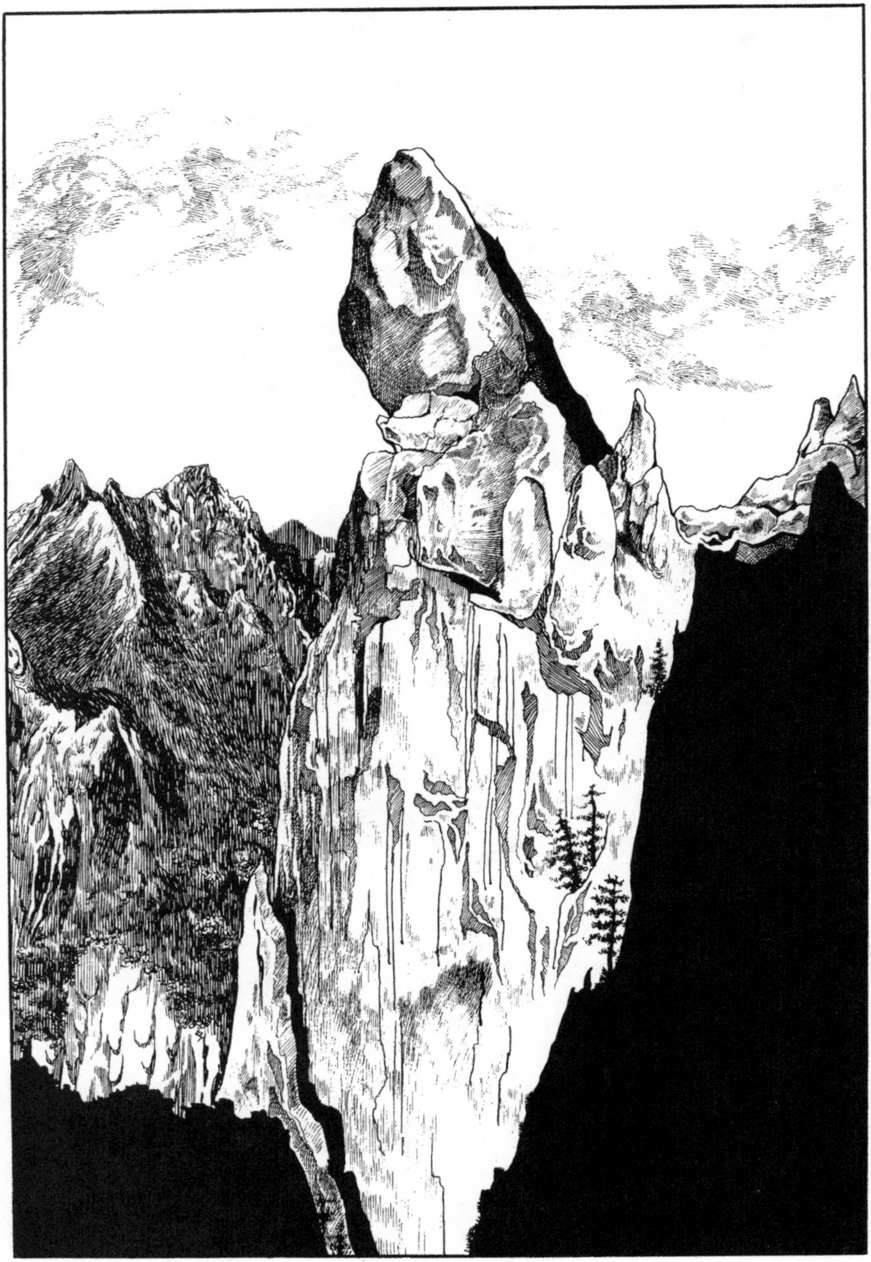

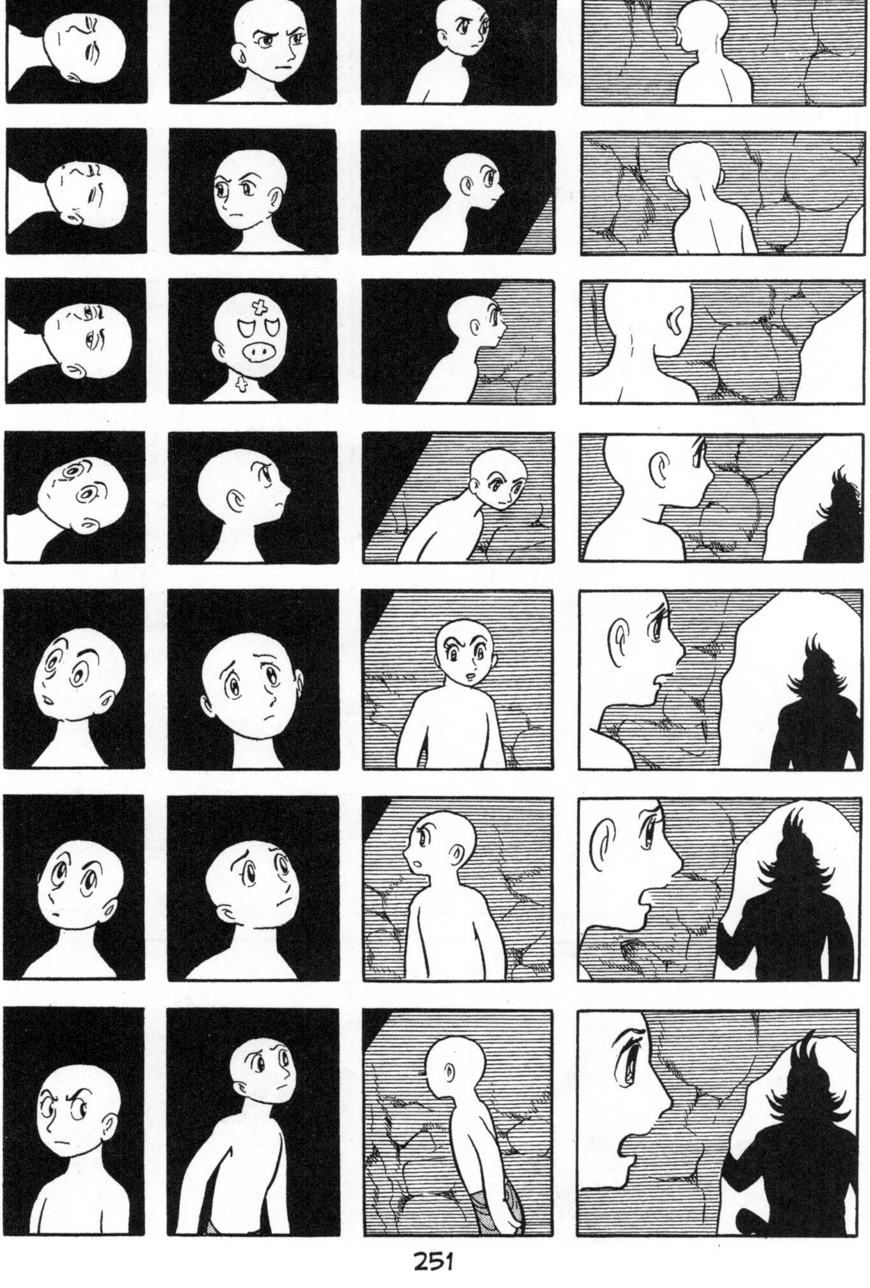

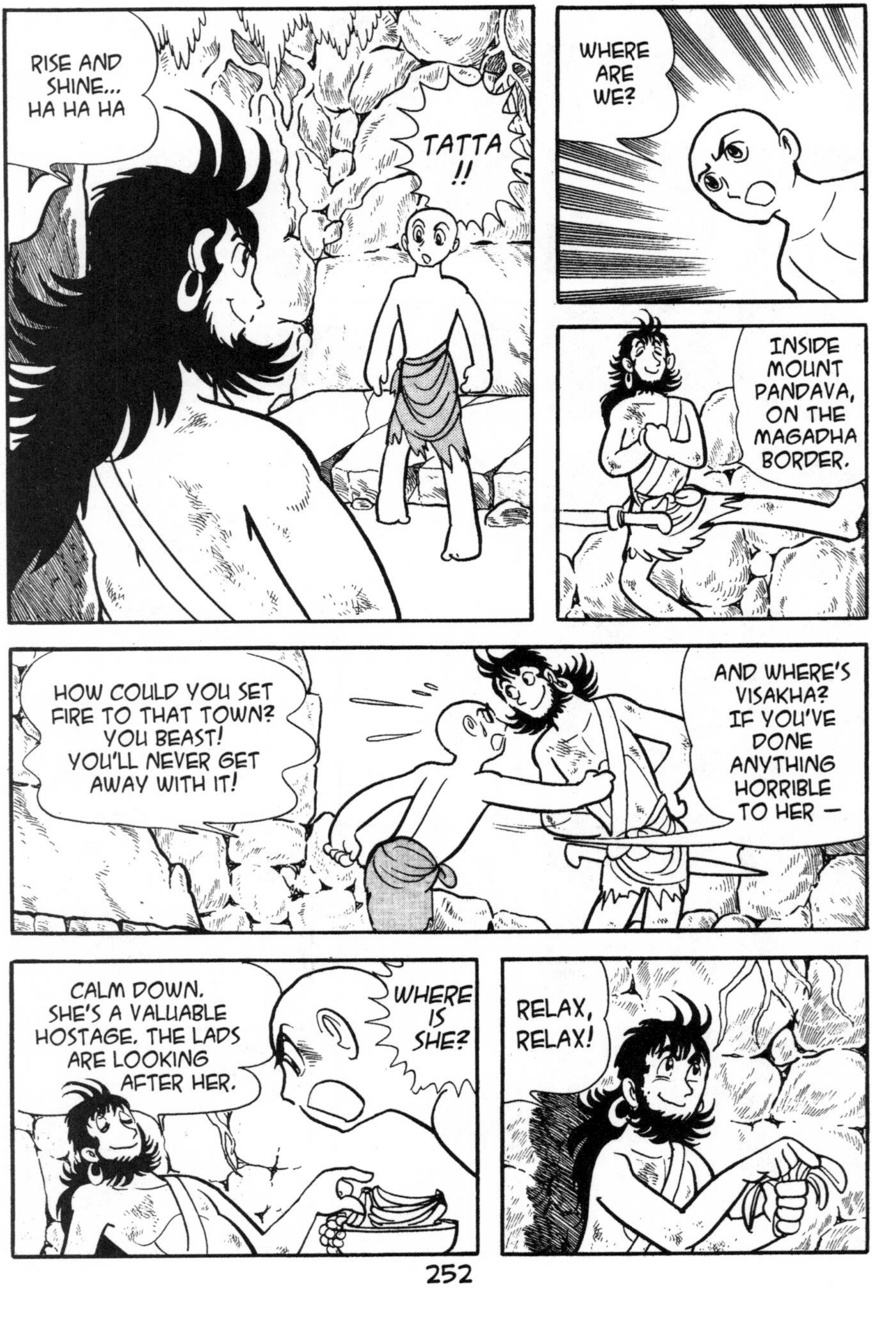
RISE AND SHINE... HA HA HA
TATTA !!
WHERE ARE WE?
INSIDE MOUNT PANDAVA, ON THE MAGADHA BORDER.
HOW COULD YOU SET FIRE TO THAT TOWN? YOU BEAST! YOU'LL NEVER GET AWAY WITH IT!
AND WHERE'S VISAKHA? IF YOU'VE DONE ANYTHING HORRIBLE TO HER —
CALM DOWN. SHE'S A VALUABLE HOSTAGE. THE LADS ARE LOOKING AFTER HER.
WHERE IS SHE?
RELAX, RELAX!

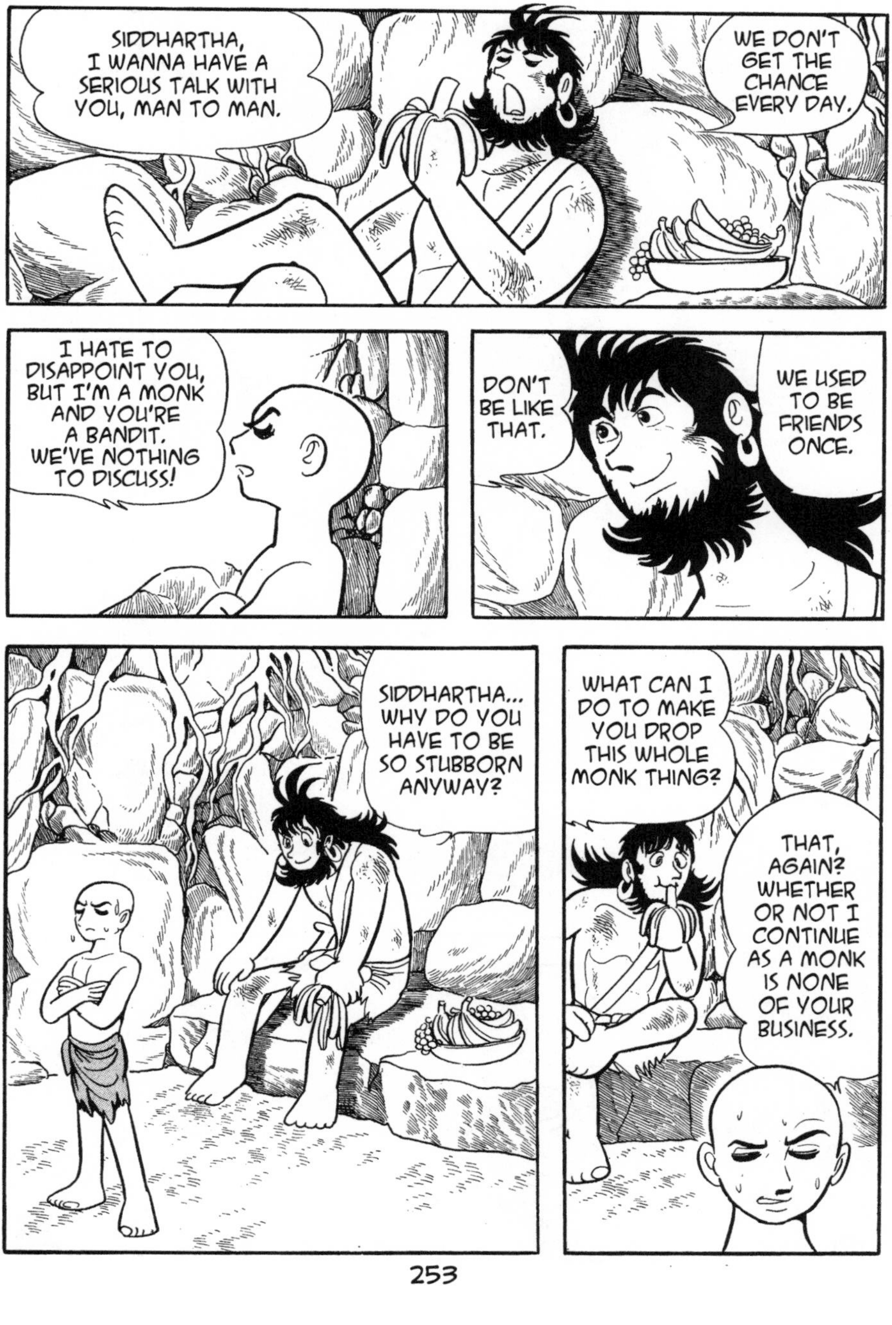
SIDDHARTHA, I WANNA HAVE A SERIOUS TALK WITH YOU, MAN TO MAN.
WE DON'T GET THE CHANCE EVERY DAY.
I HATE TO DISAPPOINT YOU, BUT I'M A MONK AND YOU'RE A BANDIT. WE'VE NOTHING TO DISCUSS!
DON'T BE LIKE THAT.
WE USED TO BE FRIENDS ONCE.
SIDDHARTHA... WHY DO YOU HAVE TO BE SO STUBBORN ANYWAY?
WHAT CAN I DO TO MAKE YOU DROP THIS WHOLE MONK THING?
THAT, AGAIN? WHETHER OR NOT I CONTINUE AS A MONK IS NONE OF YOUR BUSINESS.

254

255

256

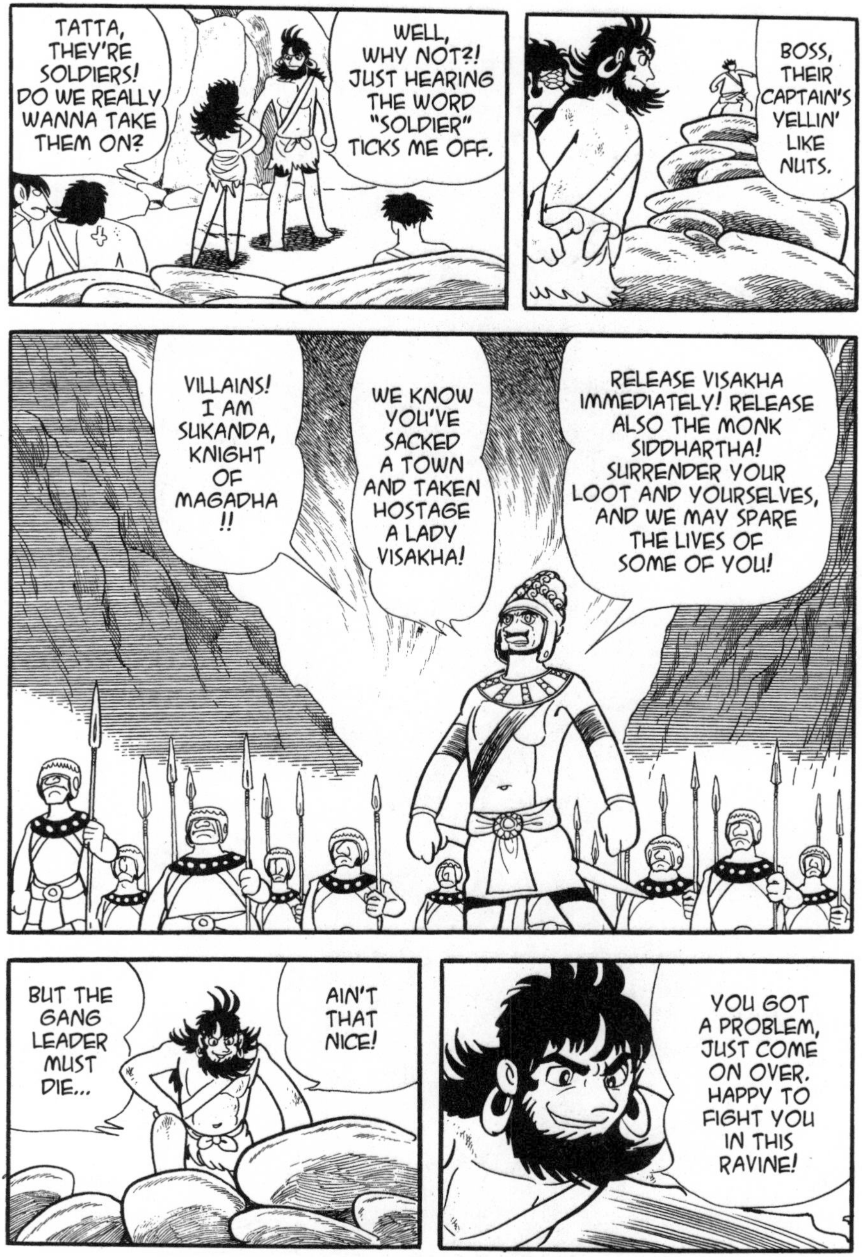
TATTA, THEY'RE SOLDIERS! DO WE REALLY WANNA TAKE THEM ON?
WELL, WHY NOT?! JUST HEARING THE WORD "SOLDIER" TICKS ME OFF.
BOSS, THEIR CAPTAIN'S YELLIN' LIKE NUTS.
VILLAINS! I AM SUKANDA, KNIGHT OF MAGADHA !!
WE KNOW YOU'VE SACKED A TOWN AND TAKEN HOSTAGE A LADY VISAKHA!
RELEASE VISAKHA IMMEDIATELY! RELEASE ALSO THE MONK SIDDHARTHA! SURRENDER YOUR LOOT AND YOURSELVES, AND WE MAY SPARE THE LIVES OF SOME OF YOU!
BUT THE GANG LEADER MUST DIE...
AIN'T THAT NICE!
YOU GOT A PROBLEM, JUST COME ON OVER. HAPPY TO FIGHT YOU IN THIS RAVINE!

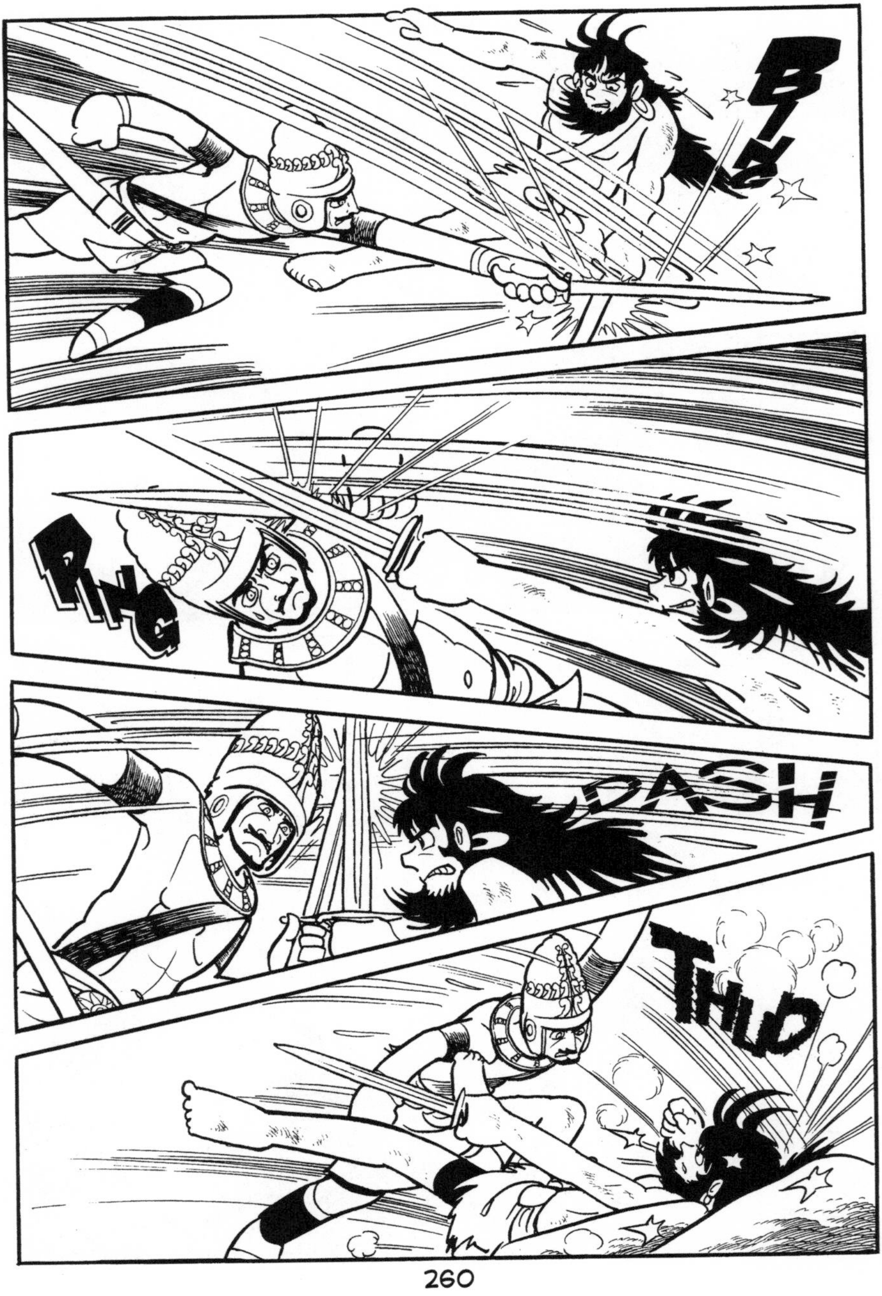
BING
RING
DASH!
THUD

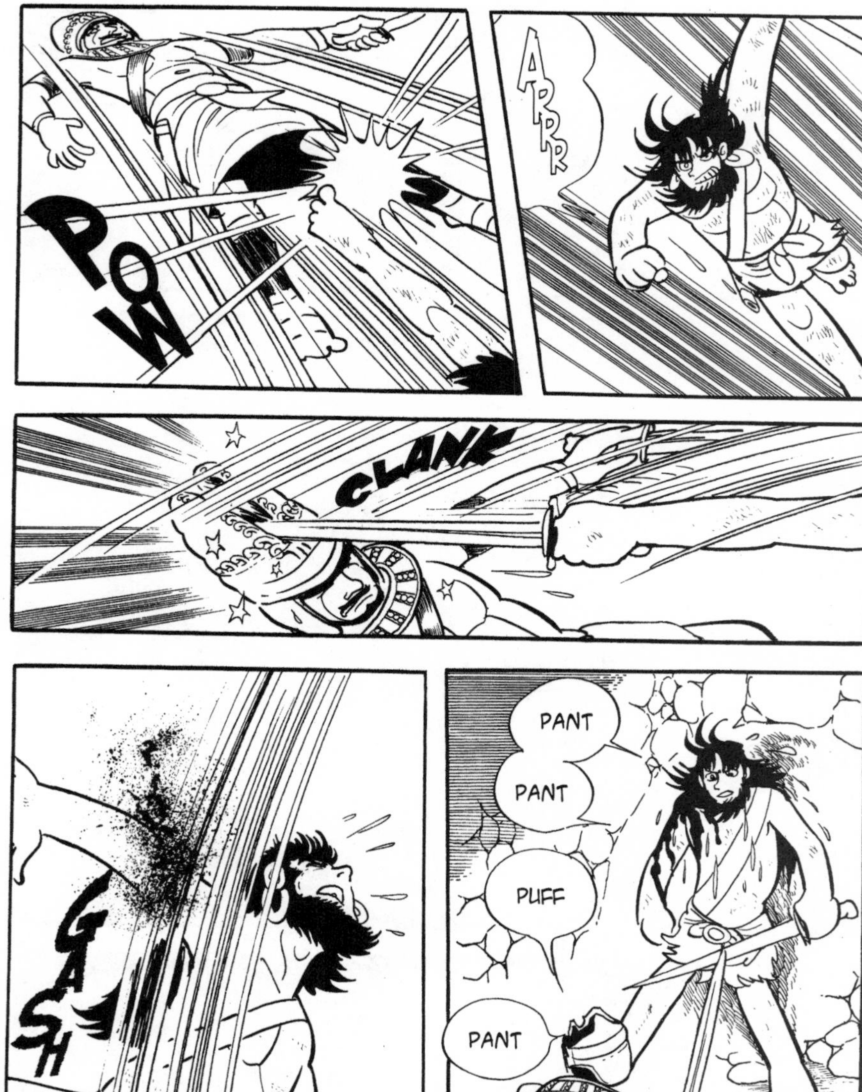
POW
ARRR
CLANK
GASH
PANT
PANT
PUFF
PANT

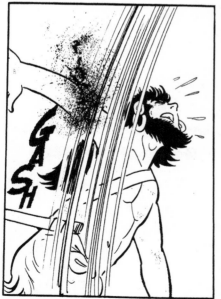

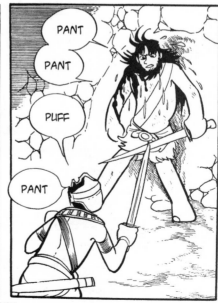

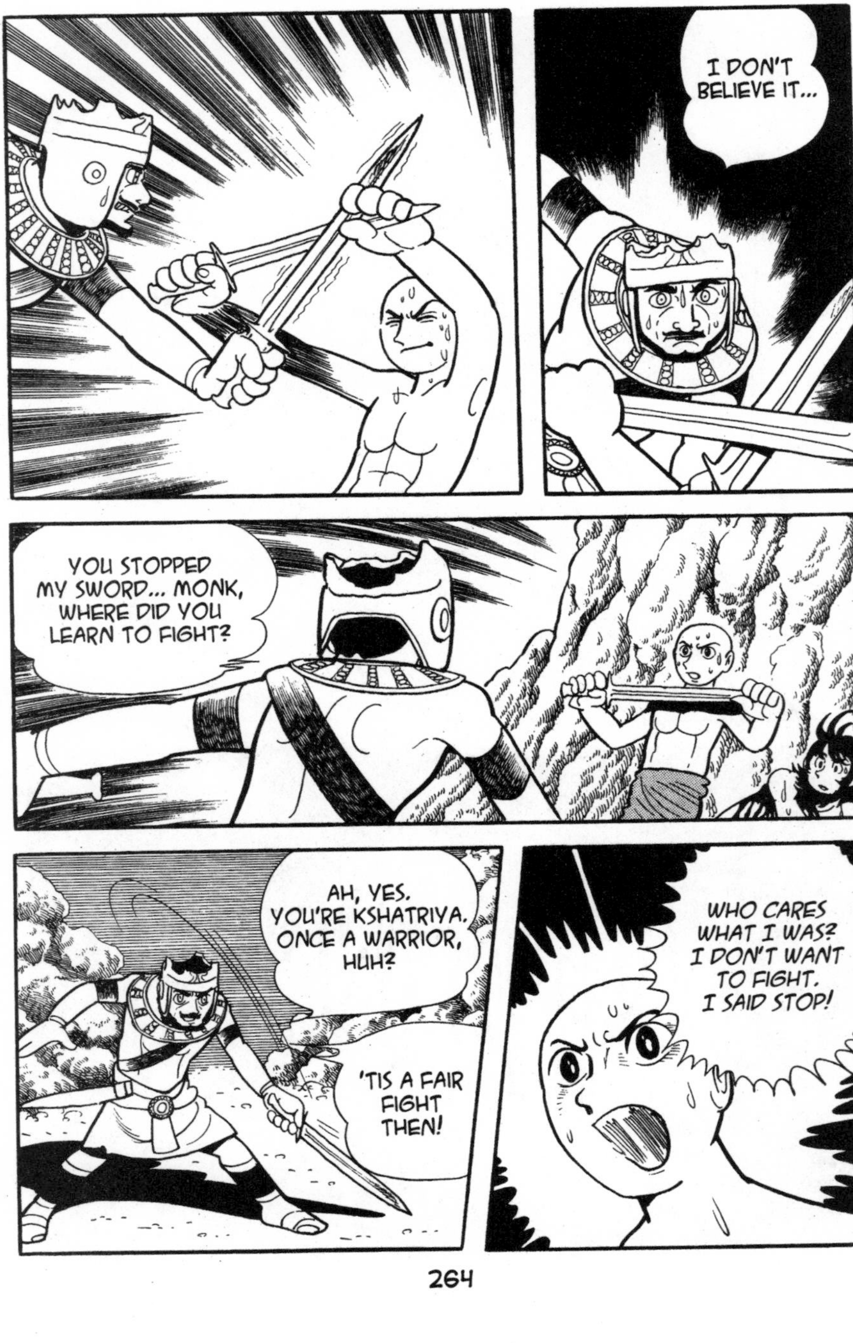
I DON'T BELIEVE IT...
YOU STOPPED MY SWORD... MONK, WHERE DID YOU LEARN TO FIGHT?
AH, YES. YOU'RE KSHATRIYA. ONCE A WARRIOR, HUH?
'TIS A FAIR FIGHT THEN!
WHO CARES WHAT I WAS? I DON'T WANT TO FIGHT. I SAID STOP!

265

266

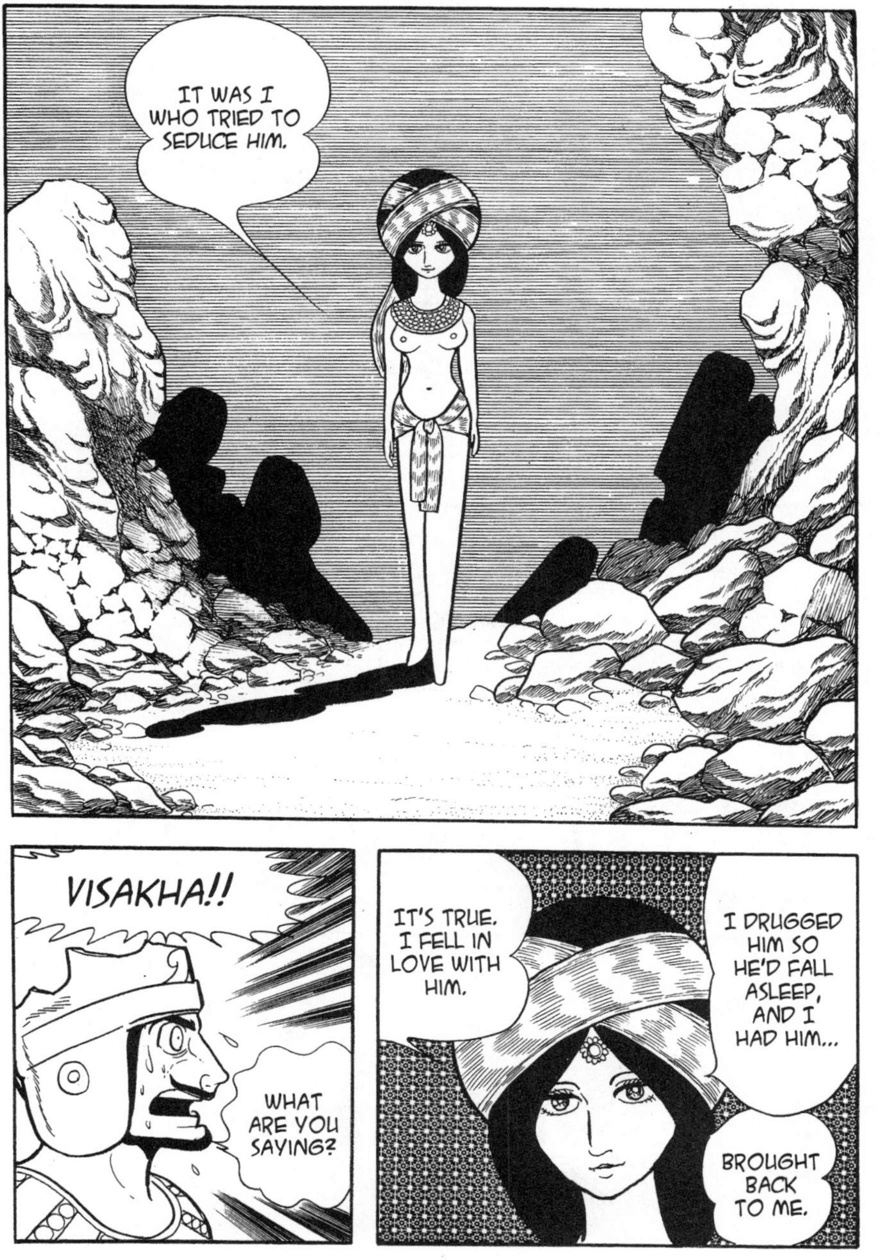
IT WAS I WHO TRIED TO SEDUCE HIM.
VISAKHA!!
WHAT ARE YOU SAYING?
IT'S TRUE. I FELL IN LOVE WITH HIM.
I DRUGGED HIM SO HE'D FALL ASLEEP, AND I HAD HIM...
BROUGHT BACK TO ME.

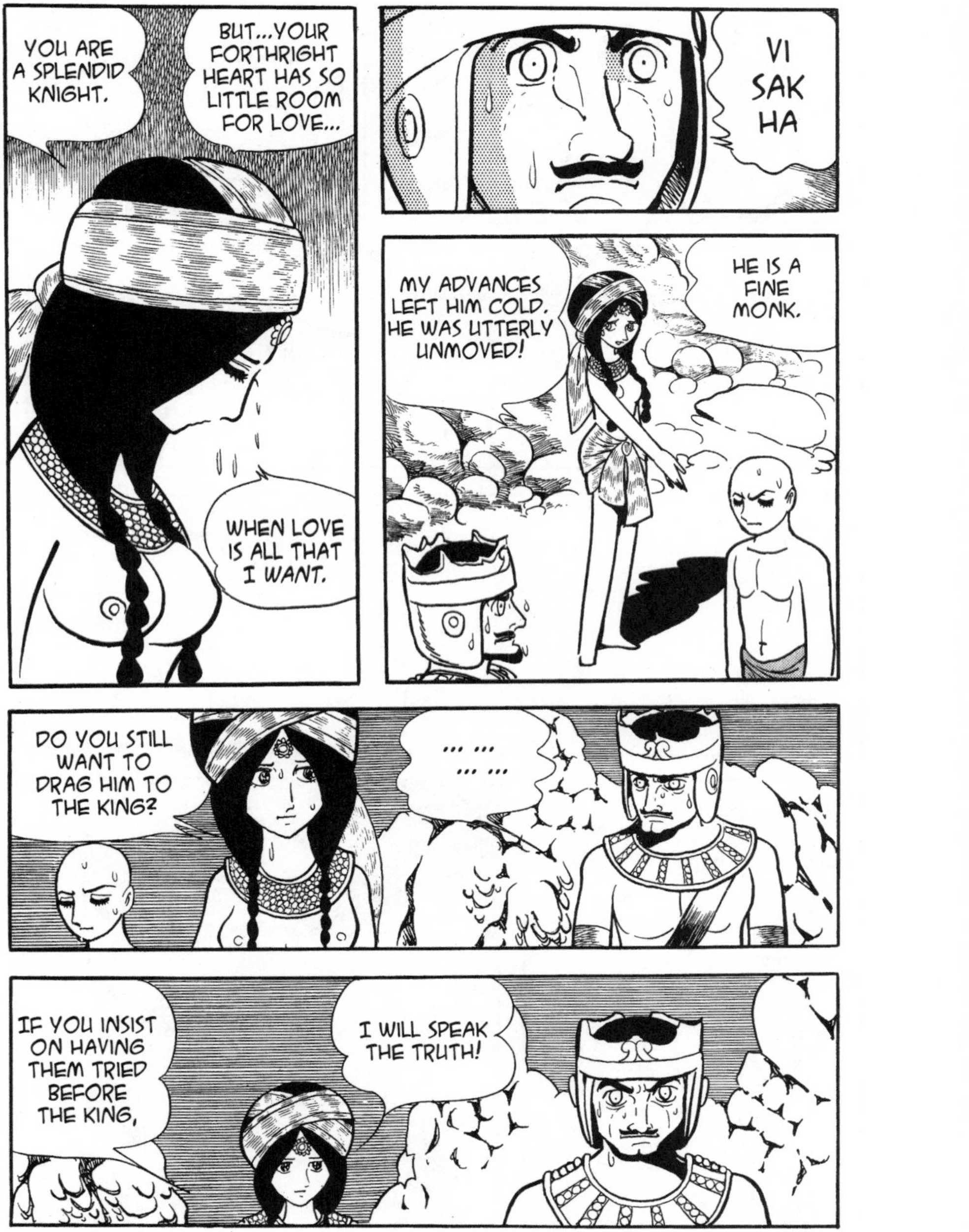
YOU ARE A SPLENDID KNIGHT.
BUT...YOUR FORTHRIGHT HEART HAS SO LITTLE ROOM FOR LOVE...
WHEN LOVE IS ALL THAT I WANT.
VI SAK HA
MY ADVANCES LEFT HIM COLD. HE WAS UTTERLY UNMOVED!
HE IS A FINE MONK.
DO YOU STILL WANT TO DRAG HIM TO THE KING?
... ...
IF YOU INSIST ON HAVING THEM TRIED BEFORE THE KING,
I WILL SPEAK THE TRUTH!

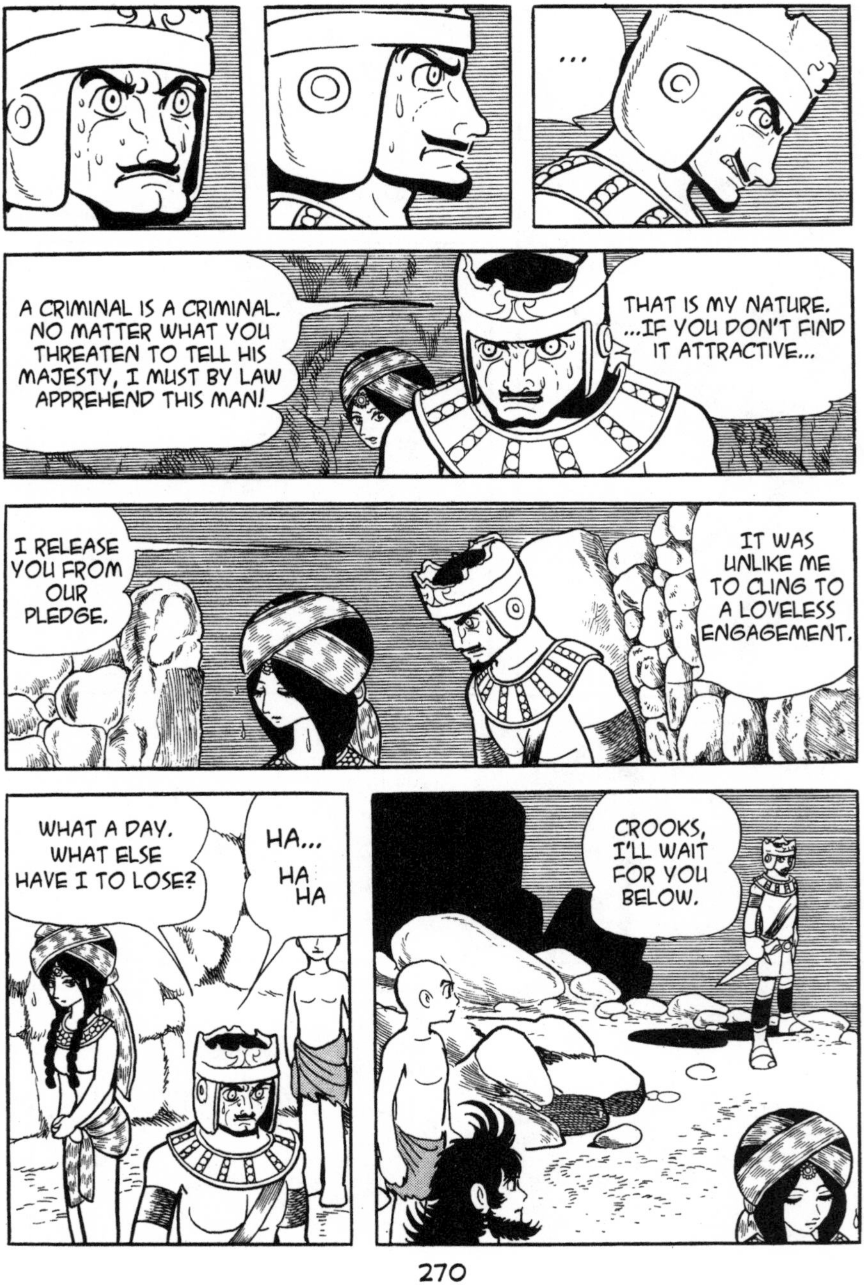
...
A CRIMINAL IS A CRIMINAL. NO MATTER WHAT YOU THREATEN TO TELL HIS MAJESTY, I MUST BY LAW APPREHEND THIS MAN!
THAT IS MY NATURE. ...IF YOU DON'T FIND IT ATTRACTIVE...
I RELEASE YOU FROM OUR PLEDGE.
IT WAS UNLIKE ME TO CLING TO A LOVELESS ENGAGEMENT.
WHAT A DAY. WHAT ELSE HAVE I TO LOSE?
HA... HA HA
CROOKS, I'LL WAIT FOR YOU BELOW.

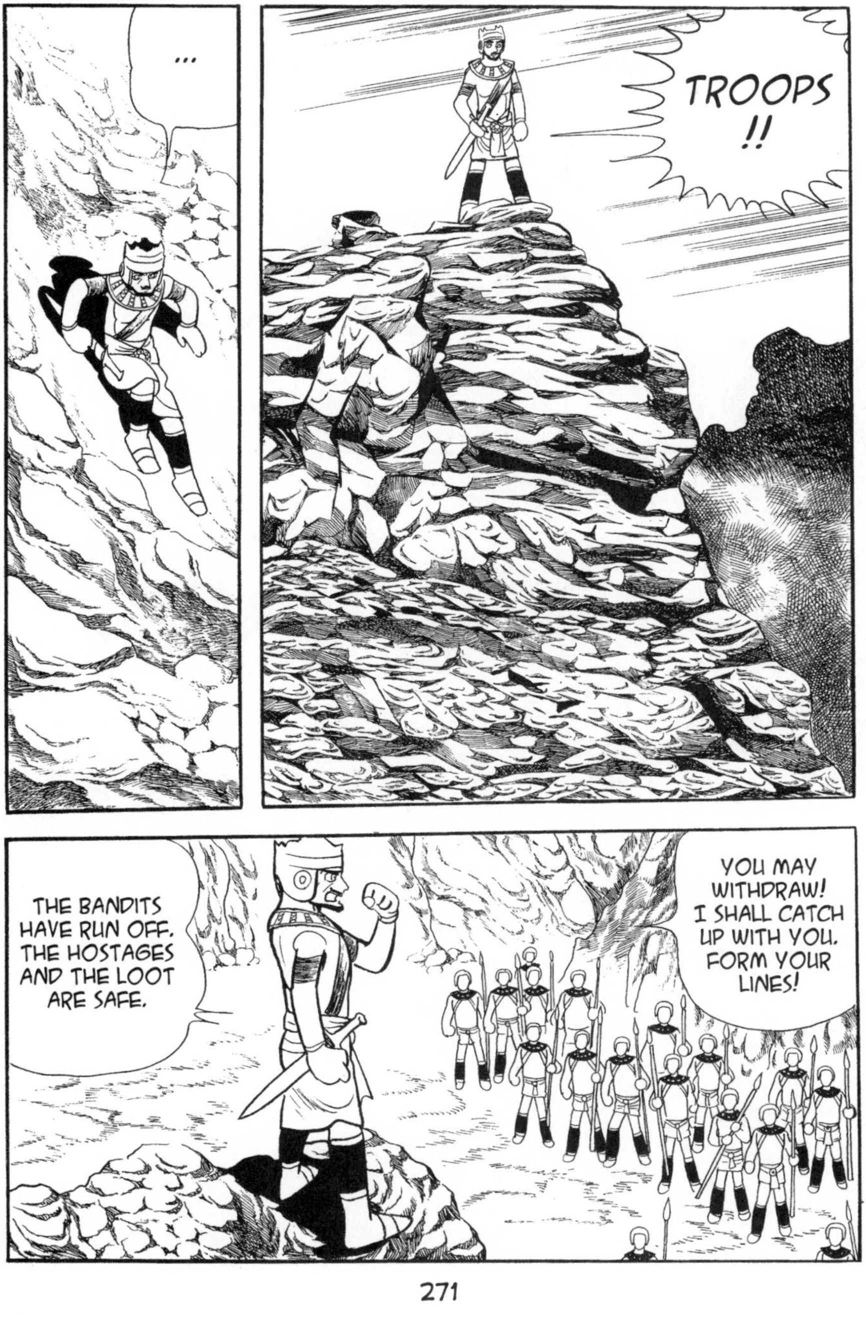
...
TROOPS !!
THE BANDITS HAVE RUN OFF. THE HOSTAGES AND THE LOOT ARE SAFE.
YOU MAY WITHDRAW! I SHALL CATCH UP WITH YOU. FORM YOUR LINES!

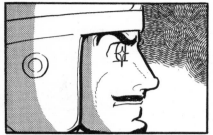

VISAKHA, I'M TERRIBLY SORRY ABOUT ALL OF THIS...

DON'T BE SORRY. YOU'RE NOT TO BLAME, SIDDHARTHA. AND I DON'T BLAME MY FATE, EITHER...

LISTEN UP!

YOU HEARD ALL THAT, RIGHT?

I HAVE TO FULFILL MY PROMISE TO SIDDHARTHA. WE DISBAND AS OF TONIGHT.

WAIT A SEC!

THAT'S PURE WHIMSY, BOSS!

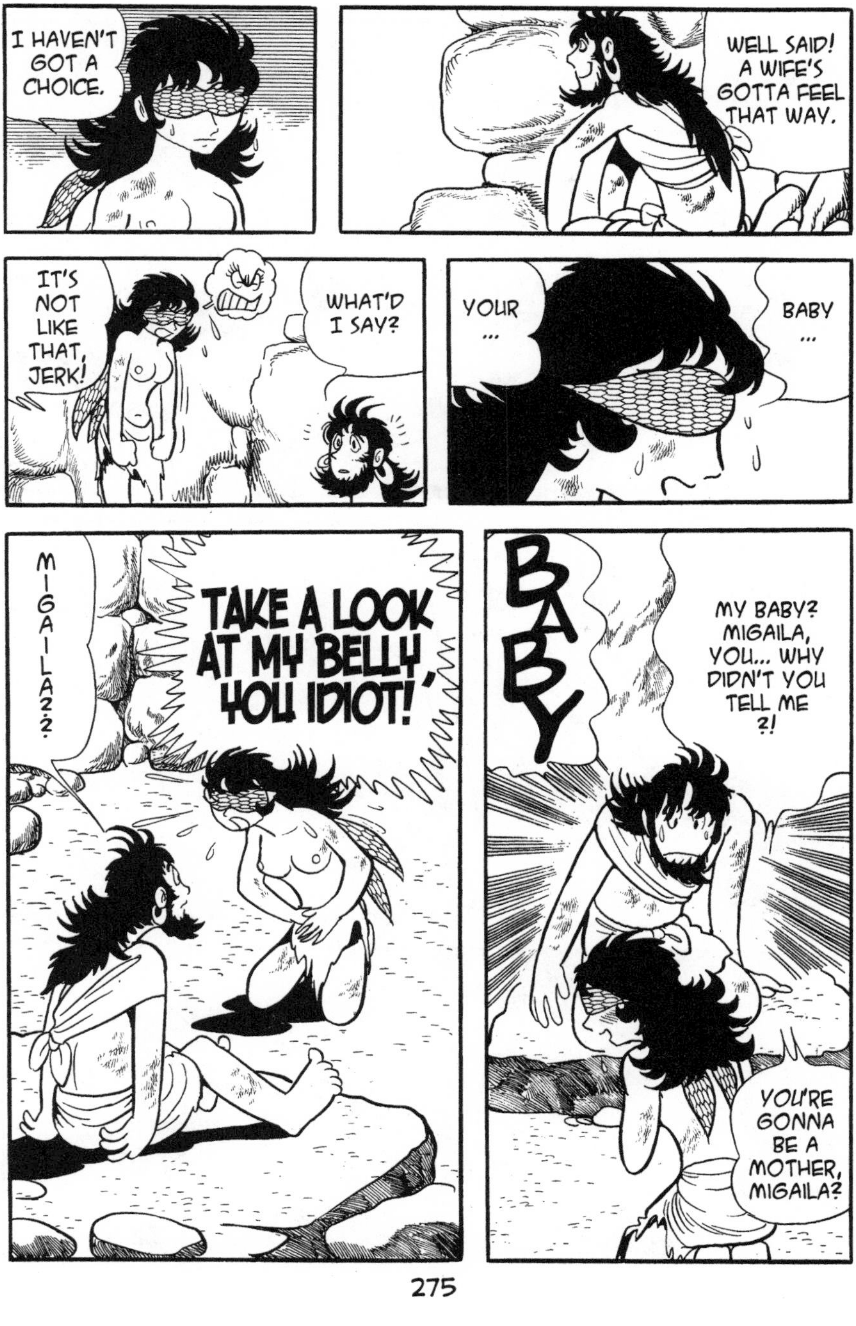

I HAVEN'T GOT A CHOICE.
WELL SAID! A WIFE'S GOTTA FEEL THAT WAY.
IT'S NOT LIKE THAT, JERK!
WHAT'D I SAY?
YOUR ...
BABY ...
MIGAILA??
TAKE A LOOK AT MY BELLY, YOU IDIOT!
BABY
MY BABY? MIGAILA, YOU... WHY DIDN'T YOU TELL ME ?!
YOU'RE GONNA BE A MOTHER, MIGAILA?

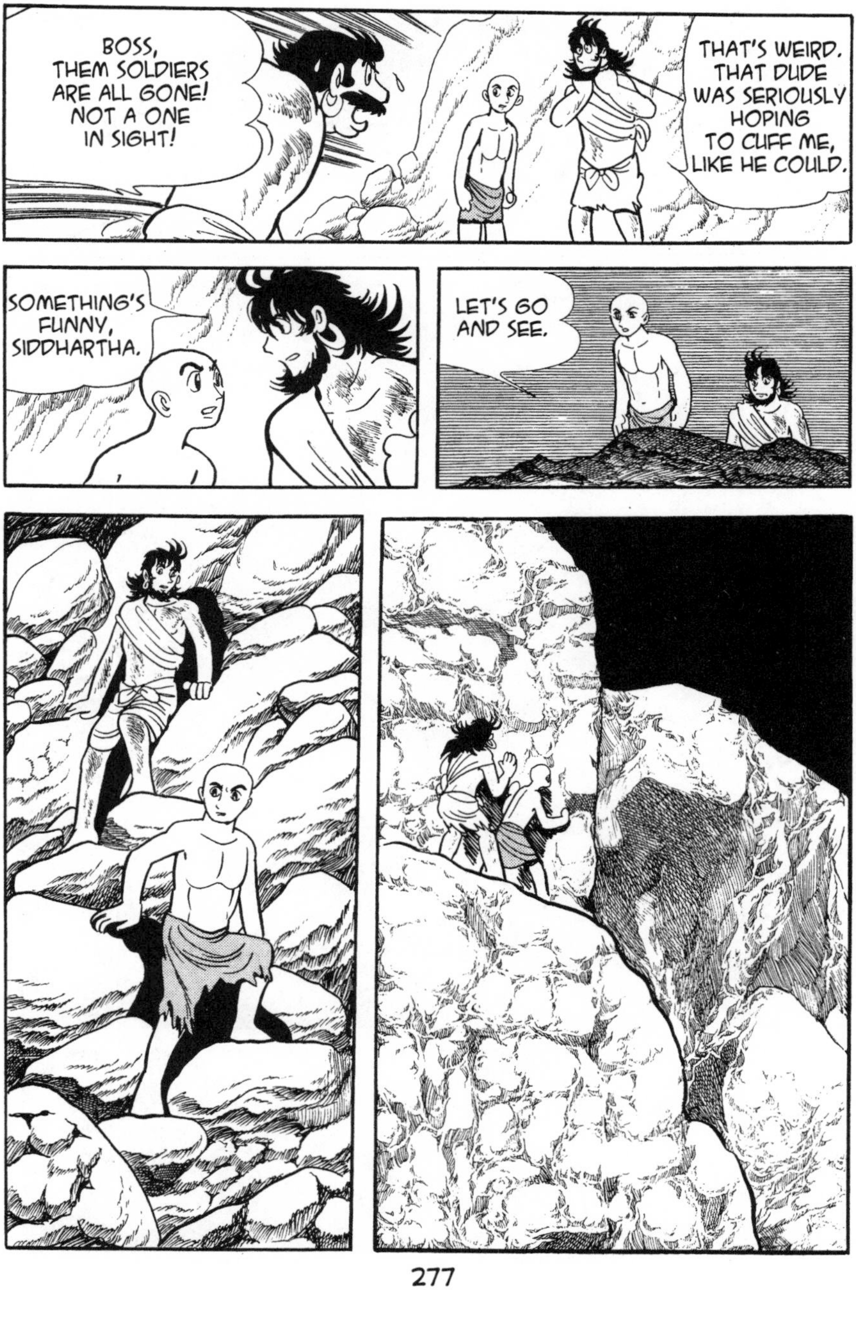
BOSS, THEM SOLDIERS ARE ALL GONE! NOT A ONE IN SIGHT!
THAT'S WEIRD. THAT DUDE WAS SERIOUSLY HOPING TO CUFF ME, LIKE HE COULD.
SOMETHING'S FUNNY, SIDDHARTHA.
LET'S GO AND SEE.

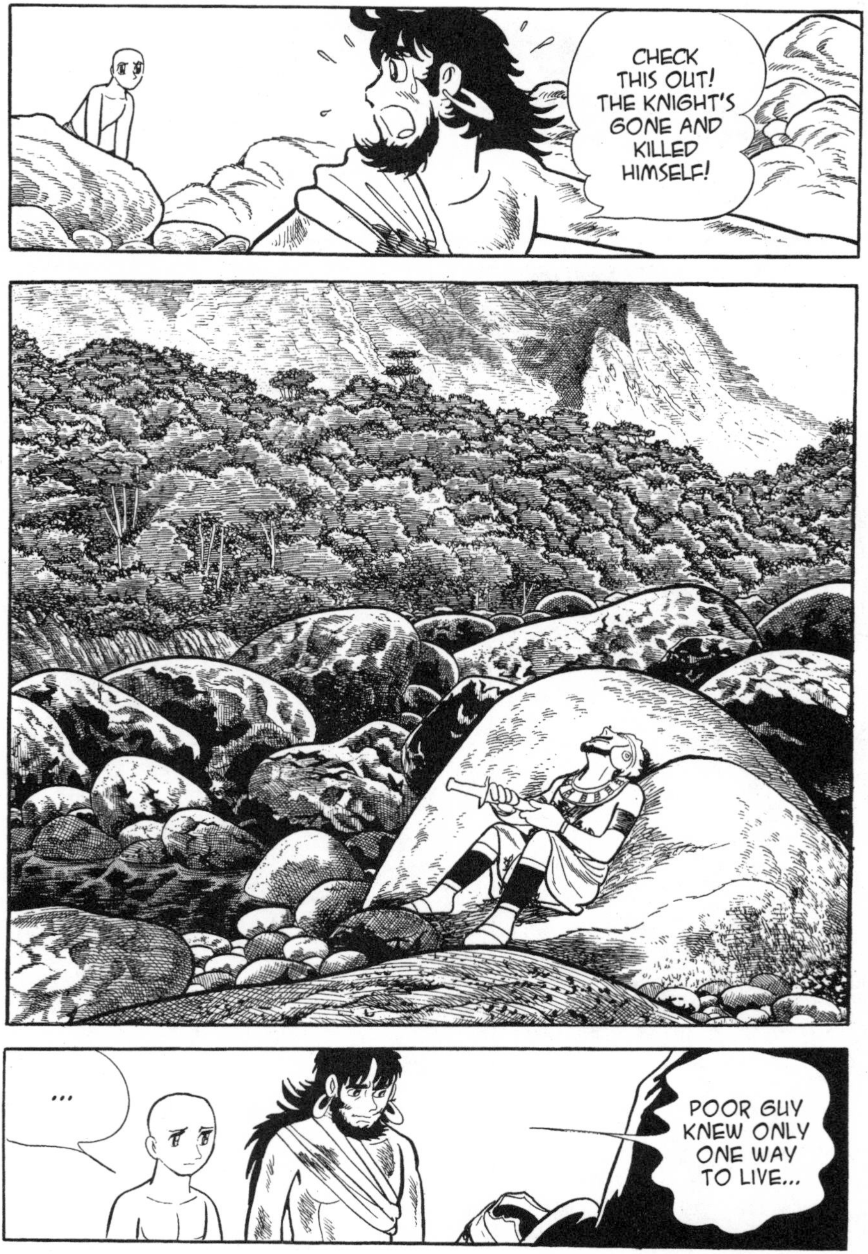
CHECK THIS OUT! THE KNIGHT'S GONE AND KILLED HIMSELF!
...
POOR GUY KNEW ONLY ONE WAY TO LIVE...

CHAPTER FIVE

INTERVIEW AT MT. PANDAVA

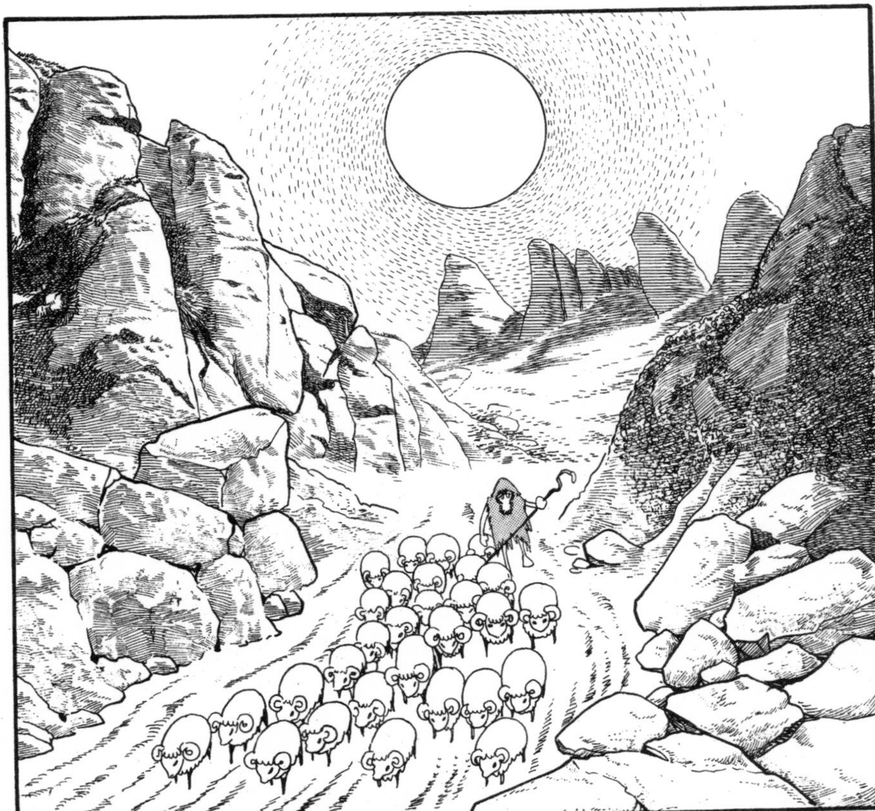

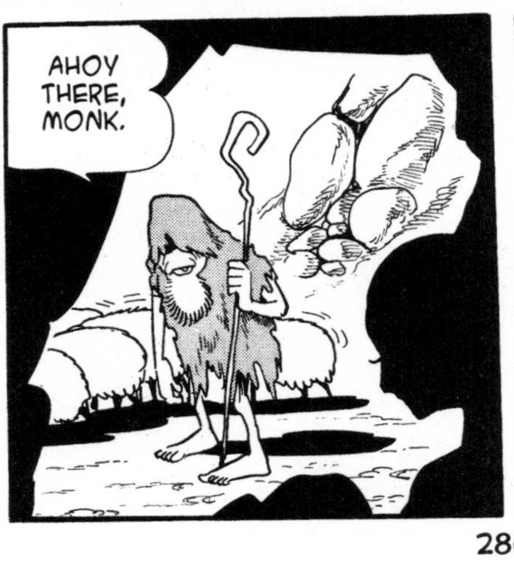
AHOY THERE, MONK.

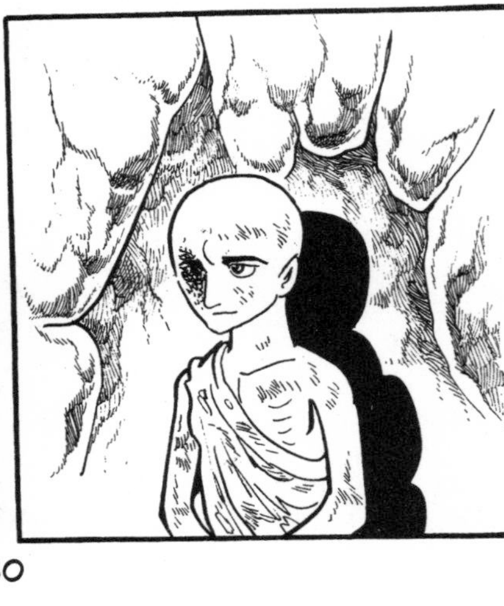

281

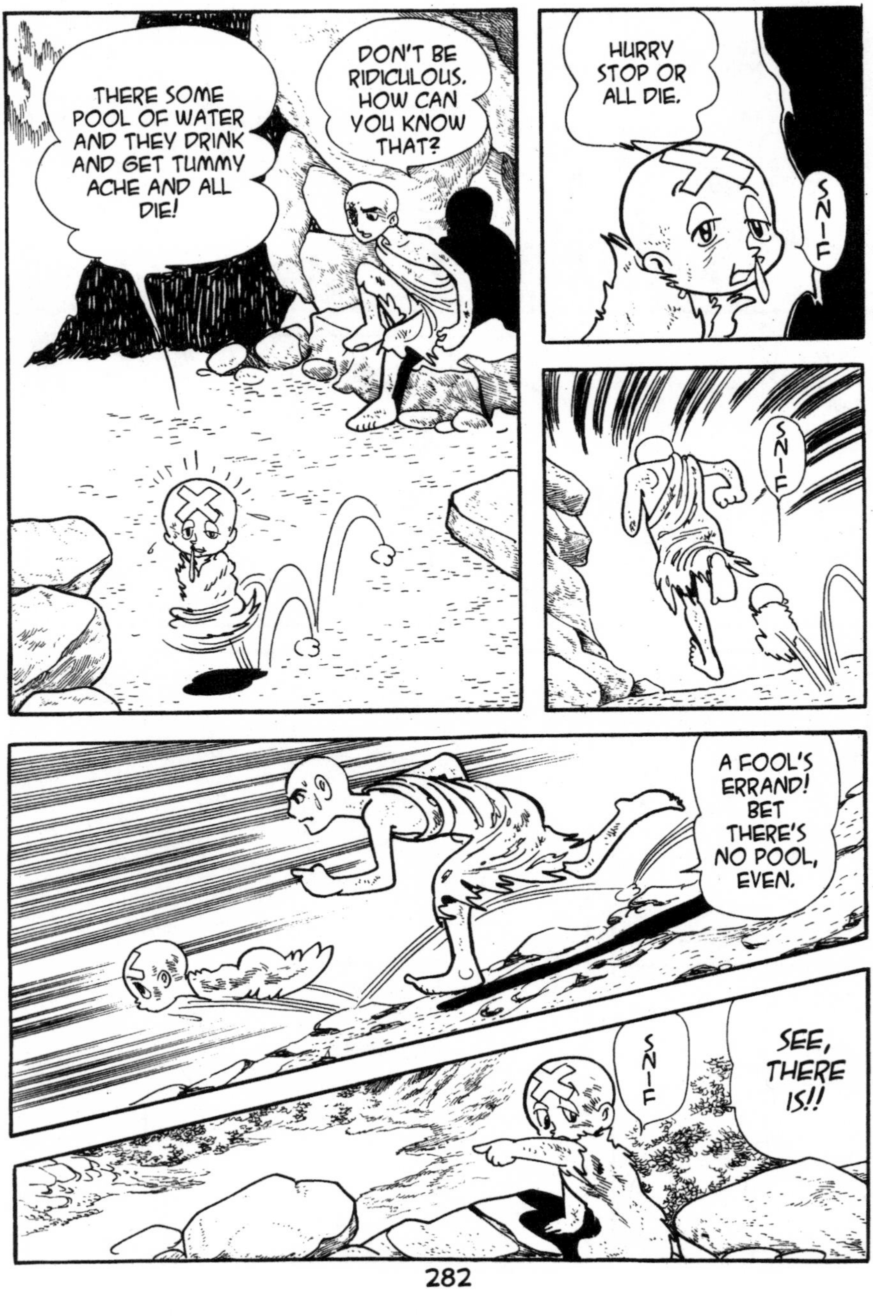
THERE SOME POOL OF WATER AND THEY DRINK AND GET TUMMY ACHE AND ALL DIE!
DON'T BE RIDICULOUS. HOW CAN YOU KNOW THAT?
HURRY STOP OR ALL DIE.
SNIF
SNIF
A FOOL'S ERRAND! BET THERE'S NO POOL, EVEN.
SNIF
SEE, THERE IS!!

283

284

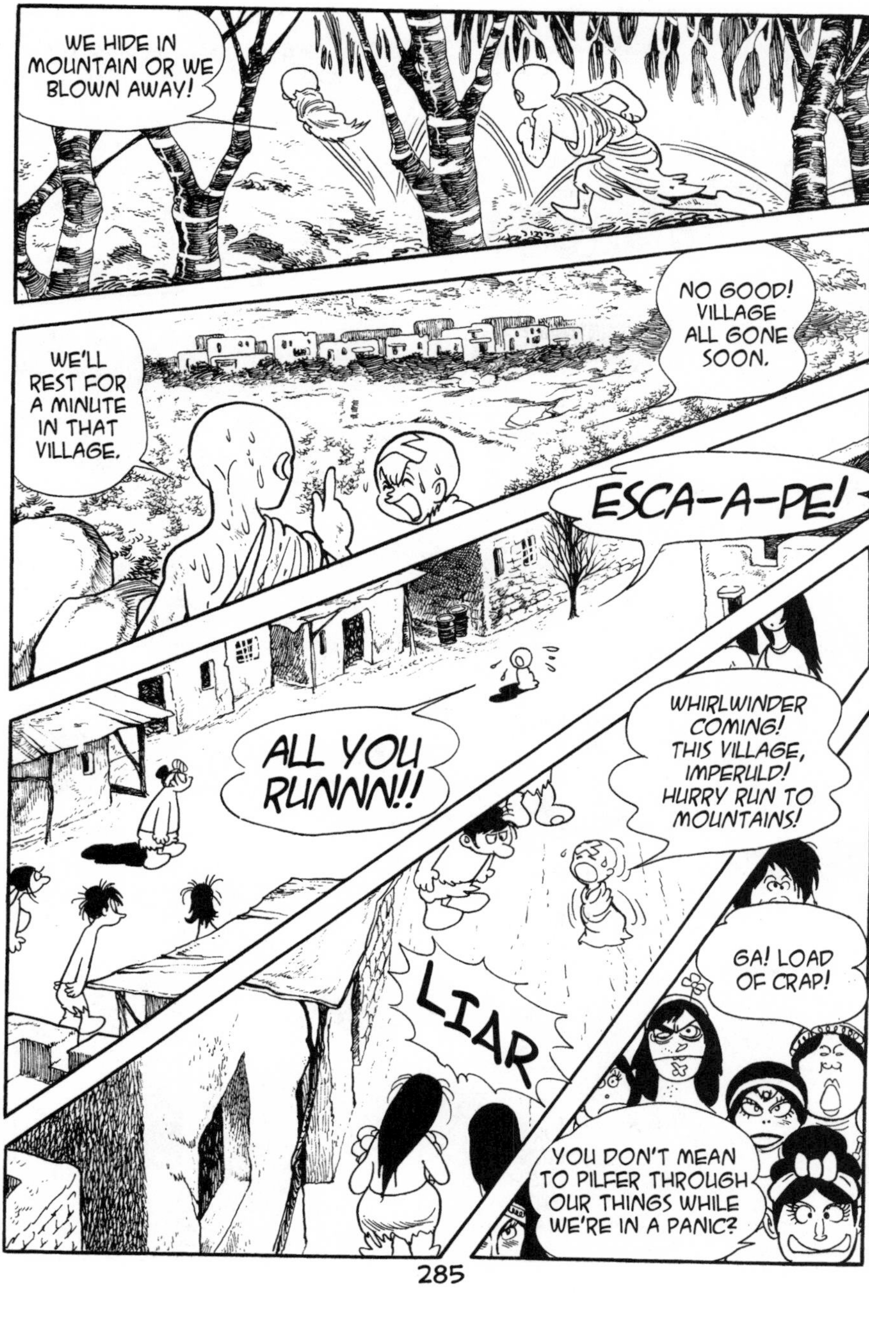

WE HIDE IN MOUNTAIN OR WE BLOWN AWAY!
WE'LL REST FOR A MINUTE IN THAT VILLAGE.
NO GOOD! VILLAGE ALL GONE SOON.
ESCA-A-PE!
ALL YOU RUNNN!!
WHIRLWINDER COMING! THIS VILLAGE, IMPERULD! HURRY RUN TO MOUNTAINS!
LIAR
GA! LOAD OF CRAP!
YOU DON'T MEAN TO PILFER THROUGH OUR THINGS WHILE WE'RE IN A PANIC?

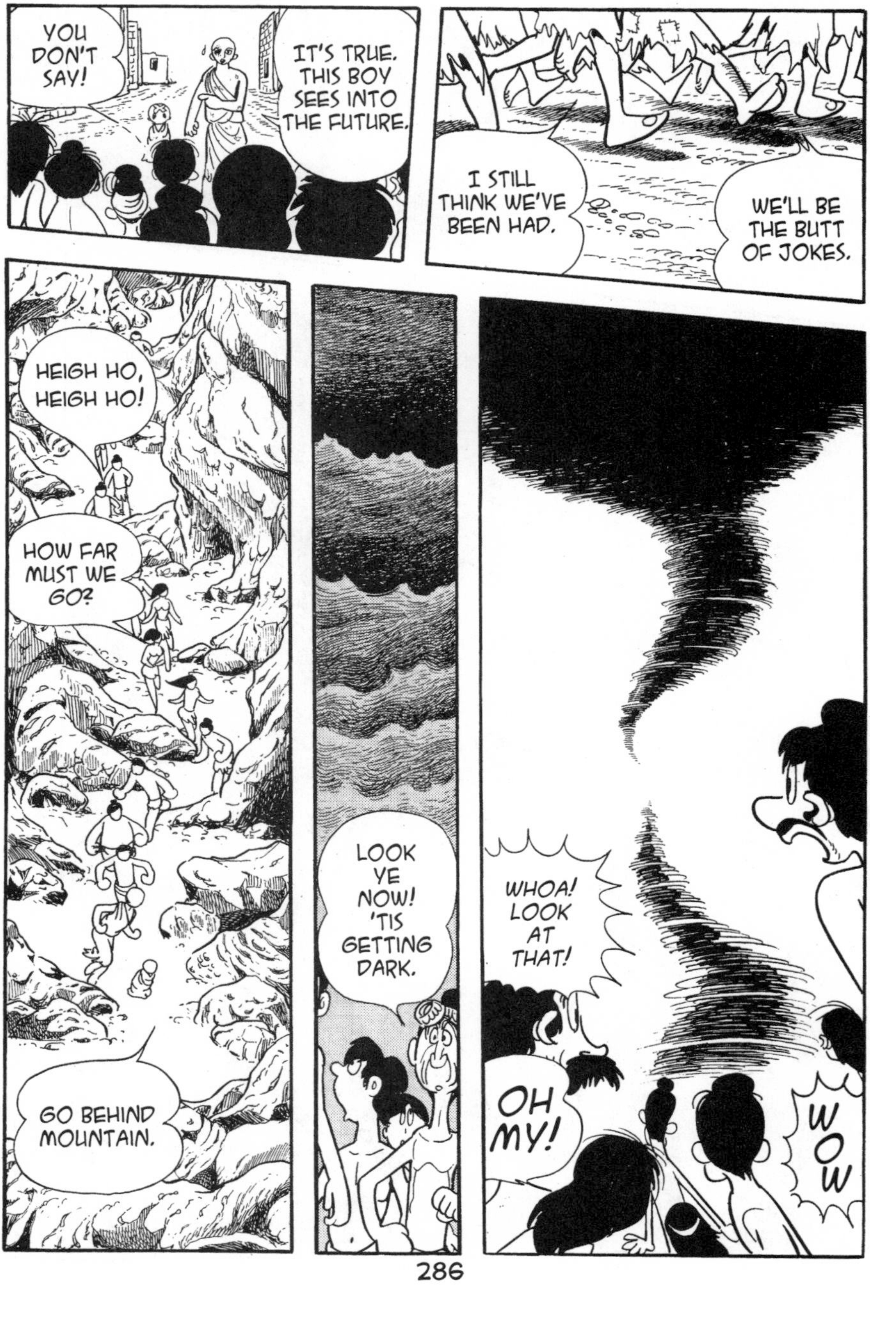
YOU DON'T SAY!
IT'S TRUE. THIS BOY SEES INTO THE FUTURE.
I STILL THINK WE'VE BEEN HAD.
WE'LL BE THE BUTT OF JOKES.
HEIGH HO, HEIGH HO!
HOW FAR MUST WE GO?
GO BEHIND MOUNTAIN.
LOOK YE NOW! 'TIS GETTING DARK.
WHOA! LOOK AT THAT!
OH MY!
WOW

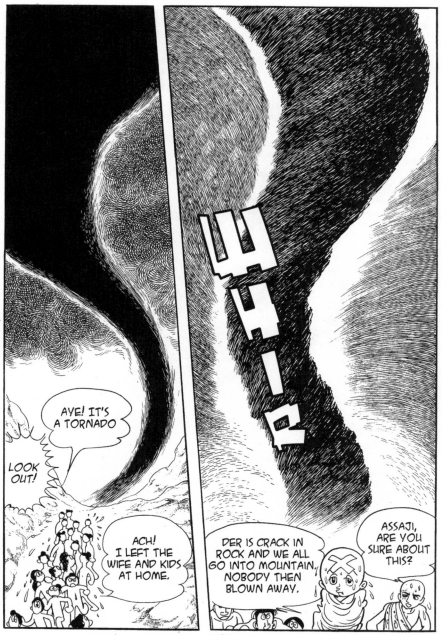

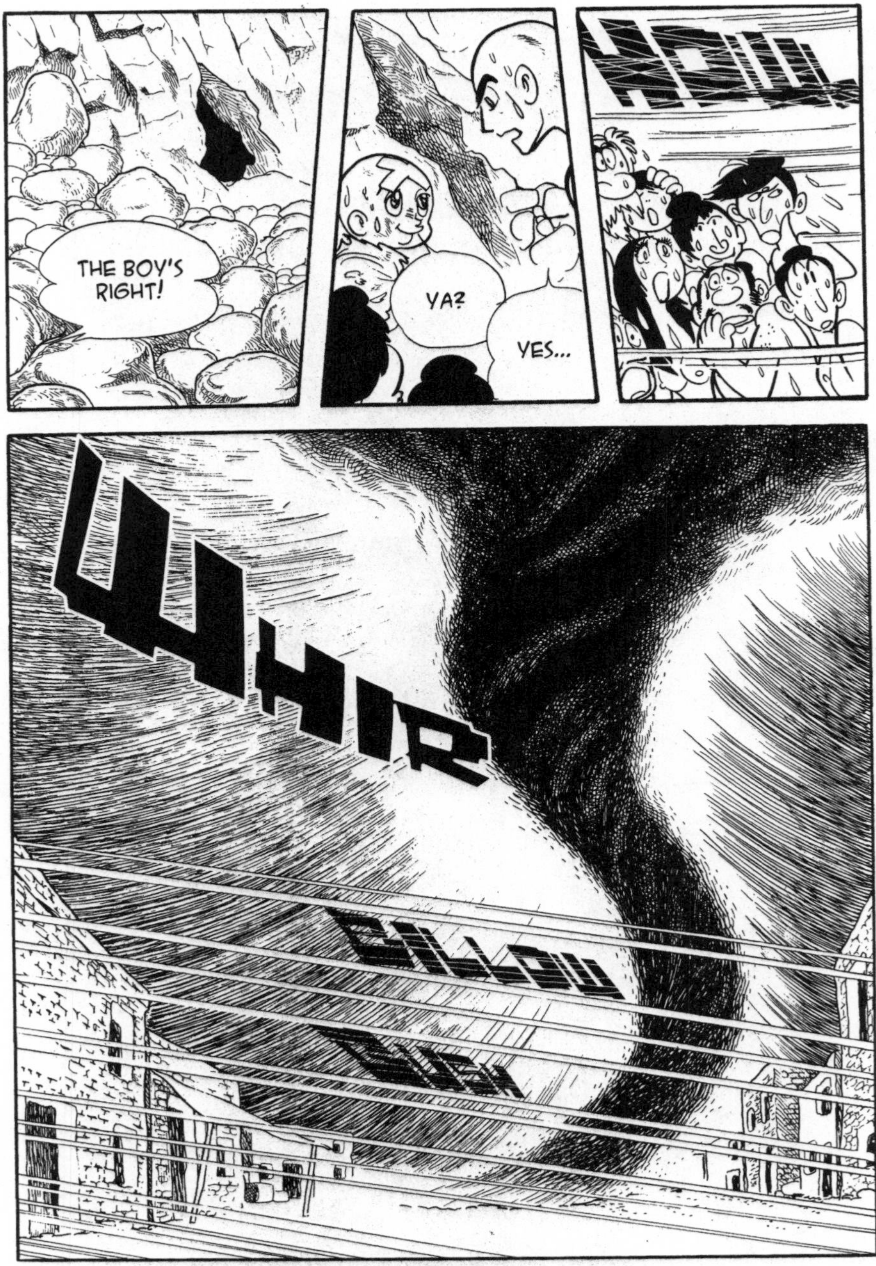
THE BOY'S RIGHT!
YA?
YES...
HOWL!
WHIR
BILLOW
RUSH

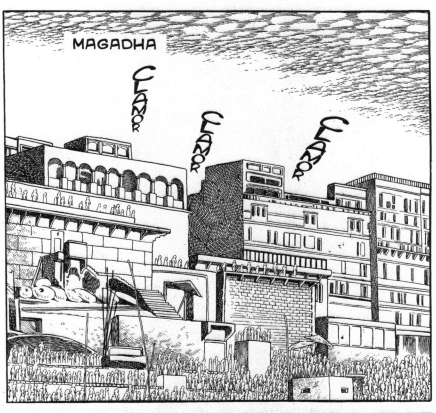

MAGADHA

CLAMOR
CLAMOR
CLAMOR

YOUR MAJESTY, I AM APPRISED OF A MOST PECULIAR TALE.

A BOY WHO SEES THE FUTURE.

I'VE HAD MY FILL OF PROPHETS!

BUT THIS IS A CHILD. HE FORETOLD A TORNADO AND SAVED THE BETTER PART OF A VILLAGE.

ALL WHO DOUBTED HIM PERISHED.

THE VILLAGERS REGARD HIM —REVERE HIM— AS A MESSENGER FROM THE GODS.

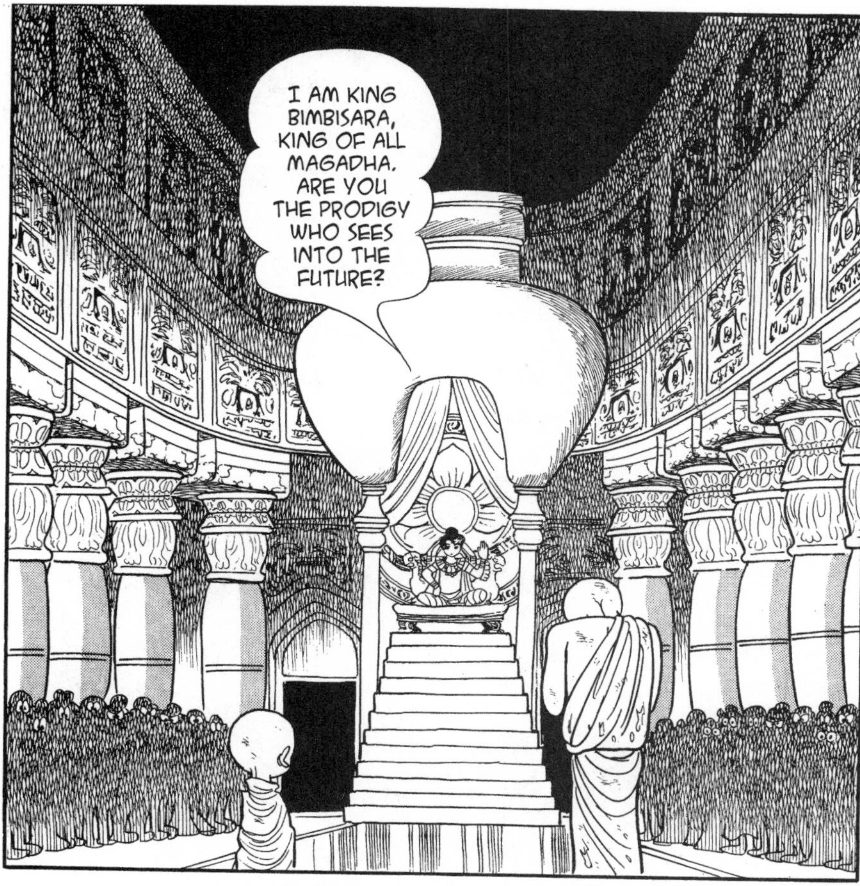
I AM KING BIMBISARA, KING OF ALL MAGADHA. ARE YOU THE PRODIGY WHO SEES INTO THE FUTURE?

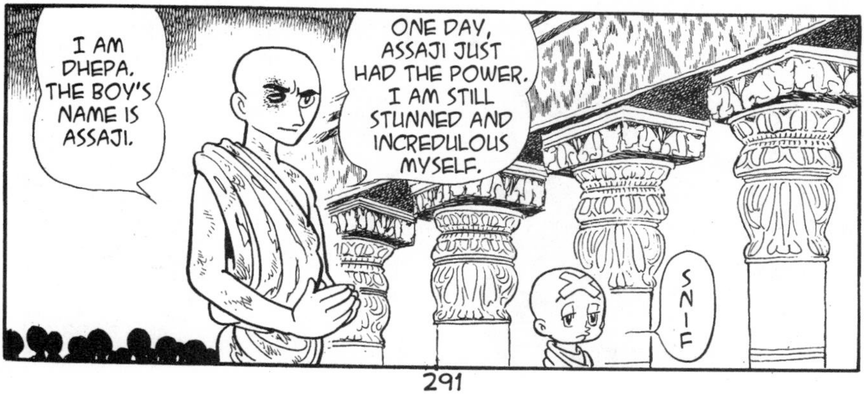
I AM DHEPA. THE BOY'S NAME IS ASSAJI.
ONE DAY, ASSAJI JUST HAD THE POWER. I AM STILL STUNNED AND INCREDULOUS MYSELF.
SNIF

VERY WELL. THERE IS A TRAP IN THIS HALL, AND YOU WILL LOSE YOUR LIFE A MINUTE FROM NOW.

UNLESS YOU DIVINE THE TRAP.

IF YOU LIVE, I WILL BELIEVE YOU.

SO TRY AND SAVE YOURSELF, HMM?

THIS IS NO JEST, CHILD!

SNIF

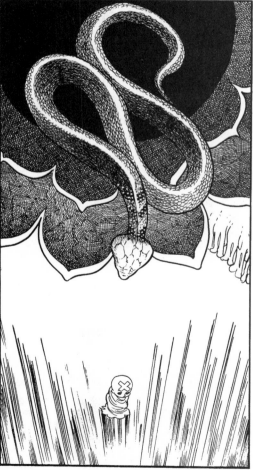

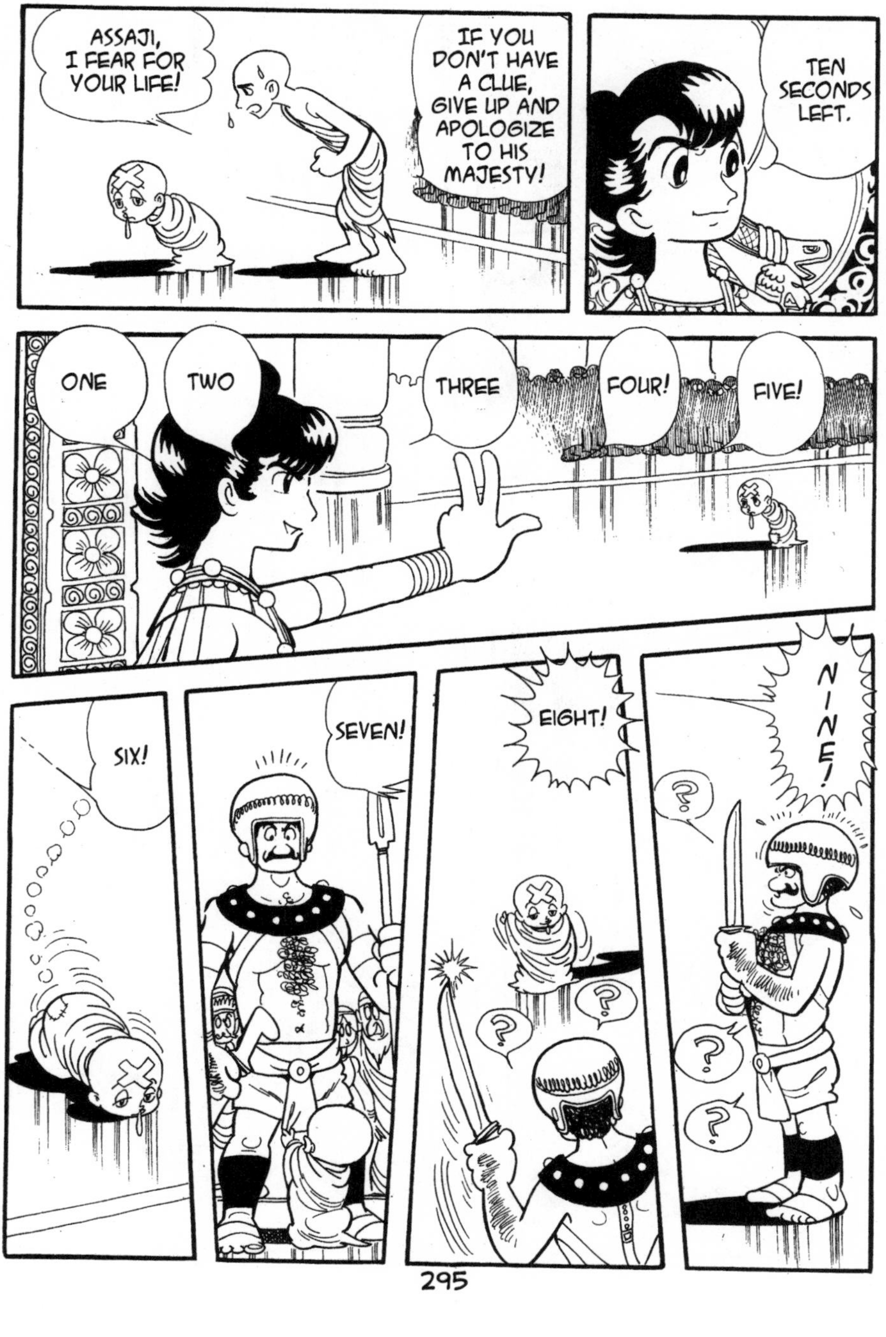
ASSAJI, I FEAR FOR YOUR LIFE!
IF YOU DON'T HAVE A CLUE, GIVE UP AND APOLOGIZE TO HIS MAJESTY!
TEN SECONDS LEFT.
ONE
TWO
THREE
FOUR!
FIVE!
SIX!
SEVEN!
EIGHT!
NINE!

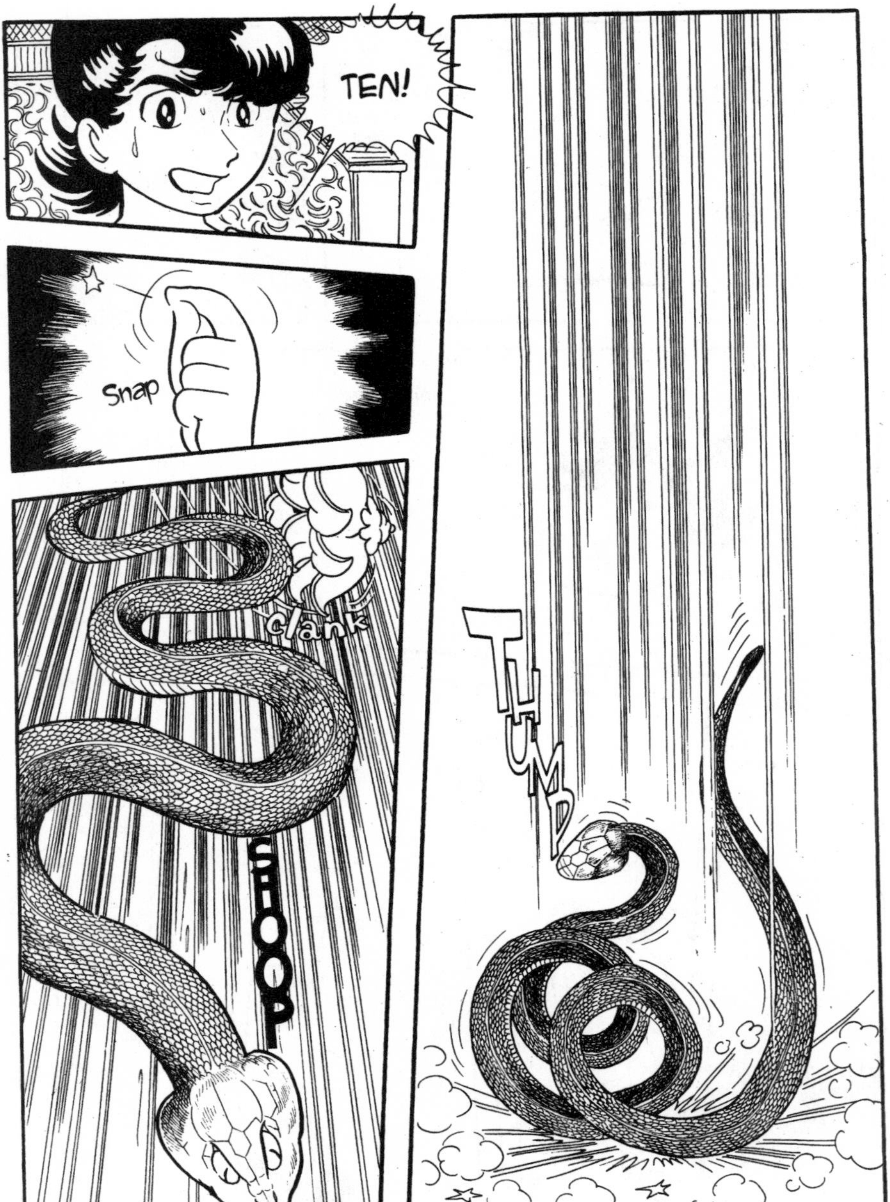
TEN!
Snap
clank
SHOOP
THUMP

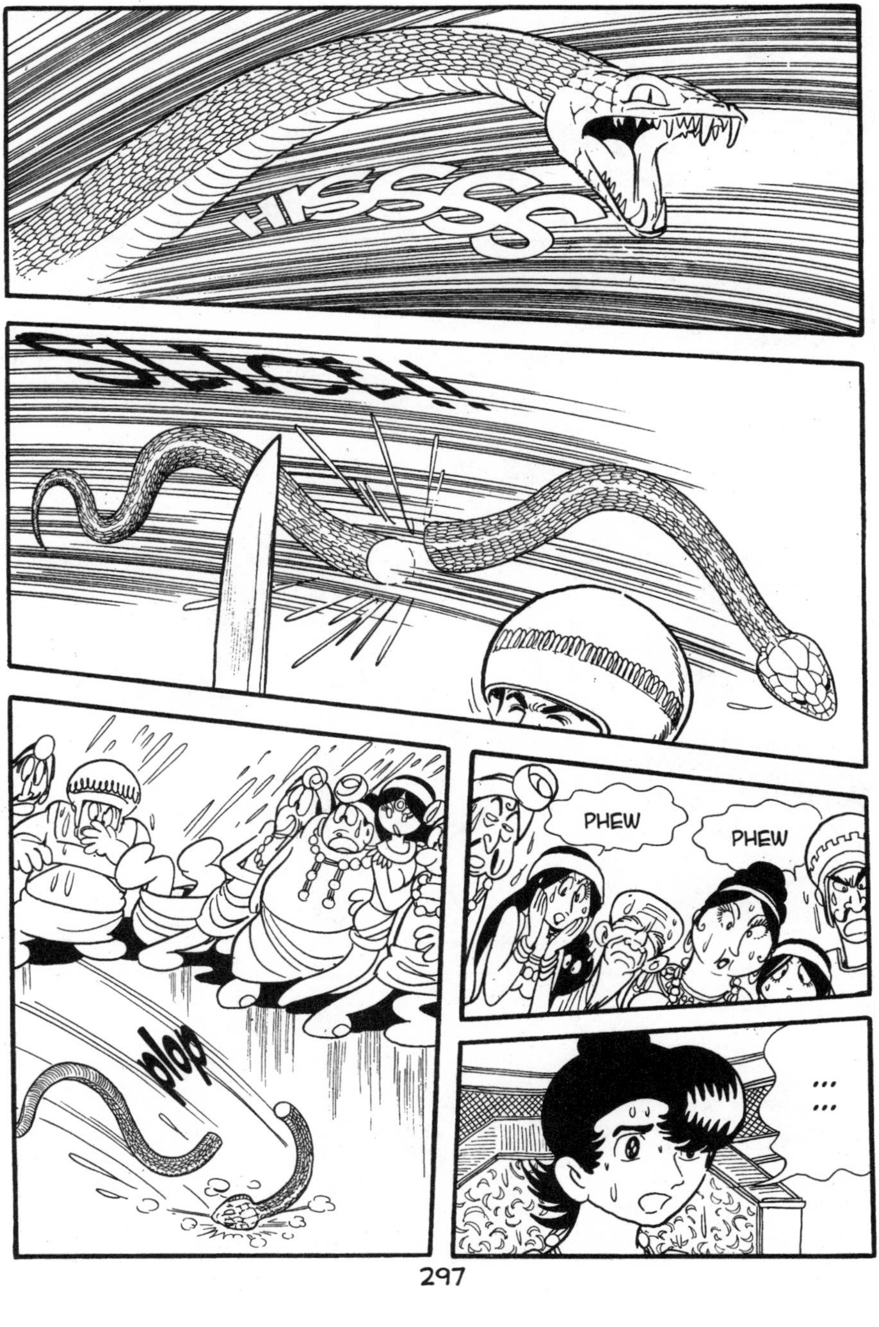
HISSSS
SLICE!!
plop
PHEW
PHEW
...
...

SO, YOU SAW THROUGH THE TRAP,

SNIF

GUESSED THE COURSE THE SNAKE WOULD TAKE,

AND PLACED A SWORD IN ITS PATH. I AM QUITE IMPRESSED.

TWITCH

AND SO, YOUR PROPHECY...

THAT IN TWENTY YEARS I AM TO BE MURDERED BY MY OWN SON...

IS NOT SO EASY TO DISMISS.

LORD, DO NOT BELIEVE HIM!

HE IS JUST A TWO-BIT FORTUNE TELLER!

THROW THE WRETCH IN THE DUNGEON!

298

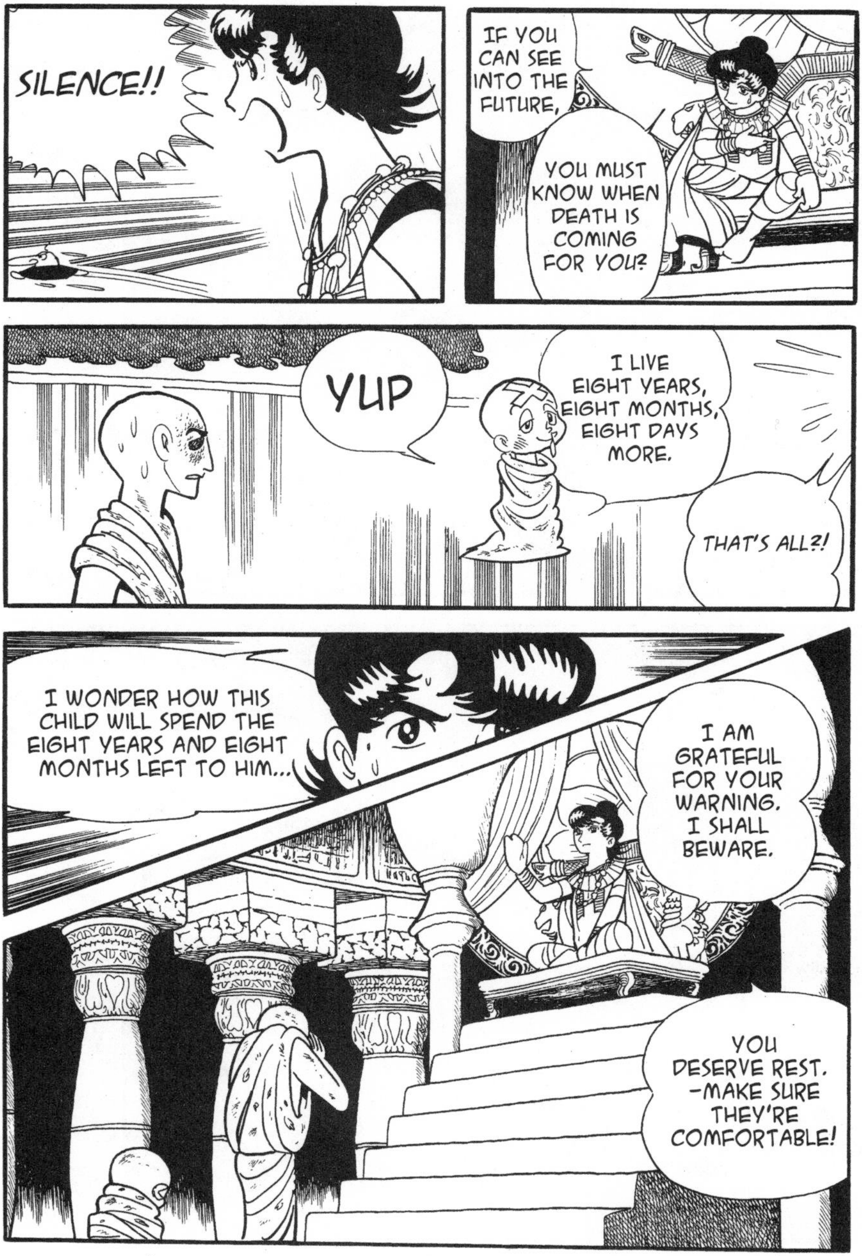

SILENCE!!
IF YOU CAN SEE INTO THE FUTURE,
YOU MUST KNOW WHEN DEATH IS COMING FOR YOU?
YUP
I LIVE EIGHT YEARS, EIGHT MONTHS, EIGHT DAYS MORE.
THAT'S ALL?!
I WONDER HOW THIS CHILD WILL SPEND THE EIGHT YEARS AND EIGHT MONTHS LEFT TO HIM...
I AM GRATEFUL FOR YOUR WARNING. I SHALL BEWARE.
YOU DESERVE REST. —MAKE SURE THEY'RE COMFORTABLE!

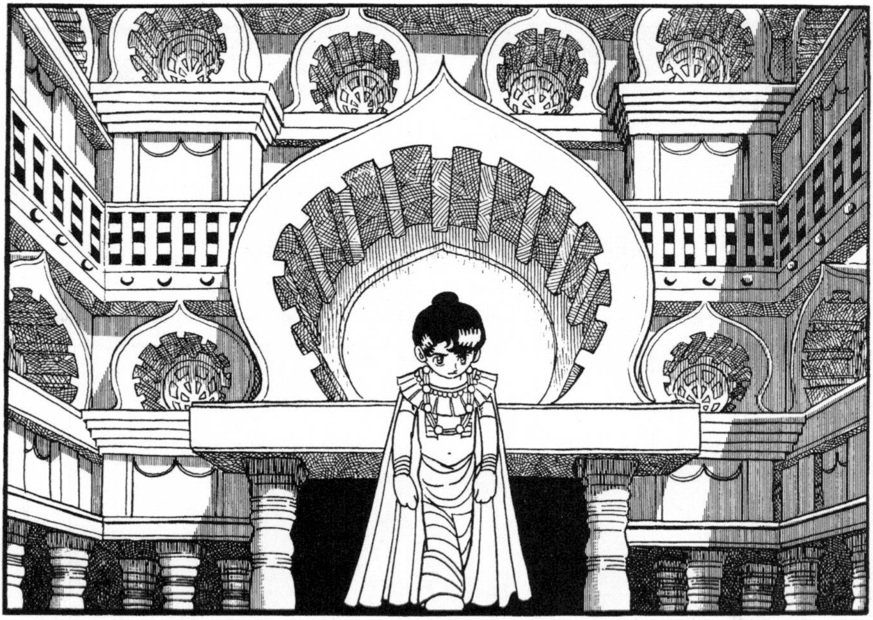

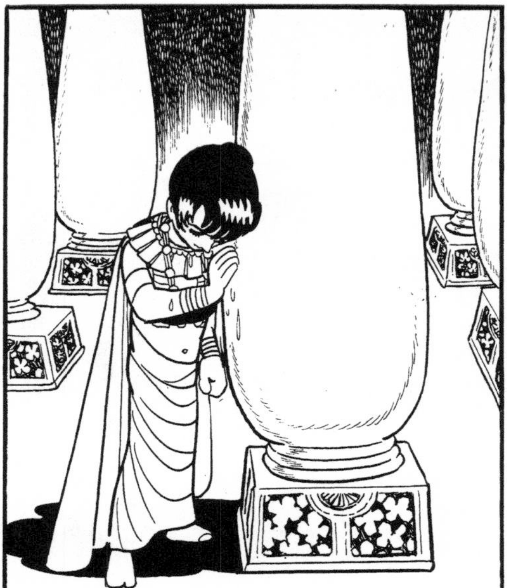

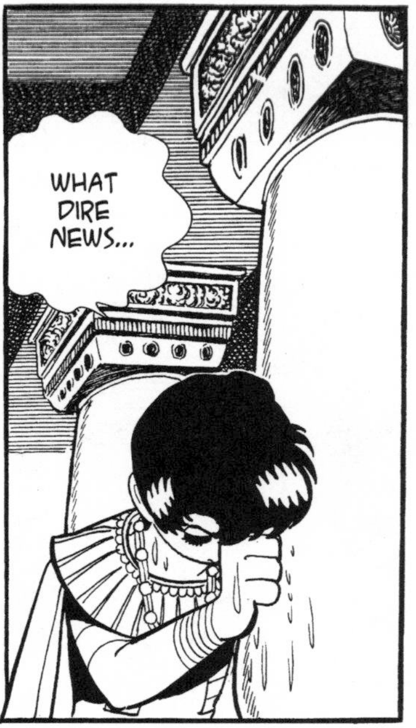
WHAT DIRE NEWS...

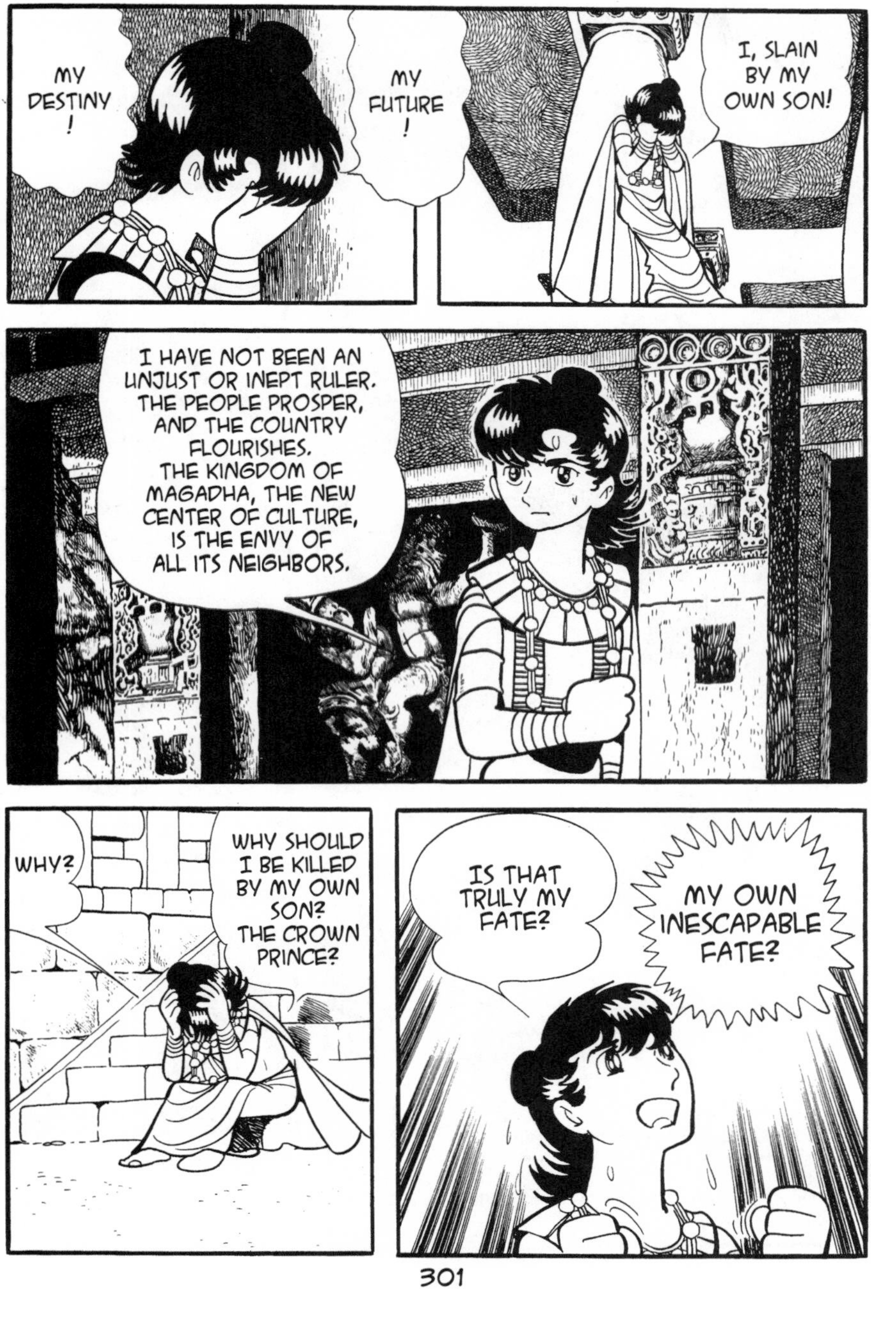
MY DESTINY !
MY FUTURE !
I, SLAIN BY MY OWN SON!
I HAVE NOT BEEN AN UNJUST OR INEPT RULER. THE PEOPLE PROSPER, AND THE COUNTRY FLOURISHES. THE KINGDOM OF MAGADHA, THE NEW CENTER OF CULTURE, IS THE ENVY OF ALL ITS NEIGHBORS.
WHY?
WHY SHOULD I BE KILLED BY MY OWN SON? THE CROWN PRINCE?
IS THAT TRULY MY FATE?
MY OWN INESCAPABLE FATE?

THERE ARE THREE WAYS TO PREVENT IT. FIRST: SIRE NO PRINCE.

SECOND: KILL AT BIRTH ANY PRINCE I BEGET.

THIRD: EXILE THE PRINCE TO A DISTANT LAND FROM WHENCE HE CANNOT REACH ME.

BUT PERHAPS ALL SUCH MEASURES ARE FUTILE.

I HAVE ONLY TWENTY YEARS LEFT!

WHAT CAN I ACHIEVE IN TWO MEASLY DECADES?

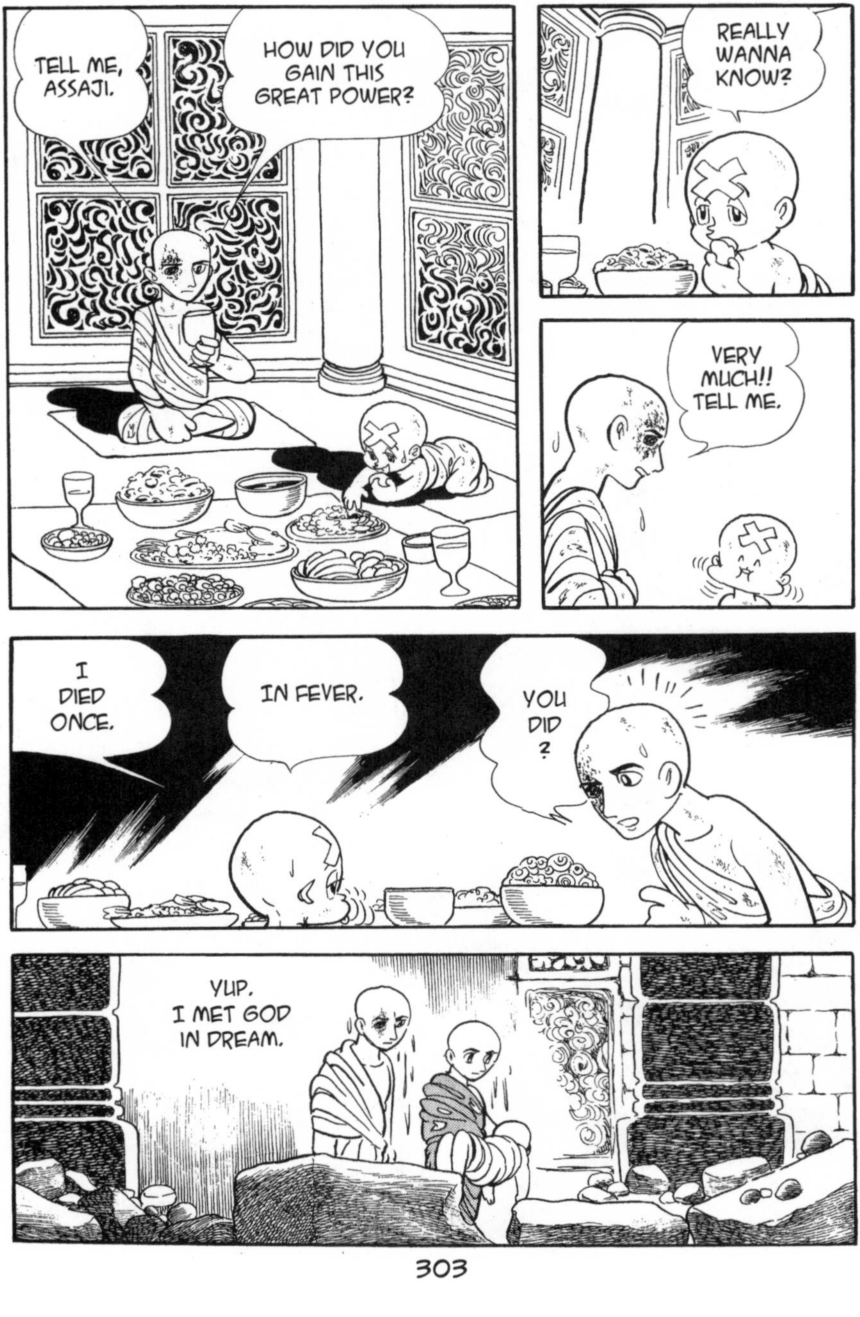
TELL ME, ASSAJI.
HOW DID YOU GAIN THIS GREAT POWER?
REALLY WANNA KNOW?
VERY MUCH!! TELL ME.
I DIED ONCE.
IN FEVER.
YOU DID?
YUP. I MET GOD IN DREAM.

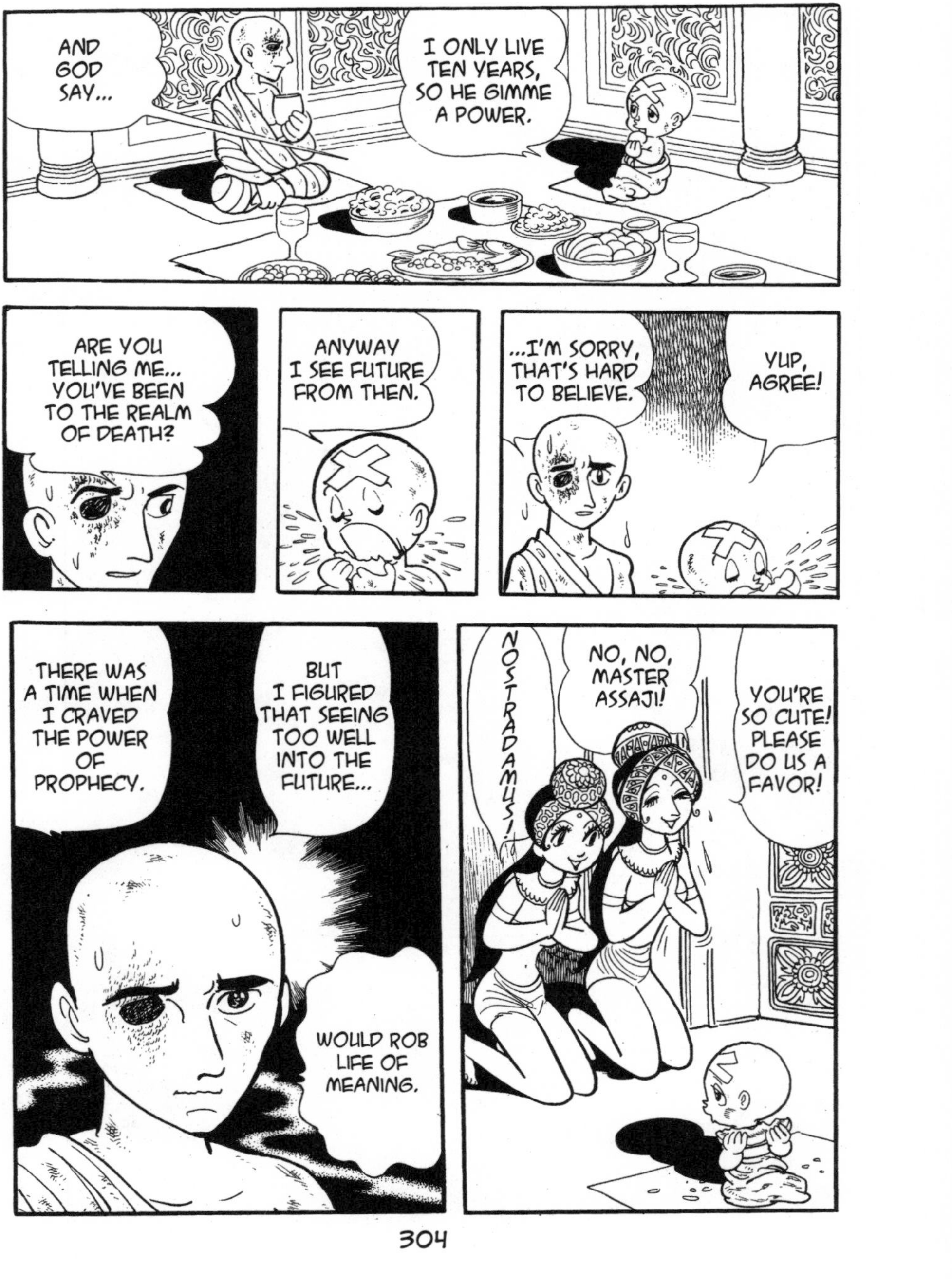
AND GOD SAY...
I ONLY LIVE TEN YEARS, SO HE GIMME A POWER.
ARE YOU TELLING ME... YOU'VE BEEN TO THE REALM OF DEATH?
ANYWAY I SEE FUTURE FROM THEN.
...I'M SORRY, THAT'S HARD TO BELIEVE.
YUP, AGREE!
THERE WAS A TIME WHEN I CRAVED THE POWER OF PROPHECY.
BUT I FIGURED THAT SEEING TOO WELL INTO THE FUTURE...
WOULD ROB LIFE OF MEANING.
NOSTRADAMUS!
NO, NO, MASTER ASSAJI!
YOU'RE SO CUTE! PLEASE DO US A FAVOR!

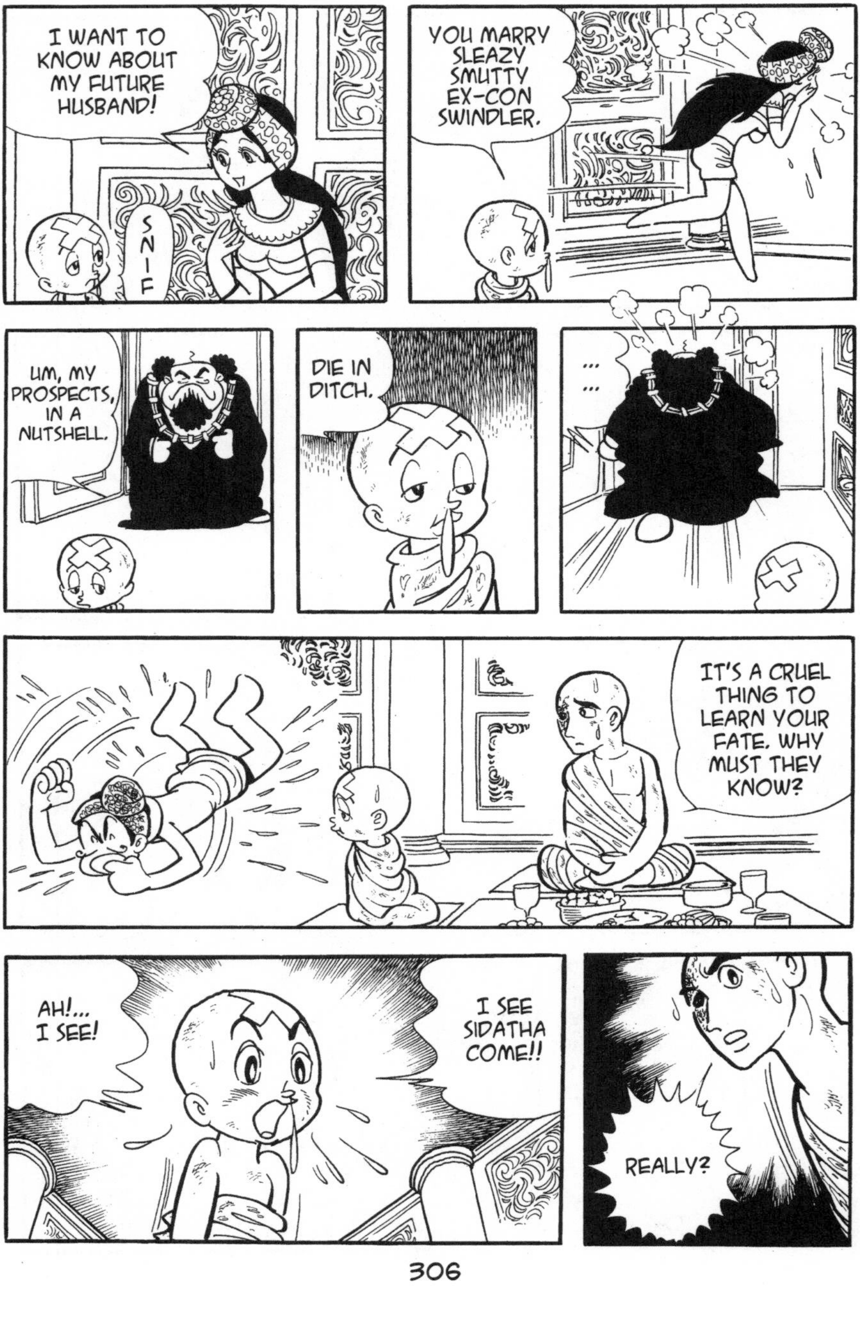
I WANT TO KNOW ABOUT MY FUTURE HUSBAND!
SNIF
YOU MARRY SLEAZY SMUTTY EX-CON SWINDLER.
UM, MY PROSPECTS, IN A NUTSHELL.
DIE IN DITCH.
... ...
IT'S A CRUEL THING TO LEARN YOUR FATE. WHY MUST THEY KNOW?
AH!... I SEE!
I SEE SIDATHA COME!!
REALLY?

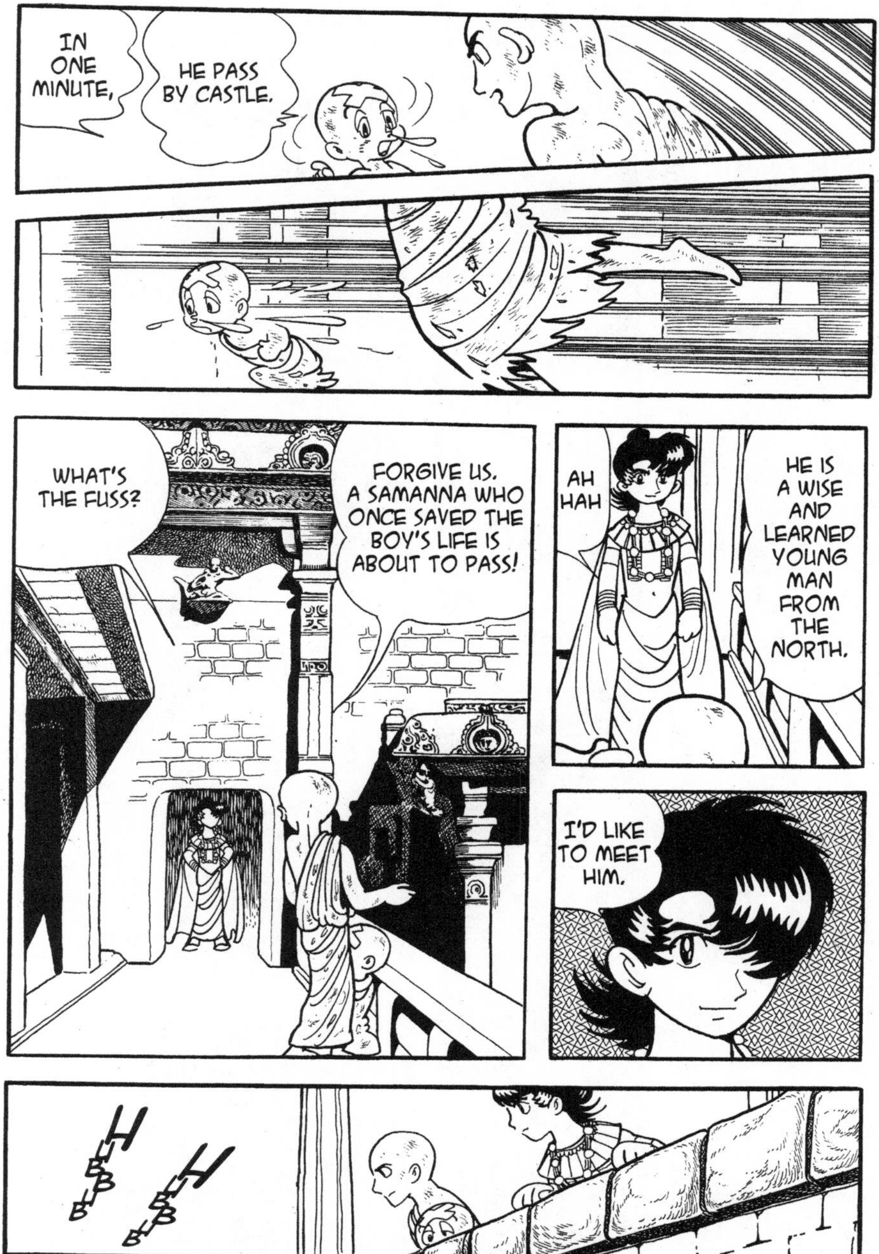
IN ONE MINUTE,
HE PASS BY CASTLE.
WHAT'S THE FUSS?
FORGIVE US. A SAMANNA WHO ONCE SAVED THE BOY'S LIFE IS ABOUT TO PASS!
AH HAH
HE IS A WISE AND LEARNED YOUNG MAN FROM THE NORTH.
I'D LIKE TO MEET HIM.
HUBBUB
HUBBUB

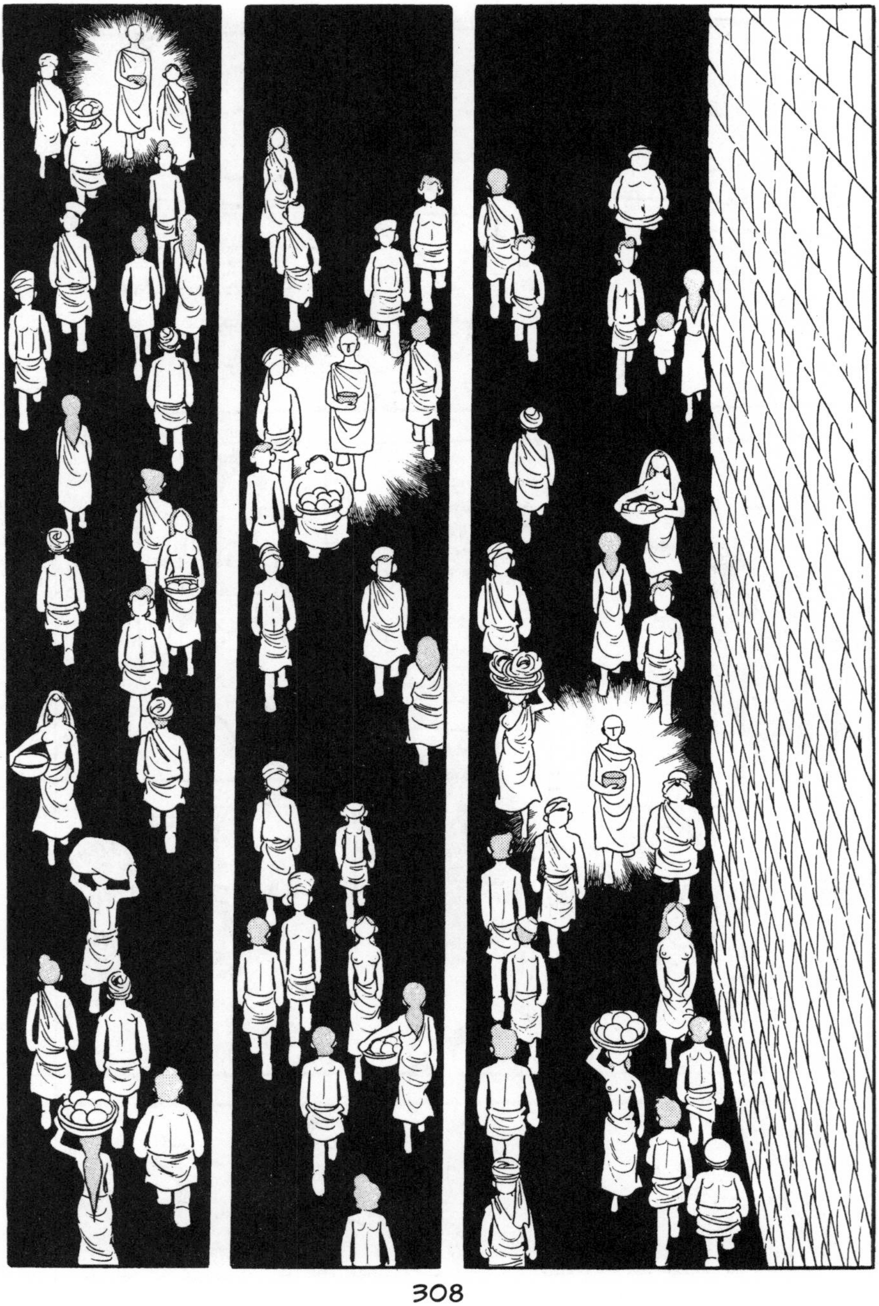

GUARD!

FOLLOW THE SAMANNA WHO JUST PASSED! FIND OUT WHERE HE STAYS AND WHERE HE MEANS TO GO!

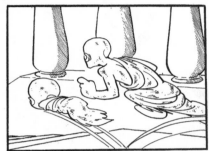

WAIT, YOU TWO!

I CANNOT LET YOU GO NOW.

WE'VE BEEN LOOKING FOR HIM!

AFTER MY MEN FIND OUT ALL ABOUT HIM, YOU MAY SEE HIM.

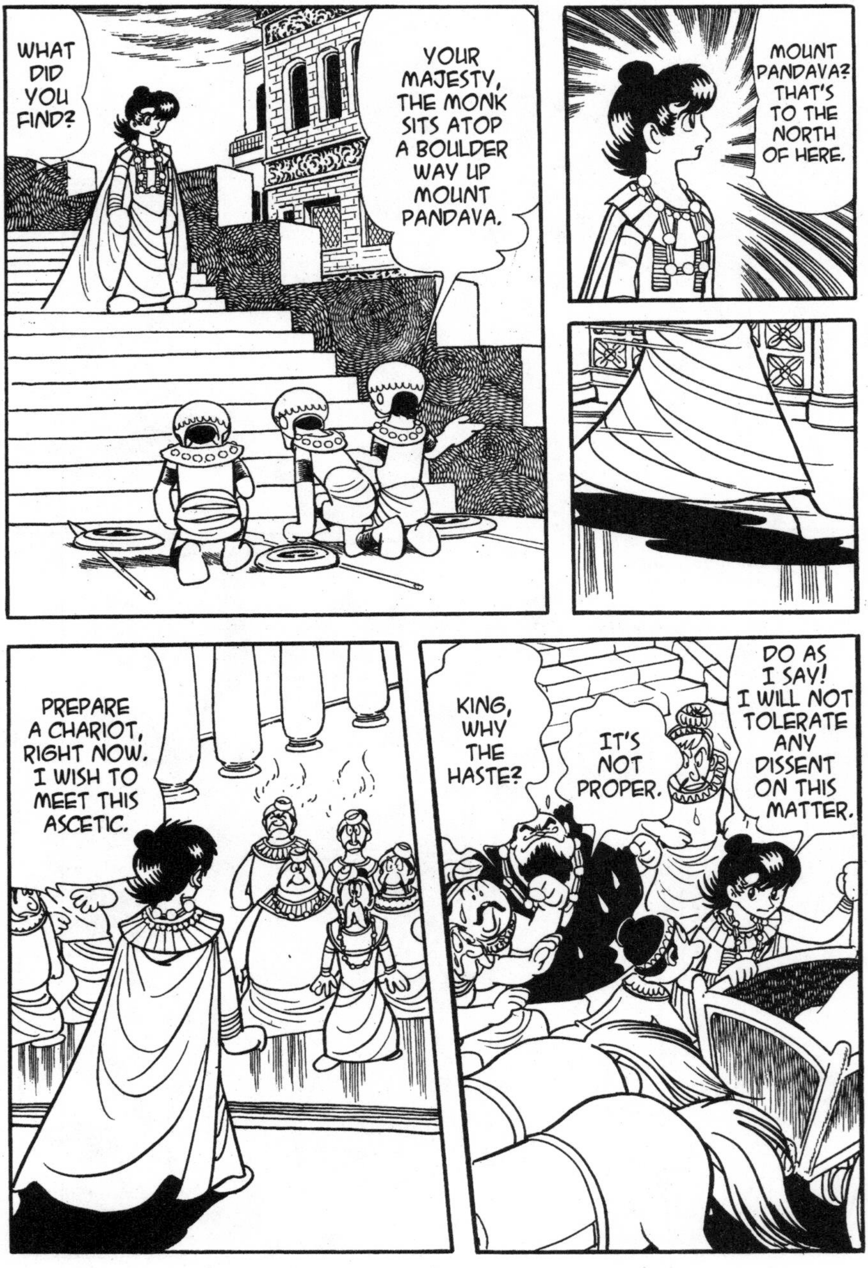
WHAT DID YOU FIND?
YOUR MAJESTY, THE MONK SITS ATOP A BOULDER WAY UP MOUNT PANDAVA.
MOUNT PANDAVA? THAT'S TO THE NORTH OF HERE.
PREPARE A CHARIOT, RIGHT NOW. I WISH TO MEET THIS ASCETIC.
KING, WHY THE HASTE?
IT'S NOT PROPER.
DO AS I SAY! I WILL NOT TOLERATE ANY DISSENT ON THIS MATTER.

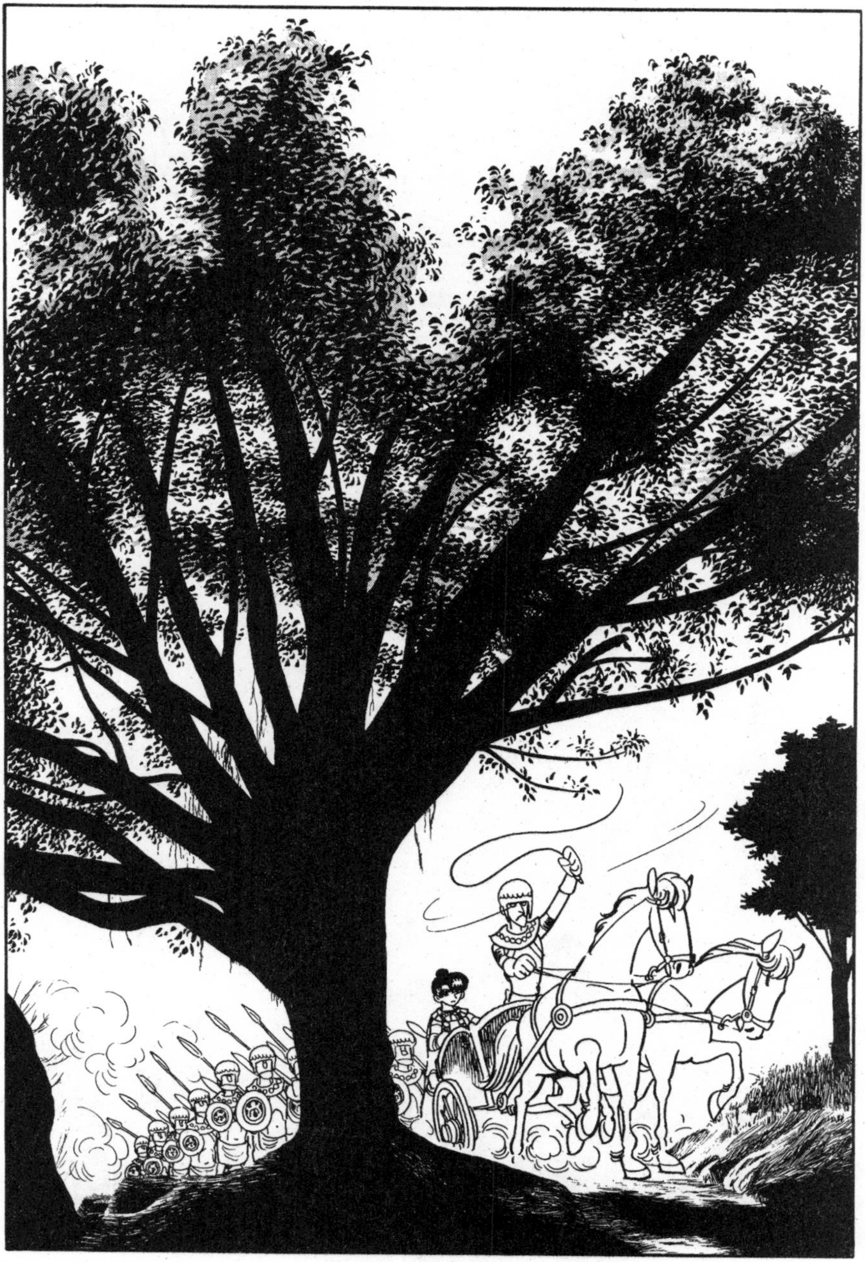

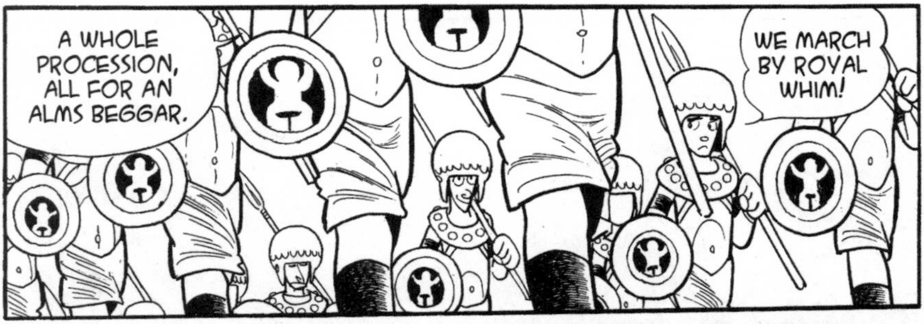
A WHOLE PROCESSION, ALL FOR AN ALMS BEGGAR.
WE MARCH BY ROYAL WHIM!

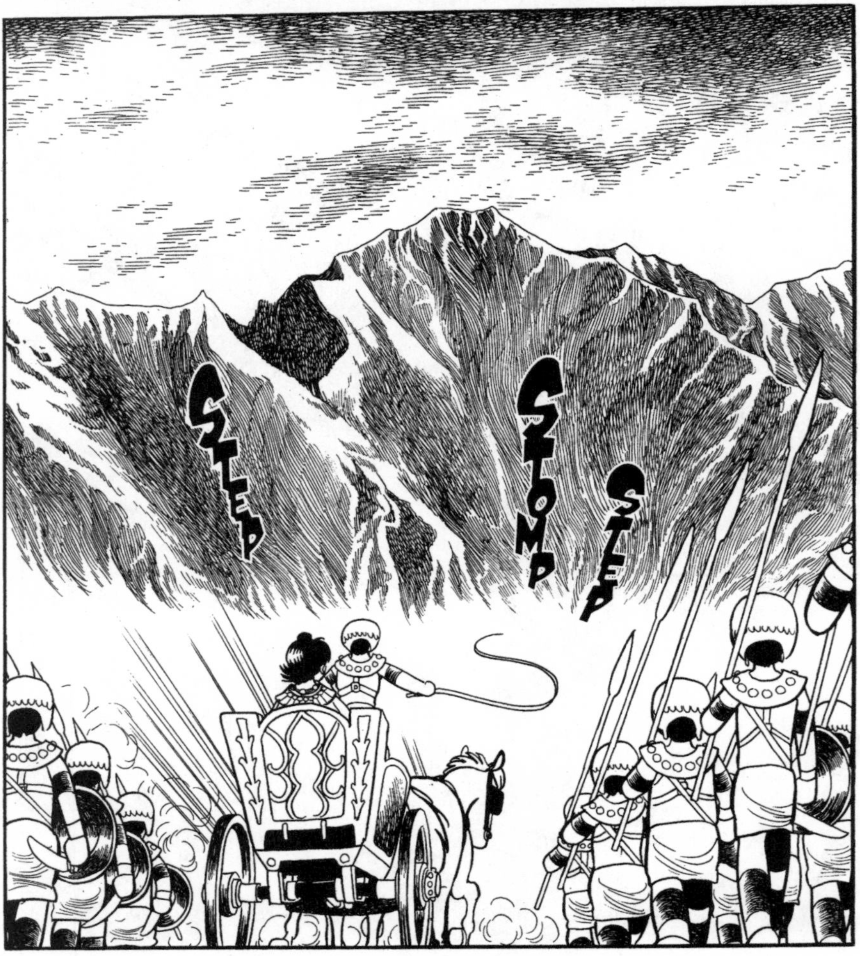
STEP
STOMP
STEP

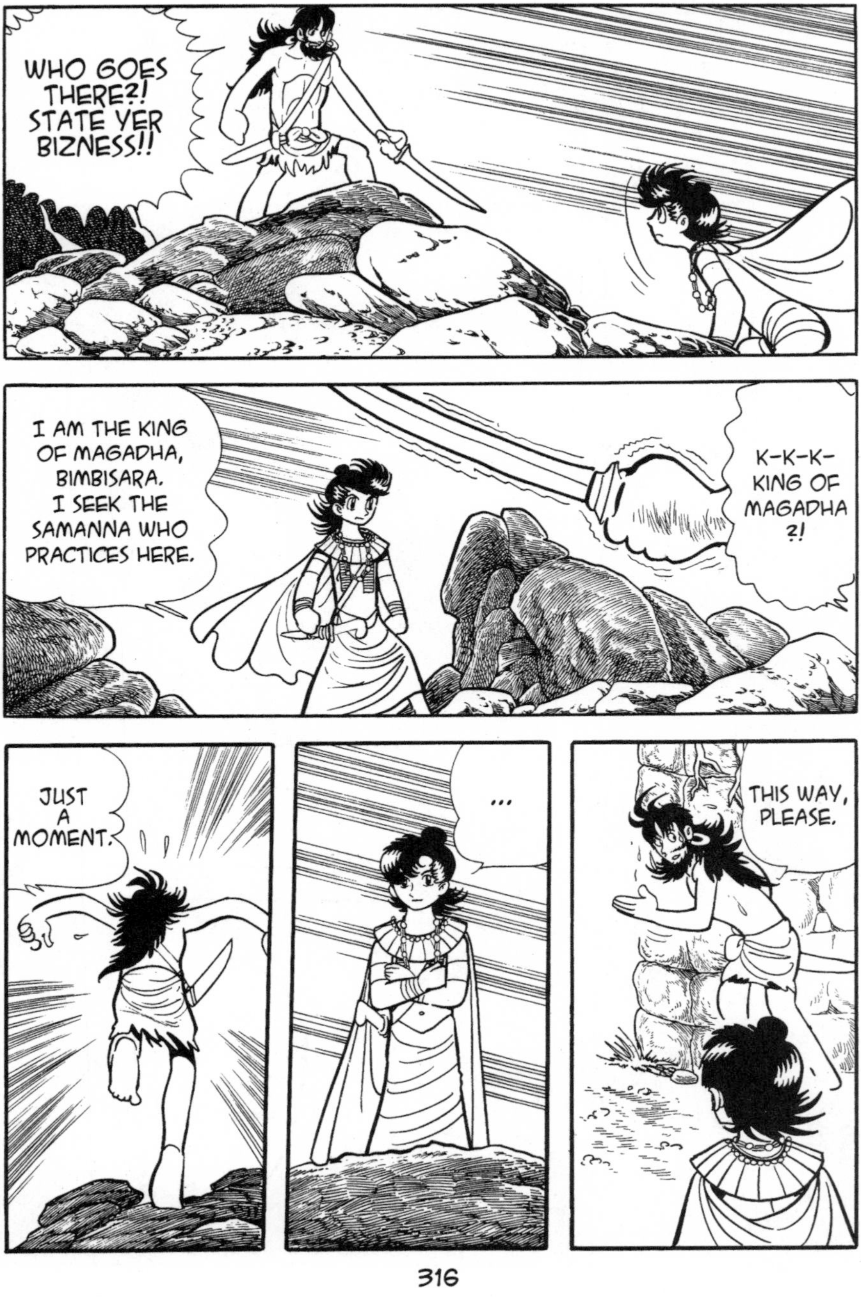
WHO GOES THERE?! STATE YER BIZNESS!!
I AM THE KING OF MAGADHA, BIMBISARA. I SEEK THE SAMANNA WHO PRACTICES HERE.
K-K-K-KING OF MAGADHA?!
JUST A MOMENT.
...
THIS WAY, PLEASE.

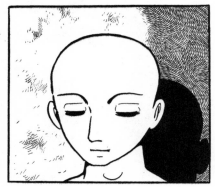

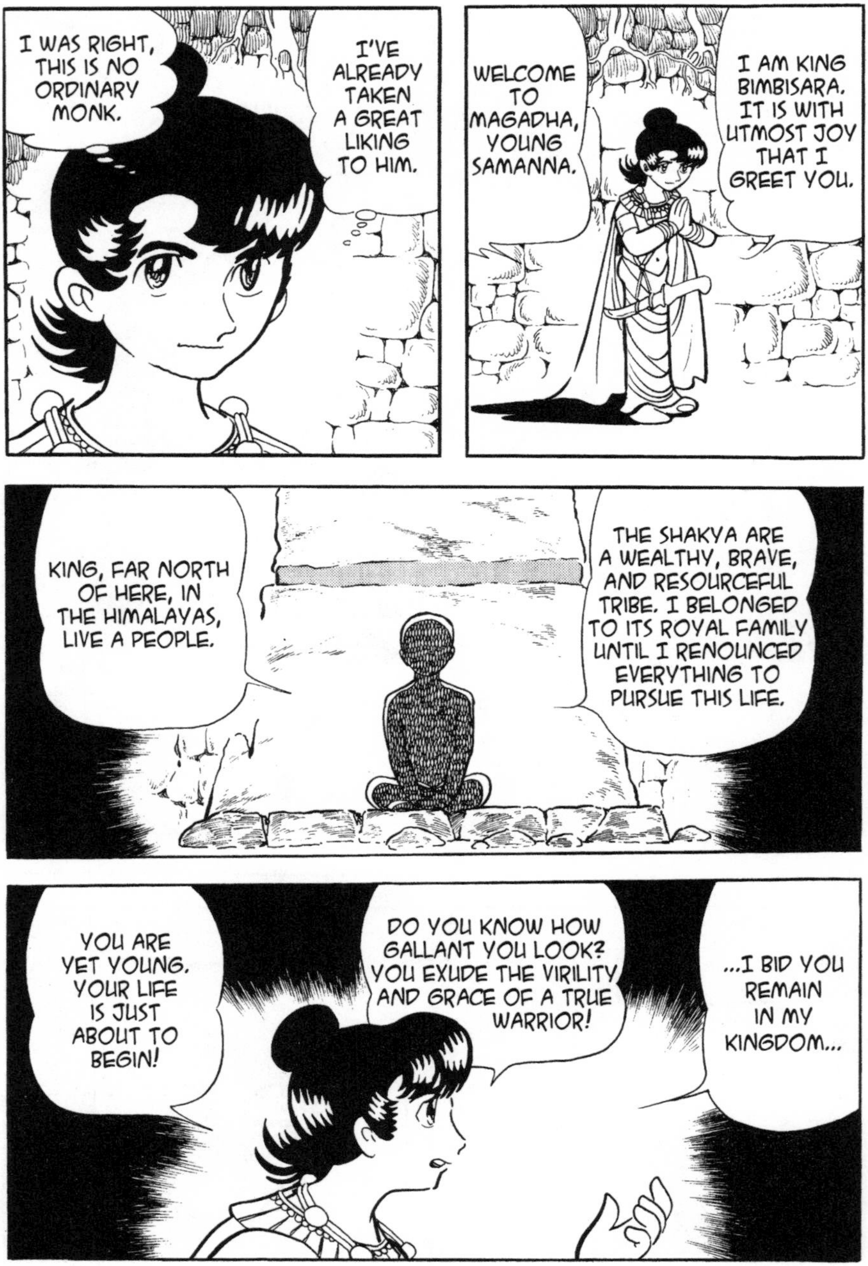
I WAS RIGHT, THIS IS NO ORDINARY MONK.
I'VE ALREADY TAKEN A GREAT LIKING TO HIM.
WELCOME TO MAGADHA, YOUNG SAMANNA.
I AM KING BIMBISARA. IT IS WITH UTMOST JOY THAT I GREET YOU.
KING, FAR NORTH OF HERE, IN THE HIMALAYAS, LIVE A PEOPLE.
THE SHAKYA ARE A WEALTHY, BRAVE, AND RESOURCEFUL TRIBE. I BELONGED TO ITS ROYAL FAMILY UNTIL I RENOUNCED EVERYTHING TO PURSUE THIS LIFE.
YOU ARE YET YOUNG. YOUR LIFE IS JUST ABOUT TO BEGIN!
DO YOU KNOW HOW GALLANT YOU LOOK? YOU EXUDE THE VIRILITY AND GRACE OF A TRUE WARRIOR!
...I BID YOU REMAIN IN MY KINGDOM...

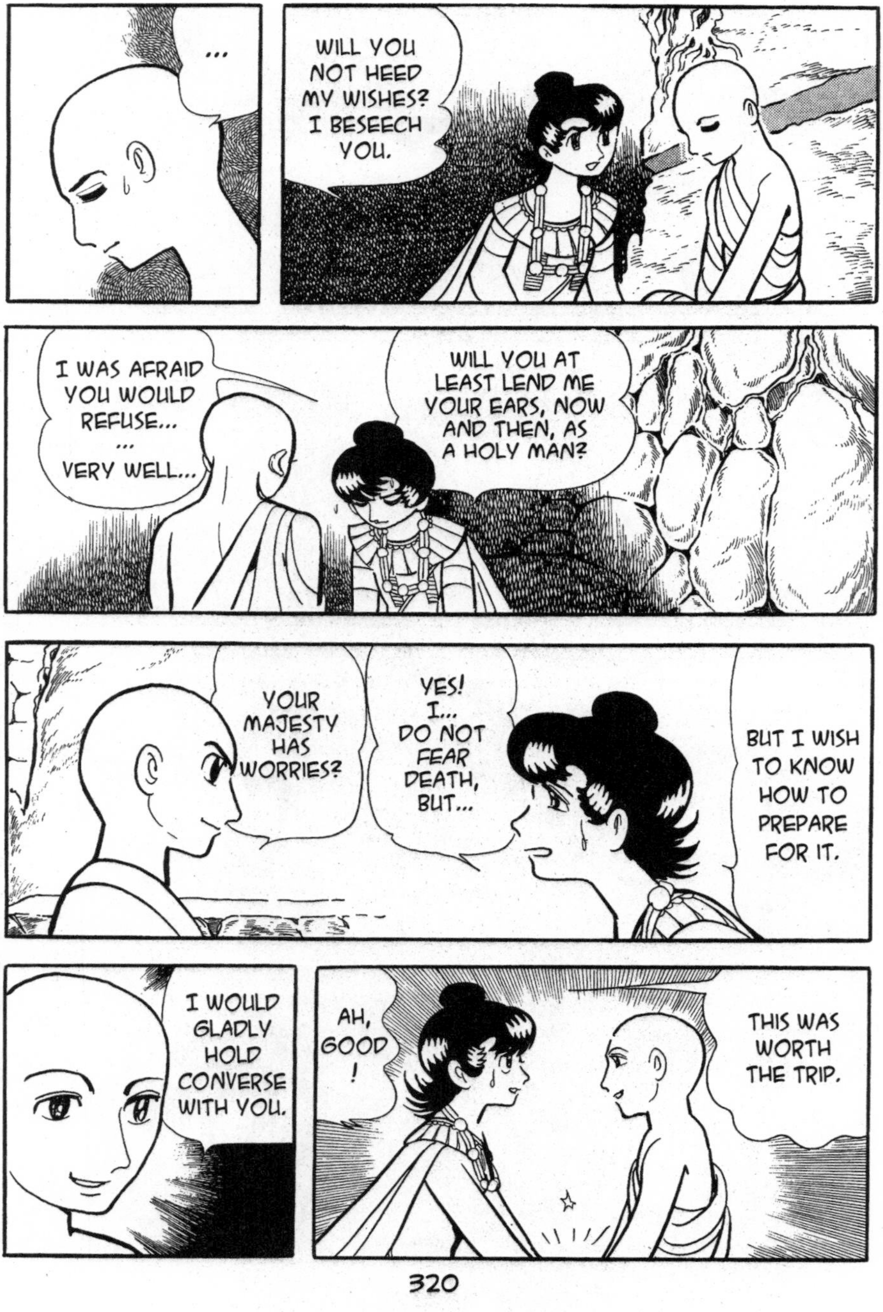
...
WILL YOU NOT HEED MY WISHES? I BESEECH YOU.
I WAS AFRAID YOU WOULD REFUSE... ... VERY WELL...
WILL YOU AT LEAST LEND ME YOUR EARS, NOW AND THEN, AS A HOLY MAN?
YOUR MAJESTY HAS WORRIES?
YES! I... DO NOT FEAR DEATH, BUT...
BUT I WISH TO KNOW HOW TO PREPARE FOR IT.
I WOULD GLADLY HOLD CONVERSE WITH YOU.
AH, GOOD!
THIS WAS WORTH THE TRIP.

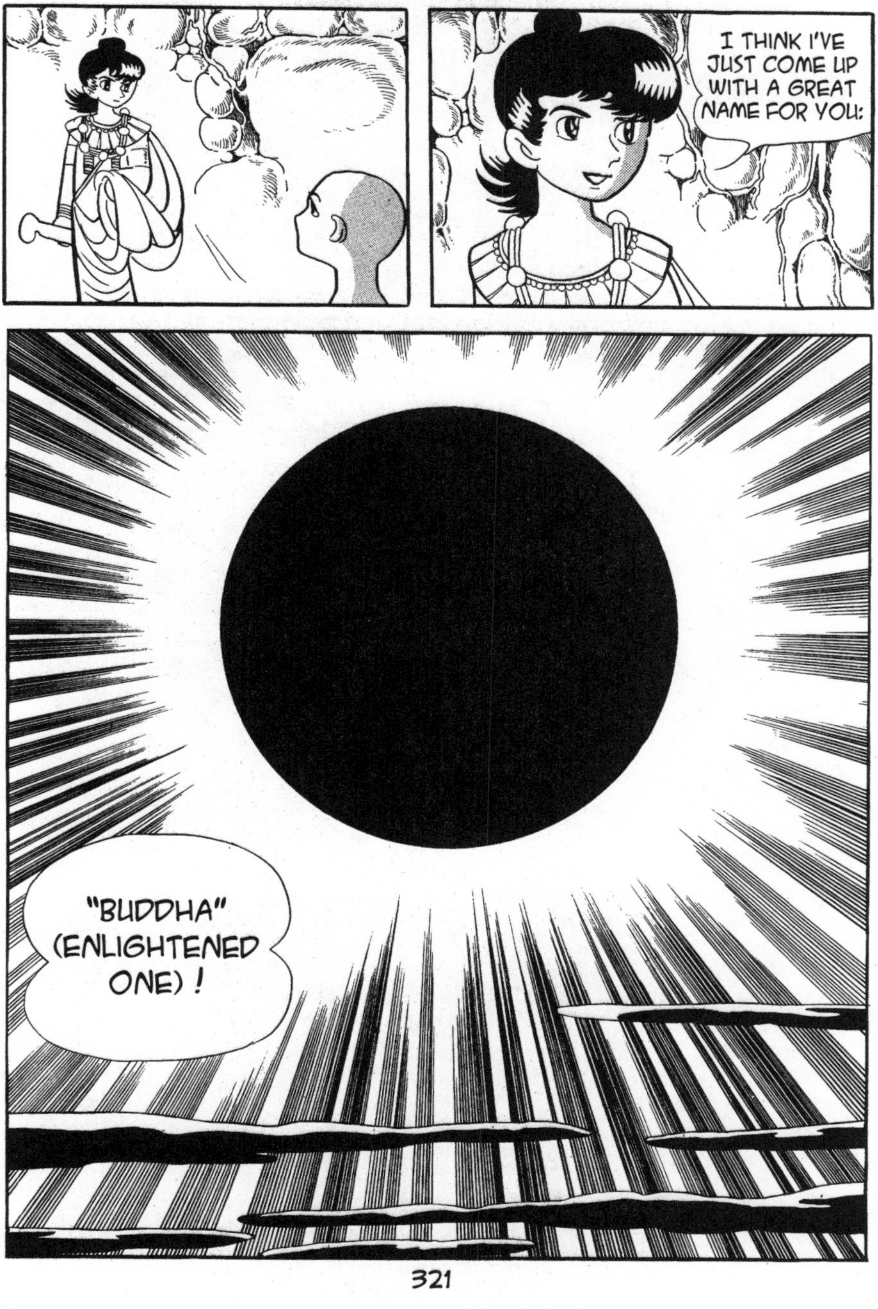
I THINK I'VE JUST COME UP WITH A GREAT NAME FOR YOU:
"BUDDHA" (ENLIGHTENED ONE)!

'TIL WE MEET AGAIN...

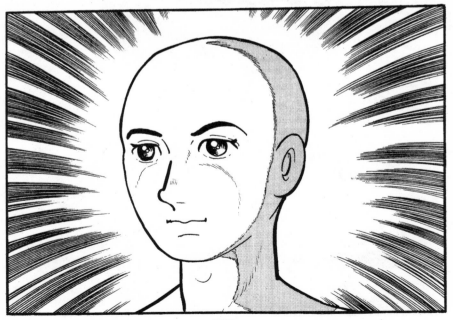

BUDDHA

OSAMU TEZUKA

VOLUME

4: *The Forest of Uruvela*

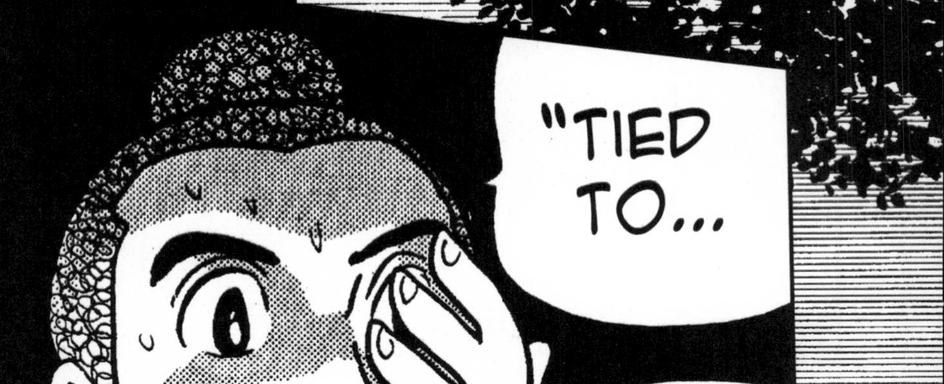
"TIED TO...
ALL THAT IS!"

November 2006